THE BEGINNING OF
CHRISTIAN PHILOSOPHY

THE BEGINNING OF CHRISTIAN PHILOSOPHY

ERIC OSBORN

PROFESSOR OF NEW TESTAMENT
AND EARLY CHURCH HISTORY
QUEEN'S COLLEGE, UNIVERSITY OF MELBOURNE

CAMBRIDGE UNIVERSITY PRESS

CAMBRIDGE

LONDON   NEW YORK   NEW ROCHELLE

MELBOURNE   SYDNEY

Published by the Press Syndicate of the University of Cambridge
The Pitt Building, Trumpington Street, Cambridge CB2 IRP
32 East 57th Street, New York, NY 10022, USA
296 Beaconsfield Parade, Middle Park, Melbourne 3206, Australia

First published 1981

Printed in Great Britain by
REDWOOD BURN LIMITED
Trowbridge

British Library cataloguing in publication data
Osborn, Eric Francis
The beginning of Christian philosophy.
1. Fathers of the Church
I. Title
189'2   BR67   80-41398
ISBN 0 521 23179 5

BR
67
.08

TO
SOPHIE CLAIRE

CONTENTS

vii

Contents

PREFACE

The earliest Christian writers were also the most creative; but
the established ways of viewing their work have largely obscured its meaning. Two things make rediscovery possible:
on the one hand there is the recent interest in second-century
issues like language about God and the problem of evil, and on
the other hand there is the mass of historical work done by the
late Jean Daniélou and others over the last twenty-five years.
As his translator claims, the relevance of the contents of
Daniélou's *Gospel message and Hellenistic culture* is not obvious.
Another step is needed, to elucidate the problems that puzzled
the second-century writers and puzzle us.

Apart from Cardinal Daniélou, others have helped considerably. In Cambridge, Professors G. W. H. Lampe,[1] C. F. D.
Moule and E. G. Rupp have helped with clarity and understanding. R. P. Claude Mondésert in Lyons and Professor
Ernst Käsemann in Tübingen have placed me frequently in
their debt. In Rome, R. P. Antonio Orbe has allowed me to
benefit from his unrivalled knowledge of Irenaeus. Closer to
home, Professor John Passmore and Dr Behan McCullagh
have lent guidance on the crucial issue of method. The intelligent enthusiasm of my students here has been a major factor.
Dr A. Lenox-Conyngham read proofs and, with Dr David
Rankin, checked references, while Mr Edwin Brown prepared
the index of citations. The staff of Cambridge University Press
have guided the book through the press with unfailing skill and
patience. To all these I offer my sincere thanks.

ERIC OSBORN

Queen's College
University of Melbourne

7 July 1978

[1] Sad news of the death of Geoffrey Lampe came during the printing of
this book. His enduring gifts to patristic learning will long be gratefully
used. By his wisdom and courage *apothanon eti lalei*. E.F.O. (September
1980).

ix

REFERENCES

JUSTIN (Goodspeed's Edition)

    1 A. 14.1 refers to the *First Apology*, chapter 14, paragraph 1.

    D. 11.1 refers to the *Dialogue with Trypho*, chapter 11, paragraph 1.

IRENAEUS (Harvey's Edition)

    H. 2.1.1 refers to *Against Heresies*, Book 2, chapter 1, paragraph 1.

    E. 14 refers to the *Epideixis*, or *Demonstration of the Apostolic Preaching*, paragraph 14 (J. Armitage Robinson's translation).

CLEMENT (Stählin's Edition)

    Prot. 4.63 refers to *Protrepticus*, chapter 4, paragraph 63.

    Paed. 1.3.24 refers to *Paedagogus*, Book 1, chapter 3, paragraph 24.

    S. 7.1.2 refers to *Stromateis*, Book 7, chapter 1, paragraph 2.

    Ecl. 2 refers to *Prophetic Eclogues*, paragraph 2.

TERTULLIAN (Corpus Christianorum)

    An. 27.1 refers to *De Anima*, chapter 27, paragraph 1.

    The titles of Tertullian's works are abbreviated as follows:

An.	*De anima*
Ap.	*Apologeticum*
Bapt.	*De baptismo*
Carn.	*De carne Christi*
Cast.	*De exhortatione castitatis*
Cor.	*De corona*
Cult.	*De cultu feminarum libri II*
Fug.	*De fuga in persecutione*
Herm.	*Aduersus Hermogenem*
Idol.	*De idololatria*
Iei.	*De ieiunio*
Iud.	*Aduersus Iudaeos*
Marc.	*Aduersus Marcionem libri V*
Mart.	*Ad martyras*
Mon.	*De monogamia*
Nat.	*Ad nationes libri II*
Orat.	*De oratione*
Paen.	*De paenitentia*
Pal.	*De pallio*
Pat.	*De patientia*

References

ABBREVIATIONS

ABR	Australian Biblical Review
ACW	Ancient Christian Writers
AeR	Atene e Roma
AGPh.	Archiv für Geschichte der Philosophie
AIPh.	Annuaire de l'institut de philologie et d'histoire orientales
ANCL	The Ante-Nicene Christian Library
AnGr.	Analecta Gregoriana
APQ	American Philosophical Quarterly
Bib.	Biblica
BJRL	Bulletin of the John Rylands Library
BKV	Bibliothek der Kirchenväter
BZNW	Beihefte zur Zeitschrift für die neutestamentliche Wissenschaft
CChr SL	Corpus Christianorum Series Latina
ClPh.	Classical Philology
CQ	Classical Quarterly
DViv.	Dieu vivant
ErJb.	Eranos-Jahrbuch
EThL	Ephemerides theologicae Lovanienses
GCS	Griechischen christlichen Schriftsteller der ersten drei Jahrhunderte
GIF	Giornale italiano di filologia
Gn.	Gnomon
Gr.	Gregorianum (Roma)
Hist.	Historia
HTh.	History and Theory
HThS	Supplement to History and Theory
HTR	Harvard Theological Review
JHS	Journal of Hellenic Studies
JR	Journal of Religion
JRS	Journal of Roman Studies
JThS	Journal of Theological Studies
KUD	Kerygma und Dogma
LCC	Library of Christian Classics
LCL	Loeb Classical Library
MH	Museum Helveticum
Mn.	Mnemosyne (Leiden)
MThZ	Münchener theologische Zeitschrift

Abbreviations

NAWG, PH	*Nachrichten der Akademie der Wissenschaften in Göttingen, Philologische-historische Klasse*
NRTh.	*Nouvelle revue théologique*
NZSTh.	*Neue Zeitschrift für systematische Theologie*
OrChr.	*Oriens Christianus*
PH	*Philologische-historische Klasse*
PhRev.	*Philosophical Review*
RB	*Revue biblique*
REG	*Revue des études grecques*
RevSR	*Revue des sciences religieuses*
RGG	*Die Religion in Geschichte und Gegenwart*
RHE	*Revue d'histoire ecclésiastique*
RHPhR	*Revue d'histoire et de philosophie religieuses*
RSR	*Recherches de science religieuse*
RThAM	*Recherches de théologie ancienne et médiévale*
SC	Sources Chrétiennes
Schol.	*Scholastik*
SE	*Studia Evangelica*
SEA	*Svensk exegetisk arsbok*
SeL	Storia e letteratura
SJTh.	*Scottish Journal of Theology*
SO	*Symbolae Osloenses*
STh.	*Studia Theologica*
STL	*Studia Theologica Lundensia*
SVF	*Stoicorum Veterum Fragmenta*, ed. von Arnim
Theol.	*Theology*
ThStKr.	*Theologische Studien und Kritiken*
Tr.	*Traditio* (New York)
TU	Texte und Untersuchungen zur Geschichte der altchristlichen Literatur
VetChr.	*Vetera Christianorum*
VigChr.	*Vigiliae Christianae*
ZKG	*Zeitschrift für Kirchengeschichte*
ZKTh.	*Zeitschrift für katholische Theologie*
ZNW	*Zeitschrift für die neutestamentliche Wissenschaft*
ZSTh.	*Zeitschrift für systematische Theologie*
ZThK	*Zeitschrift für Theologie und Kirche*

1 Christian argument

The present movement of Western civilisation away from Christianity has directed attention to earlier days when Christians were a small part of a Roman world of pluralistic beliefs;[1] they came before, we come after, Christendom. Claims for relevance, however, are always competitive and need to be argued. What drives twentieth-century Western man back to the second and third centuries? Initially there is little more than a vague feeling that Christendom was a mistake, that ecumenical councils in the fourth and fifth centuries achieved less than they claimed; that the classical dogmatic formulations are too ambiguous to be helpful. Clearly this response is not enough. Christendom was not an unqualified mistake and its assessment is the task of a lifetime and not of an impulse. The best ecumenical councils may well be those that seem to achieve little; ambiguity of creeds and councils invites further analysis before resignation.

The importance of the second century and the apologists is best seen in the emergence of Christian argument;[2] but Christians have argued about so many strange things that the area of argument is important. The claim of the enthusiast for early Christian thought is that the problems that Christians faced in a pluralistic world, then, have a close relation to those that they face now: the problems were more general and more philosophical (Is there one God? Can man speak of him? Is man free? Why is there evil in God's world?) than the dogmatic issues of the fourth and fifth centuries. To claim that Christian philosophy begins here in the second century is simply to indicate this fact; it does not mean either that the writings to be discussed were uniformly philosophical or that something like a 'system' of philosophy emerged. The problems were those commonly called philosophical and the problems are what count. For 'the philosopher – unless he be a very bad phil-

---

[1] H. I. Marrou (ed.), *A Diognète*, SC (Paris, 1951), p. 176; H. Butterfield, *Christianity and history* (London, 1954), p. 135.

[2] F. D. Maurice, *Lectures on the ecclesiastical history of the first and second centuries* (Cambridge, 1854), p. 207.

1

osopher – does not set out to construct a system; what he is trying to do is to solve problems'.[1] Where did second-century problems originate? There were four main sources that presented objections and difficulties.

The most immediate objection to Christianity was that of the State and its religion. Christians refused to fulfil the religious duties that were required of every citizen: they were atheists who could not be trusted if the State hoped for security and permanence. The Roman Empire exercised a benign tolerance towards the religion of a conquered nation. Any country might worship its gods, provided it added an allegiance to the gods who had made Rome great and whose protection was a condition of Rome's continued eminence. Christians failed to meet the required conditions. Their religion was not a local cult tied to a particular country, for they were now to be found in most parts of the empire. Nor could they claim to preserve the faith of their fathers and beg respect for their cultural heritage. They had all deserted the faith of their fathers. Their exclusiveness was their major crime; and their newness closed the loophole through which the Jews were for a time allowed to be exclusive on grounds of ancient allegiance.

Newness was an offence to philosophers too: Celsus, the Platonist, argued that what was true must be old, and what was new could not be true.[2] Any idea had to prove its antiquity to gain acceptance. Wisdom lay at the beginning of man's history, and had stood the test of time. Christians joined their novelty to a ridiculous demand for faith; they denied reason and attracted the irrational masses because they offered quick returns for the credulous. Stoics, like Marcus Aurelius, found Christians theatrical in their attitude to death,[3] and not worthy of consideration in their beliefs. Lucian had little time for philosophical claims. As a cynic he saw the variety of philosophical theories as an immediate proof of their futility. The absolute claims of Christians were a sign of their credulity rather than their credibility.[4]

---

[1] John Passmore, 'The idea of a history of philosophy', *HThS* 5 (1965), 27.

[2] Origen, *Contra Celsum*, 7.71. See C. Andresen, *Logos und Nomos* (Berlin, 1955), pp. 146ff, and H. Dörrie, in a review of Andresen, *Gn.*, 29 (1957), 195; 'Der Logos ist alt, weil er wahr ist'.

[3] M. Aurelius, *Meditations*, 8.51; 11.3.

[4] Lucian, *Peregrinus*, 11–13; cf. Origen, *Contra Celsum*, 1.9.

The Jews saw the gulf between them and the Christians widen during the second century as Jewish influence faded. At the personal level, they had supported persecution of Christians and at the theoretical level they saw no ground for this new heresy taking over the writings that belonged to the Jewish people. There was no integrity in the Christian claim, for Christians did not keep the Law, and they placed an object of shame, the cross, in the centre of their life and worship. Argument between Christian and Jew could range over the whole of the scriptures that each claimed as his own and could vary according to the method of interpretation that was used.

Finally, Christians had to argue then, as ever, more with one another than with anyone else. It is wrong to imagine a small select band, unanimous in belief, scattered through the world, fighting the three enemies we have mentioned. Christianity in the second century was torn and divided.[1] The divisions were not superficial but were concerned with fundamental points of belief. Each main centre of Christianity had its distinctive approach, but there were few centres where some divisions could not be found. Gnosticism is the name given to the most powerful force for Christian disunity. Beginning outside Christianity, it offered a higher Christian way, which could be found in simple modifications, as in the Gospel of Truth and the Gospel of Thomas, or in elaborate systems like those described without sympathy by Irenaeus and Hippolytus. Yet, for all the strength of Gnosticism, a more fundamental threat lay in the belief of Marcion. For Marcion was deeply sensitive to the wonder of the gospel; because he saw the amazing grace offered by the father of Jesus Christ, he rejected the world as God's creation, and human history, especially Jewish history, as God's activity. Both these rejections were reasonable and were prompted by honesty and sensitivity. Yet he was wrong, and Christians knew that the rejection of the creator and of the God of Abraham would be fatal to the understanding of Christian truth. A lot of argument was necessary before a clear pattern of

[1] See W. Bauer, *Orthodoxy and heresy in earliest Christianity*, ET of 2nd edition, edited by G. Strecker (Philadelphia, 1971). On p. xi, G. Strecker summarises Bauer's thesis: 'In earliest Christianity, orthodoxy and heresy do not stand in relation to one another as primary to secondary, but in many regions heresy is the original manifestation of Christianity.'

Christian truth could be found throughout the Church universal. But the way was through argument, whether the threat came from Gnosticism or Marcion, just as the way to answer the Roman state, philosophers and Jews could only be through reasoning and evidence.

Five areas may be selected as central to the widespread and many-sided debate.[1] Christians had to argue about God, that he was both real and transcendent, and that he was one. They had to argue about man, that he, for all his sinfulness, was bound to God by a likeness that could grow by grace into sonship. The world had to be defended and made rational; it had one cause, and its evils were not due to that cause but to the sin that man freely chose. History had to be made coherent around a divine purpose that was fulfilled in Jesus. Finally, the strangest thing of all was the belief that the one supreme God had become man in Jesus; yet, without this belief, Christians could believe neither in the God above, nor in man's restoration to God, nor in the goodness of the creator, nor in the unity of history. We shall look at these five areas and the aspect that they presented to each of the four groups in the Christian environment.[2]

1   The God above

The problems about the Christian God may be broken up into four main questions:

(i) Is there one God and can one speak of him?
(ii) Is God good?
(iii) Can God be three as well as one?
(iv) Is God best understood as the first cause?

Does the God of the Christians make sense? Is there one

---

[1] The five problems are not an exhaustive list; other important problems include the interpretation of scripture, the understanding of the Church, the nature of the *eschaton*.

[2] There were always Christians who did not argue and who provided ground for sceptical jeers; but they had little to offer in the fight for Christian survival. Their influence was inhibited by the catechetical instruction that was obligatory before baptism. It became harder for Christians to be ignorant of their faith. Heresy was at once seductive and disruptive; more and more Christianity became a doctrine or a philosophy.

supreme transcendent ineffable being who is different from everything else, and yet stands in sovereign majesty over all things? This God cannot be spoken of in ordinary language, but requires qualifications whenever concrete terms are used of him. Most Jews had no problem with such a God, because their God had always been above the ways of men, and because some of them had already learnt to talk in terms of Greek philosophy. The philosophers of the persuasion of Plato were ready to speak of God in negative, transcendent terms: he was to be grasped by intellectual vision and not handled or touched. Only the established religion of the day had little time for this remote and negative being. The gods of Greece and Rome were human, lively beings who got into all sorts of mischief and who left many tales of their adventures. There were other gods too, more shadowy and less colourful characters, who inhabited familiar parts of this world. Heretics, like the Gnostics, looked to a supreme God who was even more remote than the God of the Christians, Jews or philosophers; their God could not have anything to do with the world of men. Philosophy could become the chief ally on this point, but the problem remained acute. The notion of one supreme being did not come easily to the ancient world. Alexander Severus was happy to add an image of Christ to his collection of other images,[1] but he did not seem to see any point in either transcendence or exclusive unity. The God above was too remote to be useful; in words of a later day, Christians and the birds could have the heavens, provided they left the earth to others.[2]

2   Man and his freedom

(i) In what way is man related to God?

(ii) How can man's present misery be reconciled with his divine origin?

(iii) Is man free?

(iv) Of what does man consist?

[1] Lampridius, *Life of Alexander Severus*, 43.

[2] 'Did not the Nazis carry on their fight against us with the slogan: "Heaven for sparrows and Christians, earth for us"?' (E. Käsemann, *Jesus means freedom*, ET [London, 1969], p. 134).

(i.e., Has he parts such as body, soul and spirit and, if so,
how are they related?)

(v) Can man know the truth?

Christians claimed that it was possible for God by his Spirit to
live in man and to direct man's life. Man was made in God's
image and however scarred the image might be, it could be
restored to the likeness of God. God was near man and whoever
belonged to Christ had his Spirit within. Oddly enough this was
the one part of Christian belief that met little real opposition.
The Jews were prepared to acknowledge God's image in man
and the presence of his Spirit in the prophets. The philosophers
saw the reason of man as his divine part, while the pagan
religions had various ways of joining the human and divine.
The Gnostics would allow some men to possess a divine spark,
but denied that the spark could be found in all or that it was
due to anything but an inscrutable decree.

The bridge between man and God was a subject of constant attention. Christians wanted to cut this bridge and yet
to replace it with so many new bridges that God was closer than
ever. God was not to be found in any of the sacred places that
men had fondly frequented. Yet he was to be found in every
human heart and to be known as father by every man who
turned to him in faith. The optimism of this account of man
made worship of any material thing in heaven or earth absurd.
Sun, Moon and stars would not wish to bring man down to their
level but would refer him on to God.[1]

3 The world and its maker

(i) Is the world created by the one supreme God?

(ii) What has happened to make parts of the world so unlike
their creator?

(iii) Where in the world can God's hand be seen?

(iv) Is evil in the world compatible with its divine maker?

Christians claimed that the God and Father of the Lord Jesus
Christ was the creator of all things in heaven and in earth. He
was good, despite the evil in the world that he had made. Only

[1] Origen, *Contra Celsum*, 5.11; *Exhortation to martyrdom*, 7.

the Jews accepted this belief without objection. Some philosophers could not reconcile the presence of evil with the idea of a good, all-powerful Cause. Platonists and Stoics had ways of tackling the problem. The pagans allowed for many gods to produce the many things in a varied world. Supremely, Marcion and the Gnostics came out against this point. The most high God could not be responsible for the limitations, bestiality and suffering of this depraved world. Only an inferior and limited creator could have made the world in which men live. To them the reply was given: the one cause of all things was the ground of the world's order and rationality. Man could make the world his home because God ruled over it. Evil was real but it came from God's goodness in allowing man to be free. Every evil thing could be traced to sin, to the free choice of men or angels.

4   History and continuity

> (i) Is there continuity in history? Why did Jesus come so late?
> (ii) Has history a centre?
> (iii) Where do we stand in history now?
> (iv) Does man make progress in the course of history?
> (v) How will it all end?

None of the four groups could accept the unified view of history that the Christians gave. The Jews could not see their history continued in the Church, and the philosophers could not attribute any great significance to history (for the Stoics it went round in circles). The pagans denied any unity of divine activity, the Gnostics and Marcion insisted that God was a strange God, showing himself for the first time, if at all, in Jesus of Nazareth. History was appropriated by Christians. God had never ceased to care and man had never left the hands of God. What happened in Jesus was the once-for-all climax of a story that had no breaks and the correction of all that had gone wrong in that story.

5   The Word made flesh

(i) How did God's Word become flesh?
(ii) How is the Word related to God the Father?
(iii) What did the Word achieve by being both man and God?
(iv) How does the Word bring knowledge of God?
(v) How can he be particular and universal, i.e. the man Jesus or the risen Christ *and* the universal Word of God?

That God became man and lived a human life was the chief part of the Christian claim.[1] It was emphatically rejected by the Jews and the philosophers, not to mention Gnostics who could not begin to entertain such an idea. They saw this Christian claim as the rejection of the first Christian proposition, that God is supreme and transcendent. The religions of the day could accept it, but only because they did not hold the Christian idea of God. They might be happy to treat this Jesus as yet another of the many gods they knew, provided he was content to take his place in the line.

The Gospel to the Gentiles [Acts 17: 16–34]

Paul's speech on the Areopagus presents the climax of the Book of Acts: a sermon preached to Gentiles by the apostle to the Gentiles.[2] It represents the movement of Christianity into the Hellenistic world. An examination of its content provides a valuable confirmation of the problems that have been set out above. Like many sermons, it makes three points: God the creator and lord does not need temples, God has made men to

[1] John 1: 1–18 shows the central mystery of the Word made flesh.
[2] This brief account is indebted especially to E. Haenchen, *The Acts of the Apostles, a commentary*, ET (Philadelphia, 1971), pp. 515–31, where the central significance of the speech is stressed, and to M. Dibelius, *Studies in the Acts of the Apostles*, ET (London, 1956), pp. 27–83. Among other valuable literature may be mentioned O. Bauernfeind, *Die Apostelgeschichte*, Theologischer Handkommentar zum NT, 5 (Leipzig, 1939); and H. Conzelmann, 'Die Rede des Paulus auf dem Areopag', *Theologie als Schriftauslegung* (München, 1974), pp. 18–32.

seek him, and men as the offspring of God should not bow down to idols. The message is pure monotheism and only the conclusion provides a Christian note.

We begin with the unity of mankind and the uniform development of the human race. God has fixed times and bounds for nations, not in the Old Testament sense of these words, but in the wider Stoic sense: the entire life of the human race has been ordered in respect to seasons, habitations and progress in search after God. Athens was dominated by its past, and Paul is troubled by the many idols that he has seen there, which he could not regard as innocent works of art. He speaks (verse 17) in the synagogue on the Sabbath and in the market-place on week-days. The latter activity is reminiscent of Socrates and draws the attention of Epicureans and Stoics who describe him as a *spermologos* and as a messenger of new divinities. (It is hard to fix the place described as the Areopagus.) Paul is called to explain the new or strange things in which he deals; the curiosity of the Athenians (verse 21) was proverbial. Paul stands and speaks like an orator to the men of Athens, indicating his estimate of their culture and learning. He describes them as very religious people because of their abundant religious apparatus, and goes on to speak of the unknown God whom they worship in ignorance and of whom they now hear for the first time. This reference is hard to explain. No altar to an unknown God has ever been discovered, nor is any reference to it to be found in ancient literature. Probably Luke had read in some handbook that there were altars to unknown gods in Athens, and concluded from some words of Pausanias that there was an individual altar that bore the inscription 'To an unknown God'. From this transcendence Paul passes directly to the notion of creation, and quotes Isaiah 42: 5 concerning God's creation and continuing lordship and conservation of the world. Such a creator does not live in the temples men make, nor does he receive the sacrifices they offer. As the Greek enlightenment and the Hellenistic Jewish mission insisted, God has need of nothing. He gives life and breath to all, and orders the seasons and the world.

Verse 27 moves from the transcendent creator to the search for God that goes on in every man. Man tries to find God, and God is near to every man. 'For in him we live and move and are.' Aratus [*Phaenomena* 5], one of 'your' poets, is quoted concerning man's affinity to God: 'For we are of His race.' The nearness of God had been stressed by Seneca (*Ep.* 41.1: 'God is near you, with you and within you'; *Ep.* 12.14: 'He is everywhere, and He is here'). Because man is so close to God it is wrong for him to worship idols. The rational being has a natural perception of the gods, according to Dion of Prusa [*Orat.* 12.27], and man is loved by the gods because he is related to them [*Orat.* 30.26]. The same notion that we find in Romans 1 shows that idol worship is directly contrary to truth. God makes man and man makes idols. Idols are below man, while God is above him.

Verse 30 goes on to speak of God's concern with history. God overlooks men's ignorance in past times; but now men must repent, for God has fixed a day of judgement, a day of righteousness, and this day is determined through a man whom God raised from the dead. The final theme of the risen Christ completes the message. Each of the five problems has been indicated in the course of the sermon: the God above, creation, the God within, history and finally the risen man of righteousness. 'All this', comments Dibelius, 'has very little to do with the Paul of the Epistles, but a great deal to do with the exponents of a Christian philosophical system in the second century, namely the Apologists'.[1]

Method

At this point we grind to an uneasy halt. If these were the problems and concerns of second-century Christian writers, and they are plainly our problems too, why is it not more obvious? We should expect to find in the histories of early Christianity much that will bear on our own questions. Yet, at the end of Daniélou's classic treatment of this period, the English translator speaks of a reaction to the first volume as 'compounded of sheer astonishment at the bizarre character of the ideas and imagery used by the writers and relief that their works had, for the most part, sunk into oblivion'. He adds: 'The present volume also offers plenty of scope for such a response'.[2] Yet Daniélou had done far more for this period than anyone

[1] Dibelius, *Studies in Acts*, p. 82. The negative claim is not important for present purposes.
[2] J. Daniélou, *Gospel message and Hellenistic culture* (London, 1973), p. 501.

else; most histories simply represent the earlier period as a preparation for the golden age of the fourth and fifth centuries. As far as philosophy is concerned, a recent treatment of the period declares that what philosophy meant then, 'was something very different from what modern philosophers understand to be their professional activity'; there used to be a ruling interest in ethics and religion and a great respect for authority.[1]

How can we explain the violent contrast between what these early writers were saying and what historians have told us to expect? The answer is simple – it is due to the variety of methods that have been used. One is naturally hesitant to spend much time on a discussion of method for the proof of the pudding should be in the eating and not in the recipe.[2] However there is no other way out of present confusion and futility. Too many scholars believe they are doing the same kind of thing when the only hope of mutual appreciation lies in the recognition of the different intention behind different works. This does not mean that all work is equally sound or useful; but clarification of method will indicate criteria by which any work may be assessed. The rare examples of really bad work begin from an initial confusion about method.[3]

In the history of ideas, there are five questions that are commonly asked of a theory or of a statement: Does it make sense, is it true? How does it reflect the culture in which it emerged? What was said and what were other writers saying?

[1] A. H. Armstrong (ed.), *The Cambridge history of later Greek and early medieval philosophy* (Cambridge, 1967), p. 50. The suggestion that today there is little philosophical interest in ethics and religion is plainly false; the ancient respect for authority was an embarrassment to Christian thinkers, who could not deny that they had deserted the faith of their fathers, and turned gratefully to Socrates, who had anticipated their disrespect for authority.

[2] The method to be advocated in this book is problematic elucidation. This method was followed in my *The philosophy of Clement of Alexandria* (Cambridge, 1957); and *Justin Martyr* (Tübingen, 1973), as well as in other more notable recent works like G. C. Stead, *Divine substance* (Oxford, 1977); and G. W. H. Lampe, *God as Spirit* (Oxford, 1977).

[3] Many of the weaknesses in *The myth of God incarnate*, ed. John Hick (London, 1977), would have been avoided if the method of inquiry in the patristic sections had been analysed. It shows an unwarranted confidence in the stability of words and a lack of appreciation for the meaning of argument. See my review article, 'Method and myth', *Prudentia*, 10.1 (1978), 37–47.

Where does it stand in the development of ideas to point x? What problems does it attempt to solve and what methods does it use to solve them? These have been called the polemical, cultural, doxographical, retrospective and problematic approaches.[1] The best historians make some use of them all; but with the first four methods there is a tendency to absolutise one and to neglect others. When this happens, distortion is inevitable, for each of these four methods has serious limitations. The polemical approach (Is it true?) neglects the subtlety of problems and arguments, imposes its own definitions on earlier material, and ends up by telling men of straw that they have no brains. The cultural view (What setting does it reflect?) has little or no place for argument and assumes uniqueness in the social group with which it is concerned. The doxographer (What was said?) is too interested in finding parallel statements to appreciate their logical settings and different meanings. 'There are two kinds of science', said Lord Rutherford, 'physics and stamp-collecting'.[2] There are more than two kinds of history of ideas, but that most practised upon the second century, that of collecting and relating opinions (doxographical), has been dangerously like stamp-collecting. The retrospective historian (Where does it stand in a development?) does well within his limits, but is restricted by the fixed angle of his rear vision. It is obvious that he cannot do justice to the concerns of the second century that we have noted, if his point of reference is Nicaea or Chalcedon. Only the problematic historian takes account of other questions and only he supplies the logical element neglected by others; their strengths and weaknesses will be considered in greater detail at the end of this work. (See Appendix, p. 273.)

What is problematic elucidation? It starts with the claim that philosophy or theology is concerned with argument and with the attempt to solve problems.[3] There are recognisable types of problems that recur in different forms. A problematic approach will ask of a philosopher or theologian: 'What problem was he trying to solve?' 'How did this problem arise for him?' 'What new methods of tackling it did he use?'[4] There

---

[1] See Passmore, 'History of philosophy'.
[2] *My Cambridge*, ed. Ronald Hayman (London, 1977), p. 24.
[3] Passmore, 'History of philosophy', p. 28.
[4] *Ibid.* p. 29.

are difficulties in this method: it will be less concise and orderly than a general history (cultural, doxographical or retrospective); it will require some philosophical competence and thereby open up possibilities of error that a doxographer would avoid; it will appear more like a commentary than a history and its analysis may be dismissed as description. Yet such an approach 'is the only one which throws light on the inner development of philosophy',[1] for 'truth has no history, but the discussion of problems has a history'.[2] .

The problematic approach needs to answer one unfounded objection and observe two warnings. The objection is that identification of perennial problems and universal truths is only possible when the study is 'foolishly and needlessly naive'.[3] We may find such problems and truths only if we are prepared to make them so abstract and general that the range of answers will be vast, and this means 'that what *counts* as an answer will usually look, in a different culture or period, so different in itself that it can hardly be in the least useful even to go on thinking of the relevant question as being "the same"'.[4] The moral is that men should think for themselves and not lazily copy answers to their problems from ancient works. From this position, the study of thinkers of another period is of value precisely because it shows how widely assumptions and commitments vary at times and places. Every society places unrecognised restraints on the minds of its members.[5] The chief way of mitigating or destroying these restraints is through the study of what is alien. In theology and in philosophy, conceptual parochialism is the order of our day, despite constant conferences and ecumenical discussions. The first thing we may hope to learn from the past is 'the distinction between what is necessary and what is the product merely of our own contingent arrangements'.[6] What we may learn from the writings of second-century Christians may not be a final answer to our problems as we see them; but we shall learn how narrowly our grasp of things has followed a cultural or ecclesiastical pattern,

[1] *Ibid.* p. 30.
[2] *Ibid.* p. 31.
[3] Quentin Skinner, 'Meaning and understanding in the history of ideas', *HTh.*, 8 (1969), 50.
[4] *Ibid.* p. 52.
[5] *Ibid.* p. 53.
[6] *Ibid.*

and this will bring conceptual enlargement through an appreciation of alien elements in the thoughts of others. Unfortunately most philosophers 'have done nothing to enlarge the area of philosophical discussion and the historian properly passes them by'.[1]

In reply we note that this objection does not deny the importance of problems; it merely claims that the result of the investigation will be the enlargement rather than the solution of our problems. Further, the problems of the past cannot enlarge our understanding if there is no continuity at all between past and present. Since we are not dealing with problems that can, in a straightforward sense, be solved, it is to our advantage that the writers whom we consider belonged to alien settings, were genuinely puzzled and consequently untidy. 'For the problematic historian, as not at all for the doxographer, the philosopher is essentially a puzzled man.'[2] They enlarged the area of discussion and that is why they are important and useful, for the weakness of much theology is not that the answers are inadequate but that the questions are too small.

We have gained, from this objection, not a refutation but another ground for the method of problematic elucidation. For other methods have left behind an amusing trail of conceptual parochialism. Clement was once seen as an English liberal, since 'in his distrust of extremes, in his love of peace, in his reverent and sober piety, he anticipates some of the best religious characteristics of our race'.[3] On the other side of the Atlantic, Tertullian was seen to combine all the possible requirements of genius with audacity and aggression. 'It is exceedingly impressive to see Christian Latin literature Athena-like spring at once into being, fully armed, in the person of an eminently representative man, in whom seem summed up the promise and potency of all that it was yet to be.' 'Ardent in temperament, endowed with an intelligence as subtle and original as it was aggressive and audacious, he added to his natural gifts a profound erudition, which far from impeding only gave weight to the movements of his alert and robust mind.' Tertullian, we are told, had studied law, literature, medicine, military science, every form of learning including the

---

[1] Passmore, 'History of philosophy', p. 29.
[2] *Ibid.*
[3] R. B. Tollinton, *Clement of Alexandria* (London, 1914), vol. 2, p. 283.

occult. Then 'When he gave himself in his mature manhood to the service of Christianity, he brought in his hands all the spoils of antique culture, smelted into a molten mass by an almost incredible passion'. One final assessment completes the powerful picture: 'Harassed from without, the African Church was also torn from within by an accumulation of evils; apostasies, heresies, and schisms abounded. Up through the confusion were thrust Tertullian's mighty shoulders, casting off the enemies of the Gospel on every side. He was not formed for defensive warfare'.[1] What reader, in more heroic times, could resist the conviction that he had a great deal in common with Tertullian?

But we can hope for more than escape from parochialism. Since enlargement can only occur when there is continuity we can see the history of philosophy and theology as the history of certain problems. The elucidation of these problems will take the good points of other methods without suffering their disadvantages. It will respect the concern of the polemical historian for argument and for truth; but it will not force past writers into anachronistic positions and will consider the whole of their argument. It will allow the cultural historian to fill out the background of each writer and the issues he faced; but it will not allow the fuller account to shut any set of arguments off from those of other times on similar questions. It will respect the doxographer's stamp-collection, for he may indicate a fresh area for exploration and analysis. It will welcome the retrospective historian's account, for he makes clear the shape and limits of his inquiry. But it will insist that none of these methods has enabled the interests of second-century writers to emerge. If these concerns are so close to those that occupy Christian thinkers today, yet appear so remote in the classic treatments of the period, the methods require scrutiny. That scrutiny indicates inherent weaknesses in the methods no matter how skilfully they are employed. The problematic method offers ground for hope because it avoids the errors noted.

Two warnings should be added against perversity. First, when the thought of any writer is analysed, his meaning will only become clear when the different ways in which he uses terms have been set out. A perverse reader, who is innocent of

---

[1] B. B. Warfield, *Studies in Tertullian and Augustine* (Oxford, 1930), pp. 3f.

the tricks that words play, must see this process as unnecessary description and detail; he will be no wiser than the proof-reader of a street-directory who allows his reading to range over a wide area, and he will not be aware of changing patterns of meaning. 'What we should know, in studying a philosopher, is *the language he speaks*.' [1] Secondly, the same terms will keep coming back in different contexts. It is possible to find the second century, like the New Testament, so full of repetition that the perverse reader is bothered like a chess player who wonders why he must use the same kinds of pieces in successive games. Until he learns that the varying context determines the meaning of terms that appear similar, or that the important thing about chess is the different disposition of the pieces, not much can be done. If he casts his mind back to the New Testament he will know that, for all their repetition, the first three evangelists say different things and give different meanings to the same words, while the pastoral epistles use many Pauline phrases without Pauline meaning.

The problematic method determines the structure of each chapter. Each problem is subdivided into four or five questions for elucidation in each writer, whose distinctive concerns and logic will emerge in the course of the work. Passing reference may be made to recent writing in this first segment of each chapter, solely for illustration of particular points. Then at the end of the chapter, parallel contemporary problems will be considered; it should not be necessary to stress that the entire contemporary discussion of these vast areas cannot be adequately examined. The aim is to show some places where mutual illumination is possible, and to hope that readers will see many others. One positive sign may be indicated even at the beginning: when the ideas of these four writers are analysed, they illuminate and are illuminated by a diverse range of

---

[1] E. Kamenka, 'Marxism and the history of philosophy', *HThS*, 5 (1965), 103. Kamenka continues; 'This certainly means knowing the intellectual conditions and climate in which he operates, but his climate may include his past as well as his present, and his work may have an interest and a content that this climate has not'. This means more than the ability to read Greek, Latin, Coptic (to understand Gnosticism) and Hebrew (to understand the Bible); such competence remains important, but monoglot beginners who read quickly often see things that polyglot scholars, who lack the knowledge that Kamenka describes, have not seen.

twentieth-century thought. For example, their account of God gives fresh point to ideas of Ian Ramsey, Boyce Gibson, Austin Farrer, Henri Duméry, Iris Murdoch, Hans Urs von Balthasar, D. M. Mackinnon, and Eberhard Jüngel! There is no way of staying in one camp and listening to one voice.

2 People and places

The four writers, Justin, Irenaeus, Tertullian and Clement, come from four major cities and centres of Christianity: Rome, Lyons, Carthage and Alexandria.

Justin

In the second century, Rome continued to enjoy prosperity. While literature lost some of its power, building and sculpture went on vigorously. Trajan's forum, the baths of Caracalla, the palace of Septimius Severus on the Palatine, the Pantheon and Hadrian's mausoleum remain as evidence of great activity. The period of the Antonines was, said Gibbon, the greatest period of Rome.[1] Wars were few and there was prosperity on many sides. Yet disquieting signs may be found, and a recent picture of the period speaks of it as an age of anxiety:[2] men knew that the best was past and the unknown future had little to lure them on. There is truth in both these opinions, for it was the best of times and the worst of times; the general position of the empire was sound but there was intellectual insecurity.

Christians were to be found in small groups, which met in houses and recognised the oversight of a college of presbyters, and before long the presidency of one bishop. Heretics like Marcion and Valentinus met a strong opposition at Rome, for there the movement towards right belief was strongest.[3] There was tension between Rome and the East on the date of Easter, and attempts at reconciliation were not successful. Rome was becoming the centre for Christian guidance and decision, the place where local differences could be examined and corrected. Heresy was resisted more effectively because news of its varying forms could be brought together, warnings could be passed on and problems anticipated.

[1] E. Gibbon, *The decline and fall of the Roman Empire*, chapter 1.
[2] E. R. Dodds, *Pagan and Christian in an age of anxiety* (Cambridge, 1965).
[3] Bauer, *Orthodoxy and heresy*, pp. 229f.

Justin, who was born at Nablus, came to Rome by way of Asia Minor. He tells the story of his conversion at the beginning of his *Dialogue*.[1] While the facts have been dramatised and worked over, the account is confirmed by the evidence at Justin's trial.[2] Justin was a philosopher who began with a Stoic teacher who told him nothing about God, and he moved on to a Peripatetic who was more concerned about fees payable in advance than about the truth. Then a Pythagorean demanded study in music, astronomy and geometry as prerequisites for philosophy. Next, Justin came to a Platonist where at last he found some hope for the vision of God, for Middle Platonism was a deeply religious movement. Finally a Christian challenged his Platonism and showed him weaknesses in Plato and advantages in the gospel. Justin now admits the need for a direct knowledge of truth. Only those who have either seen God or heard from those who have seen can speak the truth, and the prophets alone pass this test. 'But in my soul a fire was immediately kindled and I was possessed with desire for the prophets and for those men who are the friends of Christ. As I pondered to myself his arguments, I found this to be the only safe and useful philosophy.'[3]

Justin's strength is a love of truth and a concern to follow the argument wherever it leads. He is an initiator and puts forward new ideas like that of the spermatic *logos*. Every man has some particle of divine *logos* in him. The fullness of the divine *logos* is in Christ and Christians receive all truth in him. The weaknesses of Justin spring from his position at the beginning of a new development. His key ideas remain unclear and undeveloped. As an apologist, he fights on many fronts and has little chance of bringing all his answers together. His longest work is directed towards the Jewish–Christian debate, a debate that was to have decreasing importance in the coming years.

Irenaeus

Irenaeus came from Asia Minor where he had once been a hearer of Polycarp and had learnt to reverence the apostles and

[1] *D.* 1–8.
[2] *Acta S. Justini et sociorum*, 2.
[3] *D.* 8.

the beginning of the gospel.[1] The expansion of Christianity from Ephesus into Asia Minor was more rapid than in any other place. But we learn of Irenaeus as bishop of Lyons where he succeeded to the care of the Church after Pothinus had died in prison.[2] More than forty Christians had been martyred and his task was formidable. He had gone to Rome earlier in an attempt to bring unity between churches. His chief concern was the destruction of Gnosticism, which was making heavy inroads at the time. His longest writing, *Against Heresies*, sets out what he knows of Gnostic doctrine, disproves and ridicules it, and then expounds the truth that he has received from the successors of the apostles. All that has been said about him must be qualified by the fact that his major work is clearly composite and some parts of it may be traced to different sources.[3] Nevertheless it is proper to speak of him as an identifiable theologian. No one could fight alone or disdain the help of any valuable material, and with all its tensions, the work hangs together and shows as much coherence as do the *Stromateis* of Clement.

Irenaeus is a missionary, pastor and theologian. He does theology because of the harmful effects of heresy and the pastoral problems it produces. He is concerned not simply to disprove but to destroy, and uses every argument and every detail that seems valuable. He is an optimist as far as the world and man are concerned. There is a lot of falsehood and distortion about, but man is free to choose and God's purpose brings man from childhood in Adam to maturity in Christ. His weaknesses lie chiefly in some kinds of argument that he uses. He multiplies images with rhetorical exuberance, drawing more and more parallels between Adam and Christ. His great theme of the summing-up of all things is a magnificent idea supported by slender arguments; it should be noted that the arguments would not have seemed slender to his readers, and that his techniques were entirely appropriate to his friends and foes. Another weakness is his fondness for *ad hominem* argument and the denunciation of moral faults in his opponents. Yet there is

---

[1] Letter to Florinus, in Eusebius, *H.E.* 5.20.4–8.

[2] Eusebius, *H.E.* 5.5.8.

[3] See especially A. Benoit, *Saint Irénée, introduction à l'étude de sa théologie* (Paris, 1960); F. Loofs, *Theophilus von Antiochien Adversus Marcionem und die anderen theologischen Quellen bei Irenaeus*, TU, 46.2 (Leipzig, 1930). A useful review of recent work on Irenaeus is to be found in K. N. Booth, 'Irenaeus and his Critics', *Colloquium*, 5.1 (1972), 4–11.

some evidence that the moral weakness of Gnosticism did more harm than its theology.[1] His sense of humour comes over clearly, if crudely, in places.[2] He is credulous concerning the end of the world and the thousand years in which the saints will enjoy the thousandfold blessings of the earth. Lastly, he opposes Gnostic tradition with his own tradition, and moves this idea towards the centre of Christian thought.

Tertullian

North Africa quickly became a centre of Christian faith. Carthage, the second great city of the West, received the gospel from Rome. A Latin Bible and worship in the Latin language developed here earlier than in Rome. Carthage had a dramatic and violent past. The Punic Wars ended in 146 B.C. with the destruction and cursing of the ruins of Carthage. Nevertheless attempts were made to re-establish a settlement there, and when Octavian gave land to 3000 of his veterans, the future of the colony was assured. It prospered in the second century. Roman consuls were among its citizens. Hadrian built a great aqueduct and Antoninus Pius rebuilt the forum after it had been destroyed by fire. Montanism took root in Carthage; but the chief problem for Christians was their relationship to a pagan society that was strong and vital. There were so many things that Christians could not do if they were to keep free from the pollution of polytheism.

Jerome claimed that Tertullian was the son of a Roman centurion and that he became a priest in the church at Carthage;[3] Eusebius had claimed that he was a lawyer of distinction.[4] These accounts have been shown to lack adequate

[1] This is evident, for example, in Clement's attack in *S*. 3. The lack of moral impropriety in the Nag Hammadi writings does nothing to weaken Clement's case. Gnostics could find sexual innuendoes in a cookery book, a solemn liturgy, or a gospel, as for example at Luke 6: 30 [Matthew 5: 42]; 'Give to everyone who asks you' [*S*. 3.4.27]. They would have no trouble in dimming the lights at the end of the Gospel of Thomas, with the most solemn language available. On the other hand Clement knows that there are also ascetic Gnostics, and they seem to be behind most Nag Hammadi writings.
[2] *H*. 1.1.8.
[3] Jerome, *De viris illustribus*, 5 3.
[4] Eusebius, *H.E.* 2.2.4.

foundation.[1] We have little knowledge of Tertullian's background and life. His knowledge of the law has often been either exaggerated on one hand or underestimated on the other. He writes and thinks like a lawyer, pleading a case. He belonged to the literary circles in Carthage, and therefore knew the full force of the Second Sophistic movement. He married a Christian wife, suffered a bereavement that deeply affected his theology, and became a Montanist. There is some probability that he died a comparatively young man. A rugged individualist, he stood out against pagan practice and Christian compromise. He fought heresy because he became a Montanist and was concerned for purity of doctrine. He may be called a 'Christian Sophist', provided that the title is understood in terms valid for Tertullian's day, and that it does not suggest mere verbal skill.[2]

Tertullian stands out as a defender of the faith, a preacher of the gospel, a rigorist, who could not tolerate compromise. He was pessimistic about the Church when he examined its morals, but optimistic when he saw its rapid expansion in a pagan world. His weaknesses are those of a sophist: words run away and abuse is as frequent as argument. His God is the God of the Old Testament, a God who in his justice sends bears to eat up cheeky children, and who threatens and punishes man because man is incapable of goodness without threat or punishment. His attitude to his opponents is hardly Christian and his anticipation of the suffering of persecutors in hell is as disturbing as his abuse of Marcion.

Clement

Alexandria was one of the great cities of the empire, a rival of Rome and Antioch. It dominated commerce in the eastern end of the Mediterranean, and was the gateway to Egypt. It had long been a place of learning. Despite its foundation as recently as the fourth century B.C. it treasured the wisdom of the past. The museum was founded by Ptolemy, the Jews had their schools and it was natural that Christianity should develop

[1] T. D. Barnes, *Tertullian. A historical and literary study* (Oxford, 1971), pp. 3–29.
[2] *Ibid.* pp. 211–32.

along intellectual lines. Christian teaching was not restricted to simple catechesis, but branched out into secular learning and the exegesis of scripture.

Little is known of the beginning of Christianity in Egypt. It is highly probable that the earlier Church there was dominated by Gnostic doctrine and therefore forgotten. Basilides and Valentinus are early representatives, and the Gospel of the Egyptians and the Gospel of the Hebrews show Gnostic dominance. Episcopacy developed later in Alexandria than in other places, and local churches had considerable independence.

Clement came to Alexandria at the end of his search for knowledge. He had travelled around the Mediterranean world looking for teachers.[1] In Alexandria he found Pantainos and here he settled. At last, purity of truth and richness of tradition were his. He saw Christianity as the true philosophy, and the ideal Christian as a teacher who led men away from error to the light of truth. Christianity included a process of learning: the gospel was preached to the pagans with an exhortation for them to turn from wickedness, the converted needed teaching and pastoral care in the many temptations of life, and finally each Christian should grow towards perfection as a Christian philosopher. The weakness of Clement's approach was his concentration on intellectual and ethical matters. He found it difficult to treat physical things with any great respect, although he defended the beauty and wonder of creation. God was utterly transcendent and beyond man's thought and language. The Christian struggled to be like God, free from passion and ignorance.

It would be hard to find four writers more different in approach and temperament. Justin, of whom we know least, because his surviving writings are short and entirely apologetic, provides one common denominator. His one desire is to speak and live for the truth. The love of truth dominates his whole activity. The same theme runs through the other three writers. But here the similarity must end, for Justin writes as none of the others writes and stands so close to the beginning of things. His reports on Christian behaviour, teaching and worship, show up the plain desire for truth. In his argument with Trypho his complexity first becomes obvious; he leaves his readers with many unsolved problems.

[1] Clement, *S.* 1.1.11; Eusebius, *H.E.* 6.6.

Irenaeus sees Jesus as the lord of history. The continuity of God's saving work is part of the gospel. None of it makes sense apart from the crowning event of incarnation, cross and resurrection, in which all things are summed up. With the wide sweep of historical vision, Irenaeus combines a concern for detail, finding parallel after parallel between Adam and Christ. He loves the language of sight and touch. God is seen, heard and felt. The glory of God is a living man and the vision of God is the life of man. Irenaeus analyses his opponents' theories with skill and exactness. He touches on points of detail and knows his subject. Having exposed and ridiculed the content of the heresies, he puts forward the tradition he has received and declares the gospel as he has heard it.

For Tertullian, God is creator and ruler of the world. God has made all things and there can be no other God because there is nothing for any other God to make. God is all powerful, and this means that there is no part of the universe over which he does not rule. There has to be one creator and there has to be one ruler of the world: 'Either God is one or He is not God'.[1] Coupled with his rigorism is Tertullian's hostility to every opponent. He never argues at half-speed, but throws every resource of logic and of abuse into the battle. Yet surprisingly for one who thinks with his heart and passion, Tertullian tackles more logical problems and points the way to more final solutions than most other writers of his time.

Finally, Clement sees God as truth and goodness. Men have wandered in error, but now the light has come. Their way towards the light involves a turning from sin and a readiness to learn and to obey. Their teacher is the divine Word who comes in the goodness of God, both proving and conveying divine grace to needy man. Christianity is not a simple religion, although it does begin that way. The believer is challenged to go on in daily obedience and daily fellowship with God. The limit to man's enjoyment of God's grace is not one that Clement can fix. There must be more, still more than any man has known, of God's glory to be found in a faithful life; the fullness of Christ calls men forward.

The motive of all these writers was a single-hearted love of truth, because they believed that, wherever man went, God's Word was present with him. Any fragment of truth must point

[1] Tertullian, *Marc.* 1.3.

24

to God because it was part of his purpose and his Word. Against the pagans, Gnostics and philosophers, they insisted on one God who was supreme and transcendent, one humanity freed by God to choose obedience or disobedience, one world whether in heaven or earth made by the only God for the race of men, one history of God's dealings with man from the beginning to the present and on to one end of all things, and one Word of God who declared the unity of God and who made man, the world and history into one universe under God's sovereign grace. The last word was with grace, for only grace, God's overflowing love, joined him to the one world as its creator and only saviour. Men were deceived by appearances far too easily, but when they came to themselves they acknowledged one God, one world and one saviour.

General setting

Apart from their Christian faith, the only thing that they had in common is that they were all governed by the *Imperium Romanum*.[1] What kind of a world did they live in? Militarist, aristocratic and plutocratic are the adjectives that spring most readily to mind. A military outlook dominated, for the armed force was the executive force of the government. The principate, which had emerged as a military dictatorship, retained its warrior basis; even a reflective emperor, like Marcus Aurelius, spent a great part of his life with armies in the field. Not until the twentieth century were there as many men under arms at a single time, and the brutality of war invaded the common spirit. As peace was abnormal for the Roman world so gentleness became abnormal for Roman society. Aristocracy prevailed and the strata of society were clearly and firmly delineated. The great families ruled and formed their alliances; pedigree was so important that the masks of ancestors were carried in funeral processions. Wealth was the key to advancement and the great estates were administered by efficient managers, who could be slaves or freedmen; they might hold the status of slave but they could have their own slaves and live in affluence.

[1] In these comments, I am indebted at several points to discussions with G. W. Clarke, and to chapter 4 of W. H. C. Frend, *Martyrdom and persecution in the early church* (Oxford, 1965).

Roman religion had long played an important part in the life of the nation. It is easy for the modern observer to underestimate the power of a formal creed that aroused little fervour. There was little outward zeal but there was a deep inner allegiance. Two hundred years before Christ, Polybius wrote of religion as the excellence of Rome, the source of her cohesion and fidelity.[1] Romans, unlike Greeks, could be trusted to keep their word. A hundred years later Cicero attributes the greatness of Rome to the activity of her gods.[2] The ritual and auguries of her religion were at once a sign of faith and source of guidance and stability.[3] Antiquity meant truth and efficacy, for the faith of Romans had been tested over the centuries.[4] Yet for all this ancient fidelity, Roman religion did not stand still but added new gods to its pantheon;[5] particular countries had their own special gods but the Romans had them all.[6] Within Roman religion there was room for all, with the exception of Christianity, for Christianity was neither ancient, Roman nor racial. The religion of the Jews might be repulsive, but as Tacitus put it 'defenduntur antiquitate'.[7] Christians were new and exclusive; they would not be assimilated into the total fabric of Roman religion and they would give no place to any God but their own.

By the time Christianity emerged, the emperor had moved to the centre of Roman religion. Augustus was the great Messiah who had brought peace on earth; the battle of Actium had brought in the new age. Augustus had defeated the titanic forces of disorder, just as Zeus had once subdued the Titans.[8] He might disclaim deity and insist that while his authority exceeded that of his magisterial colleagues his power was the same; but his very title raised him above ordinary mortals and he was hailed as 'god from god' and assimilated with Zeus Eleutheros Sebastos.[9] His cult was to prove a ground for opposition to Jews and Christians in many places.

[1] Polybius, 6.56.6–12.
[2] Cicero, *De natura deorum*, 2.3.5ff.
[3] Livy, 5.51.5.
[4] Ennius, *Annales*, frag. 467: 'moribus antiquis stat res Romana virisque'.
[5] Livy, 39.16.6.
[6] Minucius Felix, *Octavius*, 6f.
[7] Tacitus, *Histories*, 5.5.
[8] See Frend, *Martyrdom*, pp. 115f.
[9] *Ibid.* p. 119; see Pap. Oxy. 12, 1453, and *Corpus Papyrorum Rainerii*, ed. Wessely (Vienna, 1895), p. 224.

The treatment of Christians varied considerably during the second century. The previous century ended with the so-called 'persecution of Domitian' when charges of atheism were brought against Flavius Clemens and Domitilla, not to mention others who had lapsed into Judaism.[1] There is no evidence to establish that anything like a persecution of Christians took place;[2] it was 'a case of unnatural slaughter of kinsfolk'.[3] Pliny's correspondence with Trajan reveals a reluctance to punish except after denunciation and proof; Christians were not to be sought out, anonymous accusations received no hearing and those accused must be given a chance to recant.[4] During this early period Judaism is seen as the chief religious enemy of Rome, for Hadrian forbade all Jewish practices including circumcision. Christians stood aside during the Jewish revolts and thereby avoided the harsh treatment that their religious proximity to the Jews might have merited.

The thirty years that followed the second Jewish war have been called 'the false dawn'.[5] The laws were not changed but their administration was relaxed. Apologists came out in defence of the new faith, its moral force and its rational strength; yet popular slanders were widely believed. The martyrdom of Polycarp showed how a Christian leader who had lived in good standing with secular authorities was still not free from danger. The years of 165–80 were years of crisis, when the criticisms of Fronto, Lucian and Celsus challenged the new faith. Division within the Christian ranks arose through the Montanist movement. In the next fifty years, after considerable advances, the tide turned against Christianity. When Alexander Severus was killed, Maximinus, because of the large numbers of Christians in the imperial household, 'started a persecution, ordering that the leaders of the Church alone be put to death'.[6]

The philosophical thought of the second century is sloppy, unimpressive and easy to ignore. This is unfortunate because

---

[1] Dio Cassius, 67.14.
[2] See P. Prigent, 'Au temps de l'Apocalypse, I, Domitien', *RHPhR*, 4 (1974), 451–83; 'II, Le culte impérial au Ier siècle en Asie Mineure', *RHPhR*, 2 (1975), 215–35; 'III. Pourquoi les persécutions?', *RHPhR*, 3 (1975), 341–63.
[3] Frend, *Martyrdom*, p. 215.
[4] Pliny, *Letters*, 10, 96.
[5] Frend, *Martyrdom*, pp. 236–67.
[6] Eusebius, *H.E.*, 6.28.

the dominant trend, Middle Platonism, occasionally provides interesting parallels to Christian thought of the time. The whole shape of Platonism is now modified by a strong religious tendency. For the first time it becomes proper to speak of a Platonic theology, and not merely of Platonic propositions that may have theological relevance. The ultimate first principle is placed at the upper limit of transcendence; a widespread and deep yearning for God is linked to a strong rejection of worldly sufficiency.[1] Plato is no longer represented as the master of dialectic and logic, but rather as the teacher of that divine knowledge which is man's greatest good.[2] The world of forms is subordinate to the single-minded quest for God: there is less interest in an invisible world. The one question concerns the being of God, who is seen as first cause of all things. Aristotle helps with terminology for the ultimate cause and his transcendence, as he helps with the rejection of dualism.

The heightened transcendence of God modifies even the pattern of the 'three-principles doctrine', which had dominated Platonic thought from the beginning. For the creator becomes more than a craftsman when the ideas, which give the pattern of his work, are within his own mind.[3] Yet the two steps (making of pattern and making of world) are clearly distinguished; the two-level divinity (visible and intellectual) is the most characteristic element of Middle Platonism.[4] It does not survive into Neoplatonism, because of its lack of precision; but it is a bulwark against dualism. There is no way in which the visible god (the world) could be set over against the intellectual god (the ideas). They are both divine and they point beyond themselves to an ultimate first cause.

Celsus, known as the chief critic of Christians, has some claim to stand out from his contemporaries. His account of true *logos* is a systematic Platonic theology, which places the highest first-principle above Being, but does not identify it as the One. He seems to have probed deeper than other Platonists with whom he shared the three ways (*via eminentiae, via negativa, via*

[1] H. Dörrie, 'Die Frage nach dem Transzendenten im Mittelplatonismus' in *Les sources de Plotin*, Entretiens sur l'antiquité classique, 5 (Geneva, 1960), p. 218.
[2] *Ibid.* p. 196.
[3] *Ibid.* p. 208.
[4] *Ibid.* p. 218.

analogiae) of knowing God and a select bundle of citations from Plato. Albinus and Plutarch had already begun the movement from the 'open' philosophy of the time of Hadrian to a 'closed' or systematic account, but they had not gone far along that road. Celsus provides a clear picture of a Platonism that was a worthy opponent to Christian thought. A recent impressive account of Celsus has given him new status and significance.[1] Two comments need to be added: if Celsus rewards analysis so brilliantly, the denigration of other Middle Platonists (with which this section began) needs to be cautious until they may be shown to lack redeeming qualities; further, Celsus' failure to expound the One as a supreme principle must be due at least in part to the Christian attack on Celsus' polytheism. On this latter point the inferiority of a systematic to a problematic approach is evident.

Plotinus will take the elements of his predecessors and form something quite new. A Pythagorean tendency gives predominance to the One, and the internal duality of divinity is removed by subordinating Mind to the One and including Soul among the three ultimate principles. Plotinus avoids the threat of dualism in a different way from his predecessors. The perfection of the One overflows to produce all things in a descending order; yet it transcends them and does not embrace the forms as its thoughts. On the other hand Mind includes forms of particular things and of persons. Mind represents the One in the Soul that it causes. Soul provides order for the visible world; it is more appropriate to say that body is in soul rather than soul in body. All this means that 'Plotinus is not a metaphysical dualist. Matter is produced by the principles which come before it, and so, ultimately, by the One'.[2] Yet Plotinus is of marginal concern for the study of Justin, Irenaeus, Tertullian, Clement. He taught and wrote when their work

[1] I am indebted to the excellent study of H. Dörrie, 'Die platonische Theologie des Kelsos in ihrer Auseinandersetzung mit der christlichen Theologie auf Grund von Origenes c. Celsum, 7, 42ff.', *NAWG, PH* (1967), 19–55. The translation of Origen's *Contra Celsum* by H. Chadwick (Cambridge, 1953) opened up this area of study. Now *The Middle Platonists* (London, 1977), by John Dillon, has provided a comprehensive introduction to the period.

[2] A. H. Armstrong, 'Plotinus', in *Later Greek and early Medieval philosophy*, p. 256.

was over; he has interest chiefly because he confirms the hostility of Platonism to Gnostic dualism and because he influenced later and different forms of Christian Platonism.

3 The God above

One God was the fixed point of early Christian thought. His oneness meant that he could not be caused, described or seen. Negative attributes have an abstract ring when they are not heard properly; correctly understood, they point to the first commandment: 'Thou shalt have no other gods before me'. 'The Lord our God is one Lord and thou shalt love the Lord thy God with all thy heart, with all thy soul and with all thy mind.' The discovery of this God through the crucified Christ led Justin and others to think vigorously and to live and die faithfully. The framework was eschatological; thinking, living and dying went together: 'If we are punished for the sake of our Lord Jesus Christ we hope to be saved; for this shall be our salvation and confidence before the more terrible judgement seat of our Lord and Saviour who shall judge the whole world.' 'Do what you will for we are Christians and offer no sacrifice to idols.'[1] The meaning of the unity of God was found in the difference it made to the lives of those who accepted it.

When unity is taken seriously, it is inexpressible and transcendent. We cannot say what the One is; we can only say what it is not. Plato's *Parmenides* is logically, if not historically, relevant: 'If there is a One, of course the One will not be many. Consequently it cannot have any parts or be a whole . . . the One in no sense is . . . It is not named or spoken of, not an object of opinion or of knowledge, not perceived by any creature'.[2] Christians did not hesitate to accept the negative theology that logic required; for they wanted to destroy other gods and to insist that their God was unique. The problems about the Christian God may be broken up into four main questions:

(1) Is there one God and can one speak of him?
(2) Is God good?
(3) Can God be three as well as one?
(4) Is God best understood as the first cause?

[1] *Acta S. Justini et sociorum*, 5.
[2] *Parmenides*, 138–42.

I Is there one God and can one speak of him?

At no stage is the God of the Christians seen as one of the gods of the classical world, left alone when all the others had vanished. He was different because he was one; but how was he different? His difference lay in his transcendence over ordinary language, and his separation from common categories of thought. How did second-century writers tackle this problem? They followed the consequences of their belief in divine unity, agreeing with Plato's *Parmenides* that the One was only capable of negative description. But they said other things also.

It is Justin who first states clearly the consequences of God's unity.[1] He denies many attributes that have been given to God and insists that God is 'unbegotten', 'ineffable' and 'invisible'; for Justin wants to unravel man's introverted talk about God. Clement compares some theology to the hedgehog that rolls itself into a ball and thinks about God in terms of its own interior existence.[2] It is Justin who starts unrolling the hedgehog, and his work is continued by Irenaeus, Tertullian and Clement. Justin is the innovator; his ideas are stated in a brief and blunt way, and he is quite happy to be called an atheist. Christians are atheists as far as the so-called gods of the pagans are concerned but they are not atheists with respect to the most true God.[3]

As a Christian Justin aligns himself with Socrates, who died because he refused to believe in the false gods of his city, and because he valued truth above all else.[4] For Justin the man of truth puts even his life at a lower estimate than the truth he knows. (In company with Socrates it is easy to make fun of idols; but ridicule of idols went back to Elijah on Mount Carmel or to Deutero-Isaiah. Jews and Christians could hardly complain when pagans returned their ridicule.[5]) It is unjust to

---

[1] Antecedents are of course to be found in Philo Judaeus, not to mention Aristides, *Apol.* 1.4. and NT passages such as 1 Timothy 1: 17 and 6: 16.

[2] *S.* 5.11.68. Cf. Philo, *De sacrificiis Abelis et Caini*, 95.

[3] *1 A.* 6.

[4] *1 A.* 5 and 6. See Osborn, *Justin Martyr*, pp. 26f. and 81f.

[5] As, for example, 'Alexamenos worships his god', with picture of ass's head. See J. Preaux, *'Deus Christianorum Onokoetes'*, *Latomus*, 44 (1960), 639–54; Frend, *Martyrdom*, p. 252.

punish those who do not worship non-existent fantasies, and for love of truth, Christians will stand with Socrates as atheists. [*1 A.* 6] One practical weakness of Justin's case was that atheism was seen by his contemporaries more as an anti-social and anti-moral position than as an argued approach to theology. Impiety against the gods of the State was subversive for political reasons, and Justin's statement anticipates moral disapproval by insisting on the ethical quality of 'The most true God, the father of righteousness, moderation and other virtues, untainted by evil'. To God, Christians owe their entire allegiance.[1] The subtlety of Justin is seen in the way in which he links his negative theology to positive anthropology.[2] It is no good describing God in negative terms unless there are some positive pointers to him in the world, or in human life. For Justin, the unbegotten or uncaused God is known through the new life that he plants in the soul of a believer, the ineffable God is known through the Word or Logos he has put in the heart of every man and the invisible God is known through the quality of life that may be observed in those who gaze on his beauty and goodness.

Since this is where Justin shows clearly that he is not merely repeating negative formulae, we must look at it in detail. The Gnostics, by contrast, did not see that the terminology of transcendence was useless without a clear empirical link; yet 'It is no profit to be told what religious belief is *not*, unless some indication can be given of what it *is*'.[3] In the second century the move is invariably from an empirical fringe[4] to God. This fringe is nearly always the evidence of a new quality in human life. New possibilities and actualities of human behaviour are taken as evidence of the Christian God. The ordered world or the changing seasons had been taken as fringes of other gods. The Christian God was seen in transformed human lives.

Justin's conversion owed much to his awareness that Christians had acquired transcendence over the ordinary aims of human life. When he saw the way in which Christians behaved in the face of death, he knew that the slanders against them were

---

[1] *1 A.* 6.

[2] See E. F. Osborn, 'Empiricism and transcendence', *Prudentia*, 8.2 (1976), 115–22, which is reproduced and abridged in this section.

[3] R. B. Braithwaite, 'An empiricist's view of religious belief', in *Christian ethics and contemporary philosophy* (London, 1966), p. 88.

[4] A. Boyce Gibson, *Theism and empiricism* (London, 1970), pp. 63ff.

false. Christians are driven by a desire for eternal life in purity
and holiness with God [*1 A*. 8]. Because they look for God's
kingdom their thoughts do not dwell on the present and they
are not worried by death [*1 A*. 11]. They worship God rationally and not with blood and incense [*1 A*. 13]. Aloof from demons, they follow the one unbegotten God; from fornication
they have turned to chastity; from magic they have turned to
the good unbegotten God; from pursuit of worldly wealth they
have turned to caring for others [*1 A*. 14]. Christian behaviour
is new, concerned with heavenly treasure and does not worry
about earthly things [*1 A*. 15]. Christ's power is seen in those
who take no account of glory, fear and death [*2 A*. 10]. In
Justin there is evidence of human transcendence that enables
divine transcendence to be rationally asserted.

Justin's arguments are compact and susceptible of scrutiny;
we shall observe how intricately and exactly he joins negative
or transcendent descriptions of God with positive or optimistic
descriptions of man. In each case man is an empirical fringe or
prolongation of God, who is unbegotten, ineffable and invisible.

i   *Unbegotten*

Justin [*D*. 5] turns to the *Timaeus* 41B of Plato, where the
demiurge speaks to the gods he has made and the works he has
produced. He speaks as their father, upon whose will their
continued existence depends. His goodness ensures that their
state, which is good, will survive. What had a beginning can
have an end; but the good demiurge will preserve what he has
made because it is good. What had no beginning will not have
an end. To be God is to be uniquely unbegotten and imperish-
able. Of course, Plato was speaking enigmatically, says Justin:[1]

[1] There is a quaint discussion on the reason why Justin attributes
enigma to Plato and interprets Plato freely. Hyldahl, *Philosophie und
Christentum* (Copenhagen, 1966), E. P. Meijering, *Orthodoxy and
Platonism in Athanasius. Synthesis or antithesis?* (Leiden, 1968), p. 28,
see that Atticus' rejection of enigma could be polemical. Here
Meijering writes: 'Atticus and Justin may both use a Middle Platonic
source in which it says that Plato speaks in enigmatic language.
Justin may adopt this formulation, while Atticus – a very formalistic
Platonist – corrects his source'. The mind boggles: Justin uses a text,
which speaks of many gods, in order to prove the uniqueness of one
God; he *has* to take Plato as enigmatic or non-literal. The logical
necessity is obvious while the historical connection is not.

by 'gods' he meant the soul and things in general. Justin must modify the terms if he is to prove monotheism from a polytheist source; he redefines 'god' so as to exclude created things and to include only the one unbegotten. For the rest, the positive claims about God remain; he is father, preserver of good and giver of immortality. The positive claims about the soul and the world also remain; they are God's good creation and the soul is capable of receiving his gift of immortality. A similar strain of argument is found in Justin's argument from first cause. This argument appears first in Plato's *Laws* [893–6] and Aristotle's *Metaphysics* [1071–5], but Justin insists that it does not depend on external authorities. God is the only uncaused cause, unmoved mover and necessary being. As far as the soul is concerned [*D.* 6] this means that God lives of himself. God is life. The soul lives as God grants it life, as it participates in the life that is God. The uniqueness of God is established through the relation that he holds to other things.

ii   Ineffable

When Justin quotes the well-worn saying of Plato concerning the inaccessibility and ineffability of the father and maker of all, he seems to follow the account of Albinus.[1] Socrates, he tells us, got into trouble for his rejection of the gods of his city. Socrates' one concern was the knowledge of the unknown God and he was pessimistic about man's achievement and communication of this knowledge. Yet these very things were achieved by Christ, who is God's whole Logos and the power of the ineffable Father. The proof is public for all to see. While no one was ever persuaded to die for Socrates, now there are people everywhere, not just philosophers, but workmen too, who are prepared to despise honour, fear and death for Christ's sake [*2 A.* 10]. Here the optimism is blunt and open. It is an optimism of grace, because it springs from the word and power of God; it is born from the observation of Christian men, learned and unlearned, who have learnt from the word of the unknown God that earthly glory, fear and death do not matter. This was the way Justin himself had followed to the unknown God [*2 A.* 12]. He had heard Christians maligned but when he saw their scorn for

[1] Cf. Justin, *2 A.* 10 and Albinus, *Did.* 27.

sin and death he knew the slanders were false and made his way
to the unbegotten and ineffable God in whose sight a Christian
life is lived. In an earlier statement we learn that, unlike the
demons, God has no name [*2 A.* 6]; but the Platonist, whether
Christian or not, has then to explain what titles such as 'Father',
'God', 'Maker', 'Lord' and 'Master' do, if they are not names
of God. These titles are not names, says Justin, they are forms
of address that derive from God's benefits and works. Justin
makes three points: God does good, has works to show and is
addressed by men. We may not speak of him but we can speak
to him. This is not all. Justin goes on to speak of the son of God,
the Word who was with God, begotten of God, before all
things were made. He has the names of 'Christ' and of 'Jesus'.
'Christ' is a name in the way 'God' is not a name. It has a
discoverable meaning as well as unknown significance. 'Jesus'
means man and saviour; he came by the Father's will for the
sake of believers and for the destruction of demons. Everywhere
this name is effective against demons. Those who exorcise in
this name have cured and are curing those possessed of demons.
The demons are made ineffective and driven out [*2 A.* 6].

The same confident strain continues as Justin goes on to say
that God delays the destruction of the cosmos simply because
of the existence of Christians [*2 A.* 7]. They are the cause of the
continuance of the natural order. When this order is brought
to an end, it will not be in a general or indiscriminate way as
the Stoics suggest. It will exhibit the justice of God. Here again,
negative theology leads to optimistic anthropology, an
optimism of grace and judgement.

iii   *Invisible*

The invisible God is affirmed against the background of
polemic against idolators and Jews. The rejection of idolatry
provoked the accusation of Christian atheism. Yes, says Justin,
we are atheists as far as this kind of god is concerned. So was
Socrates and we are happier to suffer with him than to revel
with irrational men [*1 A.* 5, 6 and 13.1]. Idols are false
because God does not have the kind of shape that idols claim
to copy. To worship idols is to go against reason; for idols need
men to look after them [*1 A.* 9]. When it comes to worshipping
mice, cats and crocodiles, the absurdity is blatant [*1 A.* 24.1].

Idolatry denies the truth about God and is ultimately negative however interesting it may appear at first.

That Judaism can be classed with idolatry is strange in the face of Jewish polemic and intransigence against idols. Yet the literal interpretation of scripture must take God's hand, feet and fingers as visible objects [*D.* 114], and the whole Christian–Jewish debate hangs on the interpretation of scripture. If all Messianic prophecies must be literally fulfilled, then the Messiah has not come. Christians, on the other hand, have been circumcised with the true circumcision [*D.* 41.4] and know that the Holy Spirit has inspired the prophets [*D.* 7.1]. The Jews have forfeited their right to the scriptures because they do not understand the rational meaning of them [*D.* 29.2]. Once again a negative theology affirms what its opponents deny: it affirms spirit and reason over against letter.

How does one see the invisible? Again Justin turns to Platonic tradition, and expounds the way in which the eye of the soul sees pure being. Being itself is the cause of mental objects, is beyond all essence and has no colour, shape, size or any visible characteristic. Yet the eye of the righteous soul sees it clearly; for being appears immediately to noble souls because they possess an affinity to it and because they want to see it [*D.* 4]. Plato had spoken like this in *Phaedo* 66; the ideas had been continued by Albinus [*Did.* 10.4] and Maximus of Tyre [*Diss.* 17.1]. Once again Plato has provided the framework for Justin's negative account of God, giving it a positive content. It is because God is pure being that he does not possess physically observable qualities; further, this God is visible to pure souls, which have an affinity to him.

The logical structure is constant. As God is unbegotten, God is life and man's soul lives by participation in God [*D.* 5–7]. As ineffable, the unknown God is known through his *logos*, in which men share [*2 A.* 10]. As invisible, God is seen by the eyes of the soul through its moral excellence and purity; it has no necessary vision of God but is capable of such vision through virtue [*D.* 4.3].

Justin's account of the unknown God is far from abstract. He does not qualify divine transcendence but takes his own way through the problem. Irenaeus is more positive still: 'God the father, not made, not material, invisible; one God, the creator of all things: this is the first point of our faith' [*D.* 6].

Irenaeus begins with all the insistence on transcendence that we find in the philosophers and theologians of his day: God is not to be known by man [*H.* 4.34.1; 3.38.2; 4.34.4; 4.34.6; 2.6.1], and *man cannot properly speak of God*. The heretics, for all their lofty abstractions, are not lofty and transcendent enough. They say that God is unknown yet they give him all the thoughts and passions of men. Scripture shows that God is far above men and his ways and his thoughts are not like theirs. The only way to talk about God is the way men of religion and piety take: a simple being, without parts, entirely identical and consistent, he is total mind, spirit, thought, intelligence, reason, hearing, seeing, light, the whole source of all good things. In this account we have gone a long way beyond idols or any physical representation of God. The unity of God is comprehensive yet without parts; the stress is on his totality [*H.* 2.15.3].

Yet Irenaeus was not satisfied. 'He is, however, above these qualities and is therefore indescribable' [*H.* 2.15.4]. He is understanding, but not like the understanding of men; he is light, but not like the light that men know; and while he is Father, he has none of the weaknesses of a human father. We speak of him in these terms because we love him but our thoughts of his greatness go beyond anything we say. So the Gnostics go wrong in hypostasising divine attributes and telling stories about them. For whatever else may be said, there is no way of separating intelligence, word, life from other divine excellences that must go together if they go at all [*H.* 2.16.5]. Further, the Gnostics, so far from exalting God, still describe him in terms of abstract human thoughts and feelings; for example, in the Gnostic aeons they put Man before Word [*H.* 2.17]. So they make the same mistakes as idolators, simply using mental instead of physical attributes as they build God in the image of man. Irenaeus wants to say that they claim too little and too much: they claim too little when they separate his attributes; they claim too much when they treat these attributes as ultimate.

Yet love finds a way, for man cannot live without God and God wills man's life and salvation [*H.* 4.34.1–7]. He holds all things in his hand, gives light to heaven and earth, tests man's secret thoughts, while at the same time openly feeding and strengthening him. God's greatness is beyond our knowledge, but his love leads us to him by his Word and in obedience we learn of the infinite greatness that made, ordered and contains all things. Power and love go together where God, despite his infinite greatness, made himself visible to mortal men; for only by the vision of God could man receive life and immortality. Man without God is in darkness, corruption and death. 'For it is impossible to live without God; however, the means of life comes from participation in God, which means seeing God and enjoying his goodness: therefore men will see God, so that they may live, being made immortal by the sight and even entering into God' [*H.* 4.34.7]. The reason for this bewildering display of power and love by the most high God is man's need. Man, who had broken God's command and become his enemy, is restored to friendship by the incarnation; by grace man shares in, and is subject to, his maker. Now his sins are forgiven, for the one mediator between God and men has given himself for the propitiation of man's sins [*H.* 5.17.1]. The power that man cannot grasp is the means God uses to make himself known by men: 'since his invisible nature is powerful, it confers on all a profound mental intuition and awareness of his most powerful, indeed, all-powerful greatness' [*H.* 2.4.5]. From this initial intuition divine power leads men on to the vision of God. For Irenaeus vision is the way the unknown is known. At this point he is consistent with Plato and even the Gnostics; yet unlike them he is tied firmly to the incarnation.

The same positive note is continued in the account of the *unity of God*.[1] God is both simple and universal [*H.* 2.15.3; 2.42.2], the one universal Father of all [*H.* 5.18.2], both one and three. He includes all things, for he is himself the creator of all that is [*E.* 8]. The god of the Gnostics had deficiencies, but the God of Irenaeus has no deficiency, need or fear. As he is one God, he is worshipped day and night, while the heavens, the temple and the new covenant join in his praise [*E.* 10]. His absolute being stands over against man, as maker over against that which is made, as that which is always one and the same over against that which has a beginning, and grows toward perfection. As there is one God, so there is one salvation, although many precepts and many steps lead man to God [*H.* 4.18,19]; for the one God rules over all men in the many

---

[1] For summary of evidence see Benoit, *Saint Irénée*, pp. 204ff., where unity is taken as the chief theme of *Against Heresies*.

parts of the economy of salvation [*H.* 4.25.2]. All creation points to the one God, who is lord of all [*H.* 2.4.5].

God, by definition, is all things and there cannot be anything beyond him, otherwise he would not be God. When the heretics postulate another *pleroma* beyond God, they ignore the fallacy of infinite regress. Either there is one being who contains all things and created all things by his own will, or else there are many creators and gods who begin from one another and end in one another; but none of the beings mentioned in the second alternative could be God, for he would always lack that which belonged to his fellows. He could not be omnipotent and could not be God. The argument is: either one God or no God [*H.* 2.1.1]. The theme of the unity and sovereignty of God constantly returns: there is only one living God, who formed the world, who shaped man and, having given the faculty of growth to creation, called man upwards to greater things in his presence [*H.* 2.41.1]. So reason confirms the truth that the apostles handed down: one God, one Christ. To deny this truth is to despise the companions of the Lord, the Lord himself and the Father above [*H.* 3.1].

Irenaeus turns to one passage in the Old Testament that lights up the whole Christian position. The struggle of the prophets against the Baals is lived again by Irenaeus and other Christians. The moving scene on Mount Carmel when, after the prophets of Baal have shouted and performed their frenzies, Elijah turns in helpless solitude to the Lord God of Abraham, Isaac and Jacob, shows us where Irenaeus saw himself; he asks that whoever reads his book will know that God is God alone, and avoid heretical godless teaching [*H.* 3.6.2f.]. 'Therefore, I too call upon you, Lord God of Abraham, God of Isaac, God of Jacob and Israel, the father of our Lord Jesus Christ, the God who, through your great mercy, have been pleased to grant us knowledge of yourself.' In the loneliness and conflict of his own Mount Carmel, Irenaeus does not qualify the transcendence of the one true God but insists that the Gnostics have not made God transcendent enough. Yet the love of God leads men to him by many ways because the one God holds all things within him. He is the source of all that is and there is nothing over which he does not rule in freedom and in love.

At first Tertullian's use of *negative theology* seems less important than his loyalty to the biblical tradition. He certainly uses all the terms of transcendence; but could they mean much to a man so passionate and involved? When we look closer we see that they formed an essential part of his polemic against polytheism and are central to the extended argument of his *Apology*.

Christians are punished because they do not worship the gods; but they should be given the chance to show that these gods do not exist, and that non-existence removes any claim on worship [*Ap.* 10]. If one does believe in many gods, then one must also believe in a higher god who has made these gods. This is the god above, the god who is higher than all others; but such a god would never make more gods [*Ap.* 11]. The many gods are merely the names of heroes of ancient days, and have no substantial reality whatever. Their images are simply pieces of matter [*Ap.* 12]; household gods are bought and exchanged like any other household appliance [*Ap.* 13]. No wonder philosophers like Socrates could not accept these gods, and preferred to swear by a goat or a dog rather than by these things [*Ap.* 14]. The one God has ordered all things by his word in accordance with his sovereign will. This one true God cannot be grasped by the mind of man, but is revealed by his grace. Our faculties may form a limited idea of what he is; he can be truly known only by himself. He remains transcendent in his majesty, both known and unknown [*Ap.* 17]. Since he is the only God to whom worship is due [*Ap.* 24], Christians pray to him for the safety of their rulers [*Ap.* 30]; but they cannot call an emperor God, because that would be a falsehood. They can call the emperor Lord, provided this does not mean that he is the one true Lord, the almighty and eternal God, who is lord of the emperor as of all other men [*Ap.* 34]. God is hard to discover, as Plato insisted, and when he has been found the knowledge is difficult to communicate; but, says Tertullian, Christian workmen find God and show others what he is like [*Ap.* 46].

Against Hermogenes, a Platonic dualist, the same theme of transcendence is pursued in a more abstract vein. This universal God is one alone and there can be nothing equal to him who is unique and singular, above all and prior to all. Matter cannot be equal to God, because God is one, and he is the God above [*Herm.* 4]. As there is one God, so there is one earth that God made, and he rules over his creation [*Herm.* 26]. The wisdom of God is shown in his creation of all things out of nothing, a mysterious act that only God understands [*Herm.* 45]. Transcendence means so much to Tertullian that he is not prepared to accept Hermogenes' form of Platonism even when it would have helped him in his rejection of polytheism. On the other hand he commends the Valentinians for their awareness of God's transcendence. Heretics are not always wrong, for the followers of Valentinus acknowledge the greatness of God and declare him to be unbegotten, immense, invisible, infinite and eternal; but they err in other matters [*Val.* 7].

Before the divine mystery, no men have natural privileges;[1] only scripture and Church can explain God. That is the reason why Christian workmen have access to philosophy that the wisest Greek could not reach, and why Christians pray to God as 'Father', a name that was not given to Moses but came only through Jesus [*Orat.* 2].

Tertullian sees that Christians have an even tougher problem than divine transcendence – 'Christ, and him crucified'; but he claims that this is the way through the mystery of God. Here the philosophers are no help, since for them a crucified God would be as bad as an idol, if not worse. Tertullian professes to spurn philosophy, and infers from divine transcendence that God will act in a way that is quite different from man's expectation.

The famous passage (usually misquoted) in which Tertullian draws out this consequence is worth examining.[2] Marcion has rejected the incarnation as unworthy of the Son of God and foolish. But Paul insisted that God chose the foolish things of the world to confound the wise, and the suffering and humiliation of a crucified God are most foolish of all. Marcion must spare the only hope of all the world in his attempt to remove the 'necessary dishonour of faith'. Whatever is unworthy of God is a help to man, who is safe as long as he is not ashamed of his Lord. 'The son of God was crucified; it is not shameful because it must be an object of shame. The son of God died; it is credible, because it is inappropriate. When buried, he rose again; it is certain because it is impossible.' Christ is both man and God. 'Why halve Christ with a lie? He was truth entirely.' What Tertullian means here is neither a platitude about paradox, nor a rejection of reason. He wants to show that

---

[1] *Ap.* 34.3. See comment, J. M. Hornus, 'Étude sur la penseé politique de Tertullien', *RHPhR*, 38 (1958), 35–6.

[2] *Carn.* 5.

language about God has to be full of surprises. The Christian way through the problem does not lie in the statement of a half-truth, but in a recognition of Christian folly, which is wiser than the world. Marcion and the Gnostics settled for half the truth – they separated the divine from the human. The result for Gnosticism was a *pleroma*, which did not mix with the world but provided an archetype for worldly existence. Tertullian knows that this will not do; Irenaeus had pointed out how silly it was for spiritual aeons to cast physical shadows on the earth.

In general, we may agree with a modern comment that 'the incarnation seems to be the point for the Christian faith, where there must essentially be an intersection of religious and non-religious language; it has to be said not only that a certain person was crucified but that that person was the Son of God'.[1] However from 'It is credible because it is inappropriate' the corollary does not follow,[2] 'Because it is inappropriate it is not credible' for Tertullian wanted to insist that the fitting was not credible. There was no point in worshipping a stone, animal or even an exalted idea. The exalted idea must fit into[3] the ordinary world in some way that was not reducible to the ordinary world. Magic was not enough. If the world and God are entirely separate ('God does not reveal himself *in* the world'[4]), then religious language like that of the Gnostics will be safe but meaningless. The zenith of transcendence does not come by going beyond being but by mixing God and the world. This is Tertullian's way to meaning and transcendence, and we must return to it later.

The minimal conclusion is that there are going to be surprises when anyone tries to say what cannot be said.[5] Here again

---

[1] Bernard Williams, 'Tertullian's paradox', in Antony Flew and Alasdair MacIntyre (eds.), *New essays in philosophical theology* (London, 1955), p. 203.

[2] *Ibid.* p. 211.

[3] *Ibid.* p. 207.

[4] L. Wittgenstein, *Tractatus Logico-Philosophicus*, 6. 432 (cited by Williams, 'Tertullian's paradox', p. 202).

[5] A more useful approach than that of Williams may be found in S. Milligan, *The Goon Show scripts* (London, 1972). When the Goon Show began, it was professedly surrealist and endeavoured to end or to alternate sentences in the opposite way to what was expected. Critics saw the influence of Lewis Carroll and James Joyce in these comic scripts; one critic claimed, 'they have added a new dimension'.

Tertullian has more to say. On a scheme of logic common to all four writers the existence of one ultimate first principle was as certain as it was obscure. There had to be one first principle, but it was hard if not impossible to describe him. God was so different as to be inaccessible. Forms or first principles could be seen as efficient, formal or final causes. The efficient causes formed a series that ended in an uncaused cause. The system of definition ended in an indefinable. The series of ends or purposes stopped with an end that had no purpose or point. It is hard to see the argument from infinite regress as anything other than a disaster.

One hope lay in accepting the indefinable pointlessness and making it the criterion of being God, the upper limit of transcendence. The other hope lay in understanding God in terms of what came from him, the grace he gave and the world he made. Tertullian sees that the Gnostics and Marcion have gone wrong on both these points. They have refused to stop at the top and have added a *Pleroma* or a most high God on the other side of the first cause. At the same time they have cut the Most High adrift from the world and attenuated his causal efficacy. In stark contrast Tertullian accepts both points – that God is indefinable, beyond purpose, and that he is understood by the downward movement of his grace. So Tertullian takes yet another way through the problem of the unknown God. It was aggressive rather than abstract; the same can be said of his account of the unity of God.

Tertullian is a passionate monotheist, who ushers in African Christianity with its one all-powerful God, its loud rejection of intellectualism, its interest in demons and its Church of the saints;[1] this forceful tradition prepared the way for Islam. Marcion stirred Tertullian most deeply because two Gods meant no God: 'God is not, if he is not one'. If there is more than one being designated as God, then none of the beings so described can be the true God. God is the God above, the great and most high God, who exists forever, without beginning and without end [*Marc.* 1.3]. He must be unique and without equal,

---

[1] R. Braun, 'Aux origines de la chrétienté d'Afrique. Un homme de combat, Tertullien', *Bulletin Budé*, 5.2 (1965), 203ff. The similarity to Islam is noted on p. 208; a comment of Stephen Gsell is cited: 'De très loin Carthage a preparé les Berbères à recevoir le Coran, livre saint et code'.

in order to be the great Most High [*Marc.* 1.3], for if two gods had different parts of the world under their rule, neither would be the supreme God [*Marc.* 1.4]. The most high God is beyond comparison [*Marc.* 1.4], is independent of time and without beginning or end [*Marc.* 1.8]. God is unique in knowledge, revelation, origin and sinlessness. The knowledge of God can come from God alone, for only God can reveal what God himself has previously hidden [*An.* 1]. He is the only being who is unmade, unborn and unchangeable [*An.* 21]. God alone is without sin, and Christ is the only man without sin, because of his unity with God [*An.* 41]. The existence, nature and goodness of this one God may be known from his works [*Scap.* 2] and from the universal testimony of men in time of stress [*Scap.* 4]. Not that God needs the testimony of men, for on the last day he will judge all men. It is stupid to offer anything to the maker of all things; he needs nothing, and accepts our prayers alone [*Scap.* 2]. Tertullian also contrasts the emperor with God. The emperor is still a man and a creature; his power and his life come from God alone. Matter would be placed on the same level with God if it were considered eternal, but matter cannot be eternal, for God must be unique [*Herm.* 4.6].

There is positive talk about God too. Man can define God to a limited extent, the extent that is grasped by universal conscience: 'God is the supreme greatness established in eternity, unbegotten, without beginning and without end'. In reason and power God is the greatest that man can know [*Marc.* 1.3.2]. His sole rule or *monarchia* is a singular and unique power; but it may be exercised through others and need not be solitary.[1] God's unity is consistent with his trinity because there is one power and one will in Father, Son and Holy Spirit.

Clement presents the most extended account of the God who is not, and draws freely on philosophical ideas. He develops the terms used by Justin in ways different from Tertullian and too dangerous for Irenaeus. The danger springs from a close synthesis of Plato and Paul, which appears more striking because Clement is known especially for his *negative theology*, which was once foolishly condemned as an undigested borrowing from contemporary pagans. It was claimed that 'It is essentially a heathen conception, and can be developed consistently only on

[1] Karl Wölfl, *Das Heilswirken Gottes durch den Sohn nach Tertullian* AnGr., 112 (Rome, 1960), p. 45.

pagan principles.'[1] *Stromateis* Book 5 contains the two chief statements on this matter and each of them is set in a Pauline framework.

The first is the remarkable passage that links purification by confession with contemplative vision by analysis. Here the point, which would not have seemed strange to Clement's readers, is that men get their ideas of God wrong because they themselves are wrong.[2] The second is the extended statement on the unity and ineffability of God. We shall look at the two passages in their context, a context dominated by the themes of faith and mystery. Clement must tell his story in his own way.

From the beginning of Book 5, Clement makes it clear that faith, 'the ear of the soul', alone can find God. Faith in speaker and hearer combine to the one end of salvation, 'as our unerring witness, the apostle' speaks of the comfort of mutual faith [Romans 1: 11, 12], and adds later: 'The righteousness of God is revealed from faith to faith' [Romans 1: 17]; for the unity of faith admits plurality of growth to perfection. To reach the good we must freely choose; but 'we are saved by grace', grace that transforms our inclinations and gives us a healthy mind. Without grace our minds simply do not see intellectual objects; the senses are no help here. Paul spoke of seeing through a mirror now, and Plato also spoke of the vision that may come after death [*Epinomis* 973C]. So Paul declares the folly of the wisdom that is limited to this world [*S.* 5.1.8].

All the ancients saw the need of oracles ('know thyself') [*S.* 5.4.23] and mysteries. The wisdom of the world crucified the lord of glory [*S.* 5.4.25], and God's wisdom is hidden in a mystery [1 Corinthians 2: 7]. God has revealed to the believer what is prepared for those who love him; it is all folly to the natural man. Indeed the foundation of faith needs the building of knowledge if babes in Christ are to grow up [*S.* 5.4.26]. Plato's myths veil the truth [*S.* 5.9.58f.] and Paul speaks of mysteries [Ephesians 3: 3–5; Colossians 1: 26] of the fullness of Christ and the revelation of the eternal mystery, made known to all nations by faith [*S.* 5.10.6off.]. Plato speaks strongly of the need to guard divine mysteries and the danger of writing down the highest truths [*S.* 5.10.65; Plato, *Ep.* 2]. Plato even

---

[1] C. Bigg, *The Christian Platonists of Alexandria* (Oxford, 1886), p. 65.
[2] The removal of passions was as essential as logical argument for the contemplation of the One, according to Pythagoreans and Platonists.

spoke of the need for a higher and more difficult sacrifice before one can think about God [*Republic* 378A] and Paul speaks of such a sacrifice in Christ, our Passover [1 Corinthians 5: 7; *S.* 5.10.66]; the sacrifice God wants from men is total abstraction from the body and its passions [*S.* 5.11.67]. This is why Socrates described philosophy as the practice of death [*Phaedo* 67c and 81A].

Why do the passions have to go? Because men project their passions and their physical qualities on to God. They roll up like snails and hedgehogs and think of God in terms of themselves [*S.* 5.11.68].[1] So we come to the striking passage in which confession of sin and logical analysis go together [*S.* 5.11.71].

'We should lay hold of the way of cleansing by confession and then the way of vision by analysis, pressing on by analysis to the basis of thought, making a beginning from the things which underlie vision. We take away from physical body its natural qualities, stripping off the dimension of depth, then that of breadth, and after these, that of length. For the point which is left is unity, as it were, with position, and if we remove position from it, unity is perceived. If then, after removing all that belongs to physical bodies, and the things that are called bodiless, we cast ourselves into the vastness of Christ, and from there we go forward through holiness into the void; if we do these things we shall reach in some way the perception of the Almighty knowing not what he is, but what he is not. But shape and movement, or standing still, or throne, or place, or right hand, or left hand, are in no way whatever to be thought of as belonging to the father of all things, even if these things are written. But what each of these means will be shown in its proper place. *The first cause,* then, is not in any place, but above place, and time, and name, and thought.'

Chapter 12 [*S.* 5.78] begins with the well-worn declaration of Plato concerning the difficulties of finding and of talking about the father and maker of all things. The man in Christ (Paul), caught up into the third heaven heard unutterable words, because man cannot talk about God; the *Timaeus* is unclear on the finite or infinite number of the heavens. Paul's exclamation at the depth of divine wealth, wisdom and knowledge [*S.*

[1] Philo, *De sacrificiis Abelis et Caini*, 95.

47

5.12.80; Romans 11: 33] and other Pauline comments on divine mysteries are followed by Solon, Empedocles and John 1: 18 on the same theme.

Then comes the best-known passage [*S.* 5.12.81f.] on the unknowable God and the declaration of the unknown God by Paul [Acts 17].

(1) God, as the first principle of all things, stands at the summit of Platonic dialectic [*Republic* 509 and 511], beyond reach of man's logic and language [*Republic* 517]. 'Indeed this discussion concerning God is the most difficult discussion to deal with. For since the first principle of everything is hard to find, the absolutely first and oldest first principle is hard to show, which first principle is the cause of all things coming into being and being.'

(2) He is logically above the categories that men use to describe things. 'For how is that to be spoken of which is neither genus, nor differentia, nor species, nor individual, nor number, and on the other hand is neither an accident nor that to which an accident pertains?'

(3) God is too large for human language. 'No one can speak of him as a whole, for a whole has to do with size and he is the father of the whole universe.'

(4) There is no way of dividing him into manageable parts. God's transcendence of categories follows from his unity. He is simple and not a mixture of many ingredients [cf. Philo, *Leg. All.* 2.1]. 'Nor are any parts to be ascribed to him. For the one is indivisible.'

(5) Divine simplicity is infinite in a way that completely evades man's logical powers. There can be no dimensions, limit, form or name. Like the bare unity of Plato's *Parmenides*, God is without beginning, end, middle, limits or shape. Were he to have any of these things he would be more than one. 'Therefore it is infinite, not merely in the sense that one cannot give an exhaustive account of it, but in the sense of being without dimensions and having no limit and therefore being without shape or name.'

(6) God can have no name, for this would make him more than one. The names we give to him are not proper names. 'If we sometimes name it, we do not do so properly, calling it either the One or the Good, or Mind or Being, or Father, or God, Creator, or Lord.'

(7) These names are props to our minds, so that we will not go too far from God [cf. Plotinus, *Enn.* 2.9.1]. 'We do not speak as giving his name, but because of our lack we avail ourselves of good names, so that the intellect, not going astray in other respects, may lean on these as supports.'

(8) A name would bring God down to the level of particular beings. Indirectly the mass of names show that he is no ordinary being. 'For each by itself does not declare God, but all of them, collectively, indicate the power of the Almighty.'

(9) God's ineffability is not a mystic blank; it is capable of logical definition. Predicates must either be coextensive with their subject (species, individual) or not coextensive (genus, difference, number, accident, substance). Either type of predicate would introduce plurality. 'For predicates are applied to things, either from the things which belong to themselves or from their condition in relation to one another. But none of these can be accepted as appropriate to God.'

(10) God cannot be defined in terms of higher principles because he is at the peak of the pyramid of dialectic. 'On the other hand, he is not understood by scientific demonstration, for this depends on prior and more readily known principles, and there is nothing prior to the Unbegotten.'

(11) God therefore remains unknown apart from the gift of grace. He gives generously of his Logos.

> 'It remains for us to perceive the Unknown by the grace of God and by the Logos alone that proceeds from him. Luke in the Acts of the Apostles refers to Paul as saying, "Men of Athens, I perceive that in all things you are very religious. For in walking about, and beholding the objects of your worship I found an altar on which was inscribed, to the unknown God. Whom therefore ye ignorantly worship, him declare I to you"' [Acts 17: 22–3].

Recent Pauline study has made it easier to link Paul with this theme. His exclamation on the depth of divine mercy [Romans 11: 33] is not a piece of rhetoric but the proper conclusion from his own wrestling with his subject. The further one goes into the letter to the Romans the greater is the sense of walking between immensities or of handling mysteries. It is easier to see how people with their minds blown became Gnostics; yet the simplicity of the gospel is derived directly from the mystery of grace. Clement can help in the interpretation of Paul here as Paul helps in the interpretation of Clement.

Clement goes on to develop the theme of knowledge through divine grace. It does not matter whether we are more impressed by God's action or by our own free will; there is no way of reaching God without his special grace. Plato was well aware that virtue and wisdom come from God and that only a divine offspring can speak credibly of God [*Meno* 99 and *Timaeus* 40]. Jesus said that no one knows the Father except through the Son [*S*. 5.13.84]. Those who attack philosophy are the same people who run down faith. The rest of Book 5 shows how much the Greeks have taken from the barbarian philosophy of the scriptures. This shows God has always done good to men of every race. He will never cease to do good. Every man may, if he chooses, share in God's goodness [*S*. 5.14.141]. For Clement, God's transcendence and unity go together. If anything, God's unity comes first and from this simple unity is derived his inaccessibility to description of any kind. But God's transcendence dominates all that Clement writes. Because God cannot be directly described, symbol, parable and enigma have to be employed. These have the advantage that the presence of the divine Word can be discovered everywhere; they have the disadvantages of ambiguity and initial obscurity. Clement, in direct contrast to Justin, begins as a difficult writer; on acquaintance he becomes clearer, whereas Justin grows more obscure. The method and style of the *Stromateis* are built on the need to conceal from the unworthy and to reveal only to those who are patient [*S*. 1.2.20f.].

2 Is God good?

The problem of one God was not solved when the gods of Rome were denied. To many people, the Bible gave no consistent account of one God. The God of the old covenant could not be the God of the new covenant; most Christians took the Father of Jesus Christ as the only God and allegorised away all that

2 Is God good?

was inconsistent with him. Others took a different path. If the point where divine transcendence was to be found was the strange love of the infinitely good God, then anything that was contrary to this love must belong to an inferior being. So the very argument that gave transcendent unity a Christian stamp – infinite love – became the basis of a denial of that unity. Marcion and his followers were not foolish – they had grasped a central point.

Against them, Justin argued that there never had been and never could be a God above the creator [*D*. 11.1]. 'None is good but God alone *who made all things*' he quotes; the final words had been added to exclude Marcion [*1 A*. 16.7].[1] The goodness of God is the driving force of all divine activity [*1 A*. 10.2; *D*. 23.2].

Irenaeus insists similarly that the one God is merciful and kind, the final source of all salvation and all gifts [*H*. 4.25.2; 5.32.1], always giving generously [*H*. 4.28] and without grudging [*H*. 3 Pref.]. On the other hand, man is always receiving from a good God [*H*. 4.21.2] and is the receptacle of God's wisdom and virtue [*H*. 3.21.2]; his redemption comes from the will of the Father [*H*. 3.18.1]. God's richness and perfection are supported by his constancy; his grace never fails [*H*. 2.1–3]. He is always near to man [*H*. 5.16.1] and acts in love [*H*. 3 Pref.] and in mercy.

His freedom is a contrast to the necessity of the pagan gods, and his sovereign will is a contrast to the blind development of the Gnostic *Pleroma*. In goodness and freedom he created all things; for the world came neither from the ignorance of God, nor from a fallen aeon, but from the goodness of God [*H*. 3.41]. The one universal Father made all things [*H*. 5.18.2]. He made Adam, not because he needed men, but because he wanted an object for his benefits [*H*. 4.24.1].

The one God is both just and good [*H*. 2.47.2; 3.40.1] and his providence patiently governs all things. Marcion foolishly divides God into a good God and a just God, but goodness without justice is impossible. The excellence of the Father is the

[1] Justin uses the anti-Marcionite addition because Marcion had used the verse. The alteration of words of Jesus in the second century is discussed in L. E. Wright, *Alterations to the words of Jesus in the second century* (Harvard, 1952). On Clement see below; on Origen see E. F. Osborn, 'Origen and justification: the good is one; there is none good but God (Matt. 19. 17 et par.)', *ABR*, 24 (1976), 18–29.

wisdom by which he is lord, judge, righteous one and ruler. He is good, merciful, patient and saves men; he judges those who are worthy of judgement, and in all his justice he is good; he sends the sun to rise on all, and the rain on the just and the unjust. The clear sense of the living God of the Bible removes any suspicion that Irenaeus is concerned with an abstract Monad; yet Plato is still with him as he was with him in his account of the ineffable One. Plato stands to condemn such men as Marcion for he saw that God was both just and good and says [*Laws*, 4] that God, the ancient Word, possesses the beginning, the end and the middle of all things that exist. This God does all things rightly and exercises justice against those who depart from his Law. Further, Plato shows in the *Timaeus* that this just God, who has made all things and rules over them, is a good God. He speaks of the creator of the universe, who is good and has no envy towards anything beyond himself. The ungrudging goodness of God is seen by Plato to be the beginning and the cause of the creation of the world. The foolish Gnostics, who look for another cause, are utterly mistaken [*H.* 3.41]. It is characteristic of Irenaeus' positive account that he cannot speak of God without speaking of the world. The ineffable is known by the effects of his power and love. From his unity spring multitudinous aspects of his love and kindness. All things are governed by his providence. The notion of ultimate cause has been used to describe God's ineffability, unity and goodness. It means negatively that there is no cause beyond God and positively that all that is comes from God. For the existence of God, if you need a proof, simply look around you.

Tertullian also dwells on the goodness of the God who made and gave all things, a goodness that is as absolute as that described by Irenaeus, and even busier. God's goodness is without interruption, unchanging [*Marc.* 1.22] and essential [*Marc.* 1.25]. His goodness can be seen from his marvellous works, blessings and providence as well as from his laws, threats and warnings. In all these things God is good and merciful [*Marc.* 2.4]. No part of God's activity can be regarded as evil [*Marc.* 2.6] and he is free from all blame for the evil of the world [*Marc.* 2.9] Against man's sin he is severe in his judgement because he is good, for a good God is a just God. Justice and goodness cannot be separated, and in no way conflict [*Marc.*

2.12–16]. God's unchanging goodness is not qualified by his repentance, for he changes his mind in the face of varying circumstances; this is part of being an active God [*Marc.* 2.24]. Above all, God in his goodness may send calamities on men who neglect to worship him and who need his correction; he is perfect Father and perfect master [*Marc.* 2.13].

The best thing about God is his patience; he takes plenty of time. He sends his light on the evil and on the good, and allows all to benefit from the order of his universe. Even when his name and family are persecuted, the wonder of God's patience is still maintained [*Pat.* 2]. (No wonder that he has so few friends!) Wherever God's spirit descends, he gives the gift of patience [*Pat.* 15]. This patient God is a God of simplicity and power, working through the simple medium of water [*Bapt.* 2].

For Clement, despite all mystery, there is no ambiguity about the goodness of God. The one quality needed by a name of God is goodness. His goodness never ceases and all men share in it [*S.* 5.14.141]. God is good in a unique way and his goodness is active. Clement uses the text 'there is none good but God' twelve times; Marcion had used it to distinguish the good God from the just demiurge, and Clement, like Justin before him and Origen after him, is careful to exclude Marcion's view. For Clement the one God is good and the good God is one. It is evident from the words of Jesus that he is just and creator of all things. 'So that it is in truth clear that the one God of all alone is good, just creator, son in the Father to whom be glory for ever, Amen' [*Paed.* 1.8.74]. God's active goodness is a divine power that grips a righteous soul and sets the seal of righteousness upon it. God is blessed and eternal not because he is by nature good (although this is the case), but because he does good in his own distinctive way. 'For what is the value of good that does not act and do good?' [*S.* 6.12.104]. The notion of active goodness is reminiscent both of the Pauline notion of divine righteousness as a power [Romans 1: 17],[1] and of Plutarch, who compares unproductive goods with stagnant water, 'as none of the good they may have in them flows out, and nobody drinks of the stream'.[2]

[1] See E. Käsemann, 'God's righteousness in Paul', *New Testament questions of today* (London, 1969), pp. 181–95, translated from *Exegetische Versuche und Besinnungen*, vol. 2 (Göttingen, 1965), pp. 168–82.

[2] *Moralia*, 1129; *De latenter vivendo*, 4.

3   Can God be three as well as one?

The ineffable One has been described as good, partly because his goodness and justice had been impugned and partly because goodness is ultimate and itself falls within the category of ineffable and final. Even in the second century Christians wanted to talk about God as three as well as one. They did not see any great problem here until they had to face the Monarchian account, which denied that God could be three as well as one. Only Tertullian writes at length on this problem.

He is the first to speak specifically about the substance of God. God is spirit, and as spirit God is also body [*Orat.* 28.2]. But substance is for Tertullian the means of solving the problem of God's oneness and threeness, which was forced on him by the Monarchian heresy in its Modalist form. The error of Praxeas was an opposite error from that of Valentinus. Instead of making God too remote, he identified the Father with the Son. He put the Comforter to flight by persecuting Montanists, and crucified the Father [*Prax.* 1]. Tertullian replies that Father, Son and Holy Spirit are united in dispensation and substance. They are a trinity that is a unity, they are three not in condition, but in their degree, not in substance but in form, not in power but in aspect. God is one God, Father, Son and Holy Spirit [*Prax.* 2]. It is all very well to speak of the monarchy of God, but it is equally important to speak of his dispensation and diversity [*Prax.* 3]. The trinity does not deny the oneness of the divine rule, but it preserves the dispensation of the three divine persons [*Prax.* 8]. The Father is God, the Son is God and the Holy Spirit is God. Each is God, but there are not two Gods or two Lords [*Prax.* 13] There is one substance of God and there are three persons. Person points to the ultimate unity of substance, just as would form or species. Person is a distinct determination of a divine substance that has been differentiated into three persons.

Once again Tertullian disturbs his reader by his profound penetration of a problem and the rough edges that he leaves. He does not anticipate all that the fourth and fifth centuries were to say; but he does invent the later terminology and point the direction along which trinitarian thought was to go. What does he mean by 'substance'?[1] He may mean a particular kind of stuff, like flesh [*Prax.* 16.4], or the stuff of which all things are composed [*Herm.* 9.1]. There is also evidence that he sometimes probably meant a thing composed of a particular kind of stuff [*Herm.* 45.3], the fact of existing [*Marc.* 2.5] or nature [*Nat.* 2.4]. God's substance may simply mean 'God', or his mode of existence, his rank and character, or 'the unique stuff which is, or composes, the divine *corpus*, and which Tertullian denotes *spiritus*'.[2] It is the last sense that predominates, especially in *Against Praxeas*, which is the key work.

Unity of substance is the way in which Tertullian describes the unity of God. He affirms a real distinction between Father and Son, so that the Word is a substantial thing, existing individually as a substance. Then in order to avoid tri-theism and to preserve the divine *monarchia* he insisted that Father, Son and Holy Spirit were of one substance.[3] There has been disagreement on whether substance was for Tertullian a legal or a philosophical term; but to claim that it must be one or the other or even both is an oversimplification.[4] Unity of substance is declared by the expression 'one substance' rather than by the later adjective 'consubstantial'.[5]

Clement declares the unity of God by a different means from that of Tertullian; he applies the same titles and functions to the Father and the Son [*S.* 4.25.162; 7.1.2; 7.7.37].[6] This is similar to the logic of John 14, which applies the same predicates and activities to Father, Son and Paraclete, thereby indicating both unity and distinction, without using the language of substance and trinity. The relation between

---

[1] The following discussion is indebted to G. C. Stead, 'Divine substance in Tertullian', *JThS*, 14.1 (1963), 46–66.

[2] *Ibid.* p. 62.

[3] See J. Moingt, *Théologie trinitaire de Tertullien;* vol. 2, 'Substantialité et individualité' (Paris, 1966), pp. 297–430.

[4] *Ibid.* p. 668. See also A. Harnack, *History of dogma*, 2nd ed. (London, 1897–9) (ET of 3rd ed.), vol. 4, pp. 122f. and J. Bethune-Baker, *Early history of Christian doctrine* (London, 1951), pp. 138ff. On the general issue see further Wölfl, *Das Heilswirken Gottes*, pp. 35–117 and especially R. Braun, *Deus Christianorum. Recherches sur le vocabulaire doctrinal de Tertullien* (Paris, 1962), pp. 167–99.

[5] See Stead, *Divine substance*, pp. 202ff.

[6] See my *Philosophy of Clement*, p. 40; see also Stead, *Divine substance*, p. 187.

Father and Son is a ground for adoration rather than definition:
'O the great God! O the perfect child! Son in Father and
Father in Son!' [*Paed.* 1.5.24]. From the Son alone may the
true Gnostic receive knowledge of the cause beyond, the Father
of all things, who is to be adored with silent worship and holy
awe [*S.* 7.1.2]. The wonder, before which speech fails, is of a
God who is so distant in respect of being and so close in respect
of his power [*S.* 2.2.5]. For this reason mystery must never be
lost. Clement develops symbol and enigma in a way that had
not been done by Christians before. He has some help from
Philo. He claims: 'Therefore one may say that all who have
spoken of the divine nature, barbarians and Greeks, have
hidden the first principles of things and handed the truth down
in riddles, signs, allegories, metaphors, and similar figures of
speech' [*S.* 5.4.21]. Oblique description through symbols has
many advantages. It prevents unworthy men from gaining
access to truth and profaning it [*S.* 5.4.19]. It demands a
tradition of teaching to hand on the true interpretation. Truth,
veiled in powerful symbols, makes a deeper impression:
symbols have more than one meaning and can say many
things at once [*S.* 5.9.57].

4　Is God best understood as the first cause?

Running through each account of God, and serving a variety
of purposes is the idea of a first cause. Now, the notion of a first
cause is far from clear since it depends on denying, with
respect to itself, what is asserted of every other instance, namely
that it has been caused; it also possesses other ambiguities. If
we are to consider how these writers understood God we must
look at some of the problems linked with this term, and the
different ways in which they treated them.

The basic evidence can be briefly stated. Justin and
Tertullian have already been considered in some detail.
Irenaeus and Clement have a few more specific points to make.
For Irenaeus, God alone is the *cause of all things*; he precedes
and creates them all [*H.* 2.1.1 and 58.1]. An infinite regress of
causes is impossible [*H.* 2.1; 2.20; 4.19.2]; there is no other
beside God [*H.* 2.20.2]. Unlike the pagan gods, he does not
come from things that are made, but all things that are made

come from him [*H.* 2.37.1]. God, the one sufficient cause of all things, created all things out of nothing and through his Word [*H.* 1.15]. Man cannot make anything without material, but God had no need of matter; he was able to produce matter himself [*H.* 2.10; 2.42.4]. The things that God has made tell of his greatness and show what he is like [*H.* 2.8.1]. In describing God as first cause, Irenaeus says several positive things. He follows the rule of faith in opposition to the Gnostics, who deny all links between God and physical things; in particular they deny his creation of the universe and the resurrection of the flesh [*H.* 4.1.1; 4.9.2; 5.1.2 and 2.1]. Here the Gnostics lose out completely on both God and the world; their rejection of the world is a major reason for their ignorance of God. No man who misses the many-splendoured goodness of God in his creation, can hope to find God and understand his ways. The hand of God gives light to the heavens, tests the hearts of men, nourishes and preserves them, and works in secret ways. He who cannot discern God's open goodness will never know his secret greatness.

Clement's approach is more sophisticated but equally strong on creation. He deals with causes at length in the notes on logic that are found in *Stromateis* 8, but probably belong to the *Hypotyposes*.[1] He divides causes into original (those that initiate a process), sufficient, co-operating and necessary. A later distinction separates co-operating and joint causes. A cause must be understood in relation to its effects: a creator must create something. These and other logical points are valuable for the light they throw on Clement's own ideas, found earlier in the *Stromateis*. The variety of causes helps him to tackle problems of providence; the link between cause and effect shows why the One cannot be severed from the world it causes. There is no way of making sense of a divine *Pleroma* that has no visible effects. For this reason Clement speaks on several occasions of his transcendent God as the first cause. The peak of ascent by logic and spiritual intent is the first cause 'above place, time, name and conception' [*S.* 5.11.71]. Here the true Gnostic finds perfection in love through the firm apprehension of the first cause, learning truth from the truth itself [*S.* 6.9.78]. The God who is first cause is not like man, but man is to be

---

[1] See the well-argued discussion in P. Nautin, 'La fin des stromates et les hypotyposes de Clément d'Alexandrie', *VigChr.*, 30 (1976), 268–302.

brought to the likeness of God [*S.* 6.14.114]. The whole economy of salvation, which works through those agents nearest to every man, may be traced back to the command of the Son, whose power derives from his being next to the first cause [*S.* 6.17.161]. He is the second cause, life, knowledge, and through him the first cause made all things [*S.* 7.3.16 and 17]. Clement develops the concept of first cause from the simple notion it had been in Justin. It becomes the peak of intellectual activity and mystic vision; to know the first cause is to know the source of all things and to trace the true dialectic.

Yet Clement also saw the problems of linking a transcendent God with creation and causality. The One was not merely the last link in a causal chain. Creation came from the divine will alone. 'How mighty is the power of God! His will alone is sufficient to create the world. For God alone has made it since he is the only true God. Through simply willing, he creates. As soon as he merely wills a thing, its existence follows immediately' [*Prot.* 4.63].

The argument from first cause was used in a variety of ways by each writer. However the argument was itself capable of different meanings.[1] How did they handle these different possibilities? Did they introduce any others? None of them tried to prove the existence of something divine; the sole concern was the nature of the divinity – his unity, goodness and truth.

Justin's use of first-cause arguments begins from the negative point that the soul is not immortal. Using, with great freedom, the address of the demiurge to the lesser gods, he contrasts what is uncaused, unbegotten and incorruptible with all else. 'God alone is unbegotten and incorruptible' [*D.* 5.4]. Souls cannot be unbegotten because of their many shortcomings, changes and subordinate position. There cannot be more than one unbegotten, 'because if you refer back to infinity sooner or later you will out of exhaustion settle on one unbegotten and you will declare this to be the cause of all' [*D.* 5.6]. Here the arguments for a first cause (as in Aristotle) and first mover are linked with the argument for a necessary being. 'The soul either is life or has life' [*D.* 6.1]. If it were life it would impart life to other things just as motion imparts movement to other things, but

---

[1] The argument from first cause occurs variously in the first three of Aquinas' five ways.

although the soul lives, it does not impart life as God does. 'For life is not proper to it as it is to God' [*D*. 6.2].

In all this the simplicity of the logical move is important. Take the first cause seriously and you cannot have other gods or immortal souls as well. This is what hard-core Plato and Aristotle would imply; but, while the Platonists of Justin's day moved towards a greater appreciation of one transcendent first cause, in the eyes of Christians they did not accept the logical consequences of their ultimate monism. There is sarcasm in Justin's question whether the significance of the first-cause argument may have eluded Plato and Pythagoras. Justin saw the chief intellectual strength of the Christian position; it was more consistent with a transcendent first cause than the polytheism that Celsus and others were reluctant to abandon.[1]

Irenaeus makes the same three points in rejecting the inferior position that the Gnostics grant to the creator. He is not the fruit of deterioration or deficiency. There is nothing above him or after him. He created all things freely of his own will and plan, not moved by anything outside him, 'since he is the only God, the only Lord, the only founder, the only father, and he alone has power over all things and grants to them their existence' [*H*. 2.1.1]. He is first mover, first cause, and the necessary being, who grants being to all else. Here the argument, as in Justin, is negative and even more forceful, since Irenaeus wishes to remove not merely immortal souls but the

[1] See *Contra Celsum*, 7.47; 7.62; 7.66; 8.4; 8.5; 8.13. Polytheism was not always inconsistent with divine unity. One sovereign deity could rule the lesser divine beings or the many gods could simply be taken as the names of one divine being. Cf. Stead, *Divine substance*, p. 181. Justin's angels are subservient to, and enhance the majesty of, the one God. Origen seems to compromise his monotheism with his 'gods'. In an important passage in the *Contra Celsum*, Origen claims that there are other gods above the gods of the heathen (who are demons) and that the one God is above the lesser gods. There is an assembly of gods (Psalm 81:1) and there are many gods and many lords (1 Corinthians 8: 5). The Christian lives above these gods and far above the demons whom the heathen worship as gods. When Paul says: 'Yet to us there is one God, the Father, of whom are all things, and one Lord Jesus Christ, through whom are all things and we through him' (1 Corinthians 8: 6), 'he refers to himself and to all who have ascended to the supreme God of gods, and to the supreme Lord of lords' (*Contra Celsum*, 8.4). Service of the lower gods or demons can never be service of the supreme God.

entire menagerie of the *Pleroma*. Once the upward path of emanations is taken, where will it end? Basilides has 365 heavens and still does not look convincing. 'It is therefore much safer and more accurate, to confess the truth immediately at the beginning: that this creator God who made such a world is the only God and there is no other God beside him' [*H*. 2.20.2].[1] He has within him the plan and form of the things that he makes. He offers the only rational choice to those who grow 'weary after such extended irreligious wandering' [*H*. 2.20.2] in search of models and forms, and it is clearly better to see this and avoid the pointless regress of the heretics.

In Justin and in Irenaeus the argument for first cause has the same meaning. In each of its three forms (motion, cause and necessary being) it has a negative force. No beginning can be plural. Many gods and many aeons are alike to be rejected. Justin shows the inconsistency between philosophical monism and immortal souls while Irenaeus shows the logical weakness of the emanations of aeons. Both Justin and Irenaeus accept the disabilities of the first-cause argument: can a positive account be given of the supreme being? Justin gives some account of the divine names and points to the effect of God on human lives. Irenaeus points to the constant activity of this God in history and the vision of God that is granted to man.

Tertullian has a special concern with God as the ultimate cause of truth. We cannot understand what God is like by looking beyond him. Yet all men have some innate knowledge of him. It is not through our upward projection that he is grasped, but through his downward movement. As we have seen, it is precisely in God's joining of himself to the world that he is understood. Tertullian's keen insight is confirmed by his final claim that what is known by this divine descent is not merely unargued but unarguable. This limited rejection of reason is argued as a consequence of rationality (just as, whenever Irenaeus argues for the aptness of the incarnation, he is putting some principle above the incarnation). The whole treatise on the flesh of Christ is packed with closely reasoned argument to prove the human flesh of Christ through his birth

---

[1] 'The gradations between the infinite One and the finite many, devised by Philo, Plotinus, Spinoza, etc., conduct nearer to the abyss, but do not bridge it' (F. R. Tennant, *Philosophical theology*, vol. 2 [Cambridge, 1930], p. 125).

from the virgin and to disprove contrary opinions [*Carn.* 25]. In the well-known 'paradox' Tertullian is arguing for the foolishness of God. Only this folly can be a source for wisdom and hope. 'Spare the one hope of all the world. Why do you destroy the necessary dishonour of faith? Whatever is unworthy of God is to my advantage. I am safe if I be not ashamed of my lord.' What are the grounds of shame, which need to be overcome, if one is to be 'rightly shameless and felicitously foolish?' They all concern the son of God. His crucifixion is shameful, his death is absurd and his resurrection is impossible. These are the things of which one must be ashamed, which must be believed, which are known to be certain. How can Tertullian fit this argument into the sequence of arguments against the rationality of Docetism? It shows that the wisdom of this world, which denies the flesh of Christ, leads into absurdities; as a corollary the wisdom of God is shown in what the world finds absurd.

For Tertullian, as for Paul, this wisdom is the cross of Christ. It is ultimate because it cannot be inferred from higher principles; lacking any principle beyond itself, it is pointless and absurd. This is exactly where Plato put the Good, where 'History, God, Lucifer, Ideas of power, freedom, purpose, reward, even judgement are irrelevant. Mystics of all kinds have usually known this and have attempted by extremities of language to portray the nakedness and aloneness of Good, its absolute for-nothingness'.[1] This part of Tertullian, so far from being the point where he ceased to argue, was his most important argument. Perhaps he could have been more sympathetic with Marcion, who was overwhelmed by the wonder and mystery of the same divine love; but Marcion took off in the opposite direction from Paul, removed divine love from the world and could not have been more wrong. Perhaps Tertullian could have seen how the mystery of grace had blown the minds of Gnostics; but he could see that theosophy answered no questions and declared no gospel. The cross was the only ultimate thing man could know and it needed the earth to stand on and the universe to explain.

Clement has a similar concern with God as cause of truth, but handles the problem very differently from Tertullian. He gives the most developed account of the first cause, an account that is

---

[1] I. Murdoch, *The sovereignty of Good* (London, 1970), p. 92.

more Platonic that the others.[1] The passage that describes the *via negativa* links analysis with confession of sin. The concept of unity is reached by removing anything contingent from the account of God and removing the sin that distorts the vision. Then, with a certain bluntness, we are told to 'throw ourselves into the greatness of Christ' and to go on into the void.[2] We finish with an idea of what God is not, rather than what he is. There are no illusions about an easy way to God; instead there is the remarkable statement about the 'greatness of Christ'. The meaning of this can be seen in Clement's account of the cosmic Christ and in the close link of this concept with the life of the cross. To live beneath the cross is to live in Christ and to live in Christ is to be part of a new creation that runs from Calvary to the final triumph of God.

Clement sets out more precisely than Justin the same transcendent Platonic unity, which is above categories and names [*S*. 5.12.81f.]. The only way open is 'to perceive the Unknown by God's grace and by the sole word which proceeds from him'. The only way to knowledge of God is through the Son; but it has to be through symbol and enigma. Clement continues to underline the mystery of God and to accept the consequences of his transcendence. He is less cautious than Tertullian here; for the Word includes a universe of intellectual objects. For Clement the true dialectic leads from the first cause to the whole world of intellect and truth. Knowledge is of the *noeta* and it investigates the first cause, the structure of the universe and the function of its various parts. The truth about men and about good and evil is essential to knowledge and comes when the first cause has been understood [*S*. 7.3.17]. With such knowledge, true manhood, in independence of opinions and hardships may be gained [*S*. 7.3.18]. Not that man can ever possess the same moral excellence as the first cause [*S*. 6.14.114]. But he can from the first cause receive a knowledge of the truth from the truth itself, and the scope of this truth runs from the beginning of the world to its end, piercing through the veils of the plausible and enigmatic; like a navigator who steers by the stars, he fixes his course on earth by the

---

[1] Cf. Maximus of Tyre, *Diss.* 11.

[2] Cf. Iris Murdoch on Plato: 'The abyss of faith lies beyond images and beyond *logoi* too' (*The Fire and the Sun (Why Plato banished the artists)* (Oxford, 1977), p. 70).

forms above. He cannot be taken by surprise or deflected by difficulty [*S.* 6.9.78f.]. Like Plato's philosopher, who has seen the vision of the Good, he can return to the cave or the world and guide men according to the truth he has seen.

To sum up the accounts of a first cause, we may say that the arguments are used similarly by Justin and Irenaeus to prove the oneness of the first mover, cause and necessary being; plurality is excluded. In Tertullian and Clement, there is special interest in the ultimate cause of truth. While they both insist on one unique source, for Tertullian this remains foreign to argument, and for Clement it is the unarguable source of all argument [*S.* 8.3.7].

In looking at the whole range of problems, we have seen four parallel, but quite distinct, accounts of God. What are the special features of each? Justin has a blunt, direct approach, made obscure only by his brevity and undeveloped themes. He links the transcendent God to the world and the transformed lives he has observed; for his readers would not be moved by abstract talk. Irenaeus is also concerned to tie Christianity to the world and history; the transcendent *Pleroma* of the Gnostic is nonsense. Man finds the one God in his great act of love and self-giving in Christ; and man's life is the vision of God. For Tertullian the supreme mystery of God is not his remote excellence but his point of union with his creation. There can only be one God, the question is whether he can be a God of both love and justice, of both redemption and creation. Man finds divine wisdom in the foolishness of the cross. Clement goes beyond the Gnostics; where Irenaeus has brought the divine fullness to earth and Tertullian has made the intersection of divine love and heavenly reality the central mystery, Clement takes this mystery and never forgets its tensions. God is found above the world of things and men, and there is a path to climb. Words have no direct meaning when they speak of him; symbol and enigma are on every side. Yet this is God's world, the world in which his Son lived and died, and the world in which the friends of Christ find him on every hand.

Problems and parallels

In their different ways the four writers worked on the same problem. If God be God, he must be one God; if he be one he cannot be known. The first cause of all things is beyond ordinary explanation. Justin could point to Christian lives, Irenaeus could extol the grace that brought God near, Tertullian could praise the divine folly of the cross and Clement could deliberately accept mystery, symbolism and the need for growth in maturity and perception. What problems of modern thought can receive illumination from the questions that puzzled these writers?

1 An empirical fringe?

The empiricist philosophy that has dominated the Anglo-Saxon world during this century has invited a religious response. Logical positivism had no place for statements about God. Logical analysis offered scope for an empiricist approach to religious language.

By far the most extensive contribution was made by Ramsey, for whom language about God is language of commitment and discernment. In situations of disclosure, 'the penny drops' and the presence of God is discerned. God can only be spoken of as an object in a qualified way; 'this qualified object language becomes also currency for that odd discernment with which religious commitment . . . will necessarily be associated'.[1]

An important early contribution was also made by Austin Farrer, who accepted the point that religious language must be indirect, oblique; it was not a direct description but a parable of the truth it wished to convey. The question arose: how are these parables connected with reality and to what points of man's experience may they be referred? Farrer pointed to moral experience where the claim of a neighbour is recognised.

---

[1] I. T. Ramsey, *Religious language* (London, 1957), p. 47.

64

This claim, an absolute claim, is for the Christian exerted by God. Moral experience, argued Farrer, uncovers a point at which faith can be clearly seen to bear on human life.[1]

Boyce Gibson provided the most thorough account of empiricism and belief.[2] He rejected the attempt to whittle down religious belief to an abstract God, common to all religions. 'Neither the highest-common-factor God of eighteenth-century Deism, nor the lowest-common-denominator God of twentieth-century syncretism is in the least worshipful' [p. 57]. Of course different religions should talk to one another. 'But it is the particularities of particular religions that strike the sparks' [p. 58]. Talk about God can only arise out of a shared experience of God. There is a 'persisting experience' behind all theology; and while descriptions of the experience vary, it remains central. 'Peter's exclamation, "Thou art the Christ", was not a theory; it was forced out of him by what he saw. What he saw was so extraordinary that ordinary concepts were unable to catch it' [p. 58].

The discernment of the presence of God and a description of this discernment are possible because there are 'prolongations' of God or 'fringes' of his activity, which are accessible to human experience. These experiences are localised in the order and creativity in the world or in moral values (like freedom, which has a touch of the infinite about it).[3] The counter-evidence is met by faith, which functions as 'the courage of the spirit'. While persons and values are not God, they point beyond themselves and are transformed by the presence of God. For Boyce Gibson God cannot be proved or described in a grand scheme of metaphysics. 'But we can put together all the bits and pieces about God that come our way, . . . a mobile and still developing pattern . . . We shall always go on discovering, in the faith that there is always more to discover, and discern the presence of God throughout the unending journey' [p. 273].

[1] Austin Farrer, 'A starting point for the philosophical examination of theological belief'. *Faith and logic*, ed. B. Mitchell (London, 1957), p. 30.

[2] *Theism and empiricism.*

[3] A. D. Lindsay, *The moral teaching of Jesus* (London, 1937), p. 91, cited by Boyce Gibson, *Theism and empiricism*, p. 87.

2   Can negative theology say anything?

The claim that we can only say what God is not, and that we cannot say what he is, raises its own peculiar problems. As Clement pointed out, God does not have thousands of properties that he has given to parts of creation. But 'thousands' is surely an understatement; it is clearly impossible to begin to describe God in terms of the unlimited earthly qualities he does not possess. It is therefore almost as hard to say what God is not, with any sort of adequacy, as it is to say what he is. Again, any object is indescribable in terms of what it is not. 'Negative facts' have no stopping-point. God is not unique in this respect. Again, does not negative theology leave everything to be said, and, quite literally, say nothing? A nineteenth-century writer attributed to a certain gentleman the knowledge of only 'two tunes, one of which, he says, is "God Save The King, and the other *isn't*".'[1]

Yet, to begin within the same century, there was an excessive fondness for negative attributes when they conveyed forceful positive meaning. A strangely long line of warships was named *Invincible*, not to mention *Indefatigable*, *Inflexible*, *Indomitable*, *Irresistible*, *Implacable*, *Impregnable*, *Intrepid*[2] as well as *Dreadnought* and *Sans Pareil*. One theologian has claimed that the negative descriptions of God like 'invisible', 'ineffable', 'inconceivable' have positive meaning while positive descriptions of God like 'good' and 'loving' have negative meaning. The former point to 'ultimate self-dependency and universal responsibility' while the latter 'imply the lack of these things'.[3]

The basic features of the Jewish Christian concept of God are unity and transcendence. Transcendence can be argued as a meaningful concept, and unity may be derived from observa-

---

[1] R. S. Surtees, *Jorrocks' Jaunts and Jollities* (London, 1911), p. 108.
[2] See H. S. Lecky, *The King's Ships*, vol. 3 (London, 1914). There seem to have been four *Implacables*, four *Impregnables*, six *Indefatigables*, three *Indomitables*, four *Inflexibles*, four *Intrepids*, five *Invincibles* and four *Irresistibles*.
[3] G. L. Prestige, *God in patristic thought* (London, 1952), p. 41. This would be a difficult claim to establish, since there must be some common ground between God and the other subjects of which 'good' is predicated. It belongs to an age that was more confident of religious language.

tion of the world.[1] The oneness of God may be seen in a variety of ways: in the tradition of the Old Testament, God's unity is not abstract and philosophical, but points to a unity of purpose and character in the revelation given to prophets and priests of Israel. God is seen as a personal will or a creative demand to which man must respond. Similarly for the Christian 'God is unitary, uniting all images around that of Jesus as Lord; and God is transcendent as offering the living Lord to all men everywhere.'[2]

However, the concept of pure being is highly ambiguous.[3] 'He who is' may be the most general category applicable to things or the most mysterious because there is no predicate within reach of human reason. While Clement's *via negativa* leads to a more abstract notion, the result of stripping away all qualities, there is also the notion of divine fullness or perfect being or the sum of all positive attributes. This account is found in both Clement and Irenaeus where it is reminiscent of Xenophanes: 'All of him sees, all thinks and all hears'. In each case the verb of Xenophanes is replaced by a noun. The reason is plain enough: negative theology could leave the believer with something like the Gnostic *fructus extremitatis*, outside the divine *Pleroma*. Irenaeus and Clement had to insist that all the divine fullness was in the Father whom they worshipped. Clement applies these expressions to the Son [*S.* 7.2.5] as well as to God the Father [*S.* 7.7.37] while Irenaeus' account of the summing-up of all things in Christ also makes fullness an attribute of the Son as of the Father.

It must be stressed that Clement's *via negativa* is not inconsistent with divine fullness. One must go beyond the attributes of ordinary things and false gods to find the God who is the perfect first principle of the universe. As essence, goodness and mind, he is first principle of the spheres of being, ethical values and logic [*S.* 4.25.162]. In the *Symposium*, Plato speaks of the ultimate discovery of the one single form of knowledge, the knowledge of that beauty which is universal and eternal. This vision is not directed to a particular beautiful face, body, set of words, piece of knowledge or thing, but will be an eternal loveliness in which every lovely thing shares so that while its parts

[1] K. Ward, *The concept of God* (Oxford, 1974), p. 106.
[2] *Ibid.* p. 109.
[3] See Stead, *Divine Substance*, pp. 105–9 and 188f.

change the total beauty remains an undiminished whole
[*Symposium* 211].

But difficulties remain and one must be sensitive to the strong
objections made against the unknown God and the occasional
advocacy of that kind of divinity whom the Christians denied
and ridiculed. It has been argued that one can only worship a
necessary being, that this is an incoherent notion and that therefore a true God cannot exist. God cannot be contingent. He
must surpass all else infinitely;[1] but does this not place him
beyond the reach of knowledge and language? One careful
sceptical treatment has shown the difficulties in claiming that
paradox and the *via negativa* may point beyond themselves to
anything real at all.[2]

Further it must be admitted that the concept of God as 'the
wholly other' is odd partly because of the use of the definite
article and partly because it should only be a prelude to silence.
On the other hand, it does make good sense to say that, where
theology uses the spatio-temporal categories of our ordinary
thought, then it has to be unintelligible.[3]

The sceptic sometimes claims to accept the possibility of a
Zeus-like superman, who smashes trees and visibly intervenes
in the physical world. But this is not what believers are
interested in; they do not believe in such a god.[4] The theology
of the comic strip is the antithesis of Christian theology; such a

---

[1] See J. N. Findlay, 'Can God's existence be disproved?', in Flew and
MacIntyre (eds.), *New essays*, pp. 51f. An almost opposite objection
claims that Plato's account of logically inexpressible knowledge may
be accepted as possible; but the linking of this knowledge to an
omnipotent and omniscient being who is called God is seen to be
difficult. See H. J. McCloskey, *God and evil* (The Hague, 1974), p. 52.
However, Plato himself attributed to the form of the Good similar
qualities, insisting at the same time that it transcended being and
truth. See also Ninian Smart, *The concept of worship* (London, 1972)
pp. 55f.

[2] 'If what I have argued about ineffability and the *via negativa* is
substantially correct it cannot be correct to say or think, as some
theologians have, that the paradoxical nature of God-talk shows
the "inexpressibility of religion" – the inexpressible reality that
paradoxical religious language is designed to point toward – and it
cannot be correct to say that the religious use of language helps
"point people beyond human concepts" to the inexpressible'
(K. Nielsen, *Scepticism* (London, 1973), p. 58).

[3] M. Durrant, *Theology and intelligibility* (London, 1973), p. 196.

[4] Nielsen, *Scepticism*, pp. 90f.

domesticated God is too small, too close to the human fantasy that Christians wish to destroy. They find it hard to take seriously the scepticism that does not see the irrelevance of such a god.

Christianity has a better chance of being understood in a secular world than in a pagan religious one. For Christianity has more trouble from 'godlets' than from the godless. The recognition that God, whether he exists or not, is not a part of the world, is more important to the Christian than the vague belief that there is some divinity of some sort. This is why Christians were called 'atheists' when they rejected the immanent deities of the ancient world.

3 Destroying the images

The Platonic way that goes beyond hypotheses and images to the highest truth was as important to the early Church as it is today. Then, there were visible idols to destroy. Today, for Christianity, its own imagery fails to grip imaginations as once it did. This means that the search for God beyond imagery is deep and demanding.

> 'Art will mediate and adorn, and develop structures to conceal the absence of God or his distance. We live now amid the collapse of many such structures, and as religion and metaphysics in the West withdraw from the embraces of art, we are it might seem being forced to become mystics through the lack of any adequate imagery which could satisfy the mind.'[1]

Such an approach need not deny the value of images; it need only see them as less than ultimate. Further, the move beyond symbols need not take the direction that Plato took. For another recent writer, the way from symbol to reality is not the way of abstraction or generalisation but the way of particularity and crucifixion. Symbols are ways of presenting reality but they fall short of the reality of God and can easily become idols that protect man from exposure to divine reality. Jesus clearly accepted many of the images and symbols of the Old Testament. His life on earth brought about a 'rebirth of

---

[1] Murdoch, *The Fire and the Sun*, p. 88.

images'; symbols and parables came to life. But this is not where it ended. 'Jesus Christ clothed himself in all the images of messianic promise, and in living them out, crucified them: but the crucified reality is better than the figures of prophecy. This is very God and life eternal, whereby the children of God are delivered from idols.' Prayer repeats this process in the life of the believer; for prayer begins with vigorous images of God but must go beyond them 'to adhere nakedly to the imageless truth of God'.[1] The crucifixion of images is a gradual, incomplete and often painful process; but there is no other way to the reality of God.

But what of idols? Does it make sense to speak of idolatry in the twentieth century? The power of idols was never in their material reality but in the passions and loyalties that focussed on them. At this point little has changed and the first commandment has never ceased to express the central Christian concept of God. Modern European history points to a wide variety of faith in ultimate values such as nation, country, race, class or science. 'Men have always believed in some kind of "God" – if not in the true God, then in some kind of idols.'[2] Since true faith is to cease from fearing and loving other gods, the destruction of idols is a continuing activity and sacrilege one of the more important human duties.

4 In what sense is the One real?

Since Plato provided the chief source for the accounts of divine transcendence that we have considered, it is useful to look at two recent accounts of Platonism. Our account of the divine simplicity or oneness differs strongly from most traditional theology, including the Aristotelian stream that dominated the medieval Church. There have been two valuable new expressions of the Platonic tradition. The first was put forward by Duméry, in 1957, within the framework of phenomenology. The ultimate in religion is the One, not Being or the source of being. The job of the philosopher is to reduce, to strip religion of all that is incidental or accidental. He 'recovers the attitudes

[1] Austin Farrer, 'An English appreciation', in H. W. Bartsch (ed.), *Kerygma and myth* (London, 1957), pp. 222f.
[2] H. Küng, *Heute noch an Gott glauben?* (München, 1977), p. 47.

of the religious man' and finds God as 'pure unity, as radical spontaneity, as that by which the diverse orders and even the notion of order are conceivable'.[1] A metaphysics of the One purifies the scheme of transcendence by its simplicity. The divine attributes are not descriptive terms but must be understood in a special way. In his religious life man depends on this God; in his dialogue with God he always moves towards the One. This is not a quiescent contemplative activity, for the discovery of the One is 'less an entrance into the evidence than a militant conversion which implies detachment from everything else and from self'.[2] Duméry is at once very close to the early fathers and radically new for the twentieth century. He wants to reject most current theological talk. He puts forward an account of God in terms of pure transcendence in a world that has largely lost this sense of God; in the second century it was put forward in a world that had hardly known such a sense of God.

A different statement, also in the Platonic tradition, comes from Iris Murdoch, novelist and philosopher, in terms of the sovereignty of the Good.[3] The Good cannot be defined; it is like looking at the sun when we can only see the edges. 'We do not and probably cannot know, conceptualize, what it is like in the centre.'[4] The common degradation of any religion is the substitution of the human self for the object of veneration. Man's first need is for 'unselfing', through art, intellectual discipline or other means. 'Good art, unlike bad art, unlike "happenings" is something pre-eminently outside us and resistant to our consciousness. We surrender ourselves to its *authority* with a love which is unpossessive and unselfish.'[5] But whatever the way to the Good, the one thing that matters is that the Good should be contemplated 'not just by dedicated experts but by ordinary people: an attention which is not just the planning of particular good actions but an attempt to look right away from self towards a distant transcendent perfection, a source of uncontaminated energy, a source of *new* and quite

---

[1] H. Duméry, *The problem of God in philosophy of religion* (Northwestern University Press, 1964), p. 128.

[2] *Ibid.*

[3] Murdoch, *The Sovereignty of Good.* See also the recent lecture, *The Fire and the Sun.*

[4] Murdoch, *The Sovereignty of Good*, p. 100.

[5] *Ibid.* p. 88.

undreamt-of virtue'.[1] The Good is real in the same way as the One is real for Duméry, by producing reality in other things. The aim of morality as of art is to produce what is real. The artist does not paint 'I like it'. He paints 'There it is'. The link with experience remains constant, for one cannot prove the existence of the single, non-representable and indefinable Good: 'All one can do is to appeal to certain areas of experience, pointing out certain features and using suitable metaphors and inventing suitable concepts where necessary to make these features visible. No more, and no less, than this is done by the most empirically minded of linguistic philosophers'.[2]

5   Transcendence and crucifixion

The two accounts we have just considered give positive reasons for looking at belief in God in the way second-century writers recommended. They show the positive side of this approach to God; but there is another, less optimistic, note. In both the second and twentieth centuries people have found their way to God through negative, tragic aspects of the world.

The understanding of God's unity and transcendence is not an optional refinement for Christian belief. True, there is as Clement showed, a need to analyse and purify so that our idea of God is not that of a mountain or a mammoth; but the end of such analysis is to immerse ourselves in the vastness of Christ [cf. Ephesians 3: 18]. Both Paul and Plato agree on the pointlessness of the ultimate. Christ crucified is folly to Greeks and a stumbling-block to Jews.

Von Balthasar has written of the unknown God and of the way in which God is hidden to modern man. The habit of finding mysterious gaps in the world of nature where God might be discerned has ceased: 'The world is not God. This much is clear today to the theist as well as to the atheist'.[3] The signs of the times point to atheism, which frightens many, but may be the way forward to a more adequate idea of God. Balthasar turns to the later Platonists, whose religion had 'a certain

[1] *Ibid.* p. 101.
[2] *Ibid.* p. 74.
[3] H. U. von Balthasar, *Science, religion and Christianity* (London, 1958), p. 93.

kinship with the modern frigidity of mind'.[1] Accounts of God, such as those we considered earlier, offer a way ahead, for only Christians who have grasped the utter transcendence of God will be able to speak usefully to modern man. Here only the cross makes sense in its loneliness and silent obedience: 'For the Son has not redeemed the world by humanitarian and social works, but by the blood of his obedience shed in apparent frustration on the Cross, by which he penetrated beyond the sphere of the social as well as of the personal factors, into the nameless and faceless silence of the Godhead'.[2] So the Christian must stand with modern man in the darkness of his godless world if he is to find a way to the only God.

There is, for Von Balthasar, a positive side as well, and it is found in prayer, contemplation and love. Not that prayer and contemplation are ways of refuelling to cope with the world; they are ways of dying to self and coming to God. 'The real saints wanted only one thing, the greater glory of the love of God ... They are hidden in God, have no foothold of their own. They grow in stature, not round their own centre, but round God, whose incomprehensible grace gives ever greater personal freedom to the creature who frees himself to exist solely for God.'[3] The central reality of Christianity is love, and love alone; this is lived out in action and provides the only observable ground for credibility of the Christian message.

Christian argument demolished most of the objections to its God, by using reasons that philosophers had framed for other purposes and could hardly deny in one context what they had maintained in another. But like all Platonism it ran out in mystery, which could not be explained, and there remained some justification for the second-century graffito of a donkey's head on a cross: 'Alexamenos worships his god.'[4]

D. M. Mackinnon concludes a recent discussion of miracle, irony and tragedy with the strange episode of the raising of Lazarus and the subsequent death of Jesus. The final account of God's omnipotence is not in the miracle;[5] the tragic is what persists, and Christians could claim to provide 'a faith through

[1] *Ibid.* p. 97.
[2] *Ibid.* p. 119.
[3] *Ibid.* p. 98.
[4] See above p. 32, n. 5.
[5] D. M. Mackinnon, *The problem of metaphysics* (Cambridge, 1974), p. 121.

which they are enabled to hold steadfastly to the significance of the tragic'.[1] A consideration of the extremities of human life, as portrayed by Sophocles and Shakespeare, points to transcendence as the only refuge from the trivial. The notion of presence provides an explanation of the more significant aspects of experience. 'Moral laws . . . are often disregarded; but there is something strange in their disregard in that if it is fundamental (as in the case of radical self-deception) it is a self-destruction.'[2] Faith is 'seeing as,' seeing the world differently, because of the commitment that has been made. A dump of wrecked aircraft was seen by a landscape artist as a 'dead sea', 'A monstrous *Gestalt* of human waste'.[3] The contribution of artist and writer is one of enlarging the perception of others; faith is a similar kind of enlarged awareness. 'Jesus is received by those who use the tale of his life as a means of coming to see the world in a particular way as one who does not merely illustrate a principle but in some way . . . achieves it and brings it into being.'[4]

6 The nearness of God

The most striking point of all is Tertullian's claim that it is in God's becoming man that the glory is seen. The zenith of transcendence is not remote from the world but in the world, where the incarnation takes place. That Tertullian's claim should be regarded as hot-headed anti-rationalism is an indication that the New Testament as well as Tertullian has been misunderstood. For the Fourth Gospel, 'The Word became flesh, and we beheld his glory' is thematic, not incidental; the continued reference to Jesus' crucifixion as his being 'exalted' or 'glorified' is a simple statement of Tertullian's point. Nor is Paul's claim that he must glory only in the cross of Christ anything less than the centre of his theology. Tertullian is, contrary to most opinion, not saying anything that Justin, Irenaeus and Clement would dispute; for all of them the cross is the point where the divine transcendence is encountered, if it be

[1] *Ibid.* p. 135.
[2] *Ibid.* p. 154.
[3] *Ibid.* p. 161.
[4] *Ibid.* p. 163.

encountered at all. Yet it is only in recent years that Tertullian's argument has been analysed (and Clement's theology of the cross is still largely ignored).[1]

A recent account of the same transcendence begins with the claim that 'The being of God is in his becoming'. We only know God as he is 'for us' in the sense of Paul's 'If God be for us, who can be against us?' We only know God is 'for us' from the event of Jesus Christ. In this event God interprets for us what he is. God's being is always in relation 'for' someone, and this being is found in the relation of the Father, Son and Spirit as well as in the event of revelation. The hidden God is the same as the God who reveals himself in the event where he becomes 'for us'.[2] The link between transcendence and incarnation is here very close to Tertullian.

This view has been developed in a striking account of God as 'the mystery of the world'.[3] The Word is the means by which an absent God is present, and faith is the means by which the event of the Word is apprehended [p. 246]. Only by the unity of God with the contingent is it possible for God to be the object of thought. What is above us means nothing to us [pp. 248ff.]. The unity of God and the contingent must arise from the being of God [p. 170], from the death of the crucified God. God's being is always in his becoming; he must enter the realm of that which is not. The outward movement is the most inward act of his being.[4] Faith, love and hope express in a human way the truth that God's being is in his coming.[5] By faith one returns to the God who came from himself into the

---

[1] The belief that metaphysics forced the early Church to abandon a theology of the cross is a widespread error. See, for example, E. Jüngel, *Gott als Geheimnis der Welt* (Tübingen, 1977), p. 49.

[2] E. Jüngel, *Gottes Sein ist im Werden*, 2nd ed. (Tübingen, 1966), p. 120.

[3] Jüngel, *Gott als Geheimnis*.

[4] *Ibid.* p. 305: '*in das Nichts gehend* und dabei doch immer von sich selber her kommend. So gewiss Gott – *von* Gott kommt, so gewiss kommt er doch nicht zu sich selbst, ohne sich *dem Nichts* auszusetzen. Sein Weg *hinaus* ist nichts anderes als das *innerlichste* Werk seines Seins'.

[5] *Ibid.* p. 542: 'Im Glauben auf den von sich selbst her zur Welt gekommenen Gott zurückkommend, in der Liebe von dem auch im Tode zu sich selbst kommenden menschlichen Gott mitgenommen und in der Hoffnung dem als Gott kommenden und so der Liebe zum Sieg verhelfenden Gott entgegengehend, wahrt der Mensch Gott als das Geheimnis der Welt'.

world; by love one has gone alone with the human God who even in death came to himself; by hope one goes to meet the God who comes as God and so helps love to triumph. These are the ways in which one verifies God as the mystery of the world.

'God's being is in his coming' [p. 521]. The triune God is the mystery of the world. For God comes from God, he is his own origin and his own life. And God comes to God, but he also comes to man. 'In the person of Jesus Christ he *has come* to man' [p. 524]. In the alienation of death God comes to himself and overthrows death. Finally God comes as God; although his death is alienation, he remains source and end, joined to himself as Father and Son; 'in brief, God himself is his own mediation, and this is the third mode of his being and this is God the Holy Spirit' [p. 531].

7   Silent worship

Because of the difficulties involved in this kind of language, it has been properly suggested that the central task of theology today is to ask what kind of silence, what repudiation of every image, will best convey the ultimate love that is in 'Christ, and him crucified'. But this is no easy way, for it is 'only within the context of the most rigorous discipline of silence that we dare think such a reality'.[1]

The theme of silence before God comes forcefully in Simone Weil's account of *attention*, or 'Waiting on God'.[2] We cannot move towards God or walk vertically; we can only change the direction of our gaze and turn our eyes towards him [p. 167]. Salvation lies only in longing for God and renunciation of all else. This 'waiting or attentive and faithful immobility which lasts indefinitely and cannot be shaken' [p. 149] is like New Testament faith, which comes with empty hands and is marked by steadfastness.[3] Like faith it turns from self and fantasy, from the dream world of which self is the centre [p. 115], to God's pure reality, which it both seeks and fears [p. 129]. Obedience to God is like the transparence of a window-pane [p. 89] and

[1] D. M. Mackinnon, 'The inexpressibility of God', *Theol.*, 79 (1976), 206.
[2] Simone Weil, *Waiting on God* (Fontana, 1977).
[3] See G. Ebeling, *The nature of faith* (London, 1961), pp. 162–71.

the love of God is a unity in which plurality disappears [p. 85]. Friendship for the friends of God is the most potent aid to the vision of God [p. 40] and 'looking is what saves us'.[1]

A great deal of modern analysis of religion fails because it takes no account of worship and prayer. To reduce Christianity to a humanist ethic is to rob it of its cutting-edge, when 'the substantive concept of God is indissolubly linked to the practice of worship'.[2] No one has seen the link between prayer and knowledge more clearly than Clement and Origen. For Clement, the true Gnostic finds perfection in continual prayer [S. 7.10.56f.], which does not need words. 'It is possible, therefore to send up a prayer without speaking, by concentrating the inner spirit alone on mental speech, in undivided attention to God' [S. 7.7.43]. Such prayer anticipates the final state of knowledge, which is that which shines as an unchanging light eternally in the presence of God.

Origen is quite explicit that prayer is a test case for the knowledge of the unknown God [*Orat.* 1 and 2] and a way through man's ignorance [*Orat.* 13] by an awareness of spiritual beauty [*Orat.* 17] The doors are shut on the senses so that the Father who hears in secret may come to him who prays [*Orat.* 20]. Prayer brings growth in perception. 'Thy kingdom come' asks that this kingdom should spring up and grow to perfection in him who prays [*Orat.* 25]. Wisdom and truth remain supreme and the mind preserves the mystery of the ages [*Orat.* 27]. As, for Plato, if you could not do geometry, so, for Origen, if you could not pray, then there was no way in which you could grasp the first principle of all things. Similarly for Plotinus, prayer is a matter of the mind [*Enn.* 5.8.9] and the soul leans to God by prayer, as the alone to the Alone [*Enn.* 5.1.6].

Yet silence was not enough. The ineffability of God did not mean that words had no place. Each of the four writers wrote, and understood writing, in a different way. Each distrusted literary art even more than Plato and did not find, as he did, a mode of exposition that remains a model of literary form.

---

[1] *Waiting on God*, p. 145: 'The bronze serpent was lifted up so that those who lay maimed in the depths of degradation should be saved by looking upon it'.

[2] Smart, *Concept of worship*, p. 74. Hare, Wisdom, Ramsey, Flew, Martin and Braithwaite are the philosophers who come under censure.

Justin tried with dialogue and apology but he is memorable for moving patches of text rather than for any sustained quality. Irenaeus said he could not write, yet analysed his opponents and argued with skill, allowing the external stimulus of divine glory in Christ to give his writing depth and colour.[1] Tertullian had technical skill but wrote in a fiercely individual style. Clement wrote simply in the *Protrepticus* and *Paedagogus*; but in the *Stromateis* he explicitly renounced plain discourse and claimed that if words were to say anything about divine truth they would speak obliquely.[2] Yet he wrote plainly enough and argued firmly against Gnostic immorality, and he packed more into his sentences than most writers can. 'Art launches philosophy as it launches religion, and it was necessary for Plato, as it was for the evangelists, to write if the Word was not to be sterile and the issue of the Father was to be recognized as legitimate.'[3]

After the exploration of the difficulties that a Christian account of God must face, the contemporary conclusion is as positive as that of the second century. Now, as then, heightened awareness of the problems of speaking about God produces a deeper sense of the need to speak about him. One of the most sensitive and prolific theologians of our day insists that we are called to a fresh decision about God, to look to the appearing of a God whom modern critical man can worship in humility and joy. With a breadth of vision that is reminiscent of the second century, he insists that such a God will hold together the God of the philosophers and the God of Abraham, Isaac and Jacob, the God of Jesus Christ.[4]

[1] See F. Sagnard on 'L'hellénisme d'Irénée', *La gnose valentinienne et le témoignage de Saint Irénée* (Paris, 1947), pp. 70–7.

[2] Clement discussed the propriety of writing in the first chapter of the *Stromateis*; his argument is examined in my article, 'Teaching and writing in the first chapter of the Stromateis of Clement of Alexandria', *JThS*, 10.2 (1959), 335–43.

[3] Murdoch, *The Fire and the Sun*, p. 88.

[4] Küng, *Heute noch an Gott glauben?*, p. 48.

4 The rational laughing animal

After Socrates, Greek philosophy could never turn its back on questions about man and the life he should live. Man became the centre of the cosmos, ethics became fundamental and introspective reflection like that of Marcus Aurelius emerged. Philosophers and Gnostics asked: 'Where did man come from and how did he come?'[1] Christian thinkers had to ask about man for other reasons too. They saw a new humanity in Christ, a universal brotherhood, which broke across every barrier of race and class. The goal of history was the liberty of the children of God, a liberty shown in Christ and given to his followers. If man were central to the total purpose of things, as the Stoics also insisted he was, what was he? Further, if man's salvation were the goal of Christian preaching and of more esoteric religious propaganda, why did man need to be saved? Again, Christians claimed as evidence for the truth of their God, the moral transformation of men of all shapes and sizes; this confident but perilous claim kept man in the centre of the argument. Finally, there was only one ground on which all the critics of Christianity could be met: polytheist, philosopher, Jew, Gnostic, Marcionite, with internal divergences in most camps, had nothing but their humanity in common. When the apologists spoke as men to men, they were dealing with the only common question.

Man, according to one definition that Clement found, was a rational, mortal, earthy, walking, laughing animal.[2] Rationality came first because it showed man's affinity to God. Man was *logikos* and God was known through his *logos*. Man's knowledge of himself was the first step to God. But man had much about him that was unworthy of God, so some account of sin and salvation was needed urgently. The supreme clue to man's

[1] Tertullian, *Praescr.* 7.
[2] Clement, *S.* 8.6.21; cf. Aristotle, *De anim. membr.*, 3.10.65. This does not mean that man should be always laughing, any more than a horse should always be neighing. *Paed.* 2.5.46.

79

predicament and possibilities lay in his free will. His composition from body, soul and spirit or *logos* was important. Finally, if man began as rational, was there yet a way open for him to know the truth? The questions may be put concisely:–

(1) In what way is man related to God?
(2) How can man's present misery be reconciled with his divine origin?
(3) Is man free?
(4) Of what does man consist?
    (i.e., has he parts, such as body, soul and spirit and, if so, how are they related?)
(5) Can man know the truth?

From the beginning we should note the apparent contradiction between this account of man and the earlier account of God. After elevating the godhead beyond man's mental reach and ridiculing the many gods of the heathen, Christians indulge in what has been called the 'democratization of God'. The right to be sons of God is given to all who believe. This is what Christians said, and there is no doubt it confused many polytheists, who found the polarisation of transcendence and immanence beyond their comprehension. The Christian God was at once more remote and much closer than the gods men had known. This may be seen in Acts. In 14: 15 Paul and Barnabas protest that they are not gods but are 'men of like passions' with their uninvited worshippers, yet in 17: 23–8 Paul speaks of an unknown God, of whose stock men are and in whom they live and move and have their being. We have already seen how Justin uses an optimistic anthropology to bring his negative theology to earth.

1   In what way is man related to God?

Justin, as usual, presents a concise account, the simplicity of which evaporates to leave insoluble difficulties. His concept of spermatic Logos may be briefly stated.[1] Man is a rational

---

[1] C. Andresen, 'Justin und der mittlere Platonismus', *ZNW*, 44 (1952/3), 157–95; R. Holte, 'Logos spermatikos, Christianity and ancient philosophy according to St. Justin's Apologies', *STL*, 12 (1958), 109–68; R. Joly, *Christianisme et philosophie* (Brussels, 1973),

(*logikos*) being [*D*. 93.3], who shares [*1 A*. 46] in the complete Logos [*2 A*. 10], which is Christ. The same Logos revealed himself to Socrates, to Greeks and barbarians, and then later became man [*1 A*. 5]. He who once appeared both in a pillar of fire and in non-physical form has now become man and endured suffering [*1 A*. 63]. The difference between man's natural endowment and the fullness of Christ is the difference between an implanted seed of *logos* and knowledge or vision of the whole Logos [*2 A*. 8]. Lawgivers and philosophers were guided by a part of the Logos, but the whole Logos extends his rule to the simple and illiterate, since he is a power of the ineffable God and not the construction of human *logos* [*2 A*. 10]. The difference between the wisdom of the wisest men and the divine Logos is the difference between partial truth and the whole truth, between obscure and clear, between seed and fullness, between copy and reality [*2 A*. 13].

There has been such difference of opinion about Justin's spermatic Logos that some explanation of the controversy must be given. There are at least three clear reasons for disagreement in interpretation. First, Justin's terms are not logically precise but metaphorical. What does it mean to be a part, a seed, an obscure copy of the divine Logos? Secondly, the one philosophical term, 'participation', comes through Plato and is not susceptible of clear definition. Thirdly, Justin does contradict himself: the same Logos spoke in different forms, yet the whole Logos came only in Christ. For all these difficulties, Justin's account of *logos* remains an important, if imprecise, advance. The universality of Christ had broken through all restrictions of time and place: for man the only thing that mattered was whether he lived with or without *logos*. Justin sees man related to God rationally, universally and in different degrees.

Irenaeus[1] does not deny the place of reason in man's relation to God but he talks more about man seeing and hearing God and about life flowing from God to man. Rational elements are overshadowed by aesthetic and ontological considerations, which is an inflated way of saying: 'The glory of God is a

chapter 2; N. Pycke, 'Connaissance rationnelle et connaissance de grâce chez S. Justin', *EThL*, 37 (1961), 52–85; Osborn, *Justin Martyr*, pp. 140–7.

[1] The comprehensive work of Antonio Orbe, *Antropología de San Ireneo* (Madrid, 1969), is of basic importance.

living man, and the life of man is the vision of God'. Irenaeus has a lot to say about what we might call history, creation and the Word; but in the end he is only concerned with God and man.[1] History is the story of God's dealing with man, creation is the beginning of that story, its setting and a pledge of its continuance, while the incarnate Word is simply the union of God and man. God and man are not the separate sides of an ultimate dualism; they are interdependent. Man without God is nothing; God, without man to save, cannot be God. The one true God gave himself to men that they might be saved and their salvation meant that they should become like him and live forever. The abstractions of the Gnostics and the idols of the nations are wrong for opposite reasons: they don't recognise how far away and yet how close God is to man. These points run through the splendid statement [*H.* 4.34.7]:

> 'It was for this reason that the Word became the giver of the grace of the Father for the benefit of man, for whom he had made such great dispensations, revealing God indeed to man, but bringing man to God and preserving at the same time the invisibility of the Father, lest man at any time should become a despiser of God, so that he should always have a goal he had not reached, but on the other hand, making God visible to man through many dispensations, lest man, falling away from God altogether, should cease to exist. For the glory of God is a living man, and the life of man consists in the vision of God. For if the evidence of God which is given by creation gives life to all living creatures in the earth, much more does that disclosure of the Father which comes through the Word give life to those who see God.'

Here we have two complex truths clearly emphasised: the invisible Father does not demean or lower himself so that he might be despised, yet his glory is in the life and salvation of man; on the other hand, man finds life in the vision of God. God's glory is the living man, and the man's life is the vision of God. Irenaeus' optimism concerning the grace of God persists through his whole account of man. The starting-point is properly this nearness of God and man: man has enjoyed a special affinity to the Son of God, since man was made in God's

[1] See G. Wingren, *Man and incarnation* (Edinburgh, 1959).

image, and God's image is his Son [*E.* 22]. Man's relation to God is expressed in his reason and his freedom, not, as Gnostics claimed, in the stuff from which he was made. Reason shows man that there is one God over all [*H.* 2.4.6]. A king may paint a portrait of his son, and call it his own likeness, because it is a likeness of his son, and because he, that earthly king, has produced it. In the same way, the heavenly King and Father produces his likeness among men and he recognises the name of Jesus in all the world because the name of his son is his name, and because his son is given for the salvation of men [*H.* 4.30]. With his fondness for visual imagery Irenaeus speaks of the light of the Father shining in the flesh of Jesus so that incorruption may come to man [*H.* 4.20.2]. For man stands at the centre of the created cosmos, and man alone is capable of participating or sharing in the wisdom and power of God [*H.* 5.3.2].

Yet there are limitations to man's nearness to God. While he is the vessel to receive God's touch and to feel God's wisdom and power, he does not make God, but he is made by God [*H.* 4.64.2]. While God is always the same, man becomes [*H.* 4.21.1 and 2], and needs time to grow to maturity [*H.* 4.5.1; *E.* 12]. There are some men who irrationally transfer their frailties to God and do not realise how different God is. Man's nature has first to be shown in Christ. The heretics base their story of the divine aeons on their understanding of man. They are wrong to apply such things to God [*H.* 2.16.5]. They do not even understand man properly, and argue that he produces the Word, when the truth is that the Word produces man (*ibid.*). Man remains infinitely less than God, dependent on his grace, receiving only in part and never becoming God's equal; he cannot experience or understand things as God does. He is a creature of time, while God is uncreated. By God's goodness he may now learn what the Word of God has done for him [*H.* 2.37.3], and may offer his prayers to God, not because God needs any sacrifice, but because he who prays finds glory if his prayer is received by God [*H.* 4.31.1].

Man, so weak and yet so glorious, is a creature of purpose. His hope and perfection is the vision of God, his goal in life is to approach the Unbegotten, as he strives towards the perfection that God alone possesses [*H.* 4.63.2]. Man is made *according to* the image and likeness of God, and also *towards* the image and likeness, that is, pointing towards that which he has not yet received in full [*H.* 3.32f.; 5.1.3; 4.60.2; 5.1.1]. Even now all men still possess the image of God, but most have lost the likeness of God through rejecting his spirit [*H.* 5.6.1]. Man's greatness is in his beginning, when he was made in the image and likeness of God, and in his end, where he finds life in the vision of God [*H.* 3.19–21; 3.32.2]. As he is made like the son of God, so he is brought by him to the Father [*H.* 5 Preface, 5.1; 5.16.1]. While this likeness is moral it also affects men's bodies physically [*H.* 5.9.2]. Christ gathers those who are his own into the embrace of his Father [*H.* 5.2.1]. For Irenaeus true humanity is only possible through Christ, for Satan destroys humanity. 'Christ is righteous, and his life is whole and unimpaired human life.'[1] God is the only source of human life, and the incarnation gives man access to that source.[2]

Man becomes spiritual and perfect by the Spirit, who works together with the Son within man [*H.* 4.25.2; 4.34.6; 5.8.1]. As the Spirit inherits or takes over man's limbs, he bears them up to the kingdom of heaven [*H.* 5.9.4]. So the whole man is on the way to salvation, and the whole God (Father, Son and Spirit) began, continues and will perfect his work in man.

Irenaeus here speaks of God and man in a way that derives from John and Paul, but lacks the dualistic, sombre tendencies of these writers. The reason for his exuberance is plain. He reacts against all dualism because he is fighting the Gnostic threat at a time when 'contempt for the human condition and hatred of the body was a disease endemic in the entire culture of the period' and when 'the progressive devaluation of the cosmos' brought a 'corresponding devaluation of ordinary human existence'.[3] His confidence and enthusiasm raise the estimate of man to the highest conceivable level, for it is in a living man that God's glory is to be found.

For Tertullian the link between man and God is psychological and natural – man's soul is the breath of God. The

---

[1] *Ibid.* pp. 99 and 213.
[2] *Ibid.* p. 213. Here Wingren seems to overstate his case: 'Man, in order to be man, must continually transcend himself, and have God within himself. Man's life is dependent on communion with God, and if this communion is broken, man is lost. But it does not break and cannot break'.
[3] Dodds, *Age of anxiety*, pp. 35–7.

famous 'testimony of the soul which is naturally Christian', means two things that need careful examination: first, that the soul is linked to God and secondly, that this link is natural to all men. When God made man, thinking of Christ, who would one day be clay and flesh, he said to his Word; 'Let us make man in our image and likeness' [*Res.* 6]. This has a startling significance, since Tertullian believes that all reality, including spirit, is physical (*corpus*) and he has the earthy realism appropriate to a Christian materialist. The image of God is disfigured when the face of a man is kicked and beaten [*Spect.* 18], so brutal sports are unworthy of man [*Spect.* 22]. In these and other ways, man has cut himself off from his maker, so that he is no longer the pure work of God [*Spect.* 2]. Yet the soul still shares in the nature of God and even when it is corrupt, has 'that original, that Godlike and genuine thing which is its proper nature. For that which is from God is not so much extinguished as obscured; it can be obscured since it is not God; but it cannot be extinguished since it is from God' [*An.* 41]. The greatest testimony to God comes from the soul of man in its simple, untaught state. Not that the soul is Christian from birth; there must be a specific act for a man to become a Christian. In this Tertullian follows the Stoics, who believed that no matter how much a man has learned or how well a man lives, his conversion to wisdom belongs to a particular point of time.[1] The testimony of the soul to the Lord of all comes in exclamations like 'which may God grant!' and 'if God so will', or 'God is good!' Men speak in this way even when they are standing in pagan temples or beside the statues of pagan gods. There could hardly be a clearer proof of the reality of the God who is everywhere. The testimony of the soul is simple, true, commonplace, universal, natural and divine [*Test.* 4,5]. If man fears to become a Christian, let him ask his soul why it worships another god and still calls on the name of the Christian God [*Test.* 6]. The soul may proclaim God but still not seek to know him, and, with only a taste of Christianity, in its ignorance it may persecute Christians.

The soul is rational, and all men possess the same initial knowledge of God whether they are Egyptians, Syrians or even natives of Pontus like Marcion [*Marc.* 1.10; *Idol.* 14]. Men are

---

[1] E. Bickel, 'Fiunt, non nascuntur christiani', *Pisciculi, Festschrift für F. J. Dölger* (Münster, 1939), p. 61.

joined by this common nature into a community of which each is a member [*Idol.* 14; *Marc.* 4.16]. It is by reason that man is able to know in some way the one true God, for reason is divine in its core, not just on the surface [*Res.* 3].

The naturalness of Christianity means that the Christian becomes more human. He obeys the testimony of the soul, which, whenever it comes to itself, speaks the name of God. So man comes to himself when he obeys God, whereas idolatry is murder, since he who worships an idol destroys himself [*Idol.* 1]. Because he bears the image of God, man should give himself to God alone, just as coins, which bear the image of Caesar, are given to Caesar [*Idol.* 15]. Nature supports the rules of Christian practice, forbidding, for example, the wearing of a festal garland or crown as both unchristian and unnatural [*Cor.* 5] and also teaching all men, for God has written his law on the hearts of all men [*Cor.* 6].

Clement links man ethically and intellectually to God. As with Justin, reason comes first and the divine Logos has fallen like rain upon all men. As with Irenaeus, man lives only by seeing God. As with Tertullian, man is the image of the God whom all men know. Man is made for, by, and in the image of, God; he is much closer to God than any idol can be. Against pagans, Clement elevates man to stress the inferiority of idols; against Gnostics and philosophers Clement elevates man to claim that all men who believe can reach the heights that Gnostics and philosophers aspire to, but never achieve.

Clement begins the *Protrepticus*, and ends the *Stromateis*, amazed by joy at what God can do in man. The Word of God turns stones into men. God gives life to whom he wills and saves man from death and sin. Man is God's harp, God's pipe and God's temple; God plays upon the harp, blows upon the pipe and lives in the temple. He made man in *his own image*, to be the supreme object of his love [*Prot.* 1.6]. The image is purely rational and never physical, as it was for Tertullian; but Clement's use of the term is far from precise.[1]

The idols that men worship are clearly inferior to man. No great sculptor could work in any medium but the earth to which he belonged. None ever made an image that could breathe, or turned earth into flesh. Jupiter of Olympus is an image of an image, one step further away from truth than man.

---

[1] See J. Daniélou, *Gospel message*, pp. 408ff.

(Here there is an echo of Paul's argument in Romans 1: 23ff. or of Plato in *Republic*, Book x). Man is only one remove from God, and God's Word is the connecting link. The image of God is the divine Logos, the light that comes from light. The image of the Logos is the true man or the mind that is in man. Man has been made in the image of God and the likeness of God, but the gods of the heathen are mere earthly copies of the visible form of man. Man has been made for fellowship with God. Immortal man is a hymn of praise to God; he is established in righteousness and the oracles of truth are written within him. (In contrast to men, animals lack reason, and are unable to know God [*Prot.* 10.107].) God, who made all things, has implanted in all men some knowledge of himself, and the power of reason turns towards God, for there is no nation of men that has not some faith in a higher being [*S.* 5.14.133].[1]

So in different combinations of several themes we learn of the dependence of man on God and the nearness of God to man. Whether through implanted *logos*, true humanity, the soul that is naturally Christian, or life-giving participation in God, there is a link between God and man that cannot be entirely broken. In the imprecise language of image and likeness, the image is always there to be restored.

2 How can man's present misery be reconciled with his divine origin?

The common answer is that man has freely chosen sin and fallen from his original fellowship with God. The image of God has been scarred or stunted by sin. Justin has a pleasantly extrovert approach – one could *almost* say that there is no such thing as sin; there are only sinners. Yet the power of sin is evident, especially in the final act of man's treachery – the crucifixion of God's Son. Justin's account of man begins at the highest level. As a whole nation once took its name from Israel, so those who keep Christ's commandments are now made by him children of God; they bear his name and share the reality of his sonship [*D.* 123]. All of which disturbs Justin's

---

[1] The argument for belief in gods or God from *consensus gentium* has had many supporters in its long history. See Cicero, *De natura deorum*, 2.2 and Seneca, *Ep. moral.* 117.

Jewish hearers so much that he has to go further and explain how all Christians are made immortal, which is what sonship of God means. The explanation [*D.* 124] plunges deeper and shocks the audience to silence. He must use their scriptures, so he turns to the psalm that had been quoted in the Fourth Gospel to justify the divine sonship of Jesus. In Psalm 82 the Holy Spirit spoke of Christians gathered together by Christ to judge all nations; 'God stood in the assembly of gods; but in the midst does he judge gods'.

This immoderate claim shows the height from which *man has fallen*; 'Behold, truly you die as men and fall as one of the princes'. The passage is ambiguous but, for Justin, it contains a rebuke to men 'who were made, like God, free from passion and death, so long as they kept his commandments, and were considered worthy of being called by God, his sons; but they became like Adam and Eve and brought death on themselves'. Those who might have been gods and sons of the Most High, follow Adam and Eve into judgement, condemnation, and death.

Justin is careful to indicate that it is the voluntary disobedience of each man that brings his condemnation. Man is not born a sinner; he has to work at it and become one by his own disobedience. From Adam on, the human race had fallen to death under the power of the deceitful serpent, 'each man having done wrong through his own fault' [*D.* 88.4].[1]

Contrary to later accounts of original sin, the sin of Adam is not the greatest sin. The history of Israel is a history of sin [*D.* 13.1; 17.1; 21.1], which reaches its climax in the crucifixion of the Christ followed by the cursing of his followers: 'you even laid hands on Christ himself and persist in wickedness, cursing those who prove that he who was crucified by you is the Christ' [*D.* 93.4]. God can have nothing but the fiercest judgement for those who violently seized his beloved son [*D.* 137.2]. Yet from the suffering of Christ has come the salvation of man. 'Speak nothing evil against him who was crucified and do not mock his stripes, for by these stripes all may be healed, as indeed we have been healed' [*D.* 137.1]. He is the king who reigns from a tree [*1 A.* 41.4; *D.* 73.1] and whose cross pervades the cosmos [*1 A.* 55].

---

[1] However in *1 A.* 61, Justin contrasts the first birth of necessity and the second birth of freedom.

88

Irenaeus has a less episodic and extrovert approach to sin, which is a cosmic catastrophe, and, while man began it, the result is far beyond his control. Yet the ever-active God was more than able to cope with the disaster and, taking a long view, it is hard to see how things could have gone better! 'O felix culpa!'

Certainly man fell from his first state. He received his formation at the hands of God himself, made from the purest, finest earth and infused with God's power, made in the image of God and receiving the breath of God; he was like God both in his breath and his formation; he was made free to rule over all the earth. God gave the whole creation to him, so man gave the names to all living things and lived with Eve in innocence and purity, the breath of life making them both immune to the understanding of baser things. But man disobeyed God, and was expelled from paradise for eating forbidden fruit [*E.* 11–16]; yet the fall was his wounding rather than his death. God's power is perfected in weakness [*H.* 5.2.3], and the hearts of men are transformed by the word of the gospel, and the coming of Jesus the Lord was necessary to give man the truth concerning God [*H.* 3.12]. Man is not yet what he should be, but through God's grace and God's continual work of salvation, man will reach incorruption and immortality. For just as a doctor is proved by his patients, so God is revealed through the men he heals. He came in Jesus to make it possible for man again to perceive God and for man to dwell in God [*H.* 3.20]. And the life that comes from the revelation of God in Christ, his Word, is even more exuberant than the life of creatures from the earth [*H.* 4.34.7].

Why was man not made perfect at first? God could not make men perfect, because created things have to be less perfect than those that are uncreated. There are other important factors: man was not ready to receive perfection when he was created; he could not have received the power of God, and God's perfection; he passed through a time of infancy and growth [*H.* 4.62 and 63]. Man must come to know his weakness and then find that weakness made strong through God's grace [*H.* 4.63.3], for man is God's workmanship and he must wait for the hand of God, who does all things at the proper time. Let man give to God his heart while it is soft and tractable, so that he may keep the form in which God made him and not lose the impression of God's fingers [*H*. 4.64.2]. Although he is a disobedient son of God, who has lost his inheritance and ceased to be a son [*H*. 4.68.1], man does not escape the hands of God, and he will once again be made in God's image and likeness [*H*. 5.1.3]. While all stem from Adam and suffer from his fault [*H*. 3.33], those who were once claimed by death are now freed from death [*H*. 3.19.6], and redeemed by the blood of Christ [*H*. 5.2.1].

After Justin's episodic account of sin and Irenaeus' optimism, Tertullian's account is gloomy indeed. He sees sin as a universal epidemic. Man's seed is sick and the Church's main job is to stop the sickness and avoid contamination. There are no easy cures, but active measures are possible all along the line. To recognise the epidemic proportions of sin is the first move towards its restraint.

Man's knowledge of God was never more than partial, and, since he has not listened to the perfect teacher of righteousness, whom God has sent [*Ap*. 40], his imperfection no longer has any excuse [*Ap*. 48]. Now *man acts against God* and against reason, like a rudderless ship, for reason is the only rudder by which he may safely steer [*Paen*. 1]. The weakness of the flesh is no excuse, for man is both flesh and spirit [*Ux*. 4], and both can be instruments of sin or of righteousness [*Paen*. 3].

Irenaeus' motif of growth may be found in Tertullian, but it is overshadowed by the fall and original sin.[1] Man lost the likeness of God through sin, and while he may regain it through grace [*Bapt*. 5], his position is less happy than Irenaeus had thought, for Adam's sin brought corruption on the human race: 'totum genus de semine infectum' [*Test*. 3]. This infection is handed down as soul is transmitted from parent to child (Stoic materialism is evident here), and the corruption of man gives him a different nature [*An*. 41]. Human birth is inevitably unclean when it is surrounded by idolatrous superstitions, which ensure the presence of demons from the beginning [*An*. 39]. Yet in spite of these two sources of corruption (original sin and evil spirits), the divine part of man is never completely destroyed: while some men are very bad and others

---

[1] See N. P. Williams, *The ideas of the fall and original sin* (London, 1927), pp. 231–45; also F. R. Tennant, *The sources of the doctrines of the fall and original sin* (Cambridge, 1903), p. 328: 'The beginning was made by Tertullian'.

very good, there is some good in the worst and some bad in the best [*An.* 41]. For sinful man, repentance is the only medicine that can cure his illness [*Paen.* 7]. While God is appeased by man's penitence [*Paen.* 9], all is not quickly set right. Tertullian is ambivalent about the sinner's prospects. Sin excommunicates a member of the Church by cutting him off from the fellowship, and there is no way for a sinner to find his way back into the Church, for the Church is always the community of the saints. Penance may be done, but this brings man to the threshold of the Church and the community must continue to pray for the sinner. Tertullian also gives a second account, that the Church has powers to forgive sin, and it may exercise these when it judges it to be proper so to do.[1] The outlook is not encouraging, for while man receives grace, which is confirmed at baptism, this grace may be destroyed and wasted through sin. Further, while some sins may be forgiven, sins against God cannot be forgiven, for they bring death and destroy grace.[2] Yet Tertullian still has a place for the love and mercy of God, who forgave the Ninevites when they repented [*Pud.* 10.3], and the compassion of Christians to the penitent sinner is a sign of the law of mercy, which remained valid for Tertullian even after he had become a Montanist [*Pud.* 6.4].

A more positive point is made in the account of grace as a special divine favour and assistance [*Pat.* 1], but a legal structure dominates in the end. God is the judge who deals with every case on its merits [*Paen.* 2.11]. Beginning from baptism, when former sins are washed away, merit is earned before God, and the quantity of merit determines the rank of the believer in heavenly bliss [*Paen.* 6.1 and *Res.* 48].

Clement is neither an extrovert like Justin, a ready synthesiser like Irenaeus, nor a gloomy epidemiologist like Tertullian. Yet sin is real and sinister; it is about men all the time, in every corner, like an invisible and deceitfully pleasant form of poison gas. Clement has a strong optimism based on grace and he seems less anxious than Tertullian; but in every part of Clement there is a horror of the contagion of sin. The Scythian king was right when he shot a depraved subject [*Prot.* 2.24]

[1] E. Altendorf, *Einheit und Heiligkeit der Kirche* (Leipzig, 1932), pp. 28f.
[2] K. Rahner, 'Sünde als Gnadenverlust in der frühkirchlichen Literatur', *ZKTh*, 60 (1936), 504–6.

for too few people see the danger of sin. Only demons who hated men could condone human sacrifice to idols [*Prot.* 3.42]. In the worship of idols man does violence to his own nature, disbelieving the true God so that he may have an excuse for his indulgence [*Prot.* 4.61]. The *Paedagogus* insists that wickedness is the one proper cause for shame [*Paed.* 2.6.52] but provides incredibly detailed instruction on how to avoid this shame. Clement does not write as a fastidious Christian who wants to make a fuss about little things; he writes as one who knows and fears the power of sin in the polite circles of Alexandrian paganism. Lastly, the third book of the *Stromateis* shows Clement fighting desperately against sin that claims to be a higher righteousness and communion. 'It is to the brothels that this communion leads' [*S.* 3.4.28–30].

Against this sombre background Clement is confident. The light of man's original union with heaven, once darkened by man's ignorance, has broken out again in the pure, divine light of Christ [*Prot.* 2.27]. The need of man serves to show the greatness of man's saviour. 'The dead need life, sheep need a shepherd, children need a teacher; but all humanity needs Jesus' [*Paed.* 1.9.83] and 'all men are his' [*S.* 7.2.5]. His first quality is the love of men and his only work is their salvation [*Prot.* 9 *passim*]. Clement's final exhortation asks men as God-loving and Godlike images of the Word to take the yoke of Christ in love [*Prot.* 12.121] in order to learn from him. A great part of man's salvation is through the teaching of Jesus, who shows men how the image of God should live; for such a life was man made [*Paed.* 1.13.103]. Jesus is the incomparable teacher who trains men for true life. In the beginning he formed man from the dust, then gave him new life through water and growth through his Spirit, so that, being trained by his Word, man, who was born from the earth, might be changed into a holy, heavenly being [*Paed.* 1.12.98]. God brought men to communion with himself by giving that which was his own; God gave his own Logos and made all things for all men [*Paed.* 2.12.120].

Clement finds new words to describe the answer to sin, which is salvation. To believe is to be made one in Christ [*S.* 4.25.157] and to grow like him. The end of man is to become like God: 'assimilation to God, as far as possible, so that a man becomes righteous and holy with wisdom' is the end of faith and also the chief good of man [*S*. 2.22.133]. But it is impossible for man to gain the knowledge of God while he is under the control of his passions; he cannot become like the Lord if he is at the mercy of physical pleasure [*S*. 3.5.42], and for this reason likeness to God must include *apatheia*.

So in quite different ways for each writer, sin is seen to explain where man is now. There is no attempt to minimise the disaster. Every optimist has his dread of sin and every pessimist has his hope of salvation; of course there are different optimisms and different pessimisms. Even Tertullian, for all his gloom over a fallen race, claims to know what to do or how to find a way out.

3   Is man free?

The sense of fate hung heavy over the second century. A dread of divine decree ran back to the beginning of the classical world, and the stars increased their hold on men. Gnosticism was dangerous because its determinism was strict and it merged readily with the ordinary faith from which it claimed to advance. Yet Christian writers did not have to look far for arguments against determinism. They were on every hand[1] and were part of continuing debate among Stoics and Platonists. But they had to use them carefully because so much of their accepted belief seemed congenial to determinism: divine foreknowledge and election, not to mention man's slavery under sin.

Justin's account of free will confirms the practical extrovert picture; it is not the whole Justin, but it is part of him. He tells how he reached Christianity at the end of a long chain of choices. His personal vitality is evident in the incisive way he describes his pilgrimage, even when allowance is made for the fact that he is arguing a case to convince the waverer. There is cool decision behind the words, 'In this way, then, and for these reasons, I am a philosopher' [*D*. 8.2]. Self-determination is one of his favourite themes. He finds it in the dramatic choice, which Israel faced: 'Behold before you are good and evil; choose the good' [Deuteronomy 30: 15, 19]. It is equally

---

[1] See the extended treatment in D. Amand, *Fatalisme et liberté dans l'antiquité grecque* (Louvain, 1945).

clear in the well-worn words of Plato: 'The blame falls on the one who chooses; God is blameless'.

God must judge all men and a final judgement is unthinkable unless men are free and responsible. Men show their free will when they switch from one course of action to its opposite. Men and angels are distinct from other creatures in their power of free will. Fate does not explain the mixture of moral drives in most people and it removes the difference between good and evil [*1 A.* 28.4]. Prophecy of future events does not imply man's lack of moral responsibility, for the prophets are chiefly concerned with this responsibility, since rewards and threats take up so much of their discourse [*1 A.* 43]. The world continues because God wants men to have time to choose; the end is delayed in the interests of man's freedom [*2 A.* 6]. The course of human history is marked by periods of man's freedom and wickedness, punctuated by God's acts of judgement. God let men build Babel and bring judgement on themselves [*D.* 102] while he remained always in control, allowing men freedom to act and be judged.

Justin's use of a new word *autexousios* is a final indication of the central place he gives to responsibility and free will.[1] His motives are clear. The denial of free will by Gnostics brought moral decay to Christian ranks, while Stoic acceptance of fate made persecutors less sensitive to the wrong they were committing. There would be no point, thinks Justin, in arguing with emperors or Jews if they could not, by their own act of will, change their ways.

Irenaeus digs deeper and recognises that there is something odd about a gospel of redemption that claims that all men are free anyway. At least the Gnostics had a point: man must be captive or he would not need to be liberated. There are two kinds of freedom: that which all men have and that which man may have only through God's grace. Man is not the slave of fate, yet he is not totally free; he was given freedom of will and authority over himself and is responsible for what he is, whether that be wheat or chaff. Although he was created a rational being, he has lived without reason and against the righteousness of God. As the Psalm said, man being in honour did not understand, but became like the senseless beasts

[1] *D.* 102.4; *2 A.* 7.5; *D.* 88.5; *D.* 141.1. See W. Telfer, 'AUTEXOUSIA', *JThS* (1957), 124.

[*H.* 4.7]. Since God always worked to bring man back, he left man with the freedom to return from idolatry to obedience and immortality [*H.* 4.26.2]. Man's free will, God's free will and man's likeness to God are the three factors in man's vocation to live according to God's will [*H.* 4.60.2].

Although man's freedom reflects the freedom of God, man cannot be truly free without the grace of God. Only Christ brings man to knowledge of God as Father and to obedience to him, in action, word and thought [*H.* 4.28]. Grace restores the freedom with which man was made [*H.* 3.5.2]. The puzzle of man's freedom may be expressed in the claim that man is always free, but always a servant. When he is the servant of sin, he is responsible for his choice; when he is a servant of God he is truly free [*H.* 4.26.2].

Here Irenaeus has clarified a major distinction between freedom as free will and freedom as total liberty. With Paul he asserts free will and denies liberty; fallen man is responsible but is the slave of sin. The Gnostics deny man's generic responsibility (he is material, animal or spiritual from birth), but assert the uninhibited liberty of the spiritual kingly race to which they alone belong. Like Paul, Irenaeus sees the central question about man as: whose servant is he? what power rules over him? Only when he becomes the servant of God, can he in the end find true liberty.

Tertullian probes the paradox that the source of man's sin and tragedy is the quality that places him next to God. The legal shape of Tertullian's thought is only valid if man is responsible for the good or evil he produces. Man's soul is endowed with the power to choose, with *autexousia* [*An.* 21]. This free will is the source of evil in God's world [*Cast.* 2] and always plays a central part in the argument against Marcion. Nevertheless man's free will is his highest attribute; it constituted his original likeness to God and was confirmed by the Law that God gave, a law that confronted man with the choice between good and evil, life and death. The creation of a free agent was better than any alternative. Marcion's God is 'irrationally' good; the true divine goodness acts with purpose and plan. Tertullian's argument runs:

(1) it was good that God should be known;
(2) it was proper for something to be worthy of this knowledge;

(3) nothing is more worthy than God's own image and likeness;
(4) free will should be seen as the distinctive feature of the divine image and likeness;
(5) it was proper that the image and likeness of God should have free will;
(6) free will enables man to do good spontaneously.

Tertullian's account of divine goodness and human free will is able to provide a clearer basis for ethical activity than any that was open to Paul or the Platonists. For Paul and Plato no one was good but God; the Good was one. Man could only be good by sharing in divine grace or goodness. Tertullian sees man's freedom as the source of his ability to produce good. While God alone remains good by nature, and is the final author of all good, man is given freedom that enables him to do good spontaneously.

> 'Therefore, so that man might now have his own goodness, granted (*emancipatum*) to him by God, and so that there might now be in man a property and in some sense a nature of goodness, there was assigned to him, in his constitution, as the proof of the goodness bestowed by God, freedom and the power of choice. The result is that man can now produce his own goodness from himself' [*Marc.* 2.6].[1]

Clement takes the different view that man's freedom derives from a growing dependence on God. This means that, like Paul and Irenaeus, he distinguishes free will from freedom. While for Tertullian and the Stoics the divine spark is given and the wise man achieves freedom through independence of external things, with Clement the stress is on the perfection of freedom as total service of God and total dependence on grace.

Such fulfilment or perfection of man can only be reached by man's free choice and the help of divine grace [*S.* 5.1.7]. Faced with the threat of Gnostic determinism, Clement persistently stresses man's freedom of choice. Man is not a puppet [*S.* 2.3.11]; he is made free to choose. God is not blamed for man's choice and man judges what is right by his own conscience [*S.* 1.1.5]. When faced with the choice that scripture declares, we have chosen the way of faith and life,

---

[1] The Stoic notion of man as a divine *apospasma* was widely spread.

and we believe God in his Word ⌈S. 2.4.12⌉. The true Gnostic chooses those things that are good and desirable in themselves; he has no hidden motives [*S*. 6.12 *passim*].[1] Yet in his choice he finds freedom and owes it all to God. He is surrounded by angels who work with him to fulfil God's will [*S*. 6.17.157]. He is led by the Spirit of God and cries, 'Abba, Father'. Only in this knowledge of the Father, to whom man prays, is freedom found [*S*. 4.8.67], for while all have free will, not all are free.

This account of freedom, as it comes with different stresses from each writer, presents a double denial of Gnostic claims. For the Gnostic, men were determined to be material, animal or spiritual, and only the spiritual found freedom in personal autonomy and rejection of any external standards or claims. Against such views it is insisted, first, that all men are free to choose and are responsible for their choice, and, secondly, that growth in freedom is a growth in dependence on grace and obedience to God.

4 Of what does man consist?

I.e., has man parts, such as body, soul and spirit and, if so, how are they related? The most common error in the discussion of these terms is to treat them as a form of advanced or ghostly anatomy: having learned of legs and arms in *Anatomy I*, we are led to see body as part of a larger complex under *Anatomy II*. Now it is not like that, even if for Tertullian the soul is physical. Anthropology is used to describe man's relation to God and the universe, to life and to death. Doxographers cannot be expected to see this; but it is especially clear in the second century, where the same writer may use two different sets of terms to say different things about man, without any contradiction.

Justin gives two accounts of man's composition. In the first, man is described as body, soul and spirit [*D*. 5–7], while in the second, he is described as body, soul and *logos* [*2 A*. 10]. The reason for the different accounts is simple and follows the logic of apologetic. An apologist is concerned to defend his

---

[1] The similarity of Clement's knowledge to the vision of Beauty in Plato's *Symposium* and the purified will in Dante's *Purgatorio*, 27 is remarkable. See Murdoch, *The Fire and the Sun*, pp. 34f.

faith against a variety of attacks. There is no system in the objections that he faces, for they normally come from diverse logics. Yet he must meet each objection with a rebuttal that is intelligible and consistent with the logic of the objection. He may have his own key ideas but they cannot dominate his argument; if they do, he will not be heard by the objectors. We shall understand the diversity of Justin's apologetic in terms of objection and rebuttal.

The account of the one Unbegotten answers the objection: why one God and not many? The rebuttal to this is the argument against infinite regress. There can be only one Unbegotten, one uncaused cause, one essential life or pure being. Man receives life by the gift of the divine spirit. When this spirit is taken from man then his soul ceases to exist and returns to the place of its origin. The life-giving spirit is the same power that raised Christ from the dead and brings rebirth to the Christian at baptism. While it is certain that the soul lives,

> 'it lives not as something which is life but as something which participates in life. That which participates is a different thing from that which is participated in. A soul partakes of life because God wishes it to live. Life does not belong to it as life belongs to God; but as man does not exist always neither is body joined to soul forever. But whenever it is necessary for this harmony to be broken, the soul leaves the body and man is no more'.

In what way does the will of God have any effect? The soul is as dependent on spirit as body is on soul. The *Dialogue* continues: 'So too, whenever it is necessary that the soul should no longer be, the spirit goes from it and the soul is no more; but it too goes once again to the place whence it was received'. The last words echo the phrase from Plato's *Phaedrus*, 248; 'to the place from whence it has come', and also suggest the words of Ecclesiastes 12: 7: 'and the dust return to the earth as it was and the spirit return to God who gave it'. For Justin, however, the dust does not merely return to the earth. The flesh is to rise again. Yet there is a definite hierarchy. Body depends upon soul and soul depends upon spirit. Body cannot live without soul. Soul cannot live without spirit. Spirit can live without soul for it is life and does not merely participate in life [*D*. 5–7].

98

The account of God as ineffable and unknown is part of the reply to the objection to Christian truth: what is new cannot be true. How can Christianity claim such arrogant superiority to all other teaching when it is such a recent growth? The rebuttal to this objection is the account of the partial and perfect *logos*, of participation in *logos* and the Logos himself. Christ is the whole Logos and he appeared on earth for our sakes as body, *logos* and soul. Before this happened, men said good things by discovering and contemplating some part of the Logos. They took different parts and so they contradicted one another. Yet Christ was and is the *logos* in every man, so that all truth belongs to him. From spermatic Logos or reason, man may move either to sharing in Christ himself, or in the other direction, to his own mental constructions and final falsehood. The choice is with man [*2 A.* 10]. On this account the third element in man is *logos*, not spirit.

Justin's two accounts of man are intelligible in terms of the objections he was trying to meet and the objections are intelligible in terms of problems that require solution. In neither case is the problem anything to do with ghostly anatomy – the first is concerned with life, death, man's relation to God, while the second is concerned with the knowledge of the truth.

In the same way Irenaeus speaks of man with a special concern for his body after death. Man is made of body and soul, and needs spirit from God. The soul teaches the body and shares with it any spiritual vision that it has enjoyed. At the same time, the soul inspires and gives life to the body, ruling over the body and possessing it [*H.* 2.53]. Body is not the same as the soul, but is joined with the soul as long as God wills. The soul is not life, but may share in the life that God gives; for soul and life remain separate essences [*H.* 2.56.2]. It is the Spirit that brings the body and soul of natural man to completion. Soul and flesh need the spirit of God. The Spirit transforms soul and body [*H.* 5.6.1]. Life is given through God's grace alone. The body is to be brought to immortality and not to be discarded. Soul and flesh receive the Spirit of the Father; the Spirit saves and the flesh is saved [*H.* 5.9.3). But the soul must co-operate with the Spirit in this transformation, to make man's end like his beginning, so that the whole man is saved [*H.* 5.20.1].

The respect for the body that is found in Justin and developed in Irenaeus may be found in more striking terms in Tertullian. Tertullian wrote a special work on the soul, which was at many points derivative from the writing of Soranus of Ephesus.[1] Yet it remains a remarkable work, the first Western treatise on psychology,[2] not to be emulated by a Christian writer for another 200 years. Tertullian shows his ability to argue and analyse abstract issues, without the stimulus of an opponent he detests. Tertullian believes the soul is handed on from parent to child (traducianism), rather than pre-existent or created at birth. Soul does not precede body, nor does body precede soul; both begin simultaneously at conception [*An.* 27] and until the separation at death [*An.* 51] body and soul are a physical unity. His chief concern is always to destroy dualism (man is as much body as soul [*Res.* 32]), and his main achievement is not traducianism, which would be of antiquarian interest, but a credible account of man as a unity.[3]

While philosophers argue about the soul interminably, Christians have a concise knowledge of the matter, because they learn the truth from God. Soul must be joined to body and the senses are not to be despised in the way Gnostics and Platonists have despised them. The soul springs from the breath of God. 'We define the soul, then, as born of God's breath, immortal, corporeal, having shape, simple in substance, intelligent in itself, various in its manifestations, full in its power of choice, subject to accidental change, changeable in its faculties, rational, ruling, able to see into the future and

---

[1] Soranus (A.D. 98–178) studied at Alexandria and worked and wrote in Rome. See H. Diels, *Doxographi Graeci* (Berlin, 1879), pp. 203–13; also H. Karpp, 'Sorans vier Bücher Peri Psuches und Tertullians Schrift De Anima', *ZNW.* 33 (1934), 31–47; also J. H. Waszinck (ed.), *De Anima* (Amsterdam, 1947), pp. 21–44.

[2] 'Der Umstand, dass Schriftsteller wie Tertullian nicht einfach biblische Aussagen über die Seele sammelten, sondern die vorliegende antike Uberlieferung in ausgewählten Stellen oder sogar in einem gegebenen literarischen Zusammenhang benutzten, liess eine abendländische Psychologie entstehen, deren geschichtliche Einheit sowohl in den Fragen als auch in den Antworten von den Griechen bis in unsere Tage reicht' (H. Karpp, *Probleme altchristlicher Anthropologie* (Gütersloh, 1950), p. 231).

[3] *Ibid.* p. 90: 'Auch der scharfe, gewandte Kampf gegen die Gnosis und die Psychologie unter der Voraussetzung, dass die Seele des Menschen, dieser selbst und die ganze Menschheit eine einzige, von Gott geschaffene, aber dann verdorbene und zu erlösende Einheit sind, ist eine bedeutende literarische und theologische Leistung'.

flowing from one original source' [*An.* 22]. The soul is not, as Plato claimed, self-existent and divine. It is immortal but a long way below God (*afflatus*, not *spiritus*) and is handed on from parent to child. As a materialist, Tertullian sees the influence of many physical factors on the soul. Fitness is important; the fat man learns little, while the lean and hungry have keen minds. The mind may be sharpened by scholarly activity or blunted by torpidity and vice [*An.* 20]. The mind is sluggish in colder climates but in warmer air it is active and acute [*An.* 25].

Tertullian's account of the soul is characteristic of his thought both in its systematic argument with definitions that derive from careful investigation and in its fresh earthiness, which comes from a respectful and observant materialism. The movement of a child in the womb provides proof that the soul is already present. The senses are given by God so that man may understand and enjoy the works of God. Once the senses are discredited, the order of nature, the providence of God and human existence are all devalued [*An.* 17]. Tertullian is not as hard-headed in his empiricism as his defence of the senses might suggest. He accepts the vision of a Montanist sister who saw the physical shape of a soul; she was very good at visions and revelations [*An.* 9]. He is less happy about the story of a praying corpse; but he accepts the occurrence, and interprets the evidence in a way that does not harm his thesis that the death that is not complete is not death [*An.* 51]. The charm of his earthy abrasive humour emerges in one brief interlude. Transmigration of souls has its funny side, for Empedocles claimed he was once a fish. 'Why not a melon since he was so silly or a chameleon since he was so puffed up with conceit?' [*An.* 32]. Yet no doubt, says Tertullian, it was as a fish that he jumped into the volcanic frying-pan of Mount Aetna to continue his transmigrations [*An.* 32], without benefit of chips.

Clement lacks the driving concern of Irenaeus and of Tertullian for all that is physical, although the body is still important. He has little to add to what has been said already; yet his account of the soul is full and his terminology is both biblical and philosophical.[1] Like Justin he sees the union of

---

[1] For an extended account of Clement's view of the soul, see Karpp, *ibid.* pp. 92–131. For all the similarity between Tertullian and Clement, there are important differences. Clement rejects Stoic

body and soul dissolved at death [S. 7.12.71] and like Justin he insists that the soul depends on God for its life. His great theme is that man is a creature, the work of one God [S. 3.4.34]. Man is not related to God by a common substance, but is the product of God's will [S. 2.16.75].

From the four writers a clear picture of man as body, soul and spirit (or *logos*) emerges. Man is a creature, dependent on God for life, yet plainly the most important part of God's creation. Tertullian's detailed account tells as much about Tertullian as it does about man.

5 Can man know the truth?

This was the universal quest of the second century. The popular way was that of mystical vision, with little scope for argument and proof. Even the Platonism of the day was religious rather than logical. Gnosticism was a dominant approach, as it abandoned discursive reasoning at the beginning instead of at the end of the process of knowledge.[1] For each of our four writers, the knowledge of truth involves direct apprehension of ultimate reality; but in each case argument is important and there is need for growth and development in the knower.

Knowledge of truth was the central drive of Justin's life; but he made no attempt to provide a competitive gnosis. Man could know God through the Logos, who spoke through the scriptures and who came in Jesus. When Justin faces the failure of secular philosophy, he is directed to the prophets,

materialism and the hereditary taint of original sin. His insistence on the dominance of the rational or spiritual element in man at once prepared the way for Origen's pre-existent souls and also for later asceticism. He was concerned to show how man could advance in spirituality over a period of time. 'Die realistische Eschatologie Tertullians hat er abgeschwächt zu einem zielstrebigen Geschichtsverlauf, der für die Menschheit eine vergeistigende und versittlichende Entwicklung bedeutet' (*ibid.* p. 131). Karpp's diagnosis is accurate but his evaluation is too rapid.

[1] This was why Plato rejected art. 'Art thus prevents the salvation of the whole man by offering a pseudo-spirituality and a plausible imitation of direct intuitive knowledge (vision, presence), a defeat of the discursive intelligence at the bottom of the scale of being, not at the top' (Murdoch, *The Fire and the Sun*, p. 66).

who 'alone saw the truth and declared it to men, caring and fearing for no man. They were not subject to opinion, but spoke only what they heard and saw, when they were filled with the Holy Spirit' [*D.* 7.1]. Ultimate truth can only be known directly. It cannot be inferred from other principles without ceasing to be ultimate. Those who have heard and seen give testimony concerning the truth. The perception of God does not come naturally to men, but comes only to those who receive God's gift of the Holy Spirit [*D.* 4], and whose lives show affinity to God. The truth of the prophets is confirmed by the visible fulfilment of their prophecies. Justin concludes: 'But in my soul a fire was immediately kindled and I was possessed with longing for the prophets and for those men who are the friends of Christ' [*D.* 8.1]. On this point Justin is aggressively empirical. This central point of his epistemology provides the sole ground for regarding him as a simple, uncomplicated thinker. Yet on this point he is as much a Platonist as ever.[1] The direct apprehension of truth comes after a process of argument and inquiry. It is the ultimate knowledge that the Gnostics claim but it does not despise argument.

Irenaeus, we have already seen, provided a presentation of the vision of God that defeats the Gnostics on their own ground; he goes further to show that his kind of aesthetic excludes the fantasy of the Gnostics and sets down strict rules for the knowledge of truth. He is forever talking about 'seeing' and 'showing' evidence of the truth. He is not concerned with dreams or suppositions, but with reality, and constantly speaks of what is 'true' and 'firm' [*H.* 2.40; 2.41; 1.19.1; 1.28.1]. The Word made flesh delivers Christians from the fantasies and comic cartoons of the Gnostics. These fantasies must be totally exposed, for argument on isolated points will not show them to be untenable. When the content of this teaching is uncovered, it cannot be confused with philosophy or true knowledge; but it will be recognised as fantastic nonsense. There is no rational control over the content of the Gnostic myth; it is a product of what Augustine later called 'fornicatio fantastica'. Stories about melons and cucumbers can be fabricated in the same way and 'if anyone is free to dispose of terms as he wishes, who is going to stop us from adopting these

[1] See *Republic*, 505–11 and Maximus of Tyre, *Diss.* 17.1.

terms (melons and cucumbers), when they are much more credible (than those of the Gnostics), their usage is established and they are known by all?' [*H.* 1.5.2].

God is to be seen and his truth is to be observed by faith. Faith sees things as they are and according to their nature [*E.* 3]. God may be seen from his works [*H.* 2.46.2; 3.12.1]. Here we have an extension of Justin's empiricism. Justin was primarily concerned to discredit those who had not seen. Irenaeus nearly turns theology into aesthetics – the only thing that matters is the vision of God – yet he is a long way from Gnostic ecstasy. Knowledge or vision is governed by three laws:[1]

(1) the nature of the object should be respected and truth should be loved;
(2) the nature of the faculty that knows should be respected and the order and limits of knowledge should be observed; man cannot hope to achieve more than a small part of the sum of knowledge;
(3) man will progress in knowledge if he keeps these first two laws, and this will be his way to truth.

A selfless respect for reality and a due recognition of man's finitude comprise the humility that alone can learn God. The chief fault of the Gnostics is their restlessness [*H.* 5.20.1]. They are always trying to twist things about and to know more than man may know. Because mystery remains in God, man's claim to knowledge must always be limited [*H.* 2.41]. Finally, knowledge is found within the Church: a gift of truth comes to the bishop as the successor of the apostles, for the disciples learnt the truth from Christ and deposited its full riches in the Church.[2]

The knowledge of truth brings us to a central problem in the interpretation of Tertullian. His oft-quoted antithesis between Athens and Jerusalem and his misquoted comment on belief and absurdity suggest that he had little time for reason and argument; yet a rapid reading of *De Anima* or *Against Marcion* shows more argument than most Christian thinkers have produced. How did Tertullian understand the process of

[1] D. B. Reynders, 'Optimisme et théocentrisme chez Saint Irénée', *RThAM*, 8 (1936), 229–32.
[2] See below, p. 228, n. 1: 'charisma veritatis certum'.

knowledge? Was it the simple acceptance of the rule of faith, or was he committed to exploration into God? The traditional view has been that Tertullian was an aggressive fideist who rejected all secular culture and held fast to the core of Christian belief. It is no longer possible to hold this view of Tertullian with any conviction.

We may follow the main groups of evidence.[1] There are plenty of attacks on philosophy and philosophers to be found in Tertullian; but these have many antecedents in his predecessors and contemporaries. There are more serious objections raised against philosophers: the disagreements between them, the contrast between their lives and their teaching, their preoccupation with dialectic rather than with truth; but even these objections by Tertullian are motivated by his demand for simplicity. The philosophers have shown themselves lacking in the simplicity and poverty that are essential to the Christian.[2]

The antithesis between Athens and Jerusalem is found in Paul,[3] and Tertullian's use of rhetorical questions or parallel antitheses is widespread. In *Ap.* 46.18 and *Praescr.* 7.9 Tertullian simply maintains the superiority of Christianity to philosophy and attacks the misuse of philosophy by heretics; philosophy, as such is not condemned. The paradox 'It is credible, because it is inappropriate' has already been examined. What Tertullian is concerned to show is the depth of the divine mystery. 'One is on the wrong track if one sees in this "paradox" a kind of manifesto against reason and against philosophy.'[4] Tertullian has two aims: to preserve the originality and uniqueness of Christianity (so that it is not just one philosophy among others) and to preserve the pattern of Christian belief against distortion by heretics who play with philosophy. Philosophy prepares the way for the knowledge of God by pointing to God [*Marc.* 2.27.6; *Virg.* 11.6], immortality [*Test.* 4.1–8] and resurrection [*Test.* 4.9–11]. There are plenty of points of agreement between Christians and philosophers [*Ap.* 14.7; 22.5]; not only is Seneca 'often one of us' [*An.* 20.1] but the Presocratics [*An.*

---

[1] See J. C. Frédouille, *Tertullien, et la conversion de la culture antique* (Paris, 1972).
[2] *Ibid.* p. 316.
[3] See 2 Corinthians 6: 14–16 for style and 1 Corinthians 1 for content.
[4] *Ibid.* p. 333.

14.9], Pythagoras [*An.* 28.2] and even Lucretius [*An.* 5.6] have their points of affinity. Tertullian refers to Justin with approval as 'philosopher and martyr' [*Val.* 5.1] and he continues the theme that runs from Justin through all the early Church when he speaks of Christianity as the 'better philosophy' [*Pal.* 6]. Instead of rejecting secular culture, Tertullian demands that it be used only for the furtherance of the Gospel.[1]

With this fresh appreciation of Tertullian and philosophy we are in a position to understand that, so far from being a narrow-minded bigot who became successively dissatisfied with the compromise of all other Christians, Tertullian was a restless Christian who could not be satisfied with any position short of simple solitary dedication to Christ. Seeking must go on and on until the fullness of Christ is found [*Praescr.* 9.4]. 'No one should be ashamed of progress; for even in Christ knowledge goes through different stages' [*Pud.* 1.11–12].

In his earlier work on *Patience*, Tertullian draws heavily on Stoic thought. In his subsequent work on *Flight*, Tertullian develops his account of patience along more Christian and biblical lines. Again, while he condemns curiosity at one place, he commends curiosity and culture when they are usefully directed to a good end. The Christian may learn, but not teach, secular culture; yet in his own learning, Tertullian displays all the insatiable curiosity of his own day. Neither Apuleius nor Aulus Gellius can surpass his thirst for detailed knowledge of so many kinds. His interest in physiology is obvious. He commends Hadrian as an 'explorer of all curiosities' [*Ap.* 5.7]. Like Irenaeus, he condemns the curiosity and restlessness of the heretics;[2] like Irenaeus, he has his own Christian curiosity, which goes beyond the first simplicities [*Res.* 2.11] with a restlessness that drives him on from paganism, to faith, to Montanism and beyond. Compromise in any form is progressively discarded; one may speak of a continual conversion. The apparent tragedy of Tertullian is that he ends, not in a beatific vision, not in the spiritual garden of Clement, but in loneliness and failure.[3]

So much of Tertullian's argument is polemical and brief.

---

[1] *Ibid.* p. 357.
[2] *Ibid.* p. 432.
[3] *Ibid.* p. 442. There remain differences between Tertullian and Clement, but they are more subtle than their interpreters have seen.

He is indeed a Christian Sophist[1] who needs only one or two moves to discredit an opponent. Unlike the Sophists, he also achieves sustained, systematic and constructive argument. But one must doubt whether he knew how much he had built, for he writes as one who does not expect to trace the connections of the universal Logos or to gaze upon the wholeness of truth. In the end he is less orthodox, less conservative, less sure than his three contemporaries; he alone ended outside the limits of the visible Church. Yet his work was never discarded or disowned as that of a schismatic. Those who came after him knew, better than he, how much he had achieved. He left to theology as *habitus* a Socratic hostility towards inflated, pretentious and invalid argument; to theology as *doctrina* he left a treatment of the problem of evil, an exposition of the trinity and christology and other things yet to be made clear.

Tertullian takes the cloak of the philosopher, neither as a scandal before men, nor as a gesture of Carthaginian defiance, nor even as a Christian innovation that might point to the only worthwhile philosophy. The cloak points to 'custom' and 'discipline', to a way and not to an end; this discipline is ascetic and strange to the world [*Pal.* 5.4]. Tertullian defends his right to wear the cloak in the face of misunderstanding and alienation, and he wears it to express the constant change that marks his life and thought. For him Christians are not born but are made, no one should be ashamed of moving on, and the symbolic change is from the toga of the citizen to the cloak of the philosopher. Here we grasp the direction of Tertullian's thought. The negative side remains: he has no time for heretics who desert the rule of faith. However, the positive side is striking: there is progression and growth, which gives the Christian no rest. As a *theologia viatorum* Tertullian's work is severe; it stands close to the New Testament and especially to Paul who anticipated the restlessness, loneliness and failure of Tertullian.[2] Yet the last word for both is a word

---

[1] See Barnes, *Tertullian*, pp. 211–32.

[2] For Paul was an eschatological person who knew that there was no way to resurrection except through the cross. See C. K. Barrett, *The signs of an apostle* (London, 1969), pp. 42f., and A. Fridrichsen, *The apostle and his message* (Uppsala, 1947), p. 3. See also E. Käsemann, *An die Römer* (Tübingen, 1975), p. 17 (Romans 1: 8–15): 'Selbst am Ende seines Weges steht er im Zwielicht ungeklärter Situationen, im Widerstreit gegensätzlicher Beurteilung'.

of joy. 'Gaude pallium et exsulta' [*Pal.* 6.2]; 'Rejoice in the Lord alway and again I say, Rejoice!' [Philippians 4:4].

Clement has some of Tertullian's restlessness – 'It is a venture of noble courage to take our way to God' – but he believes the way can be trodden with hope unashamed and that there is a true gnosis to be achieved on earth and amplified in heaven. The dividing line between earth and heaven is not always clear. The Christian man is indeed a king, ruling over beasts outside him and over passions within [*S.* 6.15.115]. In the righteous man, the eternal Word is present, 'being the one saviour individually to each and in common to all'. Such a man becomes a third divine image, made, as far as possible, like the Word, who is the source of true life [*S.* 7.3.16]. *Knowledge*, to put things concisely, is the perfecting of man as man, and reaches its peak in the knowledge of divine things and in the living of a life that agrees with the divine Word. Faith, which confesses God, goes on through grace to know him as far as man may [*S.* 7.10.55]. The Gnostic who loves the one true God is 'the really perfect man and friend of God'. He is ranked as God's son, and finds spiritual rest in God [*S.* 7.11.68]. Man must work towards perfection, although no one apart from the Lord himself, has been perfect in all things at once.

This [*S.* 7] is the picture of man with which Clement is commonly linked; it has no rival in Christian literature for optimism and beauty. However it was written to surpass other accounts of man's ascent to God, and to convince critics of the piety of the true Christian [*S.* 7.1.2]. Competitive spirituality is always dangerous, because it takes too much notice of competitors and has to excel them on their ground. In *Stromateis* 4, there is a systematic account of man that shows a clearer picture. Here Clement depends closely on Paul and Plato, and puts forward a moral theology of the cross that is to have lasting influence. For in the end the early Church found perfect manhood in one place only – martyrdom. Clement begins from the question of what makes a man human. Paul saw life in separation from sin, service to God, crucifixion to the world and citizenship of heaven. True philosophy still has a place for fear, and Plato found philosophy to be the practice of death, the separation of soul from body.[1] True humanity, says Clement, is therefore to be found in the martyr,

---

[1] *Phaedo*, 67D.

whom his Saviour welcomes as a brother, because they are so alike; and man is perfected in martyrdom because it is the supreme act of love [*S.* 4.4.14]. So Plato claims that the man of gold is he who dies bravely in battle [*S.* 4.4.16]. Yet for Clement this peak is not restricted to those who die a physical death for Christ. The higher 'Gnostic' martyrdom is achieved by those who leave all for the gospel and the name of Christ. 'If confession to God is martyrdom, every soul which has lived purely in the knowledge of God, which has obeyed the commandments, is a martyr both in life and word, no matter what way it may be released from the body, pouring out faith, like blood, all along life's path until it goes from here' [*S.*4.4.15]. This definition will exclude the false martyrdom of the heretic who dies from hatred of the creator and from a false confession, as well as the coward who thinks that a confession of right belief excuses him from risking his life.

The Christian stands against the powers that threaten him; a sheep for slaughter, he emerges as more than conqueror. As Simonides said, the peak of manhood is only reached through bitter sweat and toil. Great fates, says Heraclitus, bring great destinies [*S.* 4.7.47–9]. Paul sees the apostles as destined for death and dishonour [1 Corinthians 4: 9–13] even as Plato's just man is stretched on the rack. The true Gnostic, the perfect man, looks beyond earthly things to kingly friendship with God. Shame and death will not dislodge him from his freedom and supreme love of God [*S.* 4.7.52].

Clement's ideal is less solitary than that of Tertullian. The loneliness of Christ was greater than that of those who come after him.

'Alone, then, the Lord, because of the ignorance of those who plotted against him "drank the cup" for the purification of those who plotted against him and those who disbelieved him. Following his example, the apostles, so that they might reach perfection as true Gnostics, suffered for the churches they founded. So then the Gnostics who follow in the steps of the apostles ought to be without sin and for love of their Lord should love their brother too. So then, if occasion call, for the sake of the Church, not faltering in endurance of afflictions, they may drink the cup' [*S.* 4.9.75, rejecting, for once, Stählin's emendation].

Clement's final stand is not in mystic abstraction. It is inevitable [*S.* 4.14.95f.] that those who are Christ's will suffer persecution and hostility, since they live in the middle of the devil's sphere of action. Yet in this raging inferno, nothing can separate Christians in their complete manhood from God's love in Christ their Lord; man's creatureliness and God's love come together.

Clement's perfect man, then, is marked by nearness to God, by struggle against sin, by freedom and friendship with God. His ideal is not found in the rich optimism of a spiritual paradise; in the end perfection is found in the martyr alone. This is a strange end for the rational, laughing animal. However, in Clement the two extremes of death and divinity are held closely together. When we look carefully there is plenty about martyrdom in *Stromateis* 7 and plenty of divine perfection, unity and *apatheia* in *Stromateis* 4. In Book 7, Clement writes of the highest vision:

> 'Knowledge then, readily transplants a man to that holy and divine state which is akin to the soul and by a light of its own carries him through the mystic stages, till it restores him to the crowning place of rest, having taught the pure in heart to look on God face to face with understanding and absolute certainty' [*S.* 7.10.57].

The same man lives in the world, thanking his creator and loving his fellow-men [*S.* 7.11.62]. He does not rush stupidly into physical martyrdom. He and those like him know the dangers and take reasonable precautions; but 'when God really calls them, they cheerfully offer themselves, make their calling sure because they know they have done nothing rash and put to the test their manhood, with truly rational courage (*ton andra en tei kata aletheian logikei andreiai exetazesthai parechontai*)' [*S.* 7.11.66]. So the rational laughing animal thinks and is glad to the end. And if one doubt that men can so come of age as to be a friend and son of God, 'temperate and passionless, proof against pleasures and pains as, they say, the adamant is against fire' [*S.* 7.11.67], Clement has his answer ready: 'The cause of these things is love, love surpassing all knowledge in holiness and self-rule' [*S.* 7.11.68].

Problems and parallels

Of the many problems concerning man, there are two that provide illumination for contemporary issues. The first is the relation of man to God and whether there is a sense in which man, united to Christ, may become divine. The second is the relation of free will to freedom and the question of their existence in the face of powerful external causes. The Gnostic aeons produced in second-century man the same helpless fatalism as scientific laws have produced in the twentieth century.

1 Anyone for deification?

This term has offended more modern readers than any other part of early Christian theology, and is rejected by most contemporary Christians: 'But does a reasonable man *today* want to become God? ... Our problem today is not the deification but *the humanization of man*'.[1] Everything depends on the *method* used to clarify this difficult issue. The main alternatives we saw to problematic elucidation, are cultural, doxographical and polemical methods;[2] it is important to recall the differences.

The first method is found in several expositions of the theology and ethos of the Eastern Church. Here the belief in deification is found as part of a complex of ideas and traditions.[3] A heightened sense of divine mystery, a concentration on prayer

---

[1] H. Küng, *On being a Christian* (New York, 1976), p. 442.

[2] See discussion above in chapter 1, and Passmore, 'History of philosophy', pp. 1–32.

[3] See V. Lossky, *The mystical theology of the Eastern Church* (London, 1957), especially chapters 1, 9, 10, 11. But note the implication that the Greek fathers all meant similar things when they talked about deification: T. Ware, *The Orthodox Church* (Penguin Books, 1963), p. 29, and *The Orthodox ethos*, ed. A. J. Philippou (Oxford, 1964), p. 27.

and contemplation, a more sensitive approach to the aesthetic aspects of worship – all these have their place. It is easy to see deification as part of this cultural complex; but it is hard to see what it may mean to someone standing outside, if the critical question of meaning persists. It is also wrong to accept the common assumption that this tradition is homogeneous and that there is close continuity between the ideas of the Greek fathers of the second, fourth and sixth century.[1] The cultural approach is valuable but ultimately unsatisfactory because it presupposes a unity that does not exist.

Elsewhere the account of Eastern theologians concerning the deification of man is set beside the Catholic account of created grace and the Protestant account of the battle against sin.[2] These are three different versions of the doctrine of justification and the ruling factor is again the different cultural milieu. Now, there is an obvious sense in which the opinions of theologians reflect the world in which they speak and the same things have to be said in different ways at different times and places. The Pauline account of justification is the beginning of the notion of deification. However, the labels of 'deification', 'created grace' and 'battle against sin' do not cover the Eastern, Catholic and Protestant accounts. They assume too much homogeneity within each tradition and too little homogeneity across the traditions.

Polemical history denies the autonomy of any account and assumes that each writer is discussing the same problem. Different views may therefore be set against one another and may be right or wrong. Whereas in a cultural history everyone may be right, in a polemical history everyone cannot be right. This method of investigating a problem, which studies different solutions proposed in the past,[3] is difficult in the case of

[1] There is slender evidence of continuity in the account of deification in the second, fourth and sixth centuries. For a careful analysis of fourth-century views, see D. L. Balas, '*Metousia Theou*', *man's participation in God's perfections according to Saint Gregory of Nyssa* (Rome, 1966). The difference again between these centuries and Gregory Palamas is equally striking; see J. Daniélou's introduction to M. Lot-Borodine, *La déification de l'homme* (Paris, 1970), p. 15.

[2] See E. L. Mascall, *The openness of being* (London, 1971), Appendix III, for a discussion of the report, *The theology of grace and the ecumenical movement*, ed. L. Moeller and G. Philips (London, 1961).

[3] C. D. Broad, *Five types of ethical theory* (London, 1930), p. 1, cited by Passmore, 'History of philosophy', p. 7.

deification, which touches a nerve and seems to produce a strange twitching across the centuries.[1] As a result, deification is condemned as 'the most serious aberration . . . the disastrous flaw in Greek Christian thought'.[2] Unfortunately, after listing extracts from Clement and Origen, 'there is no space further to illustrate the consolidation of the doctrine in succeeding Fathers, or its later mystical elaboration' and Daniélou's warning against an anachronistic uniformity between early and later Greek fathers is 'placed on record' but not heeded.[3] A strict verbalism hampers awareness of problems: 'Clement's eschatology is hardly consistent' because deification is viewed as begun but not perfected. Since this tension between promise and fulfilment is essential to any statement of the gospel that avoids naïve apocalyptic on the one hand and naïve enthusiasm on the other, it is in no sense a weakness. Further, Clement's subtle link [*S.* 2.22 *passim*] of Platonism's twofold end with Paul's twofold hope enables him to use the notion of participation to explain the 'inconsistency' in Christian thought in a way that had not been done before. Augustine, who preached: 'God wants to make you a god; not by nature as his Son is, but by his gift and adoption' [*Serm.* 166.14.4] is wrongly placed among good Westerners who opposed bad Easterners on the question of deification, and a closing reference to Clement as 'absurd' invites a repetition of the warning: 'Too often, indeed, such polemical writings consist in telling men of straw that they have no brains'.[4]

It is a waste of time writing on deification unless some attempt is made to elucidate the problem. Any Christian writer has to ask what it means to be born of God, to be born again, to be a child of God; he has to describe this in a way that does not remove the distinction between creature and creator, for a great deal in the New Testament is directed against man's effort towards self-transcendence. The cross confirms man's place as a creature, and condemns his every attempt to rise by

[1] B. J. Drewery, 'Deification', in Peter Brooks (ed.), *Christian spirituality, essays in honour of Gordon Rupp* (London, 1975), pp. 33–62, especially pp. 61f.

[2] B. J. Drewery, *Origen and the doctrine of grace* (London, 1960), p. 200.

[3] Drewery, 'Deification', p. 53.

[4] Passmore, 'History of philosophy', p. 13.

his own efforts to God.[1] Whether any account of deification denies this theme, can only be assessed after the problem has been identified. Clement and Irenaeus depend on the theme of *sola gratia*, and direct their account against the Gnostic claim for some divine–human identity; on the other hand they are both enthusiasts, who live in an atmosphere of martyrdom, and restraint is not their strong point. For Tertullian, also, the exclusive unity of God does not exclude, but rather defines, the deification of men. What belongs to God belongs to him alone; all that we have of him comes from him alone. So, while 'we shall even be gods' (according to Psalm 82), 'this comes from his grace, not from some property of ours, since it is he alone who can make gods' [*Herm.* 5].

The meaning of the word can be found in its usage and not elsewhere. Attention must be directed to the meanings found in the four writers we have considered. Their claims that the gods of Rome were nothing, and that there was one God only, had to be reconciled with their belief that they were all sons of God and in some sense divine. Justin [*1 A.* 21] argues in one place that there is nothing new in the story of the ascension: the gods of Rome have done this kind of thing; the only problem is that they have not lived in a way that is worthy of immortality. Justin uses 'immortalise' as equivalent to 'raise to divine status'; similarly in each of the other writers, the primary significance of deification points to immortality.[2] Clement even quotes Heraclitus [frag. 62] as 'gods are men, men are gods' when, according to other sources, what Heraclitus actually said was 'immortals are mortals, mortals are immortals' [*Paed.* 3.1.2].[3] What makes a man divine is his

---

[1] See E. Käsemann, 'The saving significance of the death of Jesus', in *Perspectives on Paul* (London, 1971), pp. 35–42, and also *Jesus means freedom*, pp. 76f.

[2] See discussion in A. von Harnack, *History of dogma*, vol. 1, pp. 119f., and in W. Völker, *Der wahre Gnostiker nach Clemens Alexandrinus* (Berlin and Leipzig, 1952), p. 614. See also J. Gross, *La divinisation du chrétien d'après les pères grecs* (Paris, 1938), pp. 142f.: 'Tous les apologistes enseignent que la vie éternelle offerte par le christianisme ne saurait être qu'une immortalité participée ... La déification du chrétien ... est nettement eschatologique. Elle n'en suppose pas moins une préparation terrestre, qui consiste surtout dans l'acquisition de la connaissance de Dieu et dans une vie parfaite'.

[3] J. Pépin, *Idées grecques sur l'homme et sur Dieu* (Paris, 1971), pp. 49f.

power through Christ, to live for ever. This is indeed an
outrageous claim and it is good to see the outrage; but
Christianity has rarely been found without some form of this
belief, so the selection of the term 'deification' for special
treatment can only arise from an ignorance of the way in
which words work, or a failure to appreciate the scandal of
immortality.

Each of the writers makes it clear that the soul is not divine
or immortal in its own right.[1] Justin turns from Platonism on
the ground that God alone is life and all souls must depend on
him for life. Tertullian does claim that the soul is immortal
but only because it is the breath of God; further, it is God's
afflatus not his *spiritus*, derivative and not essential [*Marc.* 2.9].
Clement vigorously rejects the Gnostic view that men could
be of the same virtue or substance as God.

The 'exchange formula' (*x* became *y*, that *y* might become *x*)
has been commonly misinterpreted. In the first place, it denies
an original identity or community between God and man. It is
clear 'That this deification does not imply, between the human
and divine, any community of nature, any consubstantiality'.[2]
If *x* becomes *y*, then it was originally not *y*. In the second place,
identity is not asserted; *x* and *y* do not become coextensive.
Man does not acquire all the attributes of God, any more than
God acquires all the attributes of man. There is a further
qualification in the distinction between the sonship of Jesus
and that of other men. Jesus is *monogenes* in the Fourth Gospel,
even if he is the first of many brothers in the letter to the
Romans. The 'exchange formula' sounds far more precise
than the meaning Irenaeus and others draw from it. Which
means again that there is no safe guide to meaning other than
usage.

Further, likeness to God and deification imply freedom from
passions as well as freedom from death. Clement believed that
Plato and Paul had seen that those who are dedicated to God

---

[1] See Pépin, *ibid.* pp. 8f., on the difference between *suggeneia* and
homoiosis; also note the lack of precision in the ancient mixture of
anthropology and theology that Pépin indicates in the remainder of
this chapter.

[2] *Ibid.* p. 27. On exchange-formulae (*Tauschformeln*), see A. Bengsch,
*Heilsgeschichte und Heilswissen. Eine Untersuchung zur Struktur und
Entfaltung des theologischen Denkens im Werk 'Adversus Haereses' des hl.
Irenäus von Lyon* (Leipzig, 1957), pp. 157f.

should not live a mortal life, bringing pollution on the divinity within them by their vices [*Paed.* 2.10.100f.]. The whole ethical dimension of man's existence is brought under the one heading of assimilation to God. This means that man depends on God for grace, which works his moral transformation. Clement wanted to establish that neither the passionate gods of the Greeks nor the passionate Gnostics of Alexandria could be regarded as truly divine. Likeness to God meant freedom from passion. On the link between *apatheia* and *homoiosis* the amount of argument in Clement is remarkable. For Clement insists in *Stromateis* 2 that participation in God is not a 'natural relation, as the founders of the heresies declare' but a matter of righteousness and obedience [*S.* 2.16.73f.]. God's goodness is shown in kindness to those who are other in essence. What matters is the choice of man's will [*S.* 2.17.77] his imitation of divine righteousness [*S.* 2.18.80f.]. Yet as like is dear to like, so the true Gnostic imitates God as far as is possible, in self-restraint, endurance, righteousness, control of passions, generosity and good works [*S.* 2.19.97]. Likeness to God is not physical but rational and ethical. Endurance and freedom from passions are part of likeness to God [*S.* 2.20.103f.]. In contrast to this the followers of Nicolaus indulge their lusts like goats [*S.* 2.20.118]. Yet there is no way to peace and freedom but by continual battle against lust and passion. The martyrs have shown the way to rise above the passions, as true Gnostics, and to live a divine life. The philosophers have seen the need for destroying lust, and self-control is the greatest gift that God can give. When *Theaetetus* 176 is used, Clement underlines the ethical content of likeness to God [*S.* 2.22.131f.]. Like is dear to like and the ordered, unified life agrees with the one God; the disorderly life does not agree within itself and is therefore incapable of agreeing with God or anything beyond itself [*Laws* 716CD].

Again, in *Stromateis* 3 Clement is concerned explicitly with those who claim kinship with God but indulge their lusts. 'How can he who submits himself to every lust, live according to the will of God?' [*S.* 3.4.31]. Such men belong to no royal race free from the law, for, as Paul says, anyone who sins is the slave of sin. He returns to the incompatibility of lustfulness and divinity [*S.* 3.5.42]: 'But how is it possible for him who is overcome by the pleasures of the body to grow like the Lord or to have knowledge of God?' The Logos will lead us through scripture to likeness to God. This means purification of soul from pleasures and lusts, so that the soul is dedicated only to what is divine. 'For when it is pure and separate from all wickedness, the mind is somehow capable of receiving the power of God and the divine image is set up in it.' Purity is essential to those who would hope in the Lord. 'But it is simply not possible for those who are still driven by their passions to receive the knowledge of God' [*S.* 3.5.43]. Those who have not achieved freedom from the power of physical lusts are simply ignorant of God. Pleasure cannot be the highest Good when God alone is good. As the tree is known by its fruit, so a man is known by the way he lives: he who is pleasure's slave cannot be free. 'For we have learnt that freedom is that which comes from the Lord above when he liberates us from pleasures, lusts and other kinds of passions' [*S.* 3.5.44].

The place of *apatheia* in Gnostic growth from faith to love and divine likeness may be abundantly proved from scripture, although it may seem an odd term to use (*hōs eipein*). Clement quotes one exhortation to *apatheia* so that he may not neglect the topic completely. Here the passion referred to is hostility between the saints; some of the Corinthians had gone to law against one another. The true Gnostic suffers injustice without retaliation and prays for his enemies. Those who do wrong will not inherit the kingdom of God [1 Corinthians 6: 9]. For the true Christian such things are in the past. 'With knowledge you threw off the animal passions, so as to become as close a likeness as is possible to the goodness of God's providence' [*S.* 7.14.86].

The themes of deification and assimilation to God are linked with the insistence that there is none good but God.[1] Only the good God can save sinful man and he can only save by giving himself to man. Man finds no goodness outside God. Christ is his only righteousness. To the extent that he is saved, he is deified. In the language of the second century, deification means *sola gratia*.

Further, deification of man is linked, especially in Clement, with a theology of the cross. It is the martyr who is perfect

---

[1] See E. F. Osborn, 'Origen and Justification, The Good is One', *ABR* (1976), 18–29.

man and at the same time divine;[1] he speeds straight to the
immediate presence of God; he is the true philosopher who
has practised death. Persecution produces a theology of glory
as well as a theology of the cross, for persecution means promo-
tion, not punishment. While Clement's ideal is subordinate to
the cross, one reason for his enthusiasm is simply that he knew
of men who had been perfected as martyrs; for these men he
gave God the glory and he put no limit on what God's grace
might do. Here is valuable insight into the complex relation
of a theology of the cross with a theology of glory. The greater
part of *Stromateis* 4 is concerned with the perfection of the way
of the cross; but here, as in *Stromateis* 7, the way of the cross is
always the way of glory. This was linked with the ancient
Greek ideal of manhood, which found glory in mortal conflict;
but it went further under the sign of the cross, and in the
actuality of persecution this was not always conducive to
clear thinking. Enthusiasm runs away with Clement when he
tells of Peter's joy at his wife's martyrdom and his call to her
to think on her Lord [*S.* 7.11.63].[2] It was not easy for those
who faced death rather than confess other gods, to speak of
one another as being made divine. But they knew that the
whole purpose of the incarnation was to bring many sons of
God to glory and that, contrary to appearances, when they
saw God, they would be like him. Perhaps there is no safe way
of stating this part of the gospel; but theology is a dangerous
business and a rejection of the term 'deification' does not
dispose of the problems that lie behind it.[3]

There have been modern writers who have not been afraid
of the term, but have seen it in close relation to the cross and
to man's place as a child of God. Deification in Clement may
be understood through the notion of decreation in Simone
Weil; by this act something passes into the uncreated, by
giving up its own existence and becoming nothing. Joy comes

---

[1] *S.* 4.4, 7, 9 and 11.

[2] The story shows the effects of persecution.

[3] At the same time, misunderstanding seems to have disqualified the
term 'deification' from effective use in the twentieth century as far as
the West is concerned; we end where we began: humanisation, not
deification, is the way ahead. 'For certainly man is a "useless passion",
if his passion is to be God. But his passions are not useless, if they help
him to become a little more humane, a little more civilised' (J.
Passmore, *The perfectibility of man* (London, 1970), p. 327).

through knowing that God is and we are not, through carrying the cross each day; humility refuses to exist outside God.[1] This is the way to knowledge and to immortality. Knowledge must break through false illusions and fantasy; the only way to avoid a false perspective is to go beyond the world to God.[2] Prestige is the illusion that rules society and it is a shadow and a lie. Christ had little prestige during his life and none in his death; this enabled him to show what justice was. To escape from illusion and to love truth is only possible when we have an unconditional acceptance of death. 'The cross of Christ is the only gateway to knowledge.'[3] Love of truth must constantly say 'no and no and no to the prompt easy vision of self-protecting self-promoting fantasy'.[4]

Immortality is not a matter of surviving death but of anticipating it in the way that Plato and Clement knew, where 'immortality refers to a person's relation to the self-effacement and love of others involved in dying to the self';[5] it is the culmination of a life in which death has been practised day by day. The great religions agree that man's fallen state or separation from ultimate reality, 'lies in his ego-ism, his worshipping of self rather than God'[6] and fullness is approached as he becomes less of an ego and more of a person.[7] So the way of the cross achieves fulfilment of man as a person. Man's fellowship with God is the source 'of all he knows, the ground of what is right and reasonable in him'.[8] In this fellowship man grows into that union with, and knowledge of, God that the fathers called deification, only because God is accessible 'through the Spirit's presence in our hearts, inspiring us to know that we are his sons, and to call him "Abba"'.[9] This

---

[1] Simone Weil, *Gravity and grace* (London, 1972), pp. 28–35.
[2] Simone Weil, *Intimations of Christianity among the Ancient Greeks* (London, 1957), p. 134.
[3] *Gravity and Grace*, p. 51.
[4] Murdoch, *The Fire and the Sun*, p. 79.
[5] D. Z. Phillips, *Death and immortality* (London, 1970), p. 54.
[6] John Hick, *Death and eternal life* (London, 1976), p. 454: 'his false belief in the independent reality of the "I", his *cor curvatus* [*sic!*] *in se*, the heart turned in upon itself'.
[7] *Ibid.* p. 460.
[8] F. D. Maurice, *The doctrine of sacrifice* (London, 1854), p. 4; cited Lampe, *God as Spirit*, p. 180.
[9] *Ibid.* p. 175.

cry of freedom has meaning for the whole of creation,[1] which waits for the manifestation of the children of God.

2 Freedom

The account of freedom given in the second century has seemed to be far from the captivity of man as seen by Paul.[2] This, we have seen, is not the case. Paul was concerned to insist on man's responsibility for his choices as well as the possibility of his liberation by the power of the Spirit. Clement faced the same problem in *Stromateis* 3 as Paul had faced in the Corinthian letters. There were those whose Christian liberty had proved more than they could handle. They needed to be shown that they had not yet arrived at the royal freedom that they claimed; their subjection to sin was evident from the lives they were living. The same question of Christian freedom is central today; Clement's account of Christian freedom is a restatement of the reality with an awareness of the dangers that Paul had seen.

The question of freedom versus determinism has received useful attention in recent years. By an examination of Gödel's theorem, it has been shown that mathematical systems that claim to be total are in fact incomplete. Any serious mathematical system includes some statements which it cannot prove but which must be accepted as true. A human being cannot be reduced to a set of physical variables that are determined by an earlier combination of their values. Any form of physical determinism can be shown to be logically inadequate. 'Any claim to reduce, explain, or give a complete description of, human beings and human action will stand refuted, provided only the reduction, explanation or description is in terms of regularities alone.'[3] Partial reductions or explanations of regularities do not present a problem because

---

[1] The Christian account of the world puts man in the centre for the very odd reason that man is dependent and must grow more dependent on God; for 'we have to accept our own dependence on God as some sort of clue to the way all things depend on him' (A. Farrer, *Reflective faith* [London, 1972], p. 161).

[2] See Fritz Buri, *Clemens Alexandrinus und der paulinische Freiheitsbegriff* (Zürich and Leipzig, 1939).

[3] J. R. Lucas, *The freedom of the will* (Oxford, 1970), p. 167.

they do not claim to be complete. Universal causation may be treated as a principle of method and in this capacity it presents no serious problems. But when it is accepted as a total picture of the world, it cannot provide for recognition of man's freedom of choice. Rationality is fundamental; people act from reasons, not merely from causes.

Mystery remains. 'Why *x* did *a* and not *b*' is capable of exploration and description; we may learn his reasons but we cannot explain why he thought they were adequate reasons. Nor can we explain why, in some cases, *x* considered the reasons for *b* as stronger than those for *a*, yet chose to do *a*. People from the same background, aware of the same reasons, faced with the same situation, choose differently. There is no explanation beyond 'They just did.' For 'I am answerable for my actions. I am free to choose what I shall do. But I, and only I, am responsible for my choice. The buck stops here'.[1]

The compatibility of free choice with causal sequence has been argued with equal simplicity elsewhere. A simple act, like not attending a lecture, is part of a causal nexus. 'None of this sequence of events and none of this causal necessitation need make me powerless... My not going was not the outcome of lacking the power to attend, but simply of the fact that I was disinclined to go.'[2] Freedom to do other than what one actually does is present provided there are no exceptional causal factors such as hypnosis or duress. Divine omniscience is equally compatible with human freedom. For God foreknows what I will do, not what I must do. 'If God knows that *p*, it must be the case that *p*' is true provided it means: 'Necessarily, if God knows that it is the case that *p*, it is the case that *p*'. It cannot be extended to mean: 'If God knows that it is the case that *p*, then necessarily it is the case that *p*'.[3]

There are good reasons why the problems of freedom and determinism should be re-examined. To many, the simple picture of nature that the principle of causation offers has blunted the reality of human choice. Certainly the limitations on human freedom are as evident as they have ever been; the unchosen pressures and hidden factors of environment and heredity are obvious. No one is completely responsible for all

[1] *Ibid.* p. 172.
[2] R. Young, *Freedom, responsibility and God* (London, 1973), p. 168.
[3] *Ibid.* p. 174.

that he does; but he cannot exalt this limitation into a universal negative proposition. Such a conclusion, apart from its faulty logic, would destroy the vision that Paul passed to the second century: that the frustration and groans of the world have their goal in the liberty of the children of God and to this freedom man is called, now.

Determinism is not, and was not, the chief problem associated with human freedom. The use to which free will or optative freedom is put is more important than the mere fact of its existence.[1] Natural freedom, the ability to achieve things that are good, is essential for a human life.[2] The Gnostic confusion of free will with freedom and its restriction to an elite was as dangerous as their determinism. Clement and Irenaeus insisted that all men had free will, and that all might gain freedom in the complete Christian life. Few advanced towards fullness of life; but Clement's chief concern was to encourage more to move on.

The obstacles to natural freedom were not different from those of twentieth-century Western society. 'Participants in the hedonic scramble . . . , as they contend ever more vehemently for satisfaction of their insatiable demands, become embittered, mutually distrustful, and at enmity with the system that has proved incapable of fulfilling the intemperate hopes and appetites engendered in its subjects.'[3] For all his ascent to God, the life of Clement's Christian is similarly concerned with full humanity in the world. 'The contest for freedom, then, is fought out not only by the protagonists in battles, but also at banquets, and in bed, and in the courts, by those who are anointed by the word, who are too proud to be prisoners of pleasure' [*S*. 6.14.112]. Free will is necessary but the notion of freedom is far more important. The heretics who denied the distinction and made freedom a way of self-indulgence missed the most important thing about the gospel. For Clement, freedom only came through love, and the way of liberation was the way of the cross. As Jesus drank the cup for those who persecuted him, so the Christian drinks the cup for the sake of others. Deification is not self-fulfilment but self-abandonment. Today, liberation movements still run the risk of the

[1] On optative freedom, see Benjamin Gibbs, *Freedom and liberation* (London, 1976). p. 17.
[2] *Ibid*, p. 22.
[3] *Ibid*, p. 139.

Gnostic error; but modern man will not find liberty so long as he uses the self-enclosed concepts of liberal capitalism. The Gnostics, who were obsessed with their own royal freedom, were the most pitiable slaves of sin, and lacked a concern for the liberation of others. Christianity does not solve all questions about freedom; but from the beginning it has insisted on two things:

(1) despite free will man is the slave of sin until he is made free in the service of Christ. Recent awareness of this problem deserves attention.

'Hobbes . . . would agree with St. Thomas that natural felicity is always an imperfect and impermanent condition. Progress to it, for each individual person, is arduous and slow. The minority who achieve it do so incompletely and temporarily. For a little while, they thrive and enrich humanity by their works; but all decline at last into dotage, pain and death. Perhaps this thought underlies Aristotle's remark: "In many ways human nature is in bondage".'[1]

(2) The way of freedom is the way of the cross, of love that is concerned for the liberation not of self but of others; even martyrdom goes wrong when it is achieved for selfish ends. For Clement the universal generalisation holds: 'it is always love of self which is for everyone the basic cause of all sins; therefore one must not love self and grasp after human glory, but love God and become really holy with wisdom' [S. 6.7.56]. The bourgeois liberal ideal, which is directed to self-emancipation and self-realisation, still survives in many freedom movements. However, for the Christian, freedom is found in the liberation of others; only then can it be linked with the man of Nazareth who gave his life as a ransom for many. 'It is won and preserved, not in the fortress of an unassailable inner life, but on the battlefield of the earth. . . . In Christian terms, it grows under the cross and is the power of the crucified as our exalted lord.'[2]

[1] *Ibid.* p. 26, including Aristotle, *Metaphysics*, 982B 29.
[2] See E. Käsemann, 'Protestant exegesis on the way to the world Church', *ABR* (1978), 1of.; also see, *Jesus means freedom*, pp. 59–84.

5 Cosmos and creation

Whatever hesitation there was in speaking of God, there was no hesitation in speaking of man and his relation to God; nor is there hesitation in speaking about the world. This is God's world: he made it, he orders it and he governs it. The first way into his mystery is through his transforming power in men's lives; the second way is through the world he has made. Each of the four writers takes creation seriously. Justin has an earthy optimism: God made the world out of matter for man's sake. But Justin is a city man who writes for city men – he tells us little about his world, except that he finds God in it through the cosmic cross. Irenaeus is different; he has an eye for colour and movement and a curiosity for shapes and structure. Creation is earthy, but it is beautiful too. Tertullian stands out as the staunchest defender of creation and the toughest opponent of Marcion. His heart is in the fight, for God's world fires his curiosity and interest. All creatures great and small, especially the small and complicated, tell him about God. God, he wants to argue, wouldn't be God without the world. The government of the world is no abstract activity, for God drops thunderbolts, causes earthquakes and readily smites whoever deserves to be smitten. With Clement we are back in the world of streets and men; there is interest in man's physiology, the freshness of flowers and camels on the desert; but travel is usually a mistake and there is nothing like reaching the harbour and finding rest.

The problems here may be divided into four:

(1) Is the world created by the one supreme God?
(2) What has happened to make parts of the world so unlike their creator?
(3) Where in the world can God's hand be seen?
(4) Is evil in the world compatible with its divine maker?

1   Is the world created by the one supreme God?

Justin's account of creation is concise; he simply puts Plato
and the book of Genesis together.[1] God in his goodness brought
all things into existence. He is the one unbegotten first cause,
and after him all else merely comes into being and passes
away. While God exists eternally, all else is contingent. The
purpose of creation was good, directed to the benefit of men.
This meant that Marcion was wrong in two ways – he denied
that the creator was the supreme God and he denied that the
creator was good. Justin does not always make it clear why he
is so upset by Marcion, but it is clear that Marcion is his arch-
heretic: 'There will never be any other God, Trypho, nor was
there ever any besides him who made and set in order the
universe' [*D.* 11.1]. The unity and goodness of the creator
God deserve defence at every point.

For Irenaeus, against the Gnostics, the created world is part
of the raw material of theology. The world is created by the
one supreme God, who would not be intelligible or accessible
without his creation. Men go wrong about God, because they
are wrong about the world he made. Just look at the sky, the
sun, the moon and stars! They come from God and they
continue at his word. Even more wonderful is the gift of life;
it comes by his grace and points us to him [*H.* 2.56.1f.].

If only heretics could see the wonder and variety of the
world, they would not be so presumptuous in their many
questions and answers that they reject true knowledge of God.
We ought to probe into the mystery and administration of the
living God who has done such great things for us. He brings
the child to birth and the wheat to its harvest. However, we
cannot expect to understand all the mysteries of God when
there is so much in his creation that we do not understand.
Why does the Nile rise? Where do birds go in winter? What
causes the tide to ebb? What do we know about the formation
of rain, lightning and thunder, clouds, winds, snow and hail?
What makes the moon wax and wane? What gives different
properties to different fluids, metals and stones? We may tell
a great deal of our search; but the final truth lies with God

---

[1] This has been more fully discussed in my *Justin Martyr*, chapter 3.

alone, and some questions are best left in his hands [*H.* 2.41.2].
To know God's creation is to know his power, which made all
things, his wisdom, which frames them in a harmonious
system, and his goodness, which pours out with such prodigality
[*H.* 4.38.3].

To deny creation is to err concerning God [*H.* 1.12.1].
There has to be a first cause; he may use lower beings as his
instruments but he is still the only creator [*H.* 2.2]. The silly
thing is that heretics, like everyone else, recognise one ultimate
God; but they do not draw the logical consequences from this
belief [*H.* 2.2.4]. They do not see that matter cannot be
independent of God. Men cannot make anything without
materials, but God makes his own material [*H.* 2.10.2; 2.28].
Nor do they see that angels cannot be ignorant of the most high
God, when his providence is clear to all [*H.* 2.4.5].

Further, the first cause has to be the only cause, else it would
not be first. There is nothing above or in this world that God
has not made, for, as the Gospel says 'all things were made by
him and apart from him was nothing made' [*H.* 3.8.3]. Man
is part of creation; God makes but man is made. God is
perfect in all things; but man must grow and increase towards
God. If man stands gratefully before God to receive his goodness, then man will find glory; but if man ungratefully rejects
God's goodness, then he stands under judgement [*H.* 4.11.3].
Equally condemned is he who forgets he is a creature and
claims to be wiser and better than the God who made him
[*H.* 2.39.1].

For Irenaeus, then, the world tells man of God and of
himself. By its wonderful intricacy it leads man to confess the
excellence and mystery of the creator and also the dependent
humility of the creature. There can be only one first cause and
he must be adequate to explain all that is.

Tertullian was not a happy man. Yet he glows with wonder
when he talks about the world.

'A single tiny flower from the hedge, I suggest, not to
mention wild flowers in the field; a single tiny shell-fish
from any sea, not to mention those from the Red Sea; a
single small wing from a moorfowl, not to mention the
peacock, will, I suppose, show you what a poor craftsman
their Creator was. Now, while you delight in those tinier
animals on whom their glorious creator has deliberately

lavished all sorts of instincts and powers ... imitate if you can, the buildings of the bee, the hills of the ant, the webs of the spider and the threads of the silk-worm.'

There are the tiny creatures that sting and bite, there are the greater animals and then there is man. God showed his love for man's shape when he came down as a man, and he uses water, oil, milk and honey, and bread in his sacraments. The world is good enough for God, and for man it is a source of joy and wonder [*Marc.* 1.13 and 14]. Tertullian would never have escaped from himself without the world. 'That's what it's like,' says a modern author, 'suddenly to be able to see the world and to love it, to be let out of oneself.'[1] No part of the ancient world has been recorded in richer colour than the countryside and sea that Tertullian knew and loved; the mosaics of the Bardo Museum, Tunis, are unsurpassed in colour and vitality and it is easy to see why Tertullian felt so strongly that, without the world, he could not believe in God. God was not compelled, but he freely chose to create, to show how much he loved; on the other hand, man needs the world for he knows God through it. 'No one denies, because everyone knows, the declaration of nature that God is the creator of the universe' [*Spect.* 2.4]. God is the supreme craftsman and the world is worthy of his skill.[2]

Creation has to be *ex nihilo* if it is to show God's greatness [*Res.* 11.6], so the rule of faith begins with God as creator of all things from nothing [*Praescr.* 13], and scripture, from Genesis to the Gospels, tells of God's creative act [*Herm.* 22.3]. Hermogenes, a Platonic dualist, argues that matter is as necessary as God to explain creation [*Herm.* 1]. But what does matter explain? It cannot explain evil any more than it can explain good. It is true that both good and evil are found in the world; but there is no reason to explain one by God and the other by matter. If there seems to be a duality in God, there should also seem to be a duality in matter [*Herm.* 12,13]. Why provide a special substance for evil and not for good? [*Herm.* 15]. Genesis makes no mention of pre-existent matter, but gives an ordered and concise account of the sequence of creation. The world

---

[1] Iris Murdoch, *The Italian Girl* (Penguin Books, 1967), p. 162. See also B. Nisters, *Tertullian, seine Persönlichkeit und sein Schicksal* (Münster, 1950).

[2] See Wölfl, *Das Heilswirken Gottes*, p. 32.

came into existence and will pass away; only God remains for ever.

Tertullian does some careful defining to clarify the notion of creation from nothing. Of course, grass, fruits, cattle and men come from the ground, as birds and fish come from water; but the original stuff, the 'materials', were made by God [*Herm.* 33]. Creation from nothing means that it may be said of everything (apart from God) that there was a time when it did not exist. Having demolished Hermogenes' argument, Tertullian closes with the sarcastic reflection that he would still wish to give Hermogenes credit for having painted a good self-portrait; all the qualities he has given to matter are his own qualities: 'inconditum, confusum, turbulentum, ancipitis et praecipitis et fervidi motus' [*Herm.* 45].

What then does creation mean, for man and for God? For man it means that Christians are not Indian mystics, who run away from the world and live as exiles from human life. They despise no one whom God has made, and they use the gifts that God has placed before them [*Ap.* 42]. They see creation reflected in baptism when the Spirit moves through water to make men new [*Bapt.* 3]. For God, creation means still more; it makes him credible. Marcion's supreme uncreative God is absurd. He did not create either because he could not or because he would not. If he could not, then he was not God; if he would not, then what kind of God is he? He is certainly not the God of infinite love of whom Marcion speaks [*Marc.* 1.11].

> 'It is now sufficient to observe, that no one is proved to exist to whom nothing is proved to belong. For as the creator is shown to be God, God beyond all doubt, from the fact that all things are his, and nothing is strange to him, so the rival god is seen to be no god, from the circumstance that nothing is his, and all things are therefore strange to him. Since, then, the universe belongs to the creator, I see no room for any other god. All things are full of their author, and occupied by him. Marcion's god ought to have produced as his own at least a tiny chick-pea.'

Tertullian makes the two points that Justin had stated and Irenaeus had developed: the creator God is the only God and he is wonderfully good. He turns to attack other accounts –

that of Hermogenes, which insists on more than one first principle, and that of Marcion, where the highest principle produces nothing.

Clement is not as earthy as Tertullian, yet in his world of men and books he still has a positive appreciation of the world. The austerity of the desert draws him. The waves of the sea fascinate him, as might be expected in Alexandria. There are flashes like his appreciation of the flowers that bloom in the spring and draw him out of doors. It is wrong to put these flowers in a crown on one's head where they can be neither seen nor smelt. 'As beauty, so indeed the flower gives delight when it is seen; and it is proper to glorify the creator by enjoying the sight of beautiful things.' To use, rather than to enjoy, the beauty of flowers is both destructive and wrong. Flowers quickly fade when picked [*Paed.* 2.8.70].

To conclude, we may say that the need for one creator or first cause was argued consistently without any lapse into the impoverished view of God such an argument might bring. When his oneness was established by this argument, the world did the rest. In Irenaeus, and above all in Tertullian there is such a delight in God's creation that it is clear that no God could love more or to better effect than the wonderful creator of all things.

2   What has happened to make parts of the world so unlike their creator?

For all its excellence, the world remains ambiguous and the problem of its deterioration calls for an answer. Justin insists that the good world has gone wrong, not through the creator's incompetence but through man's disobedience and sin. It all began with Adam, but it still goes on. Men have to choose whether they will follow the way of their sinful fathers and the wicked demons or whether they will turn to the way on which God in Christ is leading them. They are not unaided in their choice. Baptism involves a second birth and a liberation from the forces of necessity, which governed the first birth and the old life [*1 A.* 61.10]. Misuse of free will explains the sin of man and the disasters due to demons. Every man repeats Adam's choice for himself.

Irenaeus is less concerned with a primeval catastrophe than with the way God has stayed with his creation. The fallen world is still God's world and God's work of creation goes on. The Word comes in flesh to declare the goodness of his creation. At the marriage feast of Cana the better wine came last; but the first wine was never rejected, for it came from the earth, which the Word had made [*H.* 3.11.9]. The creator has never ceased to care [*H.* 5.12.5]; when the Word gave sight to the eyes of the blind man, after placing clay upon the eyes, he continued the work of creation. The clay declared the hand of God, which had made man out of dust, and what had been omitted from that man, namely eyesight, the creator supplied publicly. This same hand made us in the beginning, shapes us prior to birth, brings us back when we are lost, and takes us home as lost sheep on the shoulders of the shepherd [*H.* 5.15.2]. Man has sinned but he is on the way back and the *felix culpa* has brought a wonderful redeemer. The imperfection of the world springs from its incompleteness, its need for time to reach the goal of its creator.

Tertullian, the chief defender of the created order, alone smells the corruption of things. He sees a dark side to the world, for it is a prison from which the souls of men may escape by martyrdom [*Mart.* 1.2]. There is a vast difference between the purity in which things were made by God and the corruption to which they have now come [*Spect.* 2]. The world is God's but the worldly belongs to the devil [*Spect.* 15]. So Christians live in God's world, but do not follow its ways. They have their own times of feasting and celebration and have nothing to do with the joys of the world. Christians are free in the hand of God, and worldly liberty means little to them. For in the world nothing is real, but everything is a mere name [*Cor.* 13]. The world has a false sense of values; it crowns and glorifies many things that Christians know to be wrong [*Cor.* 13]. The whole world can pass away if one gains heavenly things; one should be willing to lose the lesser in order to gain the greater [*Pat.* 7].

Yet, whatever this means, it does not mean rejecting the body and the flesh. The physical senses must not be despised or separated from reason. From them come all man's industry, commerce and civilisation [*An.* 17]. Hermogenes is not to be taken seriously when he makes a foolish distinction between corporeal matter and incorporeal matter [*Herm.* 36]. Indeed, the chief point of all heresy, the only thing that heretics seem to be concerned with, is to deny the nobility and excellence of the flesh. It is for them always unclean because it is formed from the earth and is transmitted by human seed [*Res.* 4]. But Christians believe that all things were made by the Word of God, and all things include the flesh [*Res.* 5]. The evidence points their way, for no one will despise the flesh when he sees what it can do in faithfulness to the name of Christ. It may be exposed to the hatred of men, it may suffer in prison or exile, it may go without sleep, or it may be tied to a bed of straw. In the end, when all agony seems to have been endured, it makes its last offering for Christ by dying for him and suffering torment in death. Flesh that can repay to its master Christ so vast a debt is both blessed and glorious [*Res.* 8]. Flesh dies to be made again, for God's work of creation will be repeated when he recreates and restores the flesh at the resurrection [*Res.* 11].

The optimism of Irenaeus and the pessimism of Tertullian both find an echo in Clement who seems superior to the world when he is talking to Christians and pagans, and defensive when he is speaking to Marcionite or other dualists. In the *Protrepticus* and the *Paedagogus* we find the exhortation to rise above the world. God, who made all things, is not to be confused with the earth that he has made, and man is foolish to honour matter, however precious, as though it were God [*Prot.* 4]. Man may shape matter into splendid things; he can build houses, make ships, construct cities and paint pictures, but how can that be compared with what God does? The whole universe is God's work: sky, sun, angels and men are all made by him. By God's mere willing the whole universe sprang into being. Let man not make a God out of the universe, but look for the creator, who made all things, and by whose will they exist [*Prot.* 4.63]. The worship of earthy idols is a shameful business and brings degradation to those who practise it. The best idol is merely an image of an image, a copy of man's physical form. The only image of God is his Logos and the only image of the Logos is the true man, a rational soul with its affections fixed on him. Material copies of man's physical form are obviously a long way from the truth; they reflect man's mad fixation on matter [*Prot.* 10.98f.]. Such superstition and evil custom bring destruction rather than salvation; those who attend on idols are filthy with matted hair and nails like claws. God comes to his children who are in danger from idols, like a mother bird rescuing her fallen young from a snake. Surely anyone can see the monstrosity of devoting manhood, God's handwork and special property, to the enemy of God and goodness? [*Prot.* 10.92]. The Word of truth brings man to the truth and establishes the temple of God in man. God himself may dwell within man, whom he has made [*Prot.* 11.117]. Man is not to behave like a child, grasping at the earth, or rolling on the ground. He is to stretch upwards, away from the world and from sin, pursuing the holiness of wisdom although he appears to be still in the world [*Paed.* 1.5.107].

When it comes to food, man is not to hang on to matter as fire does; he looks above to the divine food of truth and finds in contemplation a taste of eternal and pure delight [*Paed.* 2.1.9]. Not that nature itself is bad; man's perverse use of nature and his preference for luxury over reality are the things that tie him down. The simplicity of the barbarians is commended: Celts and Scythians hate luxury, while young Arabs cross the desert on camels, which give them transport and all the nourishment they need. The natural unencumbered life of the barbarians points the way for the Christian to follow his Lord [*Paed.* 3.3.24f.]. When used in this way, nature is good, and there is nothing shameful about knees, legs or any part of the body, or the names given to them; wickedness is the only ground for shame [*Paed.* 2.6.52].

Clement defends the world in general, and marriage in particular, against Marcionite and other dualists. There are those who, under pretence of knowledge and superior piety, disown the world and the things that belong to it. Marriage should not be avoided, for God has given woman to help man's need, and men should marry for the sake of their country, for family continuity and for the completion of the world [*S.* 2.23.140]. Gnostics despise the body; they should realise that without the harmony of the body there cannot be understanding that leads to goodness. Plato insisted on care of the body for the sake of the soul and knowledge comes to him who follows the path of life and health [*S.* 4.4.18]. Those who are in error teach that the creator is someone other than the first God, and declare that the world is an evil place. But sin is man's work, not God's; sin is an activity of man and not something that exists in its own right [*S.* 4.13.93]. God has done all things well; he made man so that his shape points him upwards towards heaven, with his frame ordered for the good life and not for pleasure [*S.* 4.26.163]. The heavenly bodies, the stars above, were given to the nations to lead them upward to thoughts of their creator, but men fell to worshipping stones [*S.* 6.14.111].

The common response to corruption in the world is one of sturdy defence. Whatever has gone wrong cannot be blamed on God who made all things well and who cares for all he has made. Nor can it be blamed on the body or matter, which God made. One God made one world and it is good. This means we must probe deeper to see first how the world reflects God's activity and secondly how evil comes about.

3 Where in the world can God's hand be seen?

For the Bible, Plato and the Stoics alike, divine activity in the world was indicated by order and harmony. Justin puts the matter simply. God's creative act was to bring order from chaos by imposing order on formless matter [*1 A.* 59]. Justin doesn't worry about the dualistic possibilities of this formula. He has only one first cause, so matter has to come from God.[1]

Justin is concerned that God should handle matter. His kind of Platonism does not deflect him here. The resurrection has to be a resurrection of the body. The flesh will be destroyed by God; it will be no harder for God to raise bodies out of dust than it is for him to make them out of their present biological antecedents. Human seed and human dust are equally unlike a human body; birth and resurrection are seen together.

God handles matter in his own distinctive way. Plato saw this when he described the universe as shaped in its soul by the

---

[1] Atomistic verbalism has caused some of his interpreters to worry. If the words were taken in the sense that other people gave them, then 'formless matter' is inconsistent with Justin's monism; a lack of respect for the different meanings that the same words have in different contexts has been such an obvious error in patristic study that it does not require further refutation here. See discussion below, pp. 280f.

sign of the cross.[1] There are crosses everywhere – on the masts of ships, in human bodies, in the tools men use – and they show the divine activity at all points. Justin is sure that the creation is ordered and maintained by the sign of the son of man. One God creates and saves; the cross is 'the supreme symbol of his power and rule' [*1 A*. 55.2]. Those who believe and are saved become the seed of the world, the source of its life and the ground of its preservation [*2 A*. 7.1]. Here Justin expounds the already powerful image, created by Plato, of the Demiurge cutting the world soul into strips and stretching it crosswise. Christians are the soul of the world, its one hope of life and salvation.[2]

As elsewhere, Irenaeus expands Justin's flashes of insight about order and harmony. He feels or sees the order of creation; it is wrong to look for God in isolated units, in the letters or syllables of creation. Just as many different notes may form one melody or harmony, so creation fits together, in all its detail, under the hand of God [*H*. 2.37.2]. This order or plan is God's alone. It is simply another heretical absurdity to claim that the creator had to get his plan from a higher archetypal source. The plan is the creator's distinctive work and, if he does not do it, he ceases to be creator [*H*. 2.6.3]. In his order all things, whether animal, vegetable or spiritual, have their place [*H*. 2.2.3]. How seriously Irenaeus took the interrelation of things may be seen in his argument from fourfold animals and four winds to four Gospels. If Gospels fit in with the shape of things [*H*. 3.11.11], then, if they are living, they have to be fourfold and if they are universal they have to cover north, south, east and west. The heretics 'nullify the shape of the gospel' [*H*. 3.11.12]. This section of Irenaeus' argument is a classic example of the way in which what must always seem a joke to beginners – 'There must be four Gospels because there are four winds' – is seen to be important and illuminating when the context of the argument is explored. Because the one God is creator and redeemer there are observable parallels

---

[1] *Timaeus*, 36B. Plato speaks of the shape of the letter *chi*. Justin claims that Plato misunderstood Moses (Numbers 21: 9) and replaced a *stauros* with a *chi*.

[2] The image is one of 'the most memorable images in European philosophy' (Murdoch, *The Fire and the Sun*, p. 87). On Christians as the soul of the world, see *Ad Diog*. 5 and 6, and the cosmic Christ as found in Clement and in Paul's account of the body of Christ.

(like fourfoldness) between different parts of his work such as living things, winds and Gospels.

Tertullian, who is a better Stoic than them all, lives by the law and order he finds in God's world. The world is a cosmos, a place of order and proportion in its infinite variety; its beauty points to God's glory and wisdom [*Ap.* 17]. Order is the mark of nature and a ground for reverence, while whatever goes beyond nature is wrong [*An.* 27]. On the one hand, the world is daily becoming a more ordered and better place: it is easier now to travel from one place to another; dreary and desolate wastes have been turned into farms and wild animals have been replaced by flocks and herds; marshes have been drained and cities have been built [*An.* 30]. This follows the order that God in the beginning gave to creation [*Herm.* 26 and 29]. While it is the soul that points unambiguously to God, all creation bears his stamp [*Ap.* 17; *An.* 43].

Yet on the other hand men reject God's order and refuse to follow nature. They join in games where a boxer is maimed or a gladiator is mauled by a lion [*Spect.* 23]. Tertullian is no more successful with his arguments from natural order than others who come after him. It is unnatural and wrong to shave, for 'will God be pleased with him who applies the razor to himself and completely changes his features?' [*Spect.* 22]. It is against the order of nature to dye wool, for God could have made sheep with purple or blue wool; but he did not, so it is clearly not his will that there should be wool of this colour.[1] God made all things but man does not use them in God's way [*Cult.* 8]. Man's lust for something rare leads him to ignore what God has placed near him and to hunt for something remote and therefore unnatural[2] [*Cult.* 9]. The pattern of marriage is clear from creation: Adam had more than one rib but God used only one because he wanted man to have only one wife; the two were to become one flesh. Scripture, nature and discipline point the one way. A law, established by scripture, is confirmed by nature and enforced by Christian discipline. 'Scripture is God's, nature is God's and discipline is God's' [*Virg.* 16].

[1] This is the first clear statement in Christian literature of the disastrous natural-law argument that moves from statistically normal states of affairs or forms of behaviour to what is good. See D. J. O'Connor, *Aquinas and natural law* (London, 1967), p. 81.
[2] This objection is found in Clement, *Paed.* 2.1.3f. and elsewhere.

The order of the world is reflected in political structures. There is no question of the legitimacy of empire and emperor, for the empire is part of God's creation and manifests his will [*Nat.* 1.17.4]; but the emperor is to be seen within the order of creation. He is less than heaven and the maker of heaven, for he was a man before he was emperor, and must depend upon the creative and sovereign power of God [*Ap.* 30.3]. The Christian's obedience to the empire is limited at two points: to begin with, the authority of the empire can only stand by reference to God; where it is subject to him, the Christian is obedient. Further, despite the power and extent of the empire, it is only a part of the brotherhood and order that constitute the universe. The world is the true fatherland, and all men are brothers.[1]

Clement knows the same tension between God's order and man's disorder, between the beauty that God has given and the goodness that man has yet to reach. Man is called to live an ordered life as part of the cosmos. God's order controls the world, the heavens, the circling sun, the marching stars; he arranges all for the sake of man, his first work of beauty and proportion. Man has but to follow the inspiration of God's universal harmony to find his right way of life [*Paed.* 1.2.6]; yet he understands neither the wisdom of the creator nor the order of creation. Although God has given essential things like water and air freely to all and has hidden non-essentials in the earth and water, stupid men go digging and dredging gold and jewels, which they do not need. While God openly shows his presence in the glory of the heavens, men turn away to dig for hidden gold [*Paed.* 2.12.120].

Only the true Gnostic follows the divine order and lives as a king in the world and a priest before God. He praises God as he ploughs his fields; he sings hymns as he sails over the sea. (This is Clement's Alexandrine view of the world outside the city.) He does not indulge in theatres, perfumes, wines; but he offers the first-fruits of food, drink, ointments to the God who gave them all. So he thanks the God in whose presence he ever lives, for God hears, sees and knows all things; he does not run away from the world, but he rules over it and offers it back to God who made it [*S.* 7.7.36].

How can the world be recognised as God's work? As usual

---

[1] Hornus, 'Étude', p. 38.

Justin provides the theme with which the problem is answered: order points to God. Justin's image of the cosmic cross is followed by Irenaeus' many harmonies and correspondences. Tertullian has a more earthy view of an order that is universal and ethical; there is a law of nature that men and nature must follow in obedience to nature's creator. Clement has regard for nature but follows an all-embracing cosmic order through prayer rather than Law.

4 Is evil in the world compatible with its divine maker?

Attention to the order of the world challenges man to live a life governed by the same order and beauty; men choose to ignore this challenge with disastrous results. Is this the whole story, or does disaster on earth have further significance? Does it exclude belief in a good creator?

Justin's first approach to the problem of evil is uncomplicated. Evil comes from the free choice of men and angels. Man's part has already been described. The disobedient angels became demons when they broke away from their appointed tasks, transgressed the limits that God placed on their activity and were conquered by lust [*2 A.* 5]. They now work on men through dreams and charms, but above all as the gods of the heathen they bring man into cruel captivity [*1 A.* 5; *1 A.* 14]. God has set a limit on their period of busy malpractice and their judgement and destruction are close at hand [*1 A.* 28]. The certainty of their coming doom makes them all the more vicious to men as they try to cram as much into their last wicked years as they possibly can [*D.* 55, 88; cf. Irenaeus, *H.* 5.26]. Yet it is still possible for Roman authorities, like everyone else, to choose what is good and cease from evil; that, indeed, is why Justin writes. His concise account covers a wide range of ideas, which are, as ever, without clear development. God's goodness and concern for men in creation, his ordering of chaos, his toleration of evil for a time that is soon to end – all these are plain and are found elsewhere. Yet Justin manages to leave problems, like the unexplained origin of matter, the postponement of the *eschaton* because some men as yet unborn will repent, and the tension between Christian atheism and the occult. His conciseness and complexity remain troublesome. But he sees a link between creation and resurrection; creation is important for Christians who 'all come together on Sunday, since it is the first day, the day on which God changed darkness and matter and made the world, and also the same day on which Jesus Christ our saviour rose from the dead' [*1 A*. 67.7]. So the last word is with life and hope, and history will provide the final answer to evil. Irenaeus' account of the problem is chiefly in terms of his concept of history and we shall examine his response in the next chapter.

Tertullian brings all his logical and rhetorical skill to the discussion of the problem of evil. Here lay the crux of Marcion's attack on the creator God, and his insistence on two Gods, of whom the inferior was the world's creator. In his first book *Against Marcion*, Tertullian proves the non-existence of Marcion's second God: unity and perfection are essential to God. God is not God if he is not one. In the second book Tertullian deals directly with the problem of evil. Marcion's God is morally unfit to be God. Marcion's objections against the world and God are answered.[1]

Tertullian handles the problem of evil clearly because he is answering a particular opponent who has specific objections to God's goodness. His two main points are (1) the free will of man is a necessity for man's highest good; (2) goodness and justice mutually entail one another. Both these points are developed in the Stoic background on which Tertullian draws.[2]

God is the ultimate goodness, who made all things and ordered the way in which his good works should proceed.[3] There

---

[1] Tertullian's arguments stand out well enough in the text. There is, however, a concise, useful account in V. Naumann, 'Das Problem des Bösen in Tertullians zweiten Buch gegen Marcion', *ZKTh*, 58 (1934), 311–63 and 533–51.

[2] *Ibid.* pp. 331f.; K. Gronau, *Das Theodizeeproblem in der altchristlichen Auffassung* (Tübingen, 1922), p. 74 (on goodness of creator); *ibid.* p. 82, (on cosmic *sundesmos* and man's free will). Other ideas are man as *apospasma* of God (Naumann, 'Das Problem', p. 340), the connection between *bonitas* and *rationalitas*. Chrysippus defines God as '*zoion*', *athanaton, logikon, teleion e noeron en eudaimoniai, kakou pantos anepideikton, pronoetikon kosmou te kai ton en kosmoi* (*ibid.* p. 536).

[3] This is the basic premiss of Plato (*Republic*, 380B): 'Everything must be taken to combat the view that God in his goodness is in any way the cause of evils'.

was nothing presumptuous or imperfect in God's action; goodness inspired his every creative act.

(1) Sin is due to man's free choice;[1] but why did God permit man to sin?

(i) God's foreknowledge of man's rebellion does not make God responsible for that rebellion. Man has to be free, if he is to bear the image of God. Man did not have to sin; but God knew that he would and established the discipline of the Law to threaten man's disobedience [*Marc.* 2.5]. The Law would not make sense if man were not responsible for his sin [*Marc.* 2.6].

(ii) Suppose God had intervened to prevent sin and withdrawn man's liberty, then Marcion would have quickly accused God of instability and faithlessness. God's goodness is shown by the constancy of his gifts, by his protection of man's freedom [*Marc.* 2.7].

(iii) God's goodness in granting man free choice is evident from his great expectations of man: man was not merely to live but to live virtuously.[2] This plan is vindicated by the second Adam's obedience, which fulfils God's good will. For it is the same humanity that defeats the same devil by proper use of the same freedom in obedience to God [*Marc.* 2.8].

(iv) The objection, that God is still responsible for man's sin because the human soul is part of God, fails because the soul is the breath (*afflatus*) of God, not his spirit. God is spirit, man is the image of God, and *afflatus* is the image of spirit. It was possible but improper for the *afflatus* of God to disobey him [*Marc.* 2.9].

(v) The devil provoked man to sin and the devil was a creature of God; but here the free-will defence continues to operate. As the angel whom God made, he was good and free; but he freely chose evil. God in his goodness postponed the destruction of the devil and the restoration

---

[1] The point of the famous claim of *Republic*, 617E is not to explain the origin of evil, but to indicate the autonomy of man's moral action. See Hal Koch, *Pronoia und Paideusis* (Berlin, 1932), p. 201.

[2] This is the one thing that matters for Plato too. Injustice is its own punishment: *Laws*, 728B and 854D; *Theaetetus*, 177: 'The penalty they [the unjust] pay is the life they lead'.

of man, so that the devil might be more appropriately punished after his defeat at the hands of man. God's goodness is vindicated still further by his bringing man to a better paradise in the end.[1]

(2) The second objection is against the justice of God. Why does God punish man for his sin by inflicting physical evils on him? Certainly this is just, but is it good? Tertullian makes three main points:

(i) Justice and goodness must go together. 'Where the just is, there also is the good' [*Marc.* 2.12]. Justice preserves goodness ('tutela bonitatis') and is the function of God in his office as judge ('ordinem dei judicis operarium et protectorem catholicae et summae illius bonitatis'). Justice is essential for goodness. The road to destruction is so broad that all would slide down it if there were no fear of divine justice.[2] Even now, 'We dread the creator's frightening threats, and yet scarcely turn away from evil. What would happen, if his threats did not hang over us?' [*Marc.* 2.13]. Divine justice presents the fullness of God, who is perfect father and perfect master, to be loved as father and feared as master.

(ii) There is a great difference between evils of sin and evils of punishment. The former ('mala culpae') come from the devil and the latter ('mala poenae') come from God. The acceptance of physical evil as punishment from God enables man to accept all things as from the hand of God.[3] 'On all occasions it is God who meets you: he smites but also heals, he kills but also makes alive, he humbles and yet exalts' [*Marc.* 2.14]. God hardened Pharaoh's heart because Pharaoh deserved it. He punished

---

[1] Plato is also convinced that, for the just man, things work out for the best (*Republic*, 613A).

[2] For the Stoics too, natural disasters are providential warnings (*SVF*, vol. 2, 1175f.), and adversity is necessary for virtue, (*SVF*, vol. 2, 1152, 1173 and Seneca, *De Providentia*, 2.3.)

[3] The unity of the total scheme of things was grasped by the Stoics with more determination than others (*SVF*, vol. 2, 1171, 1178). The above references are collated by Koch, *Pronoia und Paidensis*, pp. 192–215, whose great merit is the limited significance that he sees in the parallels. He comments on Origen, 'Er ist gewillt, in einzelnen Punkten von den Stoikern zu lernen, aber im grossen ganzen verhält er sich sehr reserviert' (p. 215).

his own people for their ingratitude. He even sent bears
to eat up the children who called Elisha, 'Old baldhead!'
(iii) What of the feelings that severity requires, such as
anger, jealousy or sternness? In order to be a judge God
must show anger and rejection. These are his professional
tools, like the instruments of a surgeon. You can blame
the surgeon for using his instruments clumsily but you
cannot deny him their use and expect him to do his work.
Yet in God all forms of therapeutic severity transcend
their human counterpart. He may be angry, but he is
never irritated. 'He is moved by all these feelings in a way
peculiar to himself, a way which is entirely appropriate.'
He sees to it that man is moved by emotions that are
distinctively human [*Marc.* 2.16].

The rest of Book 2 continues in a highly readable way,
defending the creator God before the charges of Marcionites.
The command to spoil the Egyptians is brilliantly defended:
the Egyptians made out a claim for their gold and silver
vessels; the Hebrews put in a counter-claim for arrears in pay.
When the whole legal position is examined, it is obvious that
the Egyptians should have paid more and were let off very
lightly. 'If therefore the Hebrews had a good case, the creator
had an equally good one' [*Marc.* 2.20]. Not that Tertullian
simply defends God against the charges of Marcion; he links
these charges to the divine condescension, which culminated
in the coming of Christ. 'What in your eyes is the total disgrace
of my God, is indeed the pledge of man's salvation. God spoke
with man, that man might learn to act like God' [*Marc.* 2.27].

Tertullian's defence is too strong. He will not allow any
ground for Marcion's objections. When he cites the eating of
cheeky children by bears as an example of divine justice, he
has little chance of convincing anyone but himself. When he
retreats into an idiosyncratic platitude that God does everything, including being angry, in an entirely non-human way,
he has come close to the edge of intelligible discourse and his
God is almost as strange as Marcion's. But he does see that on
present evidence his problem is not solved. The devil is not yet
destroyed and man is not yet restored. God, in his goodness,
has provided space in history for man to use his freedom again,
not to go under but to overcome 'and so fittingly regain his

salvation through a victory'. The devil will be punished all the more for being defeated by a former victim and God's goodness will be all the more evident because he gave man the chance 'to return from this life to a more glorious paradise, with permission to pick fruit from the tree of life' [*Marc.* 2.10]. So Marcion is wrong; but some of the problem of evil remains. Tertullian makes the two strongest points in the Christian's case: God in Christ has begun to set things right and there is still time for his work to be perfected; in some way the problem is a pointer to that total disgrace of God which is the pledge of man's salvation.

Clement's answers to the problem are not as blunt and confident as Tertullian's although they build on the same Stoic foundations; but they are more subtle. Clement faces the problem of evil in a specific form. The possibility of martyrdom gave solid ground for doubt concerning the goodness or omnipotence of God. Basilides saw this clearly and his question demanded an answer: 'If God cares for you, how can you ever be persecuted and put to death?' [*S.* 4.11.78ff.]. Clement, whose thought is dominated by free will as the sole source of evil, makes four points:[1]

(1) Evil happens because God does not prevent it. God does not will the suffering of martyrs, yet nothing can happen apart from his will. 'The only possible solution left, expressed concisely, is that such things happen without the prevention of God. Only this preserves the providence and goodness of God. We must not think that God actively causes our afflictions. That is quite unthinkable; but we should hold the conviction that he does not prevent those who cause them' [*S.* 4.12.86f.]. Clement has earlier used a Stoic form[2] of this argument [*S.* 1.17.81f.]. The shield that does not protect cannot be the cause of the wound that the dart inflicts. The causes of sin are man's choice and desire, aggravated by the deception of the demons. God does all that is possible to prevent sin, short of taking away man's free will. 'Everything, then, which did not hinder man's free choice, he made conducive to virtue' [*S.* 7.2.12].

[1] See my *Philosophy of Clement*, pp. 69–78.
[2] *SVF*, vol. 2, 353.

(2) When man has sinned, God is active to transform the effects of man's sin. 'He uses up for good the wrongs which his adversaries have dared against him' [*S.* 4.12.87]. This is the chief part of divine providence, which is concerned not merely to do good, but 'above all to bring to a good and useful end what has happened through the evils contrived by any' [*S.* 1.17.86]. Plato [*Republic* 613A] as well as Paul [Romans 8: 28] considered that for the good man all things work out for the best. In the *Laws* [902f.] Plato sees to it that providence shows concern for the smallest things and for individual souls in a way more recently described: 'God is not only always doing geometry, he is always playing draughts'.[1] Clement also draws on Stoic sources, which regarded evil as a part of a good cosmos,[2] and saw the divine activity in 'bringing all things into one and good from bad'.[3] But Clement gives a much more intelligible place to this divine activity because his account of God is more personal and his estimate of history more real.

(3) Evil is especially used for discipline in a complicated way. Most people are corrected for their own sins. Jesus and his apostles received suffering and correction for the sins of others; by the suffering of the Lord we are sanctified [*S.* 4.12.87]. In Plato, the gods punish men, but only for men's good [*Republic* 380AB].

(4) Sin is an activity not an essence [*S.* 4.13.93], a work of man, not of God. This is profoundly Platonic, because it depends on a monistic structure ruled by the Form of the Good. As Platonism develops, the idea that evil is negative or privative becomes more obvious. Evil cannot come from God [*Republic* 380B], but all that is comes from God, therefore evil cannot be. This is carried to explicit conclusion in Plotinus.[4]

---

[1] Murdoch, *The Fire and the Sun*, p. 63.

[2] Plutarch, *De stoic. repugn.* 35 and 36; *SVF*, vol. 2, 1181, 1182.

[3] Cleanthes, in Stobaeus, *Anthologium*, ed. C. Wachsmuth (Berlin, 1884–1912), vol. 1, p. 25.

[4] Plotinus, *Enneads*, 1.8. The account of evil as privation is more subtle than has been recognised. On the one hand it may be held to remove the problem of evil and on the other hand it may still give an intelligible account of the power of evil. See McCloskey, *God and evil*, pp. 28ff. for discussion.

To sum up, Clement's account of the problem of evil is based on man's free will. To this is added the free will of those spiritual beings who, like Satan, have chosen to defy God. But God does not merely punish wrongdoers. He enters the game himself and turns the errors of men to some good effect. To this notion of saving history is added the Platonic and biblical theme that the good that God does goes on for ever, while human sin negates itself and falls short of true being.

Still more important is Clement's recognition that, as the world now is, man cannot see a solution to this problem. Clement points beyond this world to the death of the sinner [*S*. 3.9.64], to the cleansing fire, through which the believer passes [*Paed*. 1.7.61] and to the many mansions in which the faithful will find their appropriate dwelling [*S*. 6.13.105ff.]. With Clement, as with his contemporaries, there was no complete answer to the problem of evil in the present. He looked for the one fold under one shepherd [*Paed*. 1.7.53] to which the Lord would bring his own when he came in glory [*Ecl*. 56]. For Clement, in contrast to his contemporaries, heaven offers more hope than history; so wrong is the liberal optimism that has been laid at his feet.[1]

[1] Apart from his main arguments, there are many other factors that he mentions. There is much useful material in the work of W. E. G. Floyd, *Clement of Alexandria's treatment of the problem of evil* (Oxford, 1971), together with a puzzling uncritical acceptance of Lovejoy's scheme of the Great Chain of Being. The strong criticisms that have been made of Lovejoy are not recognised; yet Clement provides powerful objections to Lovejoy's method, which by itself:

'would have grave disadvantages: it would frequently lead us away from those features of an author's work which were most likely to be central to his motivation, and which might also be most important for his historical influence; it might also lead us to minimise the independence of an author's thought, suggesting lines of historical connection where such connections have not been established and may not have existed' (Maurice Mandelbaum, 'History of ideas, intellectual history, history of philosophy', *HThS*, 5 (1965), 41).

Problems and Parallels

I   One God, one world

The strength of the theme of creation in these four writers lay
in their rejection of a second world or a second god.[1] One God
met the challenge of Marcion and one world met that of the
Gnostics. Justin speaks plainly of God making the world out of
formless matter, which is subordinate to his will. There is no
suggestion that God needs an intermediary to bridge the gap
between him and creation; he said plainly to his Word:
'Let us make'. Irenaeus speaks of the hands of God, Christ
and the Holy Spirit, forming and holding man. The intermediate or higher world of the Gnostics was a foolish fantasy.
Platonism, for most people, means the doctrine of forms or
ideas,[2] and later Christian thought was to set great store on
the higher world. In contrast, second-century Christians used
Plato to defend the visible world against Gnostic attack; their
heaven was not built out of Platonic forms. Heaven was
important, for the martyrs were already there and the new
Jerusalem had been seen hanging in the sky. There was a
heavenly ladder to climb. All this belonged to the world of
apocalyptic rather than dialectic.[3] Tertullian's rejection of
dialectic and his fascination with the works of his creator
bring out this point as clearly as possible. Valentinus, he says,
drew his 'aeons' and 'forms' and threefold division of man
from Plato. Dialectic cannot help Christianity. It can only
dull the sharpness of the gospel and the stark demands and

---

[1] See A. Ehrhardt, *The beginning* (Manchester, 1968), p. 105: 'The
principle chosen by Philo, the ordering metaphysical principle, made
the empirical world a secondary consideration in the interpretation
of the relation between God and man, whereas the active causative
principle stated by Paul made it God's world'.

[2] See A. H. Armstrong and R. A. Markus, *Christian faith and Greek
philosophy* (London, 1960), chapter 3, pp. 16f. and 28.

[3] See J. Daniélou, *Judéo-Christianisme* (Paris, 1958), pp. 133–46; ET,
pp. 173–81.

gifts of Christ [*Praescr.* 7]. The wonderful maker of all has showered his gifts on the tiniest of creatures, demonstrating, by the bee and its cells, the ant and its anthill, the spider and its web, the silk-worm and its delicate threads, that greatness is proved in humility [*Marc.* 1.14].

On the other hand, Clement speaks of *Nous* or Logos as the place of the ideas and points the upward path of dialectic. But this path is the Word himself and the pure unity of God is grasped in this world for the true Gnostic makes his life an uninterrupted festival of praise and 'convinced that God is wholly present everywhere' sings hymns as he ploughs his fields or sails the sea [*S.* 7.7.35]. However foreign the Christian is to worldly things, he worships God in daily life. 'We are commanded to worship and adore the Word, in the conviction that he is our saviour and leader, and through him to worship the Father. We do this not on selected days, as certain others do, but continually through the whole of life, and in every way' [*S.* 7.7.35]. The Gnostic lives his life on earth by following the archetypes above, just as sailors steer by the stars [*S.* 6.9.79].

It is clear that Clement was just as keen on one world as was Tertullian. Here the doxographer is lost in bewilderment – how can Tertullian, who denounces dialectic, and Clement, who extols a true dialectic, be entirely agreed on one world? Simply because they are using words in different ways. To declare one God, one world, Tertullian pronounces intervening dialectic to be a dangerous fiction; it is superfluous because after Christ and the gospel nothing is needed. Clement says the same thing in a more subtle way.[1] Truth and dialectic do not stand between God and the world; for Christ is all truth and dialectic. He is the place of the ideas, the perfect

---

[1] In Clement the world of forms was swallowed up, or replaced logically and ethically by the Logos, in a way reminiscent of the limerick:

> 'There was a young lady of Riga,
> Who rode with a smile on a tiger;
> They returned from the ride
> With the lady inside,
> And the smile on the face of the tiger.'

The forms are the smile on the face of the Logos, and their function in early Christian thought is very different from the hierarchical purpose they fulfil in later Christian thought.

Logos, one thing as all things; in him the truth about things
visible and invisible, their real nature and purpose, come
together. In him all truth and goodness may be understood
and learnt. 'The Son is wisdom and knowledge and truth and
whatever else is related ... All the powers of the Spirit join
together, become one thing, and come together in the one
point, the Son' [S. 4.25.156]. This made him the 'knowledge
and spiritual garden' of the true Gnostic, or the whole body of
truth, from which men tear off a part that they claim as the
whole. Clement was out to catch men with ideas and to
entice the heretical Gnostic away into the true dialectic of
Christ. How successful he was we do not know; but, by looking
at problems rather than at fragmentary propositions, we do
know what he was trying to do, whereas the doxographer will
never know. Middle Platonism was ambivalent to the world
of forms, which had always found some critics in the Platonic
succession.[1] Three things increased the opposition to forms.
From the one side, the heightened significance of the first
cause made intervening causes less important;[2] from the other
side, the Stoic unified cosmos became part of Platonism and
absorbed the forms into itself.[3] Finally the Gnostic denigration
of the visible world aroused hostility, which culminated in the
attack of Plotinus.[4] Christians, like Justin and Clement, took
the two tendencies of Middle Platonism – transcendent first
cause and cosmic unity – and pushed them further in the
interests of one God and one world. On the other hand,
Tertullian rejected Platonism because he believed it was tied
to forms. The tendency towards monism was wider than
Platonism and Christianity.[5]

How far the Christians saw that they were at the height of
the contemporary theme we cannot be sure; for the roots of
the doctrine of creation lay in the centre of the Christian
gospel. From Paul onwards, creation out of nothing was
parallel to two central articles of belief: the justification of the

[1] P. Merlan, 'Greek philosophy from Plato to Plotinus', in Armstrong
(ed.), *Later Greek and early medieval Philosophy*, p. 53.
[2] H. Dörrie, 'Die Frage', pp. 202 and 218.
[3] Merlan, 'Greek philosophy', pp. 126ff. Cf. W. Theiler, 'Plotin
zwischen Platon und Stoa', *Les Sources de Plotin*, pp. 76 and 86; also
Die Vorbereitung des Neuplatonismus (Berlin, 1930), p. 72.
[4] Plotinus, *Enn.* 2.9.
[5] Dörrie, 'Die Frage', pp. 203f.

ungodly and resurrection of the dead.[1] Creation's puzzle is therefore to be preserved; intermediaries are as much an evangelical disaster as Galatian legalism or immortal souls, because they deny simple dependence on the one, all-sufficient God of grace.

2   Converted by a chick-pea?

The strong line on creation in the second century is a surprise. The utter transcendence of God and the upward flight of man suggest that the world below is best ignored or forgotten. However, the world had at least two strong claims for attention: it had been worth the incarnation and it pointed to a cause beyond itself. So there was added to the God above, to the God within, the definition of the supreme God as the Father and Maker of all.

In one way, the argument about the world was really an argument about God. For if the God of the Gospels did not make the world, then another God did; worse still, if the most high God didn't make anything, how could one believe in him, how could one drag him down from the never-never realms of fantasy? Tertullian declares himself ready to be converted to Marcion's strange God. All he needs is something, even a solitary pea, that this God has produced. Creation was necessarily a work of God, to link him to man, to anchor him from abstraction, to make the world a place in which God could be believed. It was hard to believe in a creator who was like Jesus, so Marcion did have to be taken seriously. The Jesus of the Gospels did bring something new, which could hardly fit with the oldness and harshness of the world. So creation had to be looked at again, until with Stoic help, the universe was able to join in the new song of the Logos; the whole creation pointed by its harmony and goodness to the One from whom all came into being.

3   Pure joy in the world

Two things made the creation credible: the idea of process,

---

[1] Romans 4. See Käsemann, *An die Römer*, pp. 110–21, and 'The Faith of Abraham in Romans 4', *Perspectives on Paul*, p. 92.

which Paul had grasped in Romans 8, and the sheer enjoyment of the world that emerged when the gods departed. The first was tied to a conception of history, to a recognition of pain and frustration, to a hope that man would reach his goal, not by leaving the world behind but by taking it with him or finding it again. This was a world marked by the sign of the cross, living between its new creation at Christ's resurrection and its restoration at the final consummation of all things.

The second point is equally subtle. The world was empty now of the friendly spirits that had filled its trees and rivers. What did it look like? Today, can the scientist, the secularist, see the world as clearly as the mystic sees it? It has been claimed, that

'faith makes the world what it truly is, the creation of God. It rids the world of demons and myths, and lets it again be what God wills it to be. Because faith frees us from the world, it frees us for the world . . . And because it drives out the liking and misliking of the world, it creates room for pure joy in the world.'[1]

The ancient world found it easy to venerate the world or to despise it. Christians believed that pagans and Gnostics were both wrong; the world was good but it was not God. You walked on it; you did not worship it. Fortunately there was enough *humanitas* in antiquity to see the beauty of the world and Christians could build on this; but, to the extent that they rejected both idolatry and flight from the world, they were building something new.

4   Creation as process

The idea of process has found many advocates in this century and the variety of their ideas is confusing.[2] The most useful

---

[1] Ebeling, *Nature of faith*, p. 161. Cf. the comments of D. S. Wallace–Hadrill: 'The fathers follow the NT closely in exhibiting a disturbing oscillation between world-acceptance and world-renunciation. The resolution of the tension may lie in this, that the man who is freed from the demands of nature is free to enjoy it fearlessly' (*The Greek patristic view of nature* (Manchester, 1968), p. 130).

[2] In particular, the idea of an imperfect or limited God is the opposite of the view held by the four writers considered; they used the idea of

work is that of the late Charles Raven. Raven was a theologian and a scientist, who believed that second-century Christians had understood the world better than any of their successors. He wrote,

'But this theology possessed the one thing necessary, a full and proportionate concept of God's nature and work. It had, what no subsequent age has yet recovered, a real doctrine of the continuity and energy of God's working in the world – that is, a worthy theology of the Holy Spirit... For them the constant, vitalising activity of God in his world was the essential element in their teaching.'[1]

Raven saw the importance of Romans 8. The traditional Christian dependence on Genesis had been shown wanting through the evolution controversies of the nineteenth century. On most issues the evolutionists were right and the theologians were wrong. Paul had a different account of creation, the truth of which was confirmed by scientific development and the new awareness of evolution.

'Instead of creation as an act, it is here a process; instead of its being perfect it is frustrate and incomplete; instead of its being corrupted by the devil it is made subject to frustration by God; and instead of its being acted upon by God it is itself in travail, awaiting the birth of the family of God and being assisted in its agony by God's own Spirit.'[2]

process as an alternative to the idea of a limited God. Recently it has been argued that a finite good God may be credible but can hardly be the appropriate object of worship. However, this objection is followed by an objection against worship as such, and the first objection thereby loses its force. 'There are difficulties in the way of justifying wholly yielding one's will to another, no matter how perfect' (McCloskey, *God and evil*, p. 69). A more interesting comment claims that 'The image of a morally perfect but not all-powerful Goodness seems to me better to express some ultimate (inexpressible) truth about our condition,' Murdoch, *The Fire and the Sun*, p. 52.

[1] C. E. Raven, *Good news of God* (London, 1940), p. 100. Raven always insisted that it was wrong to regard the natural universe merely as the stage for God's acts of redemption. The incarnate Word was continually at work. Raven greeted with enthusiasm an article by Daniélou (*Études*, 95 (February 1962)), who showed how important this theme had been to Teilhard. See R. W. McKinney (ed.), *Creation, Christ and culture* (Edinburgh, 1976), p. 95.

[2] C. E. Raven, *Science and the Christian man* (London, 1952), p. 35.

Raven turned with confidence to the philosophy of emergent evolution, put forward by Lloyd Morgan, because it spoke of a unified development of creation by one Spirit living in it. This means that man should turn to the visible world of nature, not to confirm or illustrate his own feelings, but to grow in understanding and to learn of God.[1] In the intricate structure of the world of nature there was enough to discover and to contemplate for an eternity.[2] The ways in which nature develops are the proper stuff of the philosopher and theologian; there is an increasing complexity and adaptation, which make for a greater fullness of life.[3] Frustration is important; Jesus has shown that love involves freedom, sympathy and sacrifice and he offers a clue to the meaning of suffering in the world. Raven quotes Fabre, a reflective scientific thinker, on the place of sacrifice in the structure of the universe and comments enthusiastically that 'woven into the very woof and warp of the universe, is the pattern of the Cross, that nature is baptised in the Spirit of Jesus, that man's creation was accomplished by the same means as his redemption'.[4] The study of nature leads man gradually to a deeper understanding of God, as artist, as teacher and ultimately as Father. Raven compares that growth with that of Clement's Gnostic from faith, to knowledge, to love and to the inheritance.[5]

In a later study, on the distortion of the gospel within a distorted Church, Raven stressed the need for the recovery of nature and an appreciation of history. In the recovery of nature, he saw an appreciation of the wholeness of nature as a valuable contribution of biologists. The Church's opportunity is to present a true valuation of nature: 'Inherent in its essential faith is the conviction of the worth, the sacramental significance, the "mystery" of nature'.[6] In his Gifford Lectures, Raven restated his position with clarity and force. There are two unique sacraments that disclose ultimate meaning: the universe and Jesus Christ.[7] There can be no reasonable faith

---

[1] C. E. Raven, *The creator Spirit* (London, 1928), p. 97.

[2] *Ibid.* p. 106.

[3] *Ibid.* p. 115.

[4] *Ibid.* p. 124.

[5] *Ibid.* p. 131. Clement, *S.* 7.10.55–9.

[6] C. E. Raven, *The gospel and the church* (London, 1939), p. 194.

[7] C. E. Raven, *Natural religion and Christian theology*, vol. 2, 'Experience and interpretation' (Cambridge, 1953), p. 105.

unless creation points to the true nature of its maker.[1] From biological evidence of evolution he points to 'a purposive urge promoting not only larger ranges of activity, fuller individuation and ultimately the emergence of personality, but a harmony in diversity, the gradual fulfilment of a plan, the integration of the several elements of the design into a complex and inclusive pattern'.[2] Much of the failure in the theology of creation may be linked with a neglect of the work of the Holy Spirit, once the Logos-doctrine had been abandoned. For the Spirit is God at work within his creation, giving energy for the response of the creature.[3] We must learn to look for God outside the accepted channels of revelation. 'All beauty, all truth, all goodness are the signs of His presence and, potentially at least, the instruments of His purpose; and we, to the extent to which we are capable of realisation and response, as in some sort "made in his likeness", can perceive and appreciate and accept His gifts.'[4] Raven's work remains important and requires fresh assessment by those who possess his competence in science as well as theology. There is no doubt that he learnt from the early fathers, especially the Alexandrines, and that his interpretation of their thought and of Paul was sound.

5   A secular world

We must stress the secularist position of the Christian and his enjoyment of a world that was seen without its gods. Here it is worth looking at a critical reaction to the mysticism of some contemporary conservationists. There is rubbish to be removed in this area and John Passmore names first 'mystical rubbish, the view that mysticism can save us, where technology cannot'.[5] He attacks the 'philosophy of wholeness' to which Raven showed some sympathy but kept under the control of his science. As Passmore points out: 'Science is not *intrinsically* atomistic', and the ecologist's concern for awareness of chain reactions does not put him above science. Nor is it any help to

[1] *Ibid.* p. 131.
[2] *Ibid.* p. 146.
[3] *Ibid.* p. 150.
[4] *Ibid.* p. 178.
[5] John Passmore, *Man's responsibility to nature* (London, 1975), p. 173.

revert to a view of nature as sacred. The 'mystery' of nature is not a mystery that resists reason but one that invites exploration. If the ecological mystics were right in this area, there would be no need for the divine nature to be protected. It is important, in finding a way through the ecological problems of the present, to recognise that 'neither man nor nature is sacred or quasi-divine'.[1] Two things must be clearly grasped: first, that man depends on nature completely, second, that nature is vulnerable to man's depredation. Both man and nature are marked by fragility or contingency; for the Christian, they are creatures and not creators.

Further, man can only live by plundering; there is an obvious sense in which he must master nature. Civilisation can only come through man's intelligent control of his environment; Tertullian's delight in nature did not blind him to the excellence of man's achievements in the draining of swamps and the cultivation of farms.

One final point is the advocacy of a more sensuous attitude to nature. Augustine and Plato, it is claimed, have turned Western man against sights and sounds. The origin of this aspect of Western man is more complex. There were two streams of Platonism and one of them provided the fiercest opposition to Gnostic dualism and the most fervent support of the beauty of the physical world. Again, Augustine never ceased to be a sensualist and could write long after his conversion [*Confessions* 2.5]:

'The eye is attracted by beautiful objects, by gold and silver and all such things. There is great pleasure, too, in feeling something agreeable to the touch, and physical things have different qualities to please each of the other senses. . . . The life we live on earth has its own attractions as well, because it has a certain beauty of its own in harmony with all the rest of this world's beauty.'

Yet there remains enough truth in Passmore's criticism to drive the theologian back to the second century, to Tertullian's delight in the world, to Clement's fascination for camels and deserts, to Irenaeus' earthy jokes against Gnostic transcendental stuffiness, and to the passionate way in which they all argued against Marcion.

[1] *Ibid.* p. 176.

6 God and evil

Three factors emerge in the account of the problem of evil: hope, the crucified God and retribution. None of the four writers looks for a solution of the problem in the present: when all has been said, only the future is assured because of what God has already done. The discussion of creation gives only half the answer to the problem of evil; the other half comes from the discussion of history. It is important that creation does not give unambiguous evidence for God; that would mean that creation was complete and perfect, and that God could be understood in terms of his world, without qualification. 'The world is not yet finished, but is understood as engaged in history.'[1] It is neither heaven nor hell, but the world of the possible. So God is understood in terms of the future; for Paul 'does not speak of the essence or the workings of the creature, of *actio*, *passio* or movement, but employs a new, strange, theological term and speaks of the expectation of the creature'.[2]

The crucified God is the theme of Moltmann's second main work. Auschwitz symbolises the power of evil in the twentieth century; but there could be no theology to account for Auschwitz in terms of guilt and sorrow if there had been no theology within Auschwitz. 'Anyone who later comes up against insoluble problems and despair must remember that the *Shema* of Israel and the Lord's Prayer were prayed in Auschwitz.'[3] That God himself hung on the gallows, that all sorrow and suffering are taken up into God, that God was in Auschwitz and Auschwitz was in God: these are the grounds of Christian hope. 'It is necessary to remember the martyrs so as not to become abstract.'[4] This is where the second-century writers stood – within a martyr Church; their account of suffering and evil is all the more important because of this fact. In the Western world today, faith is difficult for many because God has not rewarded the nations who have publicly honoured him;[5] the Deuteronomic belief that apostasy brings disaster, while

[1] J. Moltmann, *Theology of hope* (London, 1967), p. 338.
[2] *Ibid.* p. 35.
[3] J. Moltmann, *The crucified God* (London, 1974), p. 278.
[4] *Ibid.*
[5] Butterfield, *Christianity and history*, p. 52.

154

repentance and obedience bring triumph, dies hard. Men turn against God because of their private hardships or national decline. But the true God is 'not recognised by his power and glory in the world ... but through his helplessness and his death on the scandal of the cross of Jesus'.[1] There is no connection but only opposition between the gods of this world's power and wealth on the one hand and the God who is found in Jesus. Moltmann's claim: 'Only a Christian can be a good atheist', and Bloch's claim: 'only an atheist can be a good Christian' are equally valid.[2]

The idea of retribution gained credence through a consideration of Nazi war crimes and the punishment of war criminals. The belief that human wickedness accounts for perhaps four-fifths of the suffering of men[3] has been joined to the theme of tragic drama that punishment is needed to restore a moral balance to this wickedness. At the centre of Christian belief, it has even been claimed that 'The cross is as eloquent of God's concern for moral law as it is of his love'.[4] This is plainly an overstatement. On the basis of the New Testament, punishment and retribution can have no place in Christian thought. Suffering inflicted for disciplinary or deterrent purposes has often been confused with suffering inflicted for punishment and retribution; the former is consistent with the Gospel while the latter is not. It has found its way into Christian thought through confusion and misunderstanding.[5] New Testament writers work within a framework of ideas that include quantitative justice and retribution, yet their own expressions of these ideas are reduced and limited. Perhaps the Apocalypse is an exception, as in Revelation 16: 5f. and 19: 1f. the blood of the martyrs will be avenged with retributive, if not vindictive, justice.[6] The inappropriate application of retribution to the

---

[1] Moltmann, *The crucified God*, p. 195.

[2] *Ibid.*

[3] C. S. Lewis, *The problem of pain* (London, 1940), p. 77. On this question see also H. B. Acton (ed.), *The philosophy of punishment* (London, 1969), especially pp. 26f. and 56ff., and the essays by K. G. Armstrong and Alwynne Smart. My chief debt is to the work of John Cowburn, S.J., and to discussions with him.

[4] L. L. Morris, *The Cross in the New Testament* (Grand Rapids, 1965), p. 154.

[5] C. F. D. Moule, 'Punishment and retribution, An attempt to delimit their scope in New Testament thought', *SEA*, 30 (1968), 21.

[6] *Ibid.* p. 33.

central message of the Gospel must be resisted; for the language of deserts has no place in man's relationship to a loving God.[1]

Attention has recently been drawn to the persistent place given to the punishment of sinners by Justin and the other three writers. It is a surprise to those who have seen sweet reasonableness as a characteristic of Justin, Irenaeus and Clement to find that 'le doux Justin'[2] and not merely Tertullian, regards the suffering of the wicked as an important part of the Gospel [*Ap.* 18.3; 45.7; 47.12]. Because the picture of eternal torment is part of Jewish apocalyptic that Christianity took over, it has been commonly concluded that it had no deep significance for Christian understanding. This cannot be the case with the apologists. What was it that gave to the suffering of the wicked such importance? Tertullian, again, by his uninhibited zeal, points to the answer. He has shocked many generations of believers by his account of the delight of the saints as they contemplate the eternal punishment of their persecutors [*Spect.* 30.2].

Persecution was the ultimate challenge to faith. Justin indicates the injustice of a Christian being punished because of the virtuous reformation of another convert: 'What is the accusation? Why have you punished this man who is neither adulterer, nor fornicator, nor murderer, nor thief, nor robber, nor convicted of having done anything wrong at all?' [*2 A.* 2.16]. Above and behind the earthly judge stood the eternal judge, so that as an earthly judge delivered his verdict, he himself came under judgement. What mattered in the end was the judgement of God in heaven; if there were no such final judgement the Christian God would not be credible. The longing of men for true justice has been linked to their feeling after 'the wholly Other' whose transcendence will ensure 'that the murderer will not be allowed to triumph over the innocent victim'.[3]

---

[1] *Ibid.* p. 35; cf. also, C. F. D. Moule, 'The Christian understanding of forgiveness', *Theology*, 71 (1968), 435–43, esp. p. 437; 'on a fully personal level of procedure, and most of all in a Christian understanding of the way in which offence and estrangement are dealt with, *there is no place at all* for retribution'. In this area of discussion, I am also indebted to the comments of W. J. Dalton, S.J.

[2] Joly, *Christianisme et philosophie*, p. 167; see also pp. 171–82 and 196f. See below, p. 278ff.

[3] See M. Horkheimer, *Die Sehnsucht nach dem ganz Anderen* (Hamburg,

Another factor was also present: the persecution of Christians by good rulers was only possible because the wicked demons were having their final fling. They, who had freely chosen disobedience and wickedness, ruled and guided the hearts of men; but their doom was written. As surely as they now fled before the name of Christ, they would be overthrown and would suffer torment for what they had done to men. This was good news, for without it the story of Jesus was but a beautiful disaster. One of the stories from the Nuremberg war-crime trials told of the machine-gunning of a group of Jews before an open grave. As the execution squad opened fire, an aged Jew put his arm around a small boy and pointed upwards.[1] So Justin begins and ends his *Apology* with a warning to rulers and magistrates: 'You will have no defence before God if, when you know the facts, you do not act justly' [*1 A*. 3]. 'You will not escape God's coming judgement, if you persist in injustice' [*1 A*. 68]. Again the Appendix (or *Second Apology*) begins with a specific case of injustice and ends with the plea: 'May you therefore in a way that is worthy of piety and philosophy, judge justly for your own sakes' [*2 A*. 15]. So, within the assurance of coming judgement, there was still ground for compassion; Tertullian also writes to Scapula: 'not because we fear for ourselves, but because we fear for you and all our enemies' [*Scap*. 1]. No government or ruler sheds Christian blood with impunity and God starts punishing now. Fire and thunder point to the wrath to come; but already the deaths of provincial governors have been connected with their persecution of Christians. One of them, visibly afflicted with worms, tried to hide his illness lest Christians be encouraged; he repented and was almost a Christian when he died [*Scap*. 3].

The second century gives ground for caution in this area: while the apocalyptic vision of judgement is present in all writers, Clement argues against retribution in a careful way, while Tertullian argues for it in a disastrous way. Clement is concerned to replace the notion of punishment with that of

1970), pp. 61f., cited by Küng, *On being a Christian*, p. 436. It is perhaps important that Justin does not see the punishment of persecutors as relevant to his own death. This would be an example of the claim that men normally wish to make on behalf of their past against their future; 'This is the claim we had to renounce' (Weil, *Waiting on God*, p. 173).

[1] E. Gordon Rupp, *Principalities and powers* (London, 1952), p. 40.

discipline or chastisement. Most men are corrected by suffering for their own sins; the Lord and the apostles suffered for the sins of others [*S.* 4.12.87]. Martyrs suffer because of the sins of their persecutors, but God uses this suffering for the sanctification of the martyrs and others. Against Basilides, Clement insists that the martyr does not suffer to expiate his previous sin in this or another life; that would make God the author of persecution and would absolve persecutors. Basilides also wrongly argues that God only forgives involuntary sins and punishes all voluntary sins [*S.* 4.24.153f.]. This, says Clement, would be human and not divine forgiveness; God forgives what is past and chastises the sinner for his good and for the good of others. Correction looks forward while punishment looks back. 'God does not punish, for punishment (*timōria*) is a recompense for evil, but he chastises (*kolazei*) for the individual and common benefit of those who are chastised' [*S.* 7.16.102]. Yet Clement speaks of the discipline of fear, which supplements other forms of instruction [*ibid.*], and uses medical metaphors to show how pain can heal and restore [*Paed.* 1.9.88]. Fire will purify, test and sanctify souls that pass through it; this fire, says Clement, is intelligent and not material, cleansing and not destroying [*S.* 7.6.34].[1]

On the other hand, Tertullian argues for retribution with vigour. God rewards or punishes man according to the merits of each case, never faltering in his justice and providence [*Marc.* 2.23]. Tertullian's constant weakness is the total rejection of the case against which he argues. God's threats and man's fear of God's wrath are entirely good and necessary. The way of evil is broad: 'Would not all slide down its slippery path if there were nothing in it to fear?' [*Marc.* 2.13]. All the actions of the God of the Old Testament are consistent with his justice and goodness. The Egyptians deserved the plagues, Pharaoh deserved a hardened heart,

---

[1] Clement provides the first account of purgatory or cleansing fire, which is concerned 'to destroy the foreign and base elements which have taken root in a man's soul, a painful operation, which cannot be carried out without causing suffering' (G. Anrich, 'Clemens und Origenes als Begründer der Lehre vom Fegfeuer', *Theologische Abhandlungen, Eine Festgabe ... für H. J. Holtzmann* (Tübingen and Leipzig, 1902), p. 120). There is no notion of punishment in Clement's account.

'to be influenced to his own destruction, since he had already denied God, had already turned away God's envoys so often in his pride, had imposed hard labour on God's people, and finally, as an Egyptian, had for a long time been guilty before God of pagan idolatry, worshipping the ibis and the crocodile rather than the living God' [*Marc.* 2.14].

Clement and Tertullian draw common material from Stoic tradition, such as the medical/surgical need for pain that heals. This makes their diverse approaches all the more important, and here the chief factor is the different opponent. Clement argues against Basilides, who insists that suffering, including martyrdom, is retributive punishment for sin; Tertullian argues against Marcion, who denies the goodness of the just God of the Old Testament. Both Clement and Tertullian are outraged by the view that they oppose; while the former argues coolly and is aware of problems, the latter is unbending and weakens his position by the use of hard cases. As a result he loses his case against Marcion; for, if only fear can turn Christians from sin, then the New Testament has added nothing to the Old Testament. Tertullian has finished with one God only, but he is not the Father of Jesus Christ.[1]

Is there any way in which Christians can deal effectively with the problem of evil? In the first place, the problem does not place the burden of proof on the Christian to explain suffering and evil. This has been a mystery to men of all ages; there is no more reason to expect Christians to solve this mystery than to expect them to have a cure for cancer or to perform faultlessly in any examination they might choose to sit. The critic must establish that there cannot be a solution or 'that it is logically impossible that God should have a morally sufficient reason to allow evil of the sort that we encounter in the world'.[2]

There is a robust confidence in Tennant's account of evil, a confidence that shows what the last fifty years have done to the human spirit. Moral evil is necessary for the world to be a

---

[1] Cf. H. von Campenhausen, *The fathers of the Latin church* (London, 1964), p. 35.
[2] B. Mitchell, *The justification of religious belief* (London, 1973), p. 10. For a concise and clear account of the issues, see Brian Hebblethwaite, *Evil, suffering and religion* (London, 1976).

developing moral order, which is the best kind of world we can imagine.[1] 'The moral race which has emerged, though born to suffer through its freedom, nevertheless rejoices in living, approves its creator's ideal, accepts the chance of the prize of learning love: at least so long as it can believe the cost to be inevitable and the possibility of evil to be not superfluous.'[2]

Physical evil is necessary from the order of the world to which man belongs, and he does not think suffering is too much to pay for the ethical status he enjoys.[3] In many respects, Tennant's work has worn well but this account of evil is not one that commands conviction. Yet it is a similar account that forms the basis of Hick's important work.[4] The world is arranged for the training of souls who go forward through earthly trials to better things. There are two weaknesses here: first, the belief that character normally benefits from suffering, second the belief that adding fibre to the self is the way of moral excellence. Neither of these is acceptable without a lot of sustained argument. There seems more sense in Simone Weil's acceptance of suffering. Nothing can justify a single tear from a single child, yet all tears and suffering must be accepted. We do not accept these things because of their compensations but because they exist. The aim should not be to suffer less but to 'remain untainted by suffering'.[5] Through suffering, which itself is pointless and void, we may reach knowledge of a greater reality. Yet this learning is through a dark night of separation from God; there is no other way.[6]

The Christian case has rested heavily on the free-will defence. Since this has been recently attacked[7] we shall look at an important restatement.[8] It is useful to distinguish a free-will defence from a free-will theodicy. The latter attempts to

[1] Tennant, *Theology*, vol. 2, p. 188.
[2] *Ibid.* p. 192.
[3] *Ibid.* p. 204.
[4] John Hick, *Evil and the God of love*, 2nd ed. (London, 1977). This is the most comprehensive recent treatment of the subject. It has been severely criticised and some answers to objections are to be found *ibid.* pp. 372–84.
[5] *Gravity and grace*, p. 73.
[6] *Ibid.* pp. 75f.
[7] See McCloskey, *God and evil*, pp. 115ff.
[8] A. Plantinga, *God, freedom and evil* (London, 1975).

solve the problem of evil by showing ways in which the ways of God to men may be justified. The former aims to show that the problem does not exclude belief in a morally perfect, omnipotent God. This is where interest should be directed. Theodicies will always have some ambivalence and leave at least one point of weakness. On the other hand if it can be shown that evil is not incompatible with the existence of a morally perfect, omnipotent God, then a valid defence has been made.

The first step in the argument is to show that there are some possible worlds that an omnipotent God cannot create.[1] The second step is the more general claim that it is possible that X suffers from 'transworld depravity', which means that he will go wrong with respect to at least one action in any world that God may bring into being (p. 48). Now it is possible that everyone suffers from 'transworld depravity'; if this possibility were actual then God, although omnipotent, could not have created a world in which there was moral good and no moral evil.[2]

Further clarification of the problem of evil has recently been achieved by showing that there are three problems, not one: the general problem (is the existence of God compatible with any evil?), specific abstract problems (is the existence of God compatible with specific evil?), and specific concrete problems (are the conditions for compatibility met in our world?).[3] Analysis of the problems shows that there is no necessary incompatibility in any of the three cases. In the second century, our four writers argued for a positive solution of the general problem (non-prevention and ultimate harmony), of specific

---

[1] Plantinga demonstrates this as follows: M offers B a bribe of $35,000 and B accepts and complies with M's conditions. But B would have accepted and complied for $20,000. There is at least one possible world in which M offers B $20,000 and B does not accept. But God cannot create such a world for he has to leave B free and if B is free he will accept the bribe. There is therefore at least one possible world that God cannot create.

[2] Even when applied to essences that are instantiated as person the argument still holds. 'God could have created a world containing no moral evil, only by creating one without significantly free persons. But it is possible that every essence suffers from transworld depravity; so it's possible that God could not have created a world containing moral good but no moral evil' (Plantinga, *ibid.* p. 53).

[3] M. B. Ahern, *The problem of evil* (London, 1971), p. 9.

abstract problems (justice and goodness must go together) and of specific concrete problems (persecution points to demons, not to present retribution).

Today, as in the second century, while defensive arguments are important, the ground of hope is more fundamental because it answers the disquiet that no argument can dispel. Marcion, despite his arguments, ultimately *felt* that the wonder of the God of the Gospels was incompatible with creation, crucifixion or the history of the Old Testament. Gnosticism, as von Balthasar has shown,[1] is an aesthetic rather than a logical thing: God could only be contaminated or distorted by contact with the earth. Now, evil is not an unpleasant surprise to the believer. He knows God as the one who is present in a time of suffering.[2] God is tied to the mystery of the world and is inaccessible apart from it. He is known in the crucified God, for his being is in his becoming and he must enter the realm of that which is not.[3] Only in the event of Christ do we come to know that God is 'for us'.[4]

So in Tertullian, the defensive arguments against Marcion include much that is impressive; but the chief point is found in the 'humiliations and sufferings of God', which Marcion denied by his Docetism. Tertullian pleads his case:

'Was God not truly crucified? Or when truly crucified did he not truly die? Or when he had indeed truly died, did he not truly rise again? Was Paul false when he determined to know nothing among us but Jesus crucified, when he impressed on us that Jesus had been buried and taught that he rose again? If so, then our faith is false and all that we hope from Christ is an illusion . . . Spare the one hope of all the world, you who destroy the necessary dishonour of faith! Whatever is unworthy of God is of help to me. I am safe if I am not ashamed of my Lord' [*Carn.* 5].

[1] H. U. von Balthasar, 'Der ästhetische Mythos', in *Eine theologische Ästhetik*, vol. 2 (Einsiedeln, 1962), pp. 33–45.
[2] Martin Luther, 'Großer Katechismus', *Die Bekenntnisschriften der evangelisch-lutherischen Kirche* (Göttingen, 1963), pp. 566f.:
   'Hast du ein solch Herz, daß sich eitel Guts zu ihm versehen kann, sonderlich in Nöten und Mangel, dazu alles gehen und fahren lassen, was nicht Gott ist, so hast du den einigen rechten Gott.'
[3] Jüngel, *Gott als Geheimnis*, p. 305.
[4] Jüngel, *Gottes Sein*, p. 120.

6 History

'History is bunk.' The question of the continuity of past events was important for the first Christians. Yet for some, like the Gnostics, it was trivial; for others, like Marcion, it was bad, not merely bunk but bad bunk. For the Gnostics, the most it could provide was a reflection of the divine reality, for nothing really happened outside God. For Marcion, the past told of another God, and whatever it said was wrong. Yet Justin, and those who came after him, loved the story of the past, they loved talking about it, and making sense of it. They were, indeed, too keen about it for most of their readers today. Justin fills page after page with too many references to the Old Testament, with the way in which it makes sense of Jesus and Jesus makes sense of it.

With the apologists, this interest in history begins, like everything else, as a response to a challenge, a rebuttal of an objection. What right had Christians to make such extraordinary claims for their knowledge of God? If they had the truth, did they think that nothing true had ever been said before? They used the Jewish scriptures, but they did not keep the Law of the God who had spoken in them. Marcion and the Gnostics were at least consistent: they did not pretend that the most high God or the divine *Pleroma* had anything to do with the Old Testament.

The writer to Diognetus poses the problem in its simplest form: why did the Gospel come so late?[1] Even if it were not absurd that anyone should have all perfection here, why did God leave it so late to give what he had to give? For Greek and for Jew, what was true was ancient and what was new was false. Anything that had stood the test of time was true; but Christianity had come late. The problem for Christians was: how could they as late arrivals fit into the plan of a God who ruled over all history and all the world? They replied that Christ made sense of history by giving it a plan and a pivot, so that it was not the mere reflection of heavenly realities, lacking purpose or going around in circles. For Christians, the importance

[1] *Ad Diog.* 1.

163

of Jesus was that he enabled them to understand the past and to face the future; when they talked about history, they talked about a divine plan or dispensation (*oikonomia*), and about everything coming together or being summed up in Christ (*anakephalaiōsis*). The two ideas have to be kept together, because only Christ's significance as the pivot of history gave it continuity. Something of this puzzle comes through in a recent novel where a rather conservative and timid man falls in love, and in that experience sees himself able to cope with his past and future for the first time.

> 'I saw her now, a girl, a stranger, and yet the most familiar person in the world – my Italian girl and yet also the first woman, as strange as Eve to the dazed awakening Adam. I said, "It's odd, I scarcely know you, yet I feel now for the first time my past is really continuous with my future".'[1]

In brief, the first reason why Christians were concerned with history was the objection, 'Why so late?' The second reason was that they had found for the first time a sense of continuity between the past and the future, through the summing-up of all things in Christ. Thirdly, as a development of this, they saw themselves united with Christ, and in him the past and the future belonged to them. This is what Paul wrote of in 1 Corinthians, when Corinthians were splitting up their Christianity and saying, 'We belong to Paul,' 'We belong to Cephas,' 'We belong to Apollos.' Paul replied: 'All things are yours and you are Christ's and Christ is God's'.[2] In Christ they had entered into the fullness of what God had done. Justin and Clement were able to say: 'Whatever has been well said in the past belongs to us Christians'.[3] Justin was not a naïve intellectual imperialist; he was simply stating what it meant to believe that Jesus was the Logos: in Christ was all truth, and by the simplicity of the cross, by the total offering of self to God that the Christian made in faith, all things were his as Christ, the universal lord of all, was his lord, and Christ was God's.[4] So the ability to see continuity in history came from the ability

---

[1] Murdoch, *The Italian Girl*, pp. 170f.
[2] 1 Corinthians 3: 22f.
[3] Justin, 2 *A*. 13.4; Clement, *S*. 1.7.37f.
[4] Cf. Käsemann, *Jesus means freedom*, pp. 78f.

to see the totality of all things in Christ and from the discovery of new life in him.

The ideas of continuity and recapitulation are found in Romans 5: 12–21; Ephesians 1: 10 and in Ignatius of Antioch [*Eph.* 20.1]. A sense of history seems to have a hold on Asia Minor and dominates early theology from that area. Ignatius sees history as culminating in Christ, who is the beginner of a new humanity; in some ways Judaism anticipated Christ but in most ways Christ built on the failures of the past. He changed death to life, darkness to light. His cosmic stature was evident in the behaviour of the stars at his birth when one star so outshone the others that they gathered around and worshipped it. Ignatius sees the universality of Christ in time and space, in history and cosmology.[1]

This group of problems may be arranged in the following way:

(1) Is there continuity in history? Why did Jesus come so late?
(2) Has history a centre?
(3) Where do we stand in history now?
(4) Does man make progress in the course of history?
(5) How will it all end?

1 Is there continuity in history? Why did Jesus come so late?

Justin's account of history is clearly a response to the questions raised by Jews, Marcion and philosophers.[2] He is concerned with development in his account of the Law, but not in his account of the Logos. There is a progression from the imperfect Mosaic Law to the perfect Law of Christ. The Mosaic Law contained some prescriptions that were there simply because the

---

[1] Ignatius, *Eph.* 19. As introduction to the concepts of dispensation and recapitulation, see Daniélou, *Gospel message*, pp. 157–83 and the specific works on the themes by D'Alès, Daniélou, Prümm and Scharl, as listed in the bibliography.

[2] Jews denied any relationship between the God of Moses and the God of the Christians; Marcion confirmed their denial and asserted the newness of Christianity; philosophers rejected the Gospel because it was new.

people were so hard of heart [*D*. 45.3]; it was God's way of adjusting to a people who had a compulsion to sacrifice. Rather than have them sacrifice to idols like the golden calf, God told them to offer sacrifices, 'as if to his name' [*D*. 19.6]. The Mosaic Law was both a step on the way and a type or image of the Christ who was to come. The new Law of Christ is eternal, not temporary, and universal, not narrowly national. Yet there was only one God, who gave the old Law and who came in Christ.

'Now I have indeed read, Trypho, that there would be a final law and covenant supreme over all, which now all men should keep if they wish to pursue the inheritance of God. For the law given on Horeb is now old and belongs to you (Jews) only; but this law is for all men absolutely. A law placed against a previous law nullifies the previous law, and a covenant which succeeds another supersedes the previous covenant. Christ was given to us – an eternal and final law and a faithful covenant, after which there shall be no law, no precept, no commandment' [*D*. 11.2].

Here there is a unity of divine action in history. Time plays a part. What was once valid is now not valid at all. Yet even here the contrast is between an image and a reality. 'For we who have been led to God by this crucified Messiah are the true, spiritual Israel, the stock of Judah, Jacob, Isaac and Abraham' [*D*. 11.5].

The account of the Word sown in the hearts of men has already been examined. All men have received a seed of the Word, and many who came before Christ lived *meta logou*. In Christ came the wholeness of the Word and this wholeness differs from the part as reality differs from a copy.

The appearance of the Word to prophets and patriarchs is again part of history but hardly the subject of any real development.[1] For Justin has to prove a quite different point with the theophanies of the Old Testament. The appearances of God in the Old Testament are ground for plurality in the Godhead. So God said: 'Let us make', with a deliberate plural; still more

---

[1] Cf. de Lubac on the absence of the modern concept of history in both Irenaeus and Origen: *Histoire et esprit* (Paris, 1950), p. 248: 'L'"évolutionisme" de l'un, comme le symbolisme de l'autre, est avant tout affaire de doctrine.'

obviously, God the Father could not drop everything and come down on earth to visit man. When he appeared to his people, he appeared in his Son or word. This Son was uniquely and supremely Son of God [*1 A.* 23.3]. He was God's first-born and was prior to all created things [*D.* 100.2]. His incarnation is all the more credible because he had appeared on earth previously. 'If indeed we know that God appeared in so many forms to Abraham, Isaac and Moses, how are we puzzled and unable to believe that according to the will of the Father of all things, it has been possible for him to have been born man of a virgin?' [*D.* 75.4].

Justin, even in this brief examination, has three accounts of history or the plan of salvation. Only the first has any development or progression – the Law is a gradual growth from Moses through to perfection in Christ. The account of the spermatic Logos points to two stages – the partial *logos* in all men, received and obeyed by lawgivers and philosophers, and the whole Logos present in the incarnate Christ. Yet even this division is broken down when the theophanies of the Old Testament are considered; for the one Son of God and divine Word assisted at creation and appeared to the patriarchs of old. Since still further accounts of history may be found in Justin, all that may be concluded is that he has a sense of God's movement in history. God acts in history in a variety of ways. Justin's various views depend on the particular objection that he attempts to rebut. The first view meets objections of Jew, Marcionite and philosopher, the second that of the philosopher and the third that of the Jew. The one common element is a central point of reference in the incarnate Logos.

What is fragmentary and partial in Justin may be seen on a grand scale in Irenaeus, where the hints and half-thoughts are expanded with enthusiasm and imagination. Irenaeus has the deepest sense of God's activity in history, of God's plan, which is worked out with detail and particularity beyond the recognition of men. Why so late? Because men are men and their reactions to God are so different. Why so late? Because God is patient, thorough, universal, and because God uses time to achieve his purpose. These ideas were already hinted in Justin and Ignatius but they were never developed. Irenaeus takes the apologetic theme and turns it to positive advantage. If salvation had not taken so long to come, men would never have seen its universal extent in time and space. There is one God, over all time and space, who intelligently uses time as he uses space. The emptiness of the transcendent Monad has been overcome by the infinite and intelligible variety of his created works – Tertullian saw this most clearly. Irenaeus did with time what the account of creation had done with space. He claimed it all for God and he showed how it made sense whenever it was examined. (Now there are few things as tedious as the massed detail of scripture so it is essential to see the universality that dominated Irenaeus' account of God.)

It is hard not to connect Irenaeus' universal vision with his environment. True, he came from Asia Minor where these things were important. But he lived at Lyons and he had before his eyes one of the great landscapes of the world. To the east stood the Alps, visible on a clear day, and from them flowed the Rhône. From the mountains to the north came the Saône. At the foot of the steep hill on which the Forum stood, these two great rivers came together and flowed on another 200 miles to the sea. From and around this hill Irenaeus thought his long thoughts on *oikonomia*. He could hardly have had a better place. This reference to *Sitz im Leben* may be supported, in an unexpected way, from the political structure of Gaul and the position of Lyons at the centre. 'All the threads of Roman public service in this great region converged at Lugdunum and were gathered up at that centre.'[1] How far theologians, like poets, may be affected by their landscape,[2] is a matter of precarious probability; but he would be a dull reader who found nothing of Africa in Tertullian and nothing of Egypt in Clement.[3] Justin is more difficult: insulated in a military colony at Nablus, he needed the sea-side for the wide setting of his *Dialogue* and was never sure of his Roman environment.[4]

To Irenaeus, God's plan is continuous. Adam never left the hands of God [*H.* 5.1.3]. There was no break in God's work. There is one God, father, founder, maker, creator, who made

---

[1] James S. Reid, *The municipalities of the Roman Empire* (Cambridge, 1913), p. 179.

[2] See Gilbert Highet, *Poets in a landscape* (Pelican Books, 1959), for the relation between major Roman writers and their landscape.

[3] Tertullian went so far as to claim that in the frigid north, the soul became stiff, torpid and incapable of thought (*An.* 25).

[4] Justin's mistrust in his environment was, in the end, confirmed by his martyrdom.

all things in heaven and earth. He formed man, saved Noah, guided Abraham, Isaac and Jacob, spoke through Law and prophets, revealed himself in Christ, was made known by the apostles and believed in by the Church. He is one God, the father of the Lord Jesus Christ, revealed in the Son, who is his Word [*H.* 1.47.2]. The scriptures of both the Old and New Covenants point to the one and only God, who promised through the prophets and sent his herald in John and his salvation in the Word made flesh [*H.* 3.9.1].

God's plan is just. The righteousness of God lies behind both Testaments; it may appear in different ways but it is the same enduring righteousness of God [*H.* 4.44.1]. God's plan is rational. Like a great architect he drew up his plan of salvation. He chose the patriarchs to be saved and prepared his people to follow. He produced prophets so that men might learn to receive his Spirit and to speak with him. In the desert, he gave a Law that was appropriate to the place and the state of his people. Those who turned to him received his inheritance. 'There, in a variety of ways, he adjusted the human race to agreement with salvation' [*H.* 4.25.2]. There was always a reason for what God did. He gave circumcision, not as the completion of righteousness, but simply to keep the race of Abraham distinct (*H.* 4.27.1). Even Jerusalem was built and forsaken on rational grounds: the Law began with Moses and ended with John; Jerusalem began with David and ended with the New Covenant. 'For God does all things by measure and in order; nothing is unmeasured with him because nothing is out of order' [*H.* 4.6]. God's reason and plan are constantly related to time. What is right at one point is wrong at another, but it is the same God who acts justly and rationally at all times. This God made temporal things for man and through time brings man to the ripeness and fruit of immortality.

God's plan is an earthy plan. At the marriage feast at Cana, the Lord did not reject the wine that God had made in the vineyard. It was good wine, but the new wine that Christ made from water was better [*H.* 3.11.9]. The imagery of creation is constantly used by Irenaeus to describe God's ways. When defending or explaining God's temporary purpose with Jerusalem he points to destruction in the course of nature. There comes a time when the wheat is gathered and the straw discarded, when the twigs are pruned for the sake of the grapes.

169

Nature continues the ways of God. When the fruit of liberty had come in Christ and when those who bore fruit had been scattered from Jerusalem, then it was right that Jerusalem should be forsaken [*H.* 4.5].

God's plan continues to the present, although it reached its end in Christ and there is no more to be given. The covenants of Adam, Noah and Moses are summed up in the fourth and final covenant of Christ [*H.* 3.11.11]; but because this final covenant makes man new and gives him a fresh start, the plan of God goes on in the teaching of the apostles, which points to the one God who gave four covenants, who made all things and who is the father of Christ and the God of glory [*H.* 3.12.14]. The apostles lived as they taught, even fulfilling the Law of Moses to indicate the oneness of God [*H.* 3.12.9]. The faith of Abraham was the same as our faith and like him we look to the future for the fulfilment of God's promise and we see God's kingdom by faith [*H.* 4.35]. The Church now reaps the word that was sown by prophets and patriarchs concerning Christ [*H.* 4.39]. That is why the message of the apostles is authenticated by scripture, for they had a true version long before the heretics started to spread their errors [*H.* 3.24.2].

God's plan is concerned with the perception of his people and their direct relationship to himself. In the earliest days, his Law was written on their hearts; but when, in Egypt, they had lost his righteousness and love, he revealed himself as a voice, which led them out of Egypt to become his disciples and followers [*H.* 4.27.3]. Jeremiah reminded the people that God did not bring them out of Egypt to sacrifice, but to hear his voice [*H.* 4.29.3]. The Law prescribed gifts and sacrifices as types of heavenly things. Since earth and heaven were made by the same God, it is right that man's vision should be led from one to the other [*H.* 4.32]. The prophets saw the mysteries and the plans but not the face of God. The still, small voice that spoke to Elijah pointed to the man who was to come in meekness and mildness and quietness, not breaking the bruised reed or quenching smoking flax. Certainly Moses, Elijah and Ezekiel had visions of heaven, but they did not see God at any time. They saw parables or reflections of his glory, and prophecies of things to come. They saw the plan but not the end. The brightness of the Father's glory came only in his only begotten Son, in his Word made flesh [*H.* 4.34.9 and 10]. The plan of

God points to the patience of God, a God who accommodates himself to man, and man to himself as he works gently through providence.[1] Man was a child who needed to learn slowly.[2] The hands of God worked with artistic skill from Adam onwards, shaping and guiding.

God's plan is universal. The whole of human life is shaped by God, who left nothing out. Jesus lived through the different stages of human life to reach the age of fifty so that no period of man's life should be untouched by the divine word [*H.* 2.33]. In the incarnation Jesus became mediator between man and God. Prior to this event and especially in it, man became accustomed to receive God and God became accustomed to live in man [*H.* 3.21.2]. Yet God's plan has been ignored by the heretics. Marcion claims that God did not come to his own but came to what was foreign [*H.* 3.11.7]; but the God who made the world and acted always for the good of man has always been present with his creation [*H.* 5.29.1; 3.12.14; 5.16.1]. The Gnostics placed the divine economy inside the *Pleroma*, while Irenaeus put it firmly in history.[3] The unity of God's plan points to the one end of man's salvation through a providence that the Gnostics cannot see.[4] Here is the final thrust of the argument of Irenaeus. The heretics speak of a divine internal economy (from a total of 120 examples in Irenaeus, *oikonomia* is applied thirty-three times to a Gnostic

---

[1] K. Prümm, 'Göttliche Planung und menschliche Entwicklung nach Irenäus, Adversus Haereses, II', *Schol.*, 13 (1938), 364: 'Irenäus ist der Theologe der Langmut, der Anpassung Gottes, der Theologie der sanften Wege der Vorsehung'.

[2] *E.* 12. Cf. von Balthasar, *Herrlichkeit*, vol. 2, p. 78: 'einmal, dass der Mensch sich als ein Kind benimmt und erst langsam, durch Erfahrung, klug wird'.

[3] Bengsch, *Heilsgeschichte und Heilswissen*, p. 28. R. A. Markus, 'Pleroma and fulfilment. The significance of history in St. Irenaeus' opposition to Gnosticism', *VigChr.* 8 (1954), 216ff.

Bengsch sets out the parallel positions:

Gnostiker	Irenäus
Grundposition: Das Geschehen im Pleroma	Grundposition: Historische Existenz Christi
Abbild: Jesu Leben, und zwar doketisch gefasst	Vorbild: Prophetenwort, bildlich gefasst
Beweis: Prophetenwort, 'historisch' gefasst	Beweis: Evangelienstelle, wenn auch falsch gedeutet

[4] Prümm, 'Göttliche Planung', pp. 356–9.

doctrine);[1] but Irenaeus shows a divine economy that belongs to human history and goes beyond anything that Gnostics might propose.

So Irenaeus, in response to the Gnostic threat, presents the most comprehensive theology of history in early Christian thought. Only Augustine's *City of God* can stand with it. In the theology of the Old Testament, which looks back to the beginning of creation and forward to the new thing that God would do, such a vision of history might be found. Yet, for Irenaeus as for Justin, it gained ultimate significance only as the 'proof' of the apostolic preaching and needed the Platonic contrast between image and reality. The best aid in understanding is Michelangelo's ceiling of the Sistine Chapel, which sets out the first great events of saving history, under the central dominance of Christ in judgement and mercy.

In Tertullian many of the same themes recur; he finds God in history as he does in nature and in the soul.[2] Against Marcion, he insists that there is unity and coherence in history [*Marc.* 3.2]. In its pattern, the darkness of man's sin is interwoven with the righteousness of God and his redeeming love; victory remains with the righteousness of God [*Marc.* 2.29]. Tertullian follows Irenaeus also on the importance of antiquity; the writings of the prophets are at least as ancient as those of philosophers and legislators of Rome [*Ap.* 19]. The truth of a doctrine is established by its antiquity and survival [*Praescr.* 34], while heresies are marked by novelty [*Herm.* 1].

Yet Tertullian's feel for history is different: the wide sweep is less important than particular events. He could have walked straight into the motion-picture industry and produced blood-curdling biblical epics; or even better, he could have written television scripts from the Bible, with action-packed episodes every week, never needing to repeat. So he describes the ceaseless activity of God in history: God is always doing something, sending flood and fire in judgement, or messengers to proclaim his truth [*Ap.* 18]. Something is always happening for Tertullian: the Jews once enjoyed the favour of God and flourished;

---

[1] D'Alès, 'Le mot "oikonomia" dans la langue théologique de saint Irénée', *REG*, 32 (1919), 6.

[2] G. Leonhardi, *Die apologetischen Grundgedanken Tertullians, Ein Beitrag zur Apologie des Christenthums in der kirchlichen Gegenwart* (Leipzig, 1882), p. 6.

they fell through pride and are now scattered through the world, bereft of either a human or a heavenly king. Tertullian is always a slow, reluctant synthesiser; in contrast to Paul he even sees the trivialities, crudeness and irrationality of the Law as proof that it comes from the God who chooses the foolish things of the world to confound the wise [*Marc.* 5.6]. Yet the greater the particularity of his account of history, the more dramatic is its unification under one lord. The dispensation moved to fulfilment in Christ, who alone could bring fulfilment. The letter to the Laodiceans, which, he says, has been wrongly transferred to the Ephesians, tells of the mystery of God, the dispensation that only God knew, and the completion of all things in Christ [*Marc.* 5.17].

Clement goes to the opposite extreme from Tertullian. God has a wide horizon, and everything moves to his horizon according to his plan. From the beginning of history, God's purpose has never changed. His one concern is to save the flock of man. 'For this end the good God sent the good Shepherd' [*Prot.* 11.116]. Clement adds one new element: the preparation for the gospel, he insists, was carried out among Greeks as well as Jews, and philosophy was to the Greeks what the Law was to the Hebrews [*S.* 1.5.28]. God is the Father who from the beginning has sowed the one seed of his word; different times and places create different beliefs [*S.* 1.7.37]. When the Greek philosophers worshipped physical elements, they were slaves or children. 'Philosophers are children unless they have been made men in Christ' [*S.* 1.11.53]. (The central place of humility among Christian virtues has not always been obvious.) Clement argues also that the Greeks stole what truth they had, or received it from an angel, who stole it and then passed it on [*S.* 1.17.81]. This is an alternative explanation, which cannot be consistent with the earlier explanation. Clement achieves some kind of coherence by seeing philosophy as a clear example of the way in which God turns man's wrong deed to good effect.

The history of salvation moves through two phases before it comes to Christ. The newness of the gospel supersedes both Greek and Jew.

'He made a new covenant with us, for what belongs to the Greeks and the Jews is old. But we who worship him in a new way, in a third form are Christians . . . the one and only God was known by the Greeks in a gentile way, by the Jews in a Jewish way, and by us in a new and spiritual way.'

The same God has trained men under three covenants by his word. There are not three natures of men (as some heretics claim) but there are three consecutive covenants through which God has worked [*S*. 6.5.41f.].

In widening saving history to include the Greeks, Clement found it necessary to insist more strongly than ever on the one divine government of history. God gave the Law to the Hebrews, philosophy to the Greeks, and he arranged the universe to facilitate the salvation of man.

'Everything then which did not in any way obstruct man's free power of choice God made conducive to virtue and showed it to be so. So that in some way or other, even to those who can only see dimly, the true, only, one, almighty, good God might be manifest, from eternity to eternity saving by the Son, and in no way whatever the cause of wickedness' [*S*. 7.2.12].

Why so late? Is there continuity in history? Irenaeus has followed Justin's concise insights with an extended account of saving history. Tertullian preserves particularity and paradox, while Clement dwells on the universal, cosmic sweep. In each case, for different reasons, there is one keystone, which holds the construction together: Jesus Christ, the stone that human builders had rejected.

2   Has history a centre?

Can one event serve to unify a whole series of events? This was indeed the common experience of Christians but they did not find it easy to explain to others in simple terms. There was no difficulty in talking about it – Irenaeus talked about little else – but to make it clear was another matter.

There are the usual obscurities in Justin's account of the special place of Christ in God's saving plan. It seems probable that he did use the term 'recapitulation' and, more important, there is no doubt that its chief themes are present. The theme of repetition and correction is found in the Eve/Mary parallel:

'He became man through the virgin, so that just as disobedience through the serpent began, in the same way disobedience might be destroyed. For Eve, being an undefiled virgin, when she conceived the word from the serpent, bore disobedience and death. But the virgin Mary received faith and joy when the angel Gabriel brought the good news to her.'

The *Christus Victor* theme follows:

'and through her he has been born of whom, we have shown, so many scriptures have been spoken, and through whom God destroys both the serpent and the angels and men who have been assimilated to him; but he works deliverance from death to those who repent of their evil deeds and believe in him' [*D*. 100.6].

There are similar claims elsewhere. Christ became flesh, born of the virgin, to destroy the serpent and to bring shame on death [*D*. 45.4]. His death was the conquest of death [*1 A*. 63.6]. Equally clear is the metaphysical theme that Christ is the totality and perfection of that which otherwise was partial and derivative: he is *to logikon to holon*.

As with continuity, so with the necessary correlate of recapitulation, Irenaeus pours out evidence and enlarges the concept. Analysis is essential but it cannot convey all that he has to say. Within the rich imagery of recapitulation there are two sets of motifs that constantly interweave. On the one hand there are motifs of history, metaphysics and redemption: the historical theme draws parallels between the Old and New Testament, between Adam and Christ; the metaphysical theme sees in Christ the perfect form of humanity and the crowning reality of the universe; the redemptive element tells of the victory over evil that is won by the obedience of Christ. The second set of motifs is that of perfection and correction, where perfection includes universality and totality while correction includes restoration, unification, incorporation and representation. This second set of motifs is seen by Irenaeus as the righteousness of God, the power of God by which Jesus, the just man, is also justifier.

When we put the two sets of themes (history – metaphysics – redemption and perfection – correction) together, the possibilities appear to be endless. God sums up all things by bringing them to their climax, to their perfection, and this involves correcting what has gone wrong within them and what is deficient in their present state. Historically this is seen as a development in which God has been active from the beginning of creation, and his final act in the process of development is to perfect that which he had begun in Adam, and to correct that which had gone astray in Adam. God gives an historical clue by repeating, with correction, something that had happened before. Looked at metaphysically, the summing-up of all things indicates that creation as a whole and man in particular are now in a state of deficiency, sin, corruption and death; the recapitulation of all things in Christ means that this deficiency is supplied and this sin and death are removed. Redemptively, Christ the conqueror meets, as perfect man, Satan, who embodies death and sin; by his triumph man is liberated from evil and translated into the kingdom of light.

Adam never left the hands of God; the whole story, for all its detail and complexity, has to do with man and man only. The Word who made man in the beginning came in the last days as a man capable of suffering, joining himself to his own work. When he became man, he did not then commence his own existence, but he initiated a new succession of men so that what 'we had lost in Adam, to be according to the image and likeness of God, we might recover in Jesus Christ'. Man's first defeat had been so disastrous that he could not take up the fight again; but the Word came to the depths of man's defeat in divine humility and in the death that man had incurred. By this act man was saved and God's plan completed [*H.* 3.19.1 and 2]. So Jesus, the second Adam, (traced back by Luke to the first Adam) brings together all generations of men in a new humanity [*H.* 3.32].

The summing-up is complete and final. What came before was always preparatory; even the Law did not deny the Son of God but showed that the wound of the serpent would be healed by faith in one who was lifted up from the earth [*H.* 4.4.2]. But now the new Law that brings freedom is greater than the Law that brought slavery. It belongs to the whole world and not to one nation only. It is now time for the partial to give way to the perfect. For the work of God is complete in Christ and we look to him who lacks nothing. There is imperfection on our side, for we have not yet achieved what is perfect; but we know where perfection is: 'When the perfect is come we shall not see another Father but him whom we now desire to see. We shall not look for another Christ and Son of God than him who was born of the Virgin Mary, who suffered, in whom we trust and whom we love' [H. 4.19.1].

The coming of the perfect does not destroy what has gone before. The natural precepts of law were given before the Law of Moses. Now the Law of Moses is extended by the righteousness that goes beyond that of the scribes and pharisees. It believes not only in the Father but also in the Son. It goes beyond description to action, not merely saying but doing. Jesus took the Law, extended it, widened it and brought it to completion. All he does is positive and never negative. The freedom of the children of God is better than the obedience of slaves; it points man to receive more of God's grace, to love him more, and to go on from glory to glory in the presence of the Father. Freedom does not cut the link between man and God, but replaces it with an ever-deepening communion [H. 4.24].

Completion means unity and universality. It is the work of one God in one world and one history of salvation for one humanity. For the Word is able 'to join the end to the beginning, that is to join man to God' [H. 4.34.4]. To save all, he must descend into hell. He did not forget, says Jeremiah,[1] those who slept, but he went to them so that he might unite the work of salvation in every age among all men [H. 4.36.1]. There was only one way to reach all men and that was through the pain and agony of death [H. 4.55.3].

Universality cannot stay in the past, for the world continues and God has to deal with those who were neither past nor present in the time of Christ. The Lord has given to a new community of farmers his vineyard, which was once rented to the dispensation of Moses. The new farmers are the Church, which still goes on; suffering for righteousness and enduring afflictions, the Church may grow weak, but quickly increases in numbers again [H. 4.58.2; 4.54].

The heretics have settled for a very inferior goal. For all that

---

[1] At H. 3.22, Irenaeus attributes the same passage to Isaiah. Justin, (D. 72), assigns the passage to Jeremiah and accuses the Jews of excising it from their scriptures.

the Marcionites claim, their most high God has achieved the salvation of Paul and of no one else. God is not so limited in his resources that he has only one apostle who understands the dispensation of his Son. All things are caught up in Christ, who is man, visible and capable of suffering, gathering all humanity into himself, and is lord of heaven and supreme over things spiritual and invisible. As head of the Church he draws all things to himself [*H*. 3.17.6].

Universal victory and salvation were achieved by the way of the cross alone. Obedience and humility removed the results of man's disobedience. Man was made from virgin soil, disobeyed God and lost the gift of life. The new man was born from a virgin, obeyed God and brought many to righteousness and salvation. The disobedience or obedience of the one affects the many [*H*. 3.19.6]. Obedience brings life instead of death but comes only through humility. Mary is used by God as, at creation, dust was used by God, to form humanity [*H*. 3.30]. The dust points to flesh in all its substance and pain. The Word received flesh from Mary to become man and son of man. If he were not what we are, his suffering would be of little consequence; but, sharing the body of our flesh, he has summed up his own work of creation [*H*. 3.31.1]. Only the meek will inherit the earth. The flesh of Jesus is proved by his hunger, weariness and tears. As by the blood and water that flowed from his side, only by physical suffering could he save the work of his hands [*H*. 3.32.2].

His salvation is earthy as he unites with man's ancient substance to bring man to life, perfection and God [*H*. 5.1.3]. His flesh proves the salvation of our flesh and the truth of his humanity [*H*. 5.14.1]. Through his life on earth he discovered just how much his creation had suffered through the wickedness of man. So he gave himself to every kind of healing to bring life to man's manifold need [*H*. 5.12.5]. Every detail of his actions shows his concern for the variety of man's need. He healed the blind man with clay and taught him who had first shaped him and who had given him life [*H*. 5.15.3]. So many things reminded man that his present saviour was his first creator. He had called to man in the evening when Adam hid, as he called again and sought out the descendants of Adam [*H*. 5.15.4]. By hanging on a tree he pointed to the disobedience of the tree where man had been separated from God. The error,

disobedience and sin of Eve caused her to flee from God while
the good news and obedience of Mary caused her to carry God.
The cunning of the serpent is overthrown by the dove [*H.*
5.19.1].

In all these strange acts of humility man is brought back in
triumph to God. The Lord suffered on the day of man's disobedience, the sixth day of creation, the day on which man was
made. On this day the suffering of the Lord brings men from
death to the life of a new creation [*H.* 5.23.2]. Only the son of
the Father who is the one God and creator would have summed
up all things [*H.* 5.21.2]. Only a man born of woman could
have reversed the defeat that came through woman and
brought life through the victory of a man [*H.* 5.21.1]. So man's
enemy has been defeated as the serpent that led man captive in
Adam has been crushed and trampled under the heel [*H.*
5.21.1]. The Lord has led back into paradise those who have
obeyed his call. He sums up in himself the things of earth and of
heaven. He unites man to the Spirit and makes the Spirit dwell
in man. Through this Spirit we see and hear and speak [*H.*
5.20.2].

As before, Tertullian and Clement fix on different aspects,
Tertullian favouring history and Clement leaning to metaphysics. Yet neither can dispense with the element he tends to
neglect. Tertullian sees the work of Christ in summing-up as
moving the end to the beginning and the beginning to the end.
That is what it means to be Alpha and Omega. Every *oikonomia*
is taken by Christ to its end, which is at the same time a
restoration to its beginning: 'Just as Alpha rolls on to Omega
and then Omega rolls back to Alpha, so he might show in himself the way down from beginning to end and the way from end
to beginning' [*Mon.* 5.2]. The work of Christ begins a new age.
The gospel thundered forth and shattered the old system; but
the Spirit confirmed the condemnation of sacrifice, fornication
and blood and this last testament can never be changed [*Pud.*
12]. The new order of *Christiana disciplina* dates from the event
of Christ. 'No one was perfect before the discovery of the order
of faith, no one was a Christian before Christ returned to heaven,
no one was holy before the Holy Spirit came from heaven to
define the discipline itself' [*Pud.* 11.3].

Tertullian exploits the element of paradox in recapitulation.
The new creation moves to a higher level. The first man, born

from the virgin earth, is followed by the second man, born of flesh that had not been given generation but had been projected by God into a life-giving spirit [*Carn.* 17.3, 4; 19.1, 2].[1] 'O Christ, even in your newness you are old!' [*Marc.* 4.21]. The newness of Christ changes all things from carnal to spiritual [*Orat.* 1]. The prayer of the Old Covenant worked with fire, beasts and famine; but Christian prayer is spiritual and more effective, producing endurance, expanding grace with virtue and faith with knowledge. Only prayer can overcome God, but it cannot be used to bad effect [*Orat.* 28]. Further contrasts between the new order and the old can be made. The first Adam was married once; but the second Adam pointed a higher celibate way. Christians should not fall below the lesser of these two standards by marrying a second time [*Mon.* 17]. Prior to the new order of faith no one had reached perfection. Prior to Christ's ascent into heaven and the gift of the Holy Spirit there were no Christians and no holy men [*Pud.* 11]. There are still fasts and seasons to be observed: not those of the Old Testament but those of the New. Jewish ceremonies should be disregarded and the new times of celebration observed [*Iei.* 14]. The difference between the old and the new is seen in the rite of circumcision; this was given as a sign to Israel and the sign is fulfilled in those who obey from the heart [*Iud.* 3].

Yet paradox depends on unity as well as difference. Marcion has failed to see the continuity of God's work on the ground that one God can only do one thing. But how can the second god be superior to the first god, when he merely restores what the first god has created? The victory of Christ reverses the result of man's first battle with the devil. God allows the conflict to take place so that mankind might succeed where it had failed before. Tertullian shares with his contemporaries, Irenaeus and Clement, the importance of the descent into hell: it fulfilled the need for Christ to truly die and made it possible for prophets and patriarchs to share in his gospel and his grace [*An.* 55]. So for Tertullian, while the tensions of history are always striking, their variety serves but to prove the greatness of the

---

[1] Christ is born of the Father as spirit and of the virgin as man. He could not have had an earthly father because his human birth is simply an extension of his birth from the Father (*Carn.* 17.3). W. Bender, *Die Lehre über den Heiligen Geist bei Tertullian* (München, 1961), p. 73.

sole, sovereign lordship of Christ. Only a truly victorious lord could hold such extreme opposites under his sway.

With Clement unity and reason prevail; the historical aspect of summing-up is less important than is the metaphysical or the redemptive. His account of the Logos as one and many will require separate treatment. Here it will be sufficient to learn how Clement saw the universal work of Christ. So striking is his sense of metaphysical and redemptive totality, so confident is his message that in Christ all is accomplished, that there is little place for future eschatology.

Yet there is no lack of movement. The *Protrepticus* begins and ends with the triumph of Christ. The power of the new song has made men out of stones, brought the dead to life, ordered the whole universe harmoniously. It is now time, to hurry to the Lord and Saviour whose salvation first came to the Hebrews in the burning bush and pillar of cloud [*Prot.* 1.4f. and 8]. John the Baptist tried urgently to prepare men for great salvation and the inheritance of heaven in Christ [*Prot.* 1.10]. For nothing less than this is the consequence of Christ's victory: 'The Lord was laid low, and men rose up; and he who fell from paradise receives as the reward of obedience something greater than paradise, even heaven itself' [*Prot.* 11.111]. The time has come, the trumpet has sounded for Christ's army to possess in peace the kingdom of heaven [*Prot.* 11.116]. He himself calls on all men to be restored in the likeness of God to all that God can now give.

'For I desire, I long to impart to you this grace, bestowing on you the perfect gift of immortality; and I confer on you both the Word and the knowledge of God, my complete self. This I am, this God wills, this is symphony, this the harmony of the Father . . . I desire to restore you according to the archetypal model, that you may also become like me' [*Prot.* 12.120].

It is now proper to describe the good Christian as the only rich, wise and able man. He is God's image and likeness, for by Jesus Christ he is righteous, holy and wise. So the *Protrepticus* ends with an unqualified claim that in Christ all things are now complete and that therefore the confident enthusiasm of the entire work has a sure foundation.

Clement defines the sense in which there is something still to come. On the one hand, those who were once darkness are now light in the Lord and there is no intermediate state between darkness and light; on the other hand, the resurrection of believers is yet to come and only then will the end be reached. Yet this is simply the reception of what is now promised, the arrival that is already anticipated. 'For eternity and time are not the same, neither is the attempt and the final result; but both refer to the same object and concern the same person' [*Paed.* 1.6.115].

There is no limit to the present kingdom of the Son of God, nor to the scope of his salvation. Already he is supreme and he orders everything as the Father wills. He holds the helm of the universe and, with untiring power and perfect omniscience, he guides everything to its hidden divine end. He is everywhere, in unrestricted omnipresence, administering all things by his power. All men are his in different ways – some as friends, some as faithful servants and others as servants only [*S.* 7.2.5]. He cares for all and has adapted his goodness to the differences among men; he has no favourites, but has called all men equally, pouring out his goodness ungrudgingly. 'How is he saviour and Lord, if he is not the saviour and Lord of all?' [*S.* 7.2.7]. He is like the sun, which shines over the whole earth and sky, and sends his rays into every corner; nothing is too small for his notice and concern [*S.* 7.3.21]. God is all ear and eye, if one may be allowed this rash kind of language [*S.* 7.7.37].

So each writer struggles to convey the historical, metaphysical and redemptive aspects of the central event of history. Justin announces the themes, Irenaeus develops them with untiring imagination, while Tertullian and Clement emphasise opposite aspects. Nowhere can history make sense without metaphysics; even Irenaeus can say nothing without the concepts of image and reality, life and death, part and whole, particularity and perfection, the corruption of evil and the preserving power of good. On the other hand, nowhere can metaphysics stand still and dispense with history. Clement's acute sense of spiritual reality is coloured by a sense of movement and expanding novelty that is both biblical and evangelical: God makes all things new and if any man be in Christ there is a new creation.

3   Where do we stand in history now?

We stand in the time of the Church and this means different things to different writers. Justin's account of the Church is entirely dependent on his view of history or continuity and his debate with the Jews. How can Christians belong to God, when they admit that God's promise came to Abraham and his seed? He claims that the failure of ancient Israel has caused God to choose again. The claim that the Church is now the true Israel runs from the beginning [*D*. 11.3] to the end of the *Dialogue* [*D*. 123–35]. It is indeed the whole point of that work. By her sin Judaism has forfeited the right to be God's people and another Israel goes forward as the new people of God, descended from the patriarchs, who were before the Law. 'For we who have been led to God by the crucified Christ are the true spiritual Israel, the stock of Judah, Jacob, Isaac and Abraham (who received the testimony and blessing of God while uncircumcised because of his faith and was called the father of many nations) as shall be proved in the course of our discourse.' Yet Justin's simple ecclesiology does not mean that he is unaware of the Church; he has a lively awareness of Christian solidarity, and he is the first writer to make extensive use of the word 'Christian'. He defends this name and ridicules the persecution that is directed against the name alone, for men should be examined and judged on what they have done, not on the name they carry [*1 A*. 7.4]. Justin is proud of the name and wants everyone to know that he is a Christian [*2 A*.13.1], for Christians have publicly proved the power of Christ's name in the exorcism of demons everywhere [*2 A*. 6.6] and they care for one another in a practical way: 'Those of us who are wealthy help those who are in need; and we always stand by one another' [*1 A*. 67.1].

Irenaeus has a deep sense of the corporate reality of the Church as that which links him back through Polycarp, John and others to the words and works of Jesus. The claim that binds him through history to the one central event is a human chain of men who had heard and known the word of life. The warmth of this concept is chilled by the existence of rival traditions, as heresies force definitions and disputes upon all who claim to be the Church. For the present stage of the history of salvation is shown in the Church, which extends from the past through the present to the future, teaching and sanctifying, established in one place, and yet universal.[1] It is the extension of Christ in the world as he holds his redeemed members together in himself. The crowning event of his salvation stands at the centre of history, and there can be no doubt of his total triumph. All truth was received by the apostles on the day of Pentecost, and nothing can be added to their preaching [*H.* 3.1.1]. The work of the prophets was handed on to the apostles, who handed the same task on to the Church [*H.* 5. Preface]. Beginning from the centre of history, the Church possesses the perfect teaching of the apostles [*H.* 3.4.1] and is able to give nourishment to those who come afterwards [*H.* 4.41.2]. The apostles were rich in their possession of the truth, and they passed on the fullness of truth to all. The one faith and one tradition of the Church point to the simplicity of truth and its antiquity [*H.* 3.4.1.][2]

Extension and perfection go together. The true teaching must come from the succession, which begins with witnesses, it must be held firmly and constantly and it must be accessible to all men [*H.* 3.3.3; 3.12.9; 3.4.2; 3.14.1]. The teaching of the apostles is distinct from the fiction of the heretics [*H.* 4.23.2; 4.52.1]. The rule of faith provides a standard for the interpretation of scripture, for the variety of scripture must be linked with the one God and the one Christ. Apart from scripture there is no way of reaching a knowledge of salvation.[3]

On the evidence that is available, Irenaeus seems to have taken his terminology on tradition, knowledge and perfection from Gnosticism. There is no doubt that Irenaeus gives to the apostles a position of increased importance in the system of Christian truth. His account of succession is a reply to the earlier

---

[1] See L. Spikowski, *La doctrine de l'église dans S. Irénée* (Strasbourg, 1926).

[2] M. Widmann, 'Irenäus und seine theologischen Väter', *ZThK*, 54 (1957), 172f., summarises Irenaeus' attitude to Gnostics: 'Die Wahrheit ist einfach und nicht kompliziert wie eure Systeme, die Wahrheit ist alt und nicht neumodisch wie eure Meinungen, die Wahrheit ist eine und nicht vielfältig wie eure Schuldoktrinen'.

[3] Bengsch, *Heilgeschichte und Heilswissen*, p. 62: 'Ausgehend vom empfangenen Glauben, bleibt auch der "Wissende" Schüler des einzigen Lehrers Jesus Christus'.

account, which the Gnostics had put forward.[1] It remains an appropriate expression of his concern for history and continuity, as he uses the terms in his own way.

The universal sovereignty of God is shown throughout human history. The history of man is the history of God's care for his creation [*H*. 3.20; 3.32.2]. All God's actions were governed by his wisdom to suit the nature of man. There is a difference between the time when Christ was foretold and the time when Christ was finally given to man [*H*. 4.56.1]. Each period has its special character [*H*. 4.19.2; 3.17.7]. As history moves forward, salvation spreads wider to embrace all men. The Father reveals himself through his Word to all men, so that he may be seen [*H*. 4.34.5f.]. The Gentiles are raised up by the plan of salvation. The Church comes from the Gentiles [*H*. 4.46.1]. God's plan is not limited or defeated by man's failure. The guilt of the Jews does not frustrate God, and their fate serves the final end of salvation. The further salvation moves in the course of its history, the greater is the abundance of grace and the wider is its universal spread [*H*. 4.18 and 19].

Irenaeus is able to live happily and confidently between re-capitulation and parousia. There is something improper about this, for recapitulation should be the end. History, for Irenaeus, goes on under the strict condition that nothing new should be added. Grace may flow more abundantly and influence more people; but all has been accomplished in Christ and the Church possesses the fullness of Christ. The Church is where recapitulation has taken place, the goal of history in the present time; to get to the Church on *time* was the clue to history and to the meaning of the Church.[2] God in his sovereign freedom has created a new time, making all things new [*H*. 3.11.1], to remove any impropriety from the time of the Church.

Tertullian speaks with even greater enthusiasm than Irenaeus of the triumphal march of the gospel: 'We are but of yesterday, and we have filled every place among you – cities, islands, fortresses, towns and market-places, camps, tribes, companies, palace, senate and forum'. Nothing is left to the Romans but

---

[1] Cf. D. B. Reynders, 'Paradosis, Le progrès de l'idée de tradition jusqu'à S. Irénée', *RThAM*, 5 (1933), 191.

[2] For O. Cullmann, *Christ and time* (London, 1951), the saving work of Christ was done in the medium of time and found its present base in the Church.

the empty temples of their gods [*Ap.* 37]. The extent of Roman power is remarkable, but the name of Christ is spread as far, for he is adored everywhere and no king has greater favour among his subjects [*Iud.* 7]. The disciples of Christ continue his saving work and go out into all the world [*Ap.* 21]. Nothing can stop them, for the blood of Christians is the seed by which they grow [*Ap.* 50].[1] The lives of Christians confirm their testimony: 'See how they love one another and how they are prepared to die for one another' [*Ap.* 39]. If upright, pious and chaste men gather together, that is no faction; it is a *curia*. For Tertullian the Church is a community filled by the Spirit, a community of holy and good men, but not quite the divine institution of Cyprian. Yet the Church is identified by observable qualities: teaching, Law and tradition are open to examination. She receives her beginning from the apostles whose preaching laid the foundations, and whose teaching is the distinctive mark of each church they founded. The apostolic rule of faith, handed on by bishops, governs the life of the churches and provides them with a unity in every place [*Praescr.* 32]. The churches of the apostles provide the sure source of the true and original faith,[2] while the sects have no link with the apostles. Since the true home of the Church is in heaven, she is always a stranger on earth. God's Church is opposed by the church of the devil; but she is the little ship in which the apostles survive the storm.

Between the Church, the Spirit and the trinity, there is correspondence and even identity. (This comes out clearly in Tertullian's Montanist works.) Where the Spirit is, there God is. Where Christ presents himself among his members, there is the Church. Tertullian does not move beyond this notion of the Church as the community. It is never the collection of bishops, but is always that community made up of the members of Christ, who have been filled with the Spirit [*Pud.* 21]. Within the family of the Church Christians are nourished and share brotherhood under the one mother.[3] The Church is governed by pastors, by bishops, whom the apostles under providence

---

[1] Cf. T. S. Eliot, *Murder in the Cathedral* (final chorus),
   'From such ground springs that which forever renews the earth,
   Though it is forever denied.'
[2] Altendorf, *Einheit*, pp. 14f.
[3] *Ibid.* p. 23.

established [*Fug.* 23.1]. The difference between the order (*ordo*) that governs the Church and the people (*plebs*) who are governed is founded on the authority of the Church [*Cast.* 7.1]. The clergy have the more important part, the laity have a lesser part. However there is no particular sanctity attached to the office of priest, and it is wrong to imagine that some things are allowed to priests that are not allowed to the laity. Are not those who are laymen also priests, for each lives by his own faith? [*Cast.* 7.1]. The bishop does not govern by *imperium*, but by *ministerium* [*Pud.* 21.6.1]. The distinction within the Church between clergy and laity is of a practical disciplinary nature. Tertullian wants nothing of the hierarchy that Cyprian later establishes[1] but he has moved towards it at several points.

For Clement, Christians should smell differently from others, free from earthly perfumes, with a spiritual heavenly aroma [*Paed.* 2.8.65]. He has little interest in the shape and order of the Church[2] but he has great concern for the present life, in which the eschatological miracle is taking place. Present membership of heaven is decisive for conduct on earth. Gluttony leads only to death and is stupid and irrational: how much better to feast on the heavenly goodness to which the *agape* points [*Paed.* 2.1.9].

Yet the excellence of the Gnostic is never a solitary achievement and what Christ has done can be known only within his body, the Church. The gifts of God come to various parts of the *body* of Christ so that all may grow to the full stature of Christ. Perfection is found in different ways by different gifts, by prophets in prophecy, the righteous in their righteousness, by martyrs in confession and by the preachers in their preaching. The apostles were the one exception, for they were perfect in all they did, wrote, knew and preached [*S.* 4.21.133f.]. Within the Church there is an eternal springtime, a youthfulness in which wisdom flowers perpetually. God comforts his children as a mother comforts her young: 'The mother draws her children to herself, and we seek our *mother* the church' [*Paed.* 1.5.21]. The image of mother and children has three chief points: it indicates the youth of the Christian in his ageless springtime, it shows the need for growth towards perfection

---

[1] *Ibid.* p. 27.

[2] See the critical account of H. von Campenhausen, *Ecclesiastical authority and spiritual power* (London, 1969), pp. 196–212.

and it underlines the present perfection of divine activity. 'There is one father of all and one universal word: the Holy Spirit is one and the same everywhere and there is one only virgin mother. I love to call her the church' [*Paed.* 1.6.42]. The mother feeds the child with the milk of the Word. Clement tangles the metaphor vigorously but clambers out by means of recapitulation. 'The word is all to the child, both father and mother, tutor and nurse' [*Paed.* 1.6.42].

The holiness of the Church derives from the God to whose honour was established 'that precious temple built by no craftsman's skill, no, not even decorated by an angel's hand, but made into a shrine by the will of God himself'. This church is 'not the place but the congregation of the saints', the shrine most worthy of God. Of all God's creatures, the gnostic is most precious and in the righteous soul God finds his holy place. Here again Clement allows for imperfection within perfection. Those who are on the way to receiving knowledge are already consecrated in God's sight [*S.* 7.5.29].

So God is carried within those whom he carries and they are already divine and holy. They have no desires beyond God, who is within them, and they enter heaven by their knowledge, rising above all spiritual powers to the highest thrones [*S.* 7.13.82]. Such a man despises earthly treasures, for he is an intimate friend of his Lord and a prince and king, who lives in holiness and prayer. In this prayer he rules over all time; he gives thanks for past and present and for the future, which is already his through faith [*S.* 7.12.79; 6.9.75]. By constant prayer he is so joined to God that he may ask to understand the government of all creation and finally to see God face to face [*S.* 6.12.102].

Where are we now in the great divine plan? Those who believe have become part of that plan. For Justin they have been cut from the belly of Christ himself to be his new, spiritual Israel. For Irenaeus they are part of the ever-widening river of grace that flows through the apostles. For Tertullian they are the community filled by the Spirit in whose presence Christ is still to be found. For Clement they are already living the life of heaven under the constant care of their virgin mother, the Church. The striking eschatological, spiritual reality of Christian community is derived from its place after the summing-up of all things in Christ. Nothing more may be added but, almost incredibly, nothing may be lost as the river of grace spreads beyond its first banks. So the stream that unites Christian to Christian is a heavenly one that he can neither create nor fully understand. So much more terrible are the heresies that threaten this community and make its life a treasure to be guarded fiercely.

4   Does man make progress in the course of history?

Is the Christian conflict one of defence or one of conquest? This is an important factor in the problem of evil. An influential part of Irenaeus' thought speaks of progress in man's maturity and development. Some passages suggest that man, created as an infant, reaches perfection by natural development through clearly defined phases [*H*. 4.63.2 and 3]. Other passages speak rather of Adam's loss being restored by the work of Christ [*H*. 5.12.5]. There appears to be some disharmony between these two themes. On closer examination, the contradiction disappears.[1] Man has fallen in Adam, but God's grace is able to turn the racial catastrophe into part of the process of redemption. There is no doubt that the theme of progress and growth is widespread and striking in Irenaeus. It was God's plan that the animal man should precede the spiritual [*H*. 5.1.3]. Man had to reach maturity [*H*. 3.32.1]. God foresaw and knew the weakness of man and the consequences of this weakness [*H*. 4.63.3]. God is able to foresee all things for the salvation of men [*H*. 3.21.1]. Christian growth is a maturing for immortality [*H*. 5.29.1]. The Christian becomes, as Ignatius had put it, the pure bread of God [*H*. 5.28.3]. In each individual life, the word leads man through different stages to the maturity of Christ. Man's progress [*H*. 4.63.2] depends on his progressive formation by the Son. Luke's genealogy of Christ points to the history of Adam as the history of man [*H*. 3.32.1]. After the fall, man became more rational and ceased to be the slave of his passions [*H*. 3.35.1]. The theme of Adam's childhood and need for growth to maturity is not confined to one part of Irenaeus [*H*. 3.32.1; 4.62; and *E*. 14].

Man's infancy was both physical and moral, but he progressed

---

[1] See Benoit, *S. Irénée*, especially pp. 181f., and pp. 199ff. I owe this solution of the puzzle to A. Orbe, S.J., of the Gregorian University, Rome.

towards perfection and all things were disposed for his perfecting [*H.* 4.61.2]. The development from Adam to Christ
includes both divine gift and human education, and is directed
both to individuals and to humanity in its entirety [*H.* 4.62]. It is
not a natural development, but the restoration of something
that had been lost [*H.* 4.18; 5.16.1; 5.17.1; 3.33.1]. The result
of progressive revelation is that the Son gives life to those who
see God [*H.* 4.34.7]; man becomes what he should be in his
relationship to God, as a creature in relation to his creator.

There are many aspects of man's progress: man was thrown
out of paradise because God pitied him and did not want him
to remain in sin; death put a limit to sin [*H.* 3.35.2]; the Law
provided an exterior discipline to govern man, while the gospel
moved man in freedom [*H.* 4.18]. What man lost was not a
present gift, but a goal, the final reward of perfection and
immortality. God turned sin and death into part of his plan to
lead man towards the final end; recapitulation is the result of
man's education by God and the crowning of his work of
creation [*H.* 3.21.1; 5.21.3]. God fixed all things for the perfecting and maturing of man, so that he might see and grasp
God [*H.* 4.61.1]. Man needed to learn the difference between
good and evil by having to distinguish between them and by
testing them.

Finally, the account of progress in Irenaeus is not free from
tensions; for Irenaeus sometimes works less with ideas than with
pictures, impressions and words. Such words as 'life', 'death',
'resurrection', 'immortality', 'image', and 'likeness', 'spirit',
are sometimes used in a supernatural sense, sometimes in a
natural sense, and sometimes with a more elusive meaning.
He gave a place to both man's fall and his rise without always
making clear how they might fit together. Certainly this
tension underlines the grace of the saviour who, as Clement
puts it, turns all our sunsets into sunrises; but just as Clement
used more than one explanation of the origin of philosophy, so
Irenaeus used more than one account of the sin of man. The
parallel is useful because, as in the case of Clement, the logic
of objection and rebuttal is evident.

In such a vigorous pessimist as Tertullian, it may seem
strange to find any view of progress. When arguing against
transmigration of souls, he indicates that the number of souls
is not constant. The population of the world is growing and

overcrowded cities are establishing colonies to take their excess population. Waste land is settled and farmed.

'Surely it is obvious enough, if one looks at the whole world, that it is becoming daily better cultivated and more fully peopled than of old. All places are now accessible, all are well known, all open to commerce; most pleasant farms have obliterated all traces of what were once dreary and dangerous wastes; cultivated fields have subdued forests; flocks and herds have expelled wild beasts; sandy deserts are sown; stony wastes are planted; marshes are drained; and where once were at most solitary cottages, there are now large cities. No longer are islands dreaded, nor their rocky shores feared; everywhere are houses and inhabitants, and settled government, and civilized life.'

But the conclusion of it all is sad. Nature cannot feed the increasing numbers. We complain more bitterly; nature's remedy consists of plagues, famines, wars and earthquakes, all of which decrease the surplus population [*An.* 30]. Yet even this is a real theory of progress, through the blood and tears without which man cannot be trusted. Marcion's kind God, says Tertullian, could only ruin sinful men, who would never find salvation without fear.

By the end of his life, Tertullian had become a greater optimist. He found an answer to the tension between the summing-up of things in Christ and God's continued plan, in Montanism, which moved beyond Christ to yet another dispensation – that of the Spirit. Here the finality of Christ took second place to the continuity of God's saving work. The Paraclete had come to his new prophets and the final stage of the history of salvation had begun. It was the work of the one God, whose wisdom rules over all. Everything, as the Preacher said, has its time [Ecclesiastes 3.17; *Virg.* 1.5]. The kingdom of God and his righteousness grow as from a seed. The righteousness of God spent its childhood with the Law and the prophets, its youth with the gospel and now finds maturity with the Paraclete [*Virg.* 1.6.7]. Until Christ came, the hearts of men were hard, and until the Paraclete came, the flesh of men was weak [*Mon.* 14.4]. Now the Paraclete overcomes the weakness of man, bringing him truth and help [*Fug.* 14.3].[1]

---

[1] Bender, *Die Lehre*, p. 155.

With that heightened tension of opposites which characterises every part of Tertullian's thought, the age of the Paraclete only brought greater despair with the present state of the Church. Progress and perfection led him to abandon the Church first for the Montanists and then, it seems, for yet another community of his own.

Clement has some of Irenaeus' optimism when he speaks of the fall as a means of man's growth to maturity. Disobedience turned the child into a man [*Prot.* 11.111]. But the consequences of that sin brought trouble enough in the pains and disorders of the cosmos and the depravity of man. Not that corruption is passed on, as Tertullian thought; every man chooses sin on his own account. There has even been some opinion that attributed to Clement an account (like that of Origen) of the pre-existence of souls; however the evidence is not conclusive [*S.* 4.26.167].

5   How will it all end?

The claim that history has already reached its highest point, so that nothing remains to be done, gives shape to the whole development and substance to the claims of the gospel. It is, however, plainly contradicted by the continuance of history and the presence of evil. Another end must be envisaged to vindicate the perfection of the work of Christ and the righteousness of God. This problem defines Justin's approach to the end; he is the first Christian to speak of a 'second' coming and to distinguish it from the first. He finds many predictions of the cross in the scriptures and is able to answer the prime objection against the messianic status of Jesus: that he was crucified. But he cannot explain the triumphal prophecies on the basis of the earthly life of Jesus; he therefore assigns these references to the return of Christ and distinguishes between the two comings. 'For the prophets foretold his two advents, one which has already taken place, as of a dishonoured and suffering man, but the second when it has been declared that he shall come again with glory from heaven with his army of angels' [*1 A.* 52.3]. He shall return as the one who was pierced and will show the tokens of his cross [*1 A.* 52; *D.* 14.8; *D.* 32.2; *D.* 64.7]. If his first coming in humility has so disturbed the world, how much greater will be the power of his coming in glory! [*D*. 31.1]. The tension that the two advents of Christ produced was acute, especially in the second century. No clear answer was found for the continuance of history after the finished and perfected work of Christ. Justin produces the most appropriate and striking formula when he speaks of living 'in the middle of Christ's coming' [*D*. 51.2].

Irenaeus' lively visual imagination gives him a colourful view of the coming end. The kingdom of the Son [*H*. 5.36] will last for one thousand years from the first resurrection (or resurrection of the just) to the general resurrection of all men. Irenaeus brings together Revelation 20 and 1 Corinthians 15: 24ff. as well as other passages such as Matthew 26: 29 (Jesus' drinking the fruit of the vine) and Romans 8: 21 (the glorious liberty of the children of God). At the end of a thousand years the Son hands over the kingdom to the father, and God becomes all in all. The kingdom of the Son is seen in vivid concrete terms as in the lake of fire in which the wicked burn for ever. The restoration of all things must not be allegorised away [*H*. 5.32 and 35]. As Isaiah said, the lion will eat straw. This does not simply mean that creation will be restored with animals tame, subject to man, and eating the fruit of the soil. It means that the fruits will be of amazing size and quality; for 'if the straw is good enough to feed lions, what will the wheat be like?' [*H*. 5.33.4]. As surely as the vine and wheat bear fruit at their season, so human bodies that have been nourished by the eucharist will rise again to enter the divine glory [*H*. 5.2.3.]. The sign of Jonah points to the ascending of the flesh to immortality and eternity [*H*. 3.21.1; cf. *H*. 5.8.1]. (Irenaeus speaks of individual souls, bodies and spirits.) Just as God's good gifts are eternal, so the loss of them is also eternal; the wicked are desolate and are sent at the judgement into eternal fire [*H*. 5.27].

It is important to note that Irenaeus plays down the literal interpretation of eschatological wonders, in *Epideixis* 67, after having defended it in *Against Heresies* 5.33f. The reason for his caution may be a fresh danger of extreme chiliastic ideas and movements, the desire to protect the simple believer from extravagances, the criticism of other Christian teachers or simply his own wiser and maturer outlook. For Irenaeus, however, the tension between symbolic and literal was less important than that between present and future; the two antitheses went together and had no clear solution.

For all his taste in paradox, Tertullian did resolve some of the tension between recapitulation and history, between the end in Christ and the end to come. His first solution lay in future ✓ eschatology, or a theology of hope. His second solution was Montanism; but his theology of hope preceded and survived his Montanism.

Christians have confidence in the resurrection of the dead. This is the ground of their confidence and from this ground they will defend the flesh to all eternity [*Res.* 1; 8]. Tertullian speaks with certain tones to a Church living in the last days, declaring the coming fulfilment of all its hopes. With his longing for the fullness of the gift of the Spirit, with his relinquishing of the world, with his zeal for sacrifice and martyrdom, with his joyful hope in the glorious return of Christ, and the fulfilment of the kingdom, his eager anticipation of the eternal punishment of sinners, Tertullian has made future eschatology the dominant theme of his theology. In all these things Tertullian speaks with certainty and with confidence. The Church may pass now through a time of sorrow and persecution, but the way of the cross must lead to final glory.[1] Tertullian shows interest in the intermediate state of those who wait for the end after death and draws his ideas chiefly from the parable of Lazarus. The one great event of the end is the resurrection and the millenium that follows it. Everything else is preliminary, even the condition of those who wait for the resurrection, although they may anticipate some share of that final vindication.[2]

In contrast to his contemporaries, Clement finds little place for traditional eschatology. As far as time and space are concerned, the Logos is Lord of all. After death, justice is done, as we have seen, by destruction of sinners, by cleansing fire, by many mansions. The scheme of mansions may seem strange and fanciful – it is anything but fanciful. Because he is universal Lord, there can be no doubt about final victory; his victory is a thing of the past, his lordship a thing of the present. What

[1] K. Hesselberg, *Tertullians Lehre aus seinen Schriften entwickelt* (Dorpat, 1848), p. 133.

[2] Heinz Finé, *Die Terminologie der Jenseitsvorstellungen bei Tertullian* (Bonn, 1958), p. 236.

happens is that souls, like other things, find their own level. From the one first principle above, there extend downwards rank after rank of angels, then of men. All are being saved and all are saving others and all salvation derives from the one first principle. This is just like a magnet, says Clement,[1] extending its force through a long series of iron rings. The virtuous are drawn to the place nearest the source of power. The wicked drop off and fall away. They find their own level. 'For this is the law from the beginning, that he who wants virtue, must choose it' [*S.* 7.2.9].

How will it all end? Justin is concerned that the end should vindicate the crucified Messiah and reveal the fullness of his glory. Irenaeus pictures the wonder of universal restoration. Tertullian is governed by ethical concerns, by the full execution of the justice of God. With Clement, the traditional account is present, but it is secondary to a more rational and celestial scheme in which individual choice plays a dominant part.

Problems and parallels

1   The long march of man

Irenaeus has attracted attention because he offered an alternative account of the problem of evil to that given by Augustine and others; for Irenaeus, sin was a characteristic of man's infancy that delayed his growth in the likeness of God; it was not a catastrophe that destroyed his original righteousness. On the other hand, Augustine later put forward a cataclysmic view of the fall, by which man fell to disaster despite the righteousness that God has given him; evil, however, could be understood as privation or the absence of good, and when seen in cosmic perspective, its deficiencies produced a total goodness.[2]

---

[1] Perhaps drawing on Plato, *Ion*, 533.
[2] This is the central claim of Hick, *Evil and the God of love.*

It will already have been seen that this account of Irenaeus, like that of the Latin fathers, Tertullian and Augustine, is not quite accurate. Each of the second-century writers has more than one attempt at an explanation of evil in God's world. Irenaeus has a doctrine of the fall, although only Tertullian speaks of original sin.[1] The main defence in the problem of evil is the free will of man and this is supplemented by the aesthetic, privative and other explanations. Stoicism is more important than has been recognised. Plotinus was a late arrival at this point of view; among the Stoics the hymn of Cleanthes had long extolled the god who could make the odd even and fit everything together in one harmonious whole.[2] What each of the fathers saw was that the world, as it was, challenged belief in the Father of Jesus Christ; he could not have made the world just as it now is. History was necessary to make sense of it and to justify the ways of God to men. So Justin saw God's long road with Israel until the time for Christ was ripe; he also saw the need, partly for his Jewish questioners and chiefly for the justice of God, that Christ should come again. Clement saw the exalted Christ drawing all men to himself through the different saving cycles. When man did wrong, God stepped in, to turn the evil to good effect. Irenaeus saw salvation as *oikonomia*, a total plan that would not be completed until the saints had reigned on earth. Tertullian, with his sharp eye for justice, saw every affliction that man suffered as a punishment for personal sin, or the sin of another. In the second century there was a discontent with any one approach to evil; but all began with man's free will and all ended with an active God, who, with infinite variety, joined man in the overthrow of evil by turning it to good effect.

Even history, as it was already known, could not be enough. Evil was too strong and persistent. There had to be a time when the gradual process came to an end and sin and death were swallowed up in victory. There was no solution to the problem of evil and no one believed that God could let it run on unsolved much longer. Eschatology played a part in Christian theology from the beginning. In Justin, Irenaeus and Tertullian the

---

[1] 'He is the first to formulate the idea of inherited sin or corruption of nature, and to explain the process by which such corruption is handed on from generation to generation' (Tennant, *Sources*, p. 335).

[2] Stobaeus, *Anthologium*, ed. Wachsmuth, vol. I, p. 26.

hope was high and the expectation lively. Justin speaks of Christians as 'men of good hope',[1] Irenaeus looks to the one thousand grapes on every cluster and the harmony of nature,[2] while Tertullian sees with vivid detail the overthrow and torment of the rulers of this world.[3] Clement finds his hope in the present God, who will lead his children to the many mansions of their heavenly home.[4]

Eschatology is the only way for God's plan in history to gain credibility. Whatever he has done, it is not enough; that much is clear from the persecution of his people and the continuing dominion of injustice. There is a great contrast between the materialist apocalyptic of Irenaeus or Tertullian and the heavenly plan of Clement; but the message is the same: God has not finished yet, he is at work and he will go on to the end, when his triumph will be loosed from all ambiguity.

As with the account of creation, we must recognise that Christians did not answer, and have not answered, *all* the questions about providence and purpose. They did respond reasonably to each of the five questions that were thrust on them. They gave a direction to man's history, by placing Christ in the centre of it. But they did not solve the problem of evil and they did not have a theory of history as an autonomous self-contained movement. They showed how Christ made sense of things but they did not show human life as the rational existence of a purposeful being. There was too much on the debit side – innocent suffering, cruelty and lies. Human life was governed by many contingent things; by itself it did not make sense – the demons and man's sin saw to that. All they did show was that the created world could not be blamed and written off as an enemy and that history made sense when you saw Christ as its Lord. But this very confession of faith pointed to what was not yet to be seen. All things were not under Christ's feet; they were his by the power of his righteousness. To know him was to look in hope to the promised liberty of the children of God. They could deny that recalcitrant matter limited the power of a good creator; but they effectively declared the same

[1] *1 A.* 14.3.
[2] *H.* 5.33.3.
[3] *Spect.* 30.2; cf. *Scap.* 3: no state that is guilty of shedding Christian blood shall go unpunished.
[4] *S.* 6.13.105–6.14.114.

thing as far as the present age was concerned. God was working out his purpose; but his work was still incomplete.

Because of this inconclusiveness some modern writers have been unconvinced. Eschatology has been described as a Jewish sickness transmitted to Christians who took Jews too seriously. Pagan despair is better than the illusion of apocalyptic hope.[1] However, Wittgenstein knew better; apocalyptic was not a form of science fiction or fantasy about the future. To believe in the last judgement is to live by it – to behave as in the presence of God, and to look to reunion with departed friends. Evidence of survival is beside the point. Does the picture provide a framework for a life that is lived? If it does, it is an unshakeable belief.[2]

2   Upwards and onwards

While the contribution of Irenaeus to the understanding of the problem of evil has been wrongly simplified, there is no doubt that his more positive approach has been better understood since the recent prevalence of evolutionary ideas. Teilhard de Chardin grasped this with profound insight and inadequate precision; his work began from a dissatisfaction with the scholastic account of original sin, which was plainly not adequate for presenting the mystery of Christ. Romans 8 presented a picture of the cosmos that made sense to people who were used to scientific process and had much more gospel in it than did the scholastic account of Genesis.

Sin, for Teilhard, is what prevents movement forward to Christ, the Omega-point. Since Christ draws all together in his summing-up, sin is a movement away from unity, or the decline from an ordered whole to a more primitive state of organisation. 'Whatever fragments, dissipates and breaks asunder man and his world is evil. Sin retards the world's advances towards Christ; it counter-thrusts the coming of his

---

[1] R. Rubinstein, cited in Peter Baelz, *The forgotten dream* (Oxford, 1975), p. 113.
[2] See L. Wittgenstein, *Lectures and conversations on aesthetics, psychology and religious belief* (Oxford, 1966), p. 56; also see Phillips, *Death and immortality*, p. 68.

Kingdom.'[1] Sin is never merely personal, for man is part of the cosmos and the chief goal of its process. There is a 'tension between man's absolute future and his inability to reach this with any of the resources immanent to the world or native to himself'.[2] Christ alone makes possible the union with God for which man is made. Christ alone makes possible the journey through death into eternal life with the Father. Redemption is not at odds with creation but represents the crown of the creative work of God. So man may see in Adam's sin a *felix culpa*, which brought all mankind to redemption.

The detail of Teilhard's scheme is not important here. What is important is the sense of movement, of evolution. Sin is not a cosmic disaster that leaves the universe permanently crippled; it is overcome by the activity of God. Here, as in the second century, the ills of the world are not the last word; they do not prevent God and his children from going forward. This is perhaps a human necessity, but it is central to Christianity, which only moves by carrying a cross; but it does move, it does follow. The concrete nature of the suffering of the second century prevented Christians from opting out in meditation and self-pity. This is evident in Teilhard, where a family bereavement brings him to the heart of the matter.

'One of my nephews was drowned in Auvergne, when taking a swim in the pond: caught in the weeds. My brother came to see me last week; he is broken but at the same time so quiet and strong. Going on. It pays to have a faith. And really, quite seriously speaking, I don't see how we can escape the alternative: either the world is developing through good and bad chances, something "*adorable*" and then we must serve and love it; or it is simply absurd and *haïssable* and then we must reject it as much as we can.'[3]

The same incident later leads him to comment that Christianity is the only way men have found to make the world habitable by providing sweetness and warmth in a harsh and ruthless place. This is why Christianity is bound to win some way or other; it is not a matter of wishful thinking but of rational

[1] J. P. Kenny, 'Teilhard de Chardin on original sin', *Colloquium*, 7.1 (1974), 10.

[2] *Ibid.* p. 11.

[3] Teilhard de Chardin, *Letters to two friends 1926–1952* (London, 1970), p. 175.

survival. Teilhard's sensitive awareness of problems cannot be denied; as a palaeontologist he saw that science had raised the question: 'Why did Christianity come so late?' with fresh force. His sweeping optimism remains for some an adequate reason for rejecting his opinions. Is there a way in which his ideas can be taken up into a larger solution?[1]

The opposition between Teilhard's evolutionary ('Rise') theory and Augustine's catastrophic ('Fall') theory is not ultimate in practice. It seems complete because the former sees man rising to a future perfection while the latter sees him as fallen from a primitive perfection. However, evil confronts us in two distinct forms, physical and moral, or more accurately 'troubles that occur through nobody's fault' and moral evil. Both may have physical consequences. Particular cases often include both kinds of trouble. When, in spite of all care, someone dies of leukaemia, this is nobody's fault; but had men spent as much time and money on medical research as they have on war, it is probable that a cure for leukaemia would now be available. The two kinds of trouble require two different kinds of explanations. Non-moral evil is explicable on Teilhard's 'Rise' theory while moral evil is explicable on Augustine's 'Fall' theory. The two kinds of evil and the two explanations must never be mixed or confused, but they are frequently present and relevant to the same event.[2] Moral evil is not part of man's movement forward but non-moral evil can be. This distinction is yet another point of clarification, another rational gain in the problem of evil.

3   Ambiguities

Any discussion of Teilhard must lead to a recognition of the imprecision that has governed the use of the word 'history' in most theological writing. Justin has been credited with a theology based on history and this has been seen as an explanation of his thought. Speculative theories of history point to three main shapes: progressive-or-regressive, cyclic and

---

[1] The following paragraph answers this question along the lines suggested by John Cowburn in, *Shadows and the dark. The problems of suffering and evil* (London, 1979).

[2] *Ibid.* pp. 92f.

chaotic.[1] It is possible to see history as an ordered pattern of progress from small to great, bad to good, simple to complex; it is a simple matter to reverse the direction from progress to regress. On the other hand, many (like the Stoics) see circularity in history, through the repetition of the same errors, catastrophe and recovery. A third possibility is that persistent and increasing chaos is the only discernible feature of man's successive phases of existence. Now Justin uses each of these theories. There is a progress in the Law man receives from God and this reaches its summit in the new and final Law, which is Christ. There is also progress in the power and extent of sin, which culminates in the crucifixion of God's son. Yet the story of sin is circular, for each man goes through the choice of Adam and does wrong by his own choice; there is no end to the repetitions. Thirdly, as a result of both the power of sin and the repetition of man's fall, there is chaos everywhere. Apart from three accounts of history, Justin has a strong conviction that the more important things do not change. The Word who assists at creation and speaks throughout the prophets is the same Word who is present in Christ. As a result, history is tortured to find types of Christ in the Old Testament. The spermatic Logos allows for historical progress from part to whole; however the Logos of the Old Testament is not part but is already the whole.

This ambiguity helps to explain tensions in Justin.[2] When he is speaking of progress, as in the case of the Law, the later one stands on the line of history the better one is placed. The last who come are best served. On the other hand when he is speaking of identity, antiquity provides superiority. The first who come are best served; while all receive the same, some receive it first.

These ambiguities occur in the three other writers studied, and it is therefore unwise to speak of their account of history without indicating in some detail what is involved.[3] Justin

---

[1] W. H. Dray, *Philosophy of history* (Englewood Cliffs, 1964), pp. 61f.

[2] His confidence in, or pessimism over, human reason, his acceptance or rejection of the idea of historical development: these and other issues have been debated at length. See comments on this matter, E. F. Osborn, 'Elucidation of problems as a method of interpretation', II, *Colloquium*, 9.1 (1976), 10–16.

[3] Augustine has similar ambiguities built into his scheme and it is therefore unwise to contrast him with Joachim of Fiore without careful qualification. Augustine had more than one scheme of earthly

and Irenaeus certainly had hopes for a better life on this earth.[1] Tertullian also foresaw the coming to sight of Christ's kingdom on earth; the later account of the Church given by Cyprian was entirely conditioned by the need for the faithful to govern the earth under Christ as *imperator*. Clement concentrated on heaven, where there was progress through the different levels of glory. This was one way of settling the injustices that had occurred on this side of death; another way was through the punishment of sinners.

4   The finality of Jesus

Today the finality of Jesus cannot be expressed in the triumphalist terms of the Church of Christendom. The most convincing recent work draws instead on the early patristic account of God as Spirit.[2] Such an approach clarifies four elements: the continuity that leads up to Christ, the continuity that proceeds from him, the truth that he reveals, and the community that he builds. God is continuously incarnate as Spirit in the spirits of men, for creation and salvation go on together. The unique place of Jesus is that he is truly son of God and thereby truly and fully human [p. 23]. For the first time, God as Spirit truly makes a man. 'Christ, then, is not so much the "second" Adam as the true Adam, the "proper man" in whom God's plan for humanity comes to its realisation for the first time' [p. 19]. The work of God as Spirit continues. In Paul, Jesus as the archetypal Adam [p. 79] is life-giving Spirit [1 Corinthians

history and different divisions occur in different parts of his work; generally he held the opinion that there would be no further step forward until the last judgement, when the faithful would enter the sabbath of eternal joy. Certainly the civil power was not the kingdom of God on earth. On the other hand, Joachim did see a movement from the active life to the life of contemplation and then to a state of spiritual renewal on earth. 'We shall not be what we have been, but we shall begin to be other' (Joachim, *Psalterium* (Venice, 1527), cited in Frank E. Manuel, *Shapes of philosophical history* (Stanford, 1965), p. 40).

[1] See A. P. O'Hagan, *Material recreation in the apostolic fathers*, TU, 100 (Berlin, 1967).

[2] Lampe, *God as Spirit*, returns to the theme of finality at different stages of the argument.

15: 45] working in the believer so that the believer no longer lives, but Christ lives in him [Galatians 2: 20]. The Christ-event continues from the New Testament to the present day, developing and changing in the interpretations that are given to it. The Spirit who speaks through Christ moves us to reject some elements in the tradition as incompatible with him [p. 109]. The finality of Jesus does not mean that we can never go beyond beliefs that he held or that divine creativity ended after him; it means that he is the central and decisive point in God's dealing with man and that it is his Spirit who leads on further [p. 113]. In the movement forward there will always be some problem in relating the individual and social aspects of eschatology to each other. Today Marxists and Teilhard have been concerned with a collective hope. While there was a strong individual tendency in the hope of the early Church, there was always an essential corporate aspect too. The Christian in heaven as on earth, at the parousia as at the present, was part of a community [p. 173].

In contrast with this perceptive account, a recent explicit treatment of the finality of Christ is oddly insular and negative. Facing the difficulties of this belief in a pluralist world,[1] it attempts to solve them in the context of modern triumphalism. The historical beginnings in the second century are ignored and the result is an extreme conceptual parochialism.[2] Belief in the finality of Christ is the result, we are told, of European world colonisation in the nineteenth century, and has no place in the present post-Christian era [pp. 119ff.]. Contrary to this claim, we have seen that a belief in the finality of Christ preceded Christendom. Christians, it is next claimed, had to accept the Jewish theology of history in order to understand the finality of Christ [*ibid.*]; on the contrary, Justin's account of history is concerned with *logos spermatikos* in philosophers and Clement saw philosophy serving the Greeks as the Law had served the

---

[1] Don Cupitt, *The leap of reason* (London, 1976), p. 93: 'The interpretative plasticity of the world seems to make it possible for human groups to survive and flourish with very different world-views, especially if we consider a world-view as an action-guiding belief-system'.

[2] *Ibid.* chapter 10, is especially valuable for its explicit treatment of the theme, 'The finality of Christ'. For the term 'conceptual parochialism' see above, p. 13.

Jews. The debt here to the prophets was no more than to Plato and the Stoics. Further, we learn that the finality of Christ has been seen as the way he receives desperate sinners from destruction and that this is the view of the 'great Protestant anthropologies from Luther to Ritschl, Bultmann and Tillich' [p. 125]. It is interesting to have four such diverse theologians grouped together; however, the Protestant view that they allegedly promote is much more like conservative Roman Catholic doctrine than anything else. The criticism of the Protestant view that follows is given in a high moral tone, for the failure of this view is blamed for the lack of confidence so characteristic of recent years [pp. 128f.]. Since the loss of nerve is described in the context of the Anglo-Saxon world, where this sombre view has had limited acceptance, some other ground would be more convincing. It could perhaps be found in disappointed triumphalism. This probability is supported by the initial imperialism and by the conclusion that the finality of Jesus lies in 'the triumph of rapturous communion with God in the assurance of God's love for men' [p. 130]. Even the finality of Jesus' ethical teaching is asserted, because 'there can be no higher moral value than utter purity of heart, disinterestedness, and commitment to the way of love' [*ibid.*]. This is ultimate and cannot be superseded any more than can the central themes to which Jesus bears witness. All of which may well be true; but it is as hard to argue and as directly offensive to non-Christians as other accounts of Jesus' finality.

The subsequent account of Christian existence in a pluralist society is often unconvincing. For pluralism does *not* consist in 'a ferment of different world views' and the cities of today are *not* 'full of jostling philosophies' [p. 140]. Augustine is wrongly seen as a purely private person; his account of Christianity was as politicial, communal and historical as any. The rural Christianity depicted is flatly contradicted by every part of the Donatist controversy and the oppression that continued after its conclusion.

Two things emerge from this discussion: the present relevance of the question in a European context and the puzzle of early Christian intellectual claims at a time when Christians were obviously insignificant. To link Christian intellectual arrogance with nineteenth-century imperialism is historically absurd, for the early Christians claimed final truth long before Christendom; that is why their claims are so interesting.

5   Living after the end

History remains a problem. For the Christian the final word has been spoken in Christ but the end is not yet. There was no early answer to this problem. The finality of Christ could not be overruled as the Montanists wanted to overrule it; but history still went on. All things were summed up in Christ, yet all things were not yet complete. Christian hope was one way of bridging the gap and it was aided by Platonic participation. It was possible now to live by the end that was in Christ, through creative discipleship and creative love. The resurrection produced history, as it was spread through the world by the power of the cross. The truth that was in Christ could be known and shared now; the grace he gave was a present anticipation of his glory. Whatever the ambiguous position of the believer, there could be no doubt that the ultimate purpose of things was the liberty of the children of God, as shown and given in Jesus. 'Jesus is received by those who use the tale of his life as a means of coming to see the world in a particular way as one who does not merely illustrate a principle but in some way achieves it and brings it into being.'[1] Gnostics and Middle Platonists could speak of a totality of being, a summing-up in a heavenly aeon, but the New Testament and the fathers spoke of it as something that had occurred in history and was still to be found there.

[1] Mackinnon, *Metaphysics*, p. 163.

7 The short word

Each group of problems has shown two marked characteristics. In the first place there has been the untidiness of infinity, for there has never been a point at which the questions could be rounded off and completed. There was always a sense of being on the edge of the desert, or the shore of the sea. (The chief reason for stopping was that the topic was inexhaustible; enough had been seen to learn that the end would never be in sight.) The God above was shrouded in mystery or revealed in brightness too fierce for man to bear. Man, as God's image yet sinful, as free yet captive, was a rational, laughing animal who found life through the practice of death. The world, God's good cosmos, was shot through with suffering and evil. History had reached its end in Christ, but still went on in eerie confusion; another end remained but when, why or how could not be set down.

In the second place, there has been one conclusion and that a short one, to each investigation. The unknown God is known through his Word. Man is *logikos* and he learns his true nature only in the perfect man and complete Logos. The world is made and governed by the divine Word. History is long but it is summed up in the Word. The brutal brevity and simplicity of the gospel was unattractive to most people: only a slave mind could accept such a reduction of so many issues.[1] Yet Christians made no attempt to remove this simplicity and defended it against the pretentious inflation of Gnostics.

Irenaeus makes a point of the conciseness of Christ, quoting Isaiah 10: 22: 'A word brief and short in righteousness: for a short word will God make in the whole world' and comments 'not by the long-windedness of the law but by the brevity of faith and love, men were to be saved'. The Law is fulfilled by love and on the two great commandments hang all the Law and the prophets. Faith in Christ is the one thing necessary for man to be godly, righteous and good. This is God's short word in the

---

[1] *Contra Celsum*, 1.9; 3.44; 3.55; 3.75.

world: 'And therefore a short word has God made on the earth in the world' [*E.* 87].[1]

Simplicity of cure was related to simplicity of need. There was only one thing wrong with man – he had lost the likeness of God that Adam had. This loss had gone on for a long time but it was set right in a moment by the incarnation of the Word. This was 'salvation in a nutshell'. Man regained in Christ what he had lost in Adam. The son of God had always existed, 'but when he was incarnate and became man, he summed up in himself the long line (*longam expositionem*) of men, providing for us a brief compendium of salvation (*in compendio nobis salutem praestans*) so that what we had lost in Adam, the image and likeness of God, we might regain in Christ Jesus' [*H.* 3.19]. The same remarkable claim occurs in Irenaeus' account of the wine at the wedding feast at Cana [*H.* 3.17.7]. With Christ nothing is incomplete or ill-timed. The Father knew all that had to happen and the Son did it all in the right sequence at the proper time. Mary wanted to partake of 'the cup which summed things up (*compendii poculo*)'. The wine that Jesus made was a *compendium* because it pointed to the cup that was the New Covenant in his blood and also because it had the same punctiliar, instantaneous, once-for-all quality. For Irenaeus has already contrasted the old wine produced by the long natural process with the wine made all at once and simply ('compendialiter, ac simpliciter') from water [*H.* 3.11.9].

This is the key to all that Irenaeus and his contemporaries had to say about Jesus. The account of recapitulation is painfully capable of multiplication. For Irenaeus it served as a competitor to *gnosis*.[2] It was a Gnostic term, but Irenaeus stretched it unmercifully, partly because he thought there were no limits to the cosmic significance of Christ and partly because it offered a new way of seeing things that could defeat *gnosis* on its own ground. But to later readers the prolixity of Irenaeus obscures the central truth that it was a summary, a compen-

---

[1] Tertullian comments on the same verse: 'for the new testament is a short compendium, free from the detailed burdens of the law' [*Marc.* 4.1]. 'The precept in the Gospel has summary precision' [*Marc.* 4.16].

[2] See Norbert Brox, *Offenbarung, Gnosis und gnostischer Mythos bei Irenäus von Lyon* (Salzburg and München, 1966), especially pp. 184–95. Note also p. 180: 'Somit rückt die "wahre Gnosis" in grosse Nähe zum "Kanon der Wahrheit". Sie ist die Erkenntnis, das Wissen, und der Besitz der Glaubensregel'.

dium, quite literally, a summing-up. It was as brief as anything
could be. It was one thing, one thing as all things. It was not
calculated but seen directly as in a flash. The same thing came
to Justin when he declared Christ to be the whole Logos and
when he described the way in which Christ spoke. 'Brief and
concise statements came from him for he was no sophist, but his
word was the power of God' [*1 A.* 14]. It comes again in
Tertullian, where Christ is 'the same to all, king to all, judge to
all, God to all and Lord' [*Iud.* 7.9] and in Clement, who says
that the blind need a guide, the sick a doctor, but 'all men need
Jesus' [*Paed.* 1.9.83]. It was there in Origen, who saw the
significance of Moses and Elijah in the transfiguration story,
and the greater significance of their departing, with the result
that the disciples 'saw no one but Jesus alone'. The whole
gospel was in Christ, the *autobasileia*.[1] Brevity is a perennial
Christian plea: 'Hold to Christ, and for the rest be totally
uncommitted'.[2] *Solus Christus* meant for the second century the
ability to see in a flash five things: the Word made flesh, his
eternal unity with the Father, his joining of man to God, his
gifts of the knowledge of God, and his universality. All these
themes are found together in the Fourth Gospel where *verbum
dei* and *solus Christus* dominate from the first verse to the last
[John 20: 31].

These are short answers to five questions:

(1) How did God's Word become flesh?
(2) How is the Word related to God the Father?
(3) What did the Word achieve by being both man and
     God?
(4) How does the Word bring knowledge of God?
(5) How can he be particular and universal, i.e. the man
     Jesus or the risen Christ *and* the universal Word of God?

1   How did God's Word become flesh?

For anyone who has grasped the Christian account of a God
who transcends the limitations of men and idols, the incarna-

---

[1] Origen, *Comm. Matt.* 12.43 and 14.7. See de Lubac, *Histoire et esprit,*
pp. 176f.
[2] Butterfield, *Christianity and history* p,. 146.

tion must seem outrageous. How could it be presented convincingly? For Justin the incarnation is a set of facts that fulfil prophecy, not a strange irruption, but a long-awaited event. 'Now there is a village in the land of the Jews, 35 stadia from Jerusalem, in which Jesus Christ was born, as you can indeed verify from the registers of the taxation made under Cyrenius, your first procurator in Judaea' [*1 A*. 34]. For Justin the incarnation is a matter of fact and the facts have a double value. First, they give the event an earthy strength; secondly, they each fulfil a particular prophecy concerning the Messiah, add heavenly strength by proving God's activity and balance promise by fulfilment. A mere magician could not fulfil so many prophecies [*1 A*. 31f.].

The uniqueness of the incarnation is rigorously maintained, yet to make sense of what happened in Jesus, a comparison with Socrates is put forward. Socrates found and used part of the Logos and was therefore condemned. Christ is the *logos* in every man. He spoke through the prophets and then came and did what he had predicted. His uniqueness is seen in the extent and depth of his influence on human lives [*2 A*. 10].

Incarnation as the fulfilment of scripture is especially important in speaking with Jews, who cannot see why Christians put their hopes on a crucified man [*D*. 10.3]. Jews need to be shown that Christ must come twice to fulfil scripture – once to suffer shameful death and once to triumph over his enemies [*D*. 32.2 *et passim*]. All things have been foretold, from John's preparation for his first coming right through to his return in glory [*D*. 51.2]. The particular events of his life, especially his birth and his death are important for Justin. His obscure youth [*1 A*. 35.1] and his work as a carpenter [*D*. 88.8] fulfilled the prophet's prediction of formlessness [Isaiah 53: 2].

For Irenaeus, the incarnation certainly fulfils prophecy and balances prediction with fulfilment; but the idea of balance, exchange, symmetry or fitness is carried much further and the necessity of incarnation is argued at various levels. 'Because of his infinite love, *he became what we are* to make us what he is' [*H*. Pref. 5]. Irenaeus loves this kind of balanced statement or *Tauschformel*:[1] a formula that indicates an exchange between two properties or people. He tells of 'the father giving testimony to the son and the son announcing the father' [*H*. 3.6.2] and of

[1] On *Tauschformeln*, see Bengsch, *Heilsgeschichte und Heilswissen*, pp. 157f.

Christ 'through obedience destroying disobedience' [*H.* 3.19.5].
The intention is not merely rhetorical; it was necessary that
Jesus should become what we are and be 'made man among
men, visible and tangible' if he were to overcome death and
unite man and God [*E.* 6].

Why was it necessary that this exchange should take place
for man's salvation? The answers are many. Irenaeus could
never use one explanation when he could think of twenty, and
for him the incarnation explained everything. One reason
follows the initial claim. No one else could have taught men
of God but Jesus, for no one else but the Word could know
what God was like. But why become man? Because men
needed to *see and hear*, so that they could copy his life, obey his
words and become his friends. His plan of redemption was just
and not violent: he gave his soul for our souls, his flesh for our
flesh. He gave God to men, by giving them the Spirit, and he
gave men to God, by his own incarnation.

For Irenaeus, the acts of God have a balance or measure that
preserves justice and fitness.[1] This is a contrast to Tertullian's
necessary paradox. For Tertullian there had to be some
imbalance, some surprise, to provide evidence of divine
activity. With Irenaeus, God makes things right; the order of
salvation is marked by the same harmony as the order of
creation. Nearly all Irenaeus' arguments for the incarnation
have the same appeal to justice and balance.

The Gnostic system, which he attacked, appeared to have a
similar logic or aesthetic. There was, outside the *Pleroma*,
another Saviour, another Logos and another Christ, all produced to balance what was within and to set it right. The
difference is, however, that Irenaeus holds the two sides of each
divine act together: there is only one Word and he is the Jesus
who suffered; the Word who descended is the same as he who
ascended, and the flesh of Adam that was made from dust is
the flesh that the Word assumed. So the Gnostic galaxy
vanishes because the names all refer to the one Word, only-

---

[1] Of 'Gottes zeithafte Kunst' von Balthasar writes: 'Es ist die erste
grosse Theologie des Kairos, des aptum tempus, wobei die qualitative
Verschiedenheit und Einmaligkeit jeder Zeitstelle, in die ein Wesen
oder Ereignis gesetzt wird, von der freien Verfügung Gottes, seinem
jeweiligen Offenbarungswillen abhängt und auf ihn verweist'
(*Herrlichkeit*, vol. 2, p. 76).

begotten, life, light, Saviour, Christ, Son of God, who became incarnate. How did the Gnostic scheme arise? It came from ignoring the proper position and context of statements and not fitting them to the body of the truth; the failure had both logical and aesthetic causes [*H.* 1.1.19–20].

The two sides of the balance require each other; their separation leads to error [*H.* 3.17.6]. For the Word is always with men: he was united with creation according to the Father's will, became flesh himself as Christ the Lord, suffered and rose for us, will return in glory to raise up all flesh, to show forth salvation and bring just judgement, for all who were made by him.

Reasons for incarnation always follow this proportion. He became man to be tempted just as he was Word to be glorified [*H.* 3.20.3]. The prophets understood it all and their cryptic utterances never fail to provide support. Isaiah [63: 9] shows that the saviour is not merely a man nor even an incorporeal angel: 'Neither an elder, nor angel, but the Lord himself will save them, because he loves them and will spare them: he himself will set them free'; Isaiah equally insists [33: 20] that he should be a real man, visible to men: 'Behold, a city of Zion: thine eyes shall see our salvation.' Habakkuk [3: 3–5] makes the same two points when he combines God and geography: 'God shall come from the south, and the Holy One from Mount Ephraim . . . before his face shall go forth the Word and his feet shall advance in the plains.' This shows that God would come from Bethlehem and would walk on human feet [*H.* 3.22].

It is all very physical; flesh had to be received from another human being, namely Mary. 'For if he did not receive the substance of flesh from a human being, he became neither man nor Son of Man; and if he was not what we were, he did no great thing in what he suffered and endured' [*H.* 3.31.1]. Any qualification to the human birth of Jesus would destroy his incarnation, manhood and saving power. Jesus ate, was hungry and tired, wept tears and sweated blood and at the end was pierced with a spear so that blood and water flowed. These were all signs of the flesh, which he took from the earth so that he could bring the work he began at creation to its proper end, saving the work that his hands had made and summing it up in himself [*H.* 3.32.1].

Man's salvation depends on solidarity with the manhood of Jesus and this remains a matter of flesh. In the most physical of redemption theories the light of the Father transforms the flesh of the Lord from mortal to immortal and from that flesh the same light and immortality come to us [*H.* 4.34.2]; for the glory of God is a living man [*H.* 4.34.7].

Manhood and the cross are central. If, as the Gnostics claim, there were two Christs: one who suffered on the cross and one who flew away and did not suffer, we should certainly choose the first. For the Christ who suffered and asked forgiveness for his tormentors showed long-suffering, patience, compassion and goodness, while the fugitive Christ did not. We have nothing for which to thank the other Christ and he is no use to us when we suffer; he is morally perverse since he told others to suffer, to take up the cross and endure, but was not prepared to go to the cross himself. In marked contrast, the true master fought as a man and conquered, 'for he is a very holy and merciful Lord, and he loves the human race' [*H.* 3.19.5].

Similarly, Tertullian's first concern is to destroy any form of Docetism, any denial that Christ shared a human body and lived a physical life in the created world. For him, three reasons are present: a materialist disposition, affection and rational respect for the world and a deep personal attachment to Christ, who had shared man's condition. The 'necessary dishonour of my God' means that his dishonour is necessary if he is to be mine: it also means that Irenaeus' balance is replaced by something more violent. For Tertullian, as for Dostoevsky, truth was never in the middle but always at both extremes.[1] Jesus must suffer and he must be God.

The incarnation meant one thing to Tertullian – flesh. In a way that seems obsessive he returns again and again to insist that the Word became flesh. Against Marcion he argues that Christ was not a phantom; his spirit could not be true if his flesh were false. There can be no true substance within if it is not confirmed by what appears outside [*Marc.* 3.8]. Spirit cannot take on the appearance of flesh any more than flesh can take on the appearance of spirit, and in any case, appearance and likeness are not enough; the flesh of Christ must be real [*Marc.* 5.14]. In a work devoted solely to the theme 'On the

---

[1] See A. Boyce Gibson, *The religion of Dostoevsky* (London, 1973), pp. 1–7, 209–13.

Flesh of Christ' all qualifications or restrictions on the reality of this flesh are rejected [*Carn.* 1.2]. The incarnate Christ is both spirit and flesh, spirit as Spirit of God, and flesh as flesh of man; he is born of God and begotten in the flesh [*Carn.* 18.5] Nothing will take from Tertullian the need to hold fast to the flesh of Christ; his instinct here is sound and it is backed by an earthy temperament that could never follow a phantom. Only Tertullian could have summed the matter up by saying [*Marc.* 4.10] that Christ must have had a human body, for it would be easier to find a man born without heart and brains, like Marcion for example, than to find someone born without a body. The human reality of the flesh springs from the fact of the birth from Mary [*Carn.* 25]; that is why the virgin birth is an essential part of the divine plan of salvation. The Word, who made all things, was sent to be born of Mary, to be both man and God and to be called by the name of Jesus Christ. He suffered, died, rose again and ascended to the Father's right hand [*Prax.* 2]. No part of this sequence can be omitted without fatally damaging the whole.

On the other hand, there were those who, in the days of his flesh, had no trouble with the manhood of Jesus but could not see him as the Word of God. They thought he was just a magician; but no magician could have driven out devils with a single command or cured the lepers, the blind and the paralysed. This was the unique work of the Word of God. True, he was crucified, but this was by his own free choice. He had predicted his passion and when the time came he dismissed his spirit and anticipated the work of execution [*Ap.* 21]. Those who believe that he was God prove the truth of their belief by his effect on their lives [*Ap.* 45].

Clement makes sense of the incarnation by seeing it as an episode in an eternal plan, a part of a cosmic economy. The Word calls the heathen in the *Protrepticus*, guides the moral life of Christians in the *Paedagogus* and teaches all truth in the *Stromateis*.[1] Reality is held together, goodness is given, and truth is made coherent by the Word. The incarnation is tied carefully to pre-existence. The Word, who has appeared on earth, 'was in the beginning and before the beginning'. He

---

[1] On the continuity between these works see an outline of the discussion in Osborn, *Philosophy of Clement*, pp. 5f.

who had made us appeared on earth to be our teacher and to lead us to life eternal [*Prot.* 1.7].

There is some of Irenaeus' sense of balance, but Clement is worried that this will be upset by a lack of weight on the 'God' side. If Jesus were really limited by the needs of a physical body, could he be anything more than a late and inferior entrant to a well-stocked pantheon? Consequently Clement's attitude to the manhood and body of Christ is a sharp contrast to that of Tertullian, although he still rejects the position that the body of Christ was unreal. In his defence of marriage [*S.* 3] Clement has to answer the claim that celibacy is the proper imitation of Christ. He gives three reasons why Jesus did not marry: he already had a bride, the Church; he was not an 'ordinary man' who would need a helpmate; he did not need children because he was going to live forever [*S.* 3.6.49]. In an account of the virtue of *apatheia* he says that only the feelings that keep the body going (hunger, thirst) are permitted to the true Gnostic. In the case of Jesus it would be absurd to claim that the body, as a body, needed food or air to keep it going. Jesus ate in order to prevent people from thinking he was a phantom; it is just as well he did this, for sure enough, the idea did spread that his body was not real [*S.* 6.9.71].[1]

This is an odd theory, which is half-way to the view-point it is designed to oppose. Why did Clement insist on the reality of Christ's body and also on its non-natural sustenance? The reality of the body was important for the truth of the incarnation; but the same truth would be destroyed if Jesus needed food, for the Word of God needs nothing since all things are made by him. To need food would reduce him to the gods of the heathen, who also make excursions to earth, but need sacrifices of food to keep them actively propitious. Further, since the lives of all men depend on the divine Word, who creates and sustains the universe, he could hardly need anything external to sustain his own body. Clement's 'source' here would be the fourth Gospel where Jesus declares [4: 31–4] that he does not need the food that his disciples have brought, since doing the Father's will is food enough, and where he also tells them not to struggle after the food that perishes but to look

---

[1] See T. Rüther, *Die sittliche Förderung der 'Apatheia' in den beiden ersten christlichen Jahrhunderten und bei Klemens von Alexandrien* (Freiburg, 1949), pp. 58–60.

for the food that will endure forever [6: 26]. In the Fourth Gospel the incarnate Word is so full of glory that it has been asked, 'in what sense is he flesh, who walks on water and through closed doors, who cannot be captured by his enemies, who at the well of Samaria is tired and desires a drink, yet has no need of drink and has food different from that which his disciples seek?'[1] One other 'source' could be Luke 24: 36–43, where the risen Christ eats in order to prove that he is not an apparition.

2 How is the Word related to God the Father?

The message of the incarnation never lacked dramatic force; but what did it do to the concept of God? Who was the Word and how could he be God if there were one God only?

Justin is chiefly content to develop the concepts of sonship and Word in relation to these problems. Jesus is son of God in a special sense [2A. 6.3] and uniquely [D. 105.1]. As God's first-born, he is God [1 A. 63]. Like any word that is spoken, he remains the Word of the God who spoke him [D. 61.2] and God loses nothing through the expression of his Word. The fire that gives light and warmth and kindles another fire is not diminished in the process [D. 128.3, 4]. While different in number, the Logos is the same in substance as the Father [D. 56.11]. Both 'Son' and 'Word' point to unity and distinction between Son and Father or between Word and God.

More extended argument is found in Irenaeus, who has to exclude specific denials of this divine unity and to elaborate the nature of the divine Word. Irenaeus reads Genesis 1: 1 as: 'The Son in the beginning: God established the heavens and the earth'. The Son of God existed before the world was made [E. 43]. The unity of Father and Son is doubly explicit. The Father is Lord and the Son is Lord, the Father is God and the Son is God, for what is begotten of God must be God [E. 47]. He who sits at God's right hand was prior to all else and judges all the nations [E. 48]. God the Father spoke with him before he was born as a man [E. 51]. The mystery of his pre-existence is continued in the present power of his name. The name of Jesus Christ, crucified under Pontius Pilate, brings division and

---

[1] E. Käsemann, *The testament of Jesus* (London, 1968), p. 9.

215

separation among men; but whenever anyone believes on him and calls on his name, he is near to answer need and hear prayers. For he came as a man to bring us that salvation which we could never reach by ourselves [*E*. 97].

It would therefore be as wrong to deny pre-existence as to deny incarnation, to separate the Word from God as to separate him from man. 'Learn therefore, you senseless men, that the Jesus who suffered for us, who lived among us, this very person is the word of God' [*H*. 1.1.20]. 'For as he was man that he might be tempted, so he was Word that he might be glorified' [*H*. 3.20.3]. There is no middle way, no hybrid intermediary; it is the invisible who becomes visible, the incomprehensible who becomes comprehensible, the impassible who becomes capable of suffering and the Word who becomes man [*H*. 3.17.6].

One special thing about Irenaeus' account of Logos is that it is normally closer to spoken word rather than to inner reason; Irenaeus has a closer affinity with the Bible than with philosophers, for his sense of history ties him to the prophets, where 'word' is always 'word-event'.[1] Gnostic abstraction of Logos made it possible to separate Word from the God who speaks. Of course Irenaeus also has rational overtones when he calls Gnostics 'senseless' for misunderstanding the Word. But the opposite of 'word' is 'silence'; *Sige* and God could never coexist [*H*. 2.16.5]. He often exchanges 'word' for 'voice' (*phone, vox*): 'Father, whose voice is present to his creation from the beginning to the very end' [*H*. 5.16.1]. God has never ceased to speak to his creatures. So Irenaeus avoids the peculiar metaphysics of the Gnostics and others in their account of the origin of the Word. Everyone knows that in men, word comes from thought and sense [*H*. 2.15.2f.] but those things cannot be transferred to God, who is above human affections [*H*. 2.17]. It cannot make sense to introduce changes, like that from silence to speech, into the undifferentiated being of God [*H*. 2.16.4]. So Irenaeus has to do his own metaphysics when he insists on the unity of God and Word:[2] God is indeed all

---

[1] See below p. 244 and also G. Ebeling, *God and Word* (London, 1967), pp. 39ff. However, the two ideas are inseparable for the Fourth Gospel.

[2] For a different view, see J. Kunze, *Die Gotteslehre des Irenäus* (Leipzig, 1891), pp. 54ff.

reason and all word, for what he thinks, he says and what he says, he thinks [*H.* 2.42.2]. It would be more accurate to speak of 'God as Word' than to use the common expression 'Word of God' [*H.* 2.16.4].[1]

God's Word cannot be compared with any part of creation [*H.* 3.8.2] for he differs as the maker from what is made, as creator from creature [*H.* 3.8.3], and all things depend upon him who made them and sustains them [*H.* 3.11.11]. Unlike the words of men, or men themselves, he has no beginning [*H.* 2.16.4; 2.37.3] but exists eternally with God [*H.* 2.47.2]. This transcendence provides, oddly enough, the basis for his work of revelation. Irenaeus has not reacted so far against the Gnostics as to limit the mystery of the Word, whose beginning no one can tell, and who knows secrets that have been denied to men [*H.* 2.41.1f.].

Tertullian takes seriously the problems that the plurality of Godhead poses. 'Substance' is the word he introduces to solve the problems of the trinity and unity of God.[2] Within the one substance, Father, Son and Holy Spirit are undivided, for one substance means no separation. The substance of the Father and the Son is Spirit, yet both Son and Spirit spring from the Father. Substance is understood in a dynamic not a static way. God's hidden wisdom is also his reason and Word. The Word proceeds from the Father to create the world, and all things are made by him; he is both Son of God and God because of the unity of the divine substance [*Ap.* 21]. The sun and its rays are one substance; they are two but in no way separate. In the same way the light of the divine Word shines forth, and God is of the same substance with his Son [*Ap.* 21.10–14]. Justin had used the same simile [*D.* 61.2]. Father, Son and Spirit differ in grade and order, not in substance. In different works, *Apology*, *Against Marcion*, *Against Praxeas*, Tertullian comes at the unity of the Godhead in different ways, in terms of substance, unity of substance, part of the whole, condition of the same substance, fullness of fullness, of one substance, consort of the substance of the Father.

Tertullian takes the notion of *oikonomia* and applies it within

---

[1] Cf. 'God's Word is the coming of God' (G. Ebeling, *Word and faith* (London, 1963), p. 433).

[2] See Stead, 'Divine substance', pp. 46–66; see also Wölfl, *Das Heilswirken Gottes*, p. 150 and Bender, *Die Lehre*, p. 65.

God as well as to the dealings of God with men. Of course, the two themes interact. The Word was present, as reason, in God before the creation of the universe, being stirred up by God within himself [*Prax.* 5]. The nativity of the Word took place when God said: 'Let there be light'. In creation the Son was clearly with the Father, who said: 'Let us make man in our own image' [*Prax.* 12]. The Father remains invisible in the fullness of his majesty while the Son is visible by the dispensation of his existence [*Prax.* 14]. Yet God never changes and his Word remains the same for ever; for when the Word became flesh he did not cease to be the Word and become an alloy or amalgam of flesh and spirit. He is both God and man and not some third thing [*Prax.* 27]; yet he remains one person.

What of the distinction between Father, Son and Spirit? 'They are three, not in quality, but in sequence (*gradu*); not in substance but in aspect (*forma*), not in power but in its manifestation (*specie*)' [*Prax.* 2]. Sequence or *gradus* points to a stage in an ordered succession. *Species* is a particular type of existent that results from the order while *forma* is a principle of individualisation.[1]

Tertullian seems to have two frames of reference in his account of unity and plurality in the Godhead. On the one hand there is 'a plural unity which is the inner organisation of the divine substance', which does not introduce a plurality of divine subsistent beings. On the other hand there is 'a plurality of existents which have their basis, not in their own specific individuality, but in the Father's act of will, which causes the Son and the Spirit to come forth from him'.[2] In the eyes of his critics, Tertullian is a modalist in his account of divine unity and a subordinationist in his account of divine plurality. They fail to appreciate the subtlety of his intellectual initiative and the insolubility of the problems that he tackled.

His initiative may be recognised from his method.[3] While he also drew on the Apologists, he took from the Valentinians his use of *persona*, *forma* and *gradus*. He had no time for the Valentinian system, but he had a mind for logical structure and he used concepts in a new setting to find a different way through

---

[1] See J. Daniélou, *The origins of Latin Christianity* (London, 1977), p. 364.
[2] *Ibid.*
[3] Moingt, *Théologie trinitaire*, pp. 668f. See also above, p. 54.

problems. The sheer intelligence of his moves has not been evident to many interpreters, who wanted clear definitions and unambiguous formulae. *Persona* is the key word and may best be understood as that particularity which is expressed by *res, species, forma* or *gradus*. Is it a legal or a philosophical term in Tertullian's usage? The answer is that it is both, but that Tertullian has not refined it in either aspect. Yet he left to his successors a language that was to provide the basis for later definition.

Clement's christology follows the lines indicated by Justin and Irenaeus rather than the new terminology of Tertullian. What Christ does is the clue to what he is.

'Where he came from and who he was, he showed by what he taught and by the evidence of his life. He showed that he was the herald, reconciler, our saviour, the Word, a spring of life and peace flooding over the whole face of the earth. Through him, to put it briefly, the universe has already become an ocean of blessings' [*Prot.* 10.110].

The contrast between man under sin and man under Christ is so great that Clement finds it hard to grasp that so much has happened so quickly; salvation has lit up the whole earth and filled all things with the saving seed. So much could not have been done in so short a time, without divine resources. The Lord, despised in his humility, was divine Word, true God made known, equal to the Lord of all things. He took flesh and acted out the drama of man's salvation. He fought with and for his creatures. Quickly made one with man, *Christus Victor* brought, in a flash, the light of God's new day.

This high and lyrical enthusiasm is combined with a Platonism in which the Son is the highest excellence, most perfect, holy, powerful, princely, regal and beneficent. He governs all things, working through them his hidden divine purposes. He is everywhere at all times, knowing and seeing all things. But what is the point of this metaphysical exaltation? It has no other end than the salvation of men, for Clement continues: 'Therefore all men are his; some know it now while some do not know it yet; some belong to him as friends, some as faithful servants, some just as servants'. The great dialectic stretches from the tiniest part upwards to 'the first administrator of the universe, who by the will of the Father directs the salvation of all' [*S.* 7.2.5–9]. How does he go about this salvation? In general, he loads as much on the side of virtue as he can without limiting man's free will, so that somehow or other even the dullest perception may see 'the one almighty good God – from eternity to eternity saving by his Son' [*S.* 7.2.12]. In particular, he enters the souls of just men and lives there as 'the one Saviour individually to each and in common to all'. He stamps his image on the one in whom he dwells to make a third divine image [*S.* 7.3.16].

Clement's grounds for declaring the eternal unity of the Son and Father are the triumphs of God's grace among men. When it came to definition, he could only praise 'God in form of man, undefiled, servant of his Father's will, the Logos, who is God, who is in the Father, who is at the right hand of the Father and with the form of God is God' [*Paed.* 1.2.4]. Clement's account of the Logos is not strictly hierarchical, because he is prepared to assert the unity of the Logos with the Father on the one hand and with men on the other. The discovery of two divine *Logoi* in Clement [*S.* 5.1.6] is due to a misunderstanding of the text. Similarly, Photius [*Biblioth.* 109] makes a wooden analysis of the eternal reason of God and the Logos that goes forth from the Father to be incarnate. The most that can be said in favour of the confusion on this point, is that *logos* is the most ambiguous word in the language and anyone who tries to tidy it up must expect trouble and error, similar to that which has occurred concerning Justin's *logos spermatikos*.[1]

[1] Probably the most confused account is that of H. A. Wolfson, *The philosophy of the church fathers*, vol. 1 (Cambridge, Mass., 1956), pp. 204–17. Wolfson's approach to the 'Philosophy' of the fathers is governed by a twofold confusion. On the one hand, he accepts the classical statements on the trinity as philosophical categories, retrospectively relevant to the early fathers; on the other hand, all Christian thought is seen to be anticipated in Philo and to be unrolled from him.

See also Th. Zahn, *Supplementum Clementinum* (Erlangen, 1884), and for a very clear account, see Bethune-Baker, *Christian doctrine*, pp. 134f.

Wolfson succumbs to the simplistic error of counting *logoi* like billiard balls instead of like drops of water ($1 + 1 = 1$), or like the continuous sections of a beam of light. Clement uses the first analogy in his account of the Logos raining down and Justin uses the second analogy. The logical account in both Clement and Justin is based on the notion of participation and the confusion on this point is matched by the extensive discussion of Justin's *logos spermatikos*.

3   What did the Word achieve by being both man and God?

Clement has made us look at the activity of the Word in order to understand his relation to the Father. Irenaeus by his 'exchange formulae' has given us the common theme – the work of the Word is to join men to God. This peace was not won without struggle and must be linked with the theme of *Christus victor*; the battle still rages.

Justin, as ever, answers the problem with the intense compression and apparent simplicity that deceive so many of his readers. Every word and image is loaded with meaning. The work of the Word is to break the bonds and heal the wounds of men. All evil powers flee from the conquering name of Christ, and by his suffering the wounds of his people are healed: he is the king who reigns from the tree. He is a teacher whose words gain strength from their brevity, and whose power restores men to God. For God made man in his image but man chose the way of sin and death. Then God's only Son became man and taught men the truth for their 'conversion and restoration' [*1 A.* 23]. By becoming man he has joined God and a man together so that he might restore the whole race of men to God. The new Israel is cut from his belly.

Irenaeus, 'the peaceful', Eusebius [*H.E.* 5.36] tells us, was linked with the martyrs of Lyons in reconciling Christians with one another. This activity was the practical expression of his dominant concern for the unity that the gospel had brought. The work of Christ was to join the end to the beginning, to join man to God. What then are man's chances of union with God? Made in God's image, held always by his hands, is man's hope secure? For Irenaeus it was precarious and, to human eyes, impossible. Man had as much chance of reaching God as Jonah had of emerging from the whale's belly. He had been swallowed by Satan, the author of sin; yet like Jonah he cried out from his afflictions, and called on God from the belly of hell. God heard him and delivered him, so that man would never again think that he was naturally like or equal to God, but would thank and glorify God continually for his salvation [*H.* 3.21.1]. Man is but the receptacle; the power and the glory are God's [*H.* 3.21.2]. Yet man's deliverance is all the more certain because it has its origin outside him. The saviour became flesh, died and rose again, thereby uniting man to God. Joined to him man will be raised, without danger of relapse, and will join in the eternal adoration of the Father.[1] It is important to see the miracle of man's salvation. Man's growth and adjustment to God may have been gradual; but the power of evil was as strong as ever, if not stronger. The devil lied to Jesus when he claimed power over the world, just as he lied to Adam in the beginning [*H.* 5.24.1]; yet his defeat is certain, for Christ has already conquered.

One may go further and say that the union of God and his creation is based on an original opposition between maker and what is made, one being perfect, unchanging, unconditioned and the other needing to receive a beginning, a middle, addition and increase. From his birth Jesus joined man to God; his name, Emmanuel, showed that God was present in Mary and that the Christ was born on earth [*H.* 3.17.1]. The Spirit then descended on Jesus and became used to humanity, living in men, working the Father's will in them and renewing their old ways into the newness of Christ [*H.* 3.18.1]. From Pentecost on, the Spirit has worked to bring distant tribes into unity, to offer to the Father the first-fruits of the nations. The Comforter was promised 'to join us to God'. The Spirit is the water to make dough for one loaf, and to water the dry land, for the bodies of Christians are united by baptism and their souls by the gift of the Spirit; both baptism and Spirit are needed. The Word gives the Spirit to all who share in him, for he sends the Spirit into all the earth [*H.* 3.18.1], and his present work is to bring together the far and the near, to gather them together in a building of which he is the chief corner stone [*H.* 3.5.3]. To this goal of unity the plan of salvation works. One God, one Son doing the Father's will, one race of men, one wisdom of God, by which the creation, 'confirmed and incorporated with his Son, is brought to perfection': all this comes from the descent of the Word to the creature and the ascent of the creature to the Word. The Word 'contains' the creature and the creature 'contains' the Word [*H.* 5.36].

Man's union with God is described in blunt, concrete terms.

[1] G. Jouassard, 'Le "signe de Jonas" dans le livre IIIe de l'*adversus haereses* de Irénée', in *L'homme devant Dieu, Mélanges offerts au Père Henri de Lubac* (Paris, 1963), vol. 1, pp. 244ff.

Man is 'attached' to God by the incarnation [*H.* 5.1.2]. Enoch is moulded and translated by the same hands of God [*H.* 5.5.1]. Christ Jesus 'took up' man into himself [*H.* 3.17.6]. Man is 'mixed with' the Word and adopted as a son of God [*H.* 3.20.1]. Men who 'bear' or 'carry' the Spirit [*H.* 4.25.2] also 'receive' and 'carry' God [*H.* 5.8.1].

Yet the union of God and man is not a single episode. Both covenants, the old and the new, came from the same God, for the one end of salvation. 'For there is one salvation and one God; but the precepts which form man are many and the steps which lead man to God are not few' [*H.* 4.19.2]. Nor is the union of God with man a cheap thing: to sum up the race of men, the Lord had to embrace its death. He died on the sixth day, the day of Adam's death, bringing a second creation out of death [*H.* 5.23.2]. He also had to do battle with the devil. This he did, through his manhood, and put the devil under the power of man [*H.* 5.24.4].

In Clement there is no doubt that union with God is the chief gift of Christ to man. The whole of salvation is a unity, for all men are his and he could not be saviour and Lord if he were not saviour and Lord of all. Clement's use of the simile of a magnet illustrates two things – the one force that draws all men, and the variety of response:

'For on one original first-principle, which works according to the Father's will, the first, second and third depend; and then at the extreme limit of the visible world there is the blessed rank of angels; and so, even down to ourselves, ranks below ranks are appointed, all saving and being saved by the initiation and through the instrumentality of the One' [*S.* 7.2.9].

The relation of the indwelling saviour to the righteous soul, in which he lives, is one that unites the saviour with the community of the saved [*S.* 7.3.16]. The Gnostic, who climbs as high as man may and is joined to God by contemplation and love, knows that he must pray and be careful. For the angels who fall through carelessness 'have not yet succeeded in completely extricating themselves out of their tendency to duality so as to regain their former oneness' [*S.* 7.7.46].

So we move from the general scheme to the individual significance of salvation. Here Clement says explicitly that unity with God is an important definition of faith. After describing the cosmic unity of the Son as 'one thing as all things', he adds: 'Therefore also to believe in him and through him is to become something unified, being indivisibly made one in him; but to disbelieve means separation, estrangement, and division' [*S.* 4.25.157]. The rest of *Stromateis* 4 contains an exposition of this theme. Oneness in Christ means four things:

(1) freedom from sin, which separates from God: drawing on Ezekiel 44, Clement describes the way of purification, which reaches the eighth day of heaven and there finds perfect rest;

(2) to be born again to a life of righteousness and eternal peace in God. Rebirth means the purity and holiness of little children. The purity of Rebecca, whose name means 'glory to God', leads to divine glory, which is immortality;

(3) to serve God with all our being in the world, which he has made, is the first principle of all things, physical, ethical and rational, so the dualism of Basilides must be rejected. Whether we are on earth or in heaven we have the one task, which is to serve 'the one God, by whom all things are made and created, the world, and things above the world' [*S.* 4.26.167];

(4) to pass from ignorance to knowledge. This is a matter of choice and all men are free to choose. Growing like God, as far as is possible, the true Gnostic lives the life of the New Jerusalem now. This life will shine in good works for men to see.

Further intricate development of Clement's symbolism follows in support of these themes. Unity with God in a new life, which is free from sin, dedicated to service and enlightened by knowledge, is what Clement finds in the gospel. The terms he uses and the polemic against dualism and determinism indicate the Gnostic environment of his thought; he is concerned to offer what the heretics claim to offer but cannot.

4 How does the Word bring knowledge of God?

The problem of incarnation led to that of God and his Logos, which led in turn to what the Logos does; his work of uniting man to God ends in knowledge, reason and truth. What is this knowledge and how does the Logos bring it? Union with God is not irrational ecstasy; knowledge goes beyond human reason but not against it. Gnostic theosophy, in contrast to the beginning of Christian philosophy, was 'a defeat of the discursive intelligence at the bottom of the scale of being, not at the top'.[1] Yet mystery and revelation remain, for only God can give knowledge of God.

Justin sees the central place of knowledge and the need for both reason and revelation. All is done rationally, with *logos*:

'We shall prove that we worship rationally, having learnt that he is the son of the true God himself and having him in second place and the Spirit who prophesies in third place. For they accuse us of madness on the ground that we give to a crucified man the next place after the unchanging and eternally true God, who made all things. They are ignorant of the mystery which is in this, and we ask you to pay attention as we explain the mystery to you' [*1 A.* 13.3f.].

Justin tells how he entered the gates of light and found the true philosophy, rest and fulfilment. He invites his listeners to come to know the Christ of God and be initiated into perfection [*D.* 8.2]. The revelation of God has always been the work of his Word. When God appeared or spoke to his ancient people it was never the Father but he 'who by God's will is God, son of God and angel because he serves God's will' [*D.* 96.4]. The Jews did not understand this for 'Israel knew me not and my people understood me not'. Only the Son and those who receive his revelation may know the Father. The Word and Son of God 'is also called angel and apostle for he himself declares whatever should be known, and he is sent revealing whatever is to be announced, as indeed our Lord

[1] Murdoch, *The Fire and the Sun*, p. 66.

himself said, "He who hears me, hears him who sent me"'
[*1 A.* 63.4f.].

Knowledge is the universal quest of the second century. For
Irenaeus it all comes through the Word, who said: 'No man
knows the Son, but the Father; no man knows the Father, but
the Son and he to whom the Son has willed to reveal him'.
This is what the apostles put in the Gospels. But Valentinus
and others have changed the verb to a past tense: 'No one
knew the Father'. They falsely claim that the true God was
unknown until the Lord came, for the God of the prophets and
of creation was not the true God. Irenaeus is here supported by
the text of Luke where the verse has strong overtones of saving
history and summing-up. The seventy have returned from their
mission triumphant, the demons are defeated, and Satan has
fallen from heaven. Jesus is glad that children have seen what
the wise could not see. The Father has handed all things to
Jesus and none will know the Father but through the Son,
whose disciples now see and hear what prophets and kings
longed to see and hear but could not [Luke 10: 17–24].

Irenaeus objects to the unknown God of Marcion and the
Gnostics: how could his pre-Christian neglect of the world be
explained? He supplies the missing inference in the verse by
claiming that the Son is known only through the Father; if
your account of the Father is as wrong as that of Valentinus,
then you will not know the Son. Not that the Gnostics really
believed God could be known, anyway; for they claimed that
Christ told the *Pleroma* to accept their ignorance of God. How
silly it would have been for Christ to come to earth just to tell
men to forget about looking for God! What Christ did teach
was that God could be known only to those whom God had
taught. The Gnostics taught the mystery of God to keep men
out, whereas Jesus came to let men in.

The evidence is to be seen: 'The Father revealed himself to
all by making his Word visible to all' [*H.* 4.11.3]. This means
that those who see but do not believe may be justly judged.
Some visibility extends to the creation and history, for the
Word reveals God in his world and in the Law and the prophets; but in his earthly life the Word was 'visible and tangible'.
The Father is the invisible Son and the Son the visible Father.
Everyone confirmed the evidence that he was truly man and
truly God – 'the Father, the Spirit, angels, creation itself, men,

rebel spirits and demons, the Enemy and finally, death itself' [*H.* 4.11.5]. This means that those who do not believe can be justly judged.

The conclusion [*H.* 4.11.5] is that knowledge, like most else in Irenaeus, comes under the omnivorous theme of one God, one Word, one world. 'Therefore, then, in all things, and through all things, there is one God, the Father, and one Word, and one Son, and one Spirit, and one salvation to all who believe in him.' This provides the perfect transition to the final theme of one and many; but there remain two points, in some ways mutually inconsistent, that must be mentioned.

For Irenaeus, knowledge has a human face. What was perfected in Christ has now spread over all the earth through God's many messengers. With this extension in time and space goes a concentration on Christ crucified. It is much better not to know the reason for the existence of a single thing but to love and believe God. The only knowledge worth pursuing is that of the crucified son of God [*H.* 2.39.1]. This was the gospel preached by the first apostles and handed down to the present by their successors. It is set out in the rule of faith, which is the same everywhere – Germany, Spain, Gaul, Libya, Egypt and all places in the East. It carries the overtones that Polycarp learnt from the apostles and conveyed to Irenaeus. Successions of bishops are tedious, says Irenaeus, but the reality they indicate is living and human; without it, the truth cannot be found. The great company of believers has a central point of reference; all its roads lead to Rome [*H.* 3.3.1f.], which is a continuing witness to what believers hold as true. It is fitting that Irenaeus should have in Rome a geographical place of *recapitulatio* as well as a necessary objective point of reference against the danger of heretics.[1] When Irenaeus turned the Gnostic account of tradition into a weapon against Gnosticism, he made it more human by pointing to names and faces and by bringing into the open light of day what heretics wanted to hide.

[1] Just as Cyprian's account of collegiate episcopacy could not work without the primacy of one see, so Irenaeus' account of succession had to fix one public point of reference if it were to make any impact at all. How well this has worked is hard to say. Within 2 miles of my study, there are at least six ancient communions, each declaring apostolic succession, owning different geographical points of allegiance and for the greater part, not in communion with one another.

It was no longer the possession of a clique but the ever-widening river of God's grace. All the charismata were in each of the apostles but they now severally go on in others.

Secondly, the bishops have a charisma of truth.[1] Here again Irenaeus shows his careful sense of judgement. What the Church says is not true because of its succession. It is true in its own right. Rival pedigrees are profoundly and ultimately irrelevant, for Irenaeus does not put his final confidence in a succession or even in Christ himself. He argues that the Gnostic claims are false; he shows their logical inadequacies and their distortion of facts, for whatever has been said, from whatever source, has no value if it be not true. Like Justin, Irenaeus is driven by a love for truth alone and he quotes with approval some words of Justin: 'I would not have believed the Lord himself, if he had declared any other God than him who shaped us, made us, and sustains us' [*H.* 4.11.2].

Tertullian has little to add here, for his concentration on *solus Christus* is extreme and is not elaborated by many metaphors as in Irenaeus. 'Once we have found Christ Jesus we have no more need to be curious, once the Gospel is ours we do not need to inquire further' [*Praescr.* 7.13]. Certainly, there is progress in the deeper knowledge of Christ [*Pud.* 1.11f.] but it is not capable of exposition or elaboration. With Clement the opposite is the case: he finds it hard to stop. Knowledge is Clement's whole theme in his *Stromateis of Gnostic notes concerning the true philosophy*. Some account has already been given. It will be enough here to show how knowledge and the Logos are tied together, with the same indissoluble use of reason and revelation that we have seen in Justin and Irenaeus.

In the first place the Logos is the same as truth. Truth is one coherent whole. Error occurs when a limb is torn from the body of truth or a part taken from the whole. The different schools of philosophy have done to truth what the Bacchic women did to Pentheus: they have torn it apart. 'Each claims that the part he has obtained is the whole truth.' But just as the light breaks

[1] For discussion of this expression, see L. Ligier, 'Le "charisma veritatis certum" des évêques', *L'homme devant Dieu*, pp. 247ff. and Norbert Brox, 'Charisma veritatis certum', *ZKG*, 75 (1964), 327–31, who shows that Irenaus defended the Church's claim to authority against the Gnostics and pneumatics, 'indem er nachweist dass die wahren, überlegenen Pneumatiker in der Kirche zu finden sind' (p. 331). The term invites anachronistic interpretation.

over the whole earth at dawn, so all who have looked for the truth have received some part of its light. Now these parts come together in that instantaneous plurality or simultaneity that is so important to Clement and Irenaeus. 'Eternity indeed unites in one moment present and future besides the past as well. But truth is more capable than eternity of bringing together its own seeds though they have fallen on foreign soil.' The parts of truth will fit together because they are parts of the Logos, who is eternal. The different philosophies are torn from 'the *theologia* of the Logos, who exists eternally. He who brings together again the divided parts and makes them one, shall certainly, without danger of error, gaze on the perfect Logos, the truth' [*S.* 1.13.57]. Love of truth, in other days, has been an abstract theme; in the four writers we are examining, it is a dominant and highly personal theme. All truth was part of Christ; to know more of truth was to know Christ better.

This comes out even more clearly in Clement's account of the true dialectic [*S.* 1.28.177f.]. This is, as in Plato, a logical skill; but it does not stop at the highest form or power. 'The true dialectic, then, is linked with the true philosophy. It examines things and tests powers and first principles, rises from them gradually to the supreme essence of all, and dares to go beyond to the God of all things.' Plato used the allegory of the cave, where the philosopher must struggle beyond appearances to the light of truth, to explain how dialectic works. Dialectic uses reason, not the senses, to find out what each reality is, and does not give up, until by sheer intellect the goal is reached, the apprehension of the highest reality, the Good [*Republic* 532]. For Clement the upward climb is only possible through the saviour or the Logos. 'It does this, not without the saviour, who by the divine Word has removed, from the eye of the soul, the dark film of ignorance, which is caused by a sinful way of life, and who has given us the best faculty of all so that we may clearly recognise God and mortal man.'[1]

From this point it is easy to pass to Clement's definition of knowledge: 'Our knowledge and spiritual garden is the saviour himself, into whom we are now planted, after being transferred and transplanted from the old life into good soil. The change of soil leads to fruitfulness. The Lord then, into whom we have been transplanted, is the light and true knowledge' [*S.* 6.1.2].

---

[1] Cf. Homer, *Iliad*, 5.127f.

This account of knowledge is only possible through the concept of the Logos, where the rational object of knowledge is at the same time a person to be trusted and loved. The move from dialectic to contemplation is much easier than it could be for a plain Platonist. Nor is the end the only thing that is easier; the way is also given. Since man starts at a disadvantage, through his passions and sin, there is need for a power outside him to get him started. This power is the new life, the good soil into which he has been planted. The garden or paradise in which the believer is planted is the same garden in which the tree of life is planted; this tree is the cross, which bears the fruit of knowledge [*S.* 3.17.104]. The Logos was planted in the world and grew to the tree of the cross, by which alone man finds knowledge [*S.* 5.11.72]; in fellowship with Christ he grows to knowledge where he sees God no longer merely as reflected in a brother, but face to face [*S.* 1.19.94]. The face of God is his Son and to see him is the highest blessing man can know [*S.* 7.3.13]; properly it belongs after death but the Gnostic anticipates, while he is on earth, where he reaches a rational death, a separation of body from soul.[1] The second aspect of knowledge is continual prayer, which is just as dependent on the Logos as is the vision of the face of God. For the Logos is the total presence of God in every place and at every time. 'We are commanded to worship and adore the Logos, persuaded that he is our saviour and leader, and through him to worship the Father. We do not do this, like certain others, just on selected days, but we do it continually through the whole of life and in every way' [*S.* 7.7.35]. In this conquest of time and place, knowledge grasps past, present and future as they are revealed by the Son or wisdom of God [*S.* 6.7.61]. The final peak of knowledge is love, a love that is only reached by a freedom from passion that derives from the Logos, who is *logikos*. When the passions go, love may take control, 'for love is no longer the desire of the lover but a loving assimilation, which has restored the Gnostic to the unity of faith, independent of time and place' [*S.* 6.9.73]. He lives then by the archetypes above, just as navigators use the stars to steer their ship; everything superfluous is left behind, for knowledge is the only thing that matters [*S.* 6.9.79].

In conclusion, we may say that knowledge is related in every

---

[1] See above, p. 109.

aspect to the Logos. He is the total truth, of which most men have but a fragment; he leads men up the path of true dialectic to the highest knowledge; his cross is the tree of life, from which knowledge is to be picked; he is the face of God, on which men gaze.

5 How can he be both particular and universal, i.e. the man Jesus or the risen Christ *and* the universal Word of God?

For Justin, the Word combines universal with particular, plurality with unity. He is perfect reason, whose seeds are found in every man: what was partial in philosophers is complete in him. The philosophers contradict one another because they have different parts: he is the whole Logos, Word or Reason, who extends to all time as well as all space. His many names in scripture tell of his excellence: he is king, priest, God, Lord, angel, man, chief, captain, stone and child. These and other names show how rich is the variety of his being and activity [*D*. 33; 34; 61; 62; 126].

In Christ the gifts of the Spirit come together. Under the Old Covenant the powers of the Spirit were many and various [*D*. 87; 88]. The prophets had one or two powers. Solomon had wisdom, David understanding and counsel, Moses power and piety, Elijah fear, Isaiah knowledge and so .on. 'So then the Spirit rested or in other words ceased, when Christ came.' The gifts were no longer evident in Israel, for they had come to rest in Christ. Then came a new dispensation in which the powers were distributed again. The early life of Christ was a time of restraint as he ate and grew like any man. Yet all the powers were there. The infant Christ was able to save the Wise Men from the devil in Damascus [*D*. 78.9].[1] He did not need to be baptised, or to ride into Jerusalem to obtain power. But for the human race, for men's sake, Justin repeats, he did these things.

---

[1] See *D*. 77.4 and 88. The wise men came from Damascus, which belonged to Arabia [*D*. 88.10]. Damascus and Assyria had sinister associations from prophetic times. The fact that the wise men came from Damascus pointed to their liberation by the power of Christ, who even at his birth was able to overthrow the devil in fulfilment of Isaiah 8: 4.

When he did come to Jordan, his infinite power was evident. The water caught fire, the Spirit flew down like a dove and the voice of God thundered: 'You are my Son; today I have begotten you'. From that day he was known by men for what he was and therefore this was for them his birth. The signs of righteousness and living energy were seen by men [*D*. 87 and 88]. Now he pours out the gifts again upon the new Israel and the Spirit works his many powers through all who believe. This should be obvious to the Jews, for the gifts they have lost are now blatantly evident among Christians [*D*. 82]. Christ has captured those who were once slaves of error and now he gives them gifts. They are the faithful seven thousand, for whose sakes God holds back the wrath of his judgement. Every day Christ gains new disciples and gives them different gifts [*D*. 39.2].

Justin sees the world soul of Plato in the sign of the cross, which marks the universe. Plato, when speaking of the nature of things, spoke of the son of God, 'placed crosswise in the universe' [*1 A*. 60].[1] Indeed the cross of Christ does dominate the shape of things in the world, as 'the greatest symbol of his power and rule'. It is universal and yet peculiar to Christ, for the demons never understood it and did not put it in the myths they made [*1 A*. 55].

The universal Christ continues to bring all together, to call men to 'friendship, blessing, repentance and family life' [*D*. 139.4] in the land of the saints. 'And so men come, from every direction, both bond and free, believing on Christ, knowing the truth contained in his words and the words of his prophets, and they know that they will be together with him in that land, and will inherit the things of eternity which cannot pass away' [*D*. 139.5]. So for Justin the Logos is one and many, particular and universal, a complete unity, who brings together the many parts of truth, many divine names, many gifts of the Spirit, and many believers. As a cosmic sign his cross shapes the universe and men turn to him from every part of the world. Cosmos and history find their unity in him. This theme is expanded in Irenaeus' multi-coloured account of recapitulation.

'Semper et nunc' ('always and now') could be a motto for Irenaeus, whose account of unity and plurality in the Word would include most of what he said on any subject. For the

---

[1] See above, p. 134.

Word makes God known in many ways: he comes as true man to all men, he creates and holds together all things [*H*. 3.11.8],[1] and he weaves for God that pattern in history which makes sense only as he sums it up. For the complex unity of the saving Word belongs to the dimension of time first, and then of space. Whatever else Irenaeus said, he left no doubt that God and his Word did their best work in the medium of history. Men might work with wood or clay to produce art and beauty; God worked with time and produced a plan or pattern. In Christ, the pattern is complete, the circle closed, the end joined to the beginning and the Spirit made one with the flesh. The Word was always the same, he spoke truth in the prophets and in the apostles [*H*. 4.57.2], he mediates for sinful men, restoring them to friendship with God, offering himself as the propitiation for their sin [*H*. 5.17.1].

His cosmic unity does not belong merely to past and present, but supremely to the future. He is the first to rise from the dead, and the head of the body, which, with all its members, will rise in the body of the risen Christ [*H*. 3.20.3]. This is the second great theme that Irenaeus took from Paul.[2] Christians live between the resurrection of Christ and the final resurrection. Their lives are defined by reference to these two points. They become members of the risen Lord, who is on his way to take his throne and to rule. This body (again from Paul) is a physical unity [*H*. 5.2.2ff.; 5.6.2]. Creation is crowned as the Word brings together flesh and spirit. Only he could have achieved in the beginning, and always maintained, the order of creation, the arrangement of matter in measure and order, wisdom and reason. To creation and incarnation he now adds the Church, which has its unity and shape, within which the Spirit and all grace are present [*H*. 3.38.1]. Order and unity of many parts are signs of the truth that the Word presents and of the community that bears his name.

Why then does Irenaeus not see all that happens as a continuation of the Easter victory, which the Word has won? Why does he describe the body of Christ as an ass, a crucified beast of burden? Because humiliation is the lot of him who bears man's sin [frag. 21]. The movement from resurrection to

---

[1] Kunze, *Irenäus*, p. 56.
[2] Käsemann, 'The faith of Abraham in Romans 4', in *Perspectives on Paul*, pp. 79–101.

parousia is not mystical but earthy; it is more travail than triumph. It is marked not by the empty tomb but by the way of the cross, which is the only way to resurrection [*H.* 3.19.5]. The cross was the only way for the body to follow its head ('consequente corpore suum caput').[1]

Irenaeus lived where two great rivers joined and flowed on together to reach the sea. Not long before, there had been cruel persecution and the ashes of martyrs had been thrown into the great river, to prevent the resurrection of their bodies. In the same way, I think, he saw that the course of saving history, the uniting of men with Christ, was marked by suffering and death until the end of the journey was reached. Eusebius later wrote:

> 'Our story of God's commonwealth will record on ever-lasting monuments the most peaceful wars waged for true peace of soul, and of those who in these wars were valiant for truth rather than for country, for piety rather than for their loved ones. It will proclaim to be remembered forever the dogged resistance of the athletes of piety, their bravery which endured so much, their defeat of devils too, and victories won over unseen opponents, and the crowns at the end of it all. Now Gaul was the country where the arena was packed for these events. Its capital cities were Lyons and Vienne, whose fame outstrips that of other cities of that land; and through them both the river Rhône flows, its wide stream crossing the whole countryside.'[2]

Tertullian has little place for the cosmic unity of the Logos but the unification of mankind is very important to him; he gives it a distinctly political twist, which is to be found again in Cyprian.[3] The total sovereignty of Christ is manifest in the Church, which is universal; Christ has made men one, for he rules over all men and all that is. His death was for all men [*Marc.* 5.17]. Christ is 'the same to all, king to all, judge to all, God to all and Lord' [*Iud.* 7.9]. His rule extends over the barbarians, among whom he surely dwells, and a soldier's crown or garland of victory may well be stained with the tears of Christian wives and mothers, whose husbands or sons he has

---

[1] *H.* 4.34.4. See P. Gächter, 'Unsere Einheit mit Christus nach dem hl. Irenäus', *ZKTh*, 58 (1934), 525f.

[2] Eusebius, *H.E.* 5.1.

[3] See W. Telfer, *The office of a bishop* (London, 1962), chapter 7.

killed [*Cor.* 12.4]. The whole world is one commonwealth under Christ and nothing is foreign to those who are his [*Ap.* 38.3]. At the end of its history, the Word will appear as 'power of God, spirit of God, reason of God, Son of God, all things of God' [*Ap.* 23.12].

He has already drawn together what was once divided. As Isaiah foretold, the flower of the rod from the root of Jesse receives the whole substance of Spirit. Every energy of the Spirit, every power and gift came to rest on him, and on the apostles too. The finality of his work was matched by the completeness of his spiritual endowment [*Marc.* 5.8.4]. Law and prophet end in him, who has the entire spiritual substance of God [*Marc.* 5.8].[1]

Now he has ascended on high, endowed with all spiritual wealth, he gives to men the gifts that the prophets foretold. In these last days, Christ is 'dispenser of spiritual things', as he pours out the Holy Spirit on all flesh [*Marc.* 5.8].[2] In view of these total claims, why does not Tertullian elaborate, like Justin and Irenaeus, the perfection of Christ within the cosmic scheme? There are three reasons. First, there is his earthy, practical disposition. Secondly, there is his scorn for the pseudo-metaphysical nonsense that the Gnostics have produced. He sarcastically compares Jesus, the fruit of the Valentinian *Pleroma*, a bunch of flowers from every bush, with Pandora's box, Nestor's honey cake and other classical miscellanies [*Val.* 12]. Lastly, his eschatology is more future than realised; the powers of darkness still rule and refuse to acknowledge the universal sovereignty of Christ. Men are still slaves of sin and death. Only at the end of history will the one commonwealth of Christ appear unchallenged and unhindered. That was why for Tertullian, as for Cyprian later, the Church had to be pure. If God's city were divided, there was no way in which it could replace the cities of this world. Certainly for Tertullian and for Cyprian the end was near; but until that end, the rule of *Christus imperator* was hidden to the world.

On all these points, Clement differs. His hold on the earth is not as firm and death is the road to perfection. Further, he has no hostility towards metaphysics. Like Justin and Irenaeus, he defeats the Gnostics at their own game. His account of the

---

[1] Bender, *Die Lehre*, p. 106.
[2] *Ibid.* p. 109.

Logos does not merely play with abstractions, but argues for a description in terms of many powers united in one point. Finally Clement has no hesitation about the totality of Christ's rule. Tribulation remained for Christ's people on earth but they were confident that he had overcome the world [John 16: 33]. Their own suffering, like his, was not a denial of his glory but a present manifestation of it.

Clement's description of the Logos as 'one thing as all things' is so striking that it is sometimes forgotten how prevalent the theme is throughout his work. It is obvious that his accounts of the Word's universal salvation with its many aspects and titles, of the 'one saviour individually to each and in common to all', of the believer who is made one, and of the knowledge that, like eternity, sees all things in a flash – all these point to 'one thing as all things'. Clement was more concerned with the universality of Jesus, the Word, than with anything else. He caught the Johannine and Pauline vision of the Word who was in the beginning, who made all things, to whom all things belonged and to whom all things will be subjected. This vision carried him from the exuberant invitation of the *Protrepticus*, to the enthusiastic detail of the *Paedagogus*, to the spiritual adventure of the *Stromateis*. The glory was too much for him. Like John, he could not see how the Word could have needed food or why men could not become divine.[1] Like Paul, he revelled in freedom from the law of sin and death and saw that all things work for good. If God is for us, what, indeed, can be against us?[2] It is possible for us to die, so that we no longer live but Christ lives in us.[3] The cosmic sovereignty of Christ, as in Ephesians, Colossians and in Paul generally was the chief message of the gospel.[4] The universal Word is like the sun, who shines into every corner and whose brilliance gives light to the heavens and the earth [*S.* 7.3.21].

It is, let it be remembered, the account of the martyr as the true man that leads Clement to talk of Christian perfection in Book 4. Clement knows of no one who was perfect in all things at once except the Word, who wore our humanity. The various

---

[1] John 4: 32; 1: 12; 10: 34; see Käsemann, *Testament of Jesus*, chapters 1 and 3.
[2] Romans 8: 2, 28, 31.
[3] Galatians 2: 20.
[4] Ephesians 1: 15–23 and 4: 1–16; Colossians 1: 15–23; Romans 5: 12–21.

gifts of the Spirit show the variety of perfection that others may achieve. The perfection of the one who knows is marked by disinterested love, freedom from passion, a settled disposition, likeness to God, tranquillity and divinity. Clement pauses at the beginning of chapter 25 to let the philosophers catch up. Plato had talked of the same kind of perfection. The man who looks on the divine forms or ideas, looks on God and is himself divine, a god among man. In the *Sophist* [216B] the man who does dialectic is a god and in the *Theaetetus* [176] the leader in philosophy lives above the common level, searching the heavens. Only the wise live, as Homer and the scriptures show.

But what is the object of this vision? What, for Clement, are these eternal ideas on which the philosophers gaze? They cannot be God, the Father, because he is above all things in his solitary unity. How is the unknown God related to the man who knows things divine and human? 'God, then, is indemonstrable and consequently cannot be the object of knowledge; but the Son is wisdom, knowledge and truth and all that is related to these things. Indeed proof and description can be given of him.' Knowledge is possible because the Son bears the stamp of the Father's glory and teaches the truth concerning God [S. 7.10.58]. The Word is the image [S. 5.14.94], thought [S. 5.3.16] and face [Paed. 1.7.57], who reveals the Father's nature [S. 5.6.34]. He mediates power as well as knowledge, for he is the power [S. 7.2.7], servant [Paed. 3.1.2], instrument [Prot. 1.6] of God, the arm of the Lord [Prot. 12.120]. He became flesh to be seen by men [S. 5.3.16].

Yet the Son is not a simple object of knowledge. It would be a mistake to see him merely as a visible, earthly picture of the Father. He is understood and known as God when his own complex nature has been comprehended. 'All the powers of the Spirit become collectively one thing and come together in the same point – the Son.'

Clement has mentioned at least two distinct 'sources' [S. 4.21.132; S. 4.25.155]. In the first place, the Pauline *charismata*, which were dispersed among prophets and kings in the Old Testament, all came together in Jesus Christ to be distributed by him after his ascension. As he now gives gifts to men, they are exercised within his body so that the gift is not parted from the giver. So the Lord is the complex world of spiritual powers as they work in the world as members of his body. In the second place we have the Platonic world soul of the *Timaeus*, which Justin linked with the cross,[1] and the world of forms of the *Republic* and other Platonic writings. In Middle Platonism the increasing transcendence of the One or the first God was matched by the multiplicity of the second and third gods, who were to be the Mind and Soul of Plotinus.[2]

Poseidonios saw cosmic sympathy in terms of a system of powers. These served the function of immanent reason or divine fire in earlier Stoicism and the function of the forms or ideas in Plato.[3] They became subsequently demonic powers intermediary between a transcendent God and the world.

For Clement the powers converge in the Son, who does the entire will of God. They are the ladder by which the true dialectic ascends to the highest or best essence, the Son. Philo called the Logos, 'the idea of ideas'. The powers, forms or ideas are the efficient, final and formal causes of things. So that the Son is the ultimate efficient cause, representing the supreme power who moves all things. He is also the ultimate final cause representing total purpose and the supreme good. He is, thirdly, the ultimate formal cause, the source of all rationality and definition.

'But one cannot describe him with a list of his individual powers. The Son is not simply one thing as one thing nor many things as parts, but one thing as all things.' Clement means here that the Logos cannot be split up into an executive cabinet.[4] (Philo had six ruling powers.) Nor could he be described in his many parts, supposing one could list all the powers in succession. We are back with the idea that has dominated the whole chapter: the idea of complex unity, of many things brought together in a flash. 'All things come from him. For he is the circle of all the powers rolled into one and united.' Universality is in no way compromised by unity, for the circle offers completeness and perfect wholeness. 'Therefore the Logos is called Alpha and Omega. In him alone the end becomes the beginning and ends again at the original beginning without any gaps' [*S*. 4.25.157]. Clement is blocking off any possibility of incompleteness or of plurality through subdivision.

---

[1] Justin, *1 A*. 60 and Plato, *Timaeus*, 36.
[2] See above, p. 28f.
[3] K. Reinhardt, *Kosmos und Sympathie* (Munich, 1926), pp. 111ff.
[4] See especially *Prot.* 11 and 12.

If the Word is not perfectly one he cannot be the Word. If he is not all-inclusive he cannot be the Word. The Alpha and Omega symbols were already established in Christian thought as symbols of eternity. 'I am Alpha and Omega . . . he who is, who was and is to be, the almighty' [Revelation 1 : 8].

There have, of course, been those who have regarded this section of Clement, for all its evangelical setting, as an undigested borrowing from non-Christian sources. Undigested it is not, for it runs through Clement's three main works and is found in his Christian contemporaries too. The *Protrepticus* ends with a call to initiation into the truly sacred mysteries of light. Those who answer the call will dance with the Word around the one true God. The one, great, high priest calls: 'Come to me and be set in order under the one God and one Word of God'. He offers the gifts of immortality, *logos* and knowledge of God, as he offers himself. 'For this is what I am, this is what God wills, this is symphony, this is the harmony of the Father.' He is Son, Christ, Word of God, arm of the Lord, power of the universe, the will of the Father. He is not concerned with vague mysticism. His call is ethical, to the remaking of man in accordance with the true pattern or archetype (which the Word is) to the naked righteousness by which alone man finds God. This righteousness comes only through the faith that Christ gives, which is the only way to escape the corruption of death. It is a call to rest from the heavy burdens and to know the meekness and lowliness of Christ. His easy yoke joins together the whole of mankind, whom he drives as his chariot team to the heavenly Jerusalem. There is no time for hesitation when the offer is so great and the end is so sure. Just as Christ led ass and foal yoked together into the earthly city, so now he brings all mankind under his yoke to heaven. What a sight for the Father, to see his Son returning in victory with all men surely his. To be his means to be a son of the most high God, adopted to a life of obedience. 'The entire life of men who have come to know Christ is good.'

In all this Clement speaks as one whose mind is overwhelmed by the offer God makes. Almost incoherent at times, the themes remain rational and ethical, with extraordinary twists and recoveries.

'Enough, I think, of words. Perhaps I have, for love of men, run on too long in pouring out what I have received from

God, as is only to be expected when one is inviting men to salvation – the greatest of all things . . . But to you there still remains the final act, which is this: to choose which is better – judgement or grace. As far as I am concerned, I do not think there is any doubt at all which is the better of the two; indeed it is wrong even to compare life and destruction' [*Prot.* 12.123].

God's short word is a word without end; his brevity is the brevity of daybreak, not of death.

The answers to the five problems have produced a more coherent response than that found earlier. Tertullian is, of course, the odd man out as he anticipates later christological formulas. For the rest, there is an intelligible progression from the fact of incarnation, to the person of Christ, to his saving work and gift of knowledge, then to his universality. Such coherence is rare in apologetic writing, which has to face varied problems and questions that do not allow a co-ordinated response. The coherence springs from the one concept of Logos as the short but universal Word.

Problems and comment

In this final section of comment, there is need for a clarification of the ways in which the New Testament, Clement and others have been handled, rather than an independent exposition of parallel problems. The account of Logos, Spirit and cosmic reconciliation in the New Testament and the fathers have received considerable attention; except for a brief reference to Ebeling, we shall look at the problems that emerge in recent exposition.

1   The need for logical method

When we ask the doxographer's question: 'What did x say and how is it related to what other writers said?', we come to some very strange conclusions. For example, the account of divine transcendence in Clement has parallels and yet remains extreme; from which it is wrongly concluded: 'The transcendence of God necessarily implies his aloofness'.[1] For no one can deny that Clement's God is more intimate and immediate in his fellowship with man than is the God of almost any other theologian. The wrongness of the conclusion points to a weakness in the method of interpretation. When it is applied to Clement's account of the Logos, we are told that there are three distinct stages in Clement's Logos: 'the mind of God, the totality of ideas, the world-soul'.[2] The oddness of the division is striking from the first, when passages [*S.* 4.25.155 and *S.* 5.11.73] that speak of the 'place' of the ideas are quoted as evidence of the first stage. Clement, it is claimed, depends on Philo for the concept, although Clement thinks it comes from Plato and it is found in Aristotle, Albinus, Plutarch and elsewhere. The second stage sees the Son as the world of ideas, as the first principle of created things. Here we look at *S.* 4.25.156 where the Son is 'one thing as all things'. Again in Philo there is some parallel; but we need to go to Plotinus and Plato's *Parmenides* for the notion of a complex unity. The third stage of the Logos finds it immanent in the universe as a world soul. Here Philo has it all; but the same concept is found in Albinus, Plutarch, Atticus and Numenius, and its Stoic origin was evident to Pohlenz.[3]

Now all this might be useful because it shows the width of Clement's concept; it is also all wrong. First, the doxographer breaks a writer up into single propositions or phrases and looks for verbal coincidences; it is possible to discern the three elements and others in the account of Logos and to find parallels elsewhere. With this verbal atomism, it has even been argued that nothing new happens after Philo.[4] What is new after Philo

---

[1] S.R.C. Lilla, *Clement of Alexandria, a study in Christian Platonism and Gnosticism* (Oxford, 1971), p. 215.

[2] *Ibid.* pp. 199–212; Lilla follows Wolfson (see below, n. 4) on this point.

[3] M. Pohlenz, 'Klemens von Alexandreia und sein hellenisches Christentum', *NAWG, PH* (1943), 158ff.

[4] E.g., 'Not exactly a departure from Philo but only an addition to him is the doctrine of the Incarnation, for in its ultimate formulation the Incarnation became a new stage in the history of the Philonic Logos' (Wolfson, *Church fathers*, vol. 1 (Harvard, 1956), p. viii). See also p. 244, n. 2 below.

is the way in which Clement and others combine many ideas in different ways. Source criticism may share the same atomistic errors and even add an element of nescience fiction.[1] Where there are so many different verbal parallels it is probable that the idea was so widespread that the search for literary source is superfluous. Even if the key phrase 'one thing as all things' were found elsewhere, it would be sounder to conclude the presence of persistent logical problems (one and one–many) rather than recurrent doctrines.[2] There is clear evidence of the logical importance of the concepts of one and one–many from Plato's *Parmenides* onwards, as distinct from the direct historical influence of any 'doctrines'. Philosophy does not work within a strict doxographical framework, which looks for words and phrases rather than for arguments.

On Clement's account of the Logos, however, doxography is in a worse case than ever:

> 'The Logos is, first of all, the mind of God, which contains his thoughts; at this stage, he is still identical with God. In the second stage, he becomes a separate hypostasis, distinct from the first principle; in this stage, he represents the immanent law of the universe or, in other words, the world-soul. Let us examine each of these three stages.'[3]

Now Clement is concerned to state that the opposite is the case: the Logos is 'not one thing as one thing nor many things as parts but one thing as all things'. He is concerned to argue for the unity not just of the so-called 'stages' of the Logos but for the unity of God as *anarchos arche*, Logos in God, ideas in Logos, world soul, believers, heaven and earth, In other words, there is only one *arche* of all things.

[1] Lilla, *Clement of Alexandria*, p. 207: 'It is possible, although it cannot be proved directly, that the common source of these parallelisms between the Logos of Clement and the *Nous* of Plotinus is represented by Ammonius Saccas'. Everything that does not contradict known laws of nature may be held to be physically possible, and everything that is not a formal contradiction is logically possible. It is possible, although highly improbable, that Simon Stylites wrote the original version of the hymn, 'Nearer, my God, to thee', although it is not possible that he sang it as the *Titanic* went down; heaven and re-incarnation do not satisfy known laws of nature.

[2] See Osborn, *Philosophy of Clement*, pp. 17–24.

[3] Lilla, *Clement of Alexandria*, p. 201. I can only count two stages in this statement.

The argument of the context, as always, gives the clue to interpretation. Clement speaks of the unity of the pantocrator with the true Gnostic, who frees himself from lust that he may be joined to God. 'For the plan of creation is good and all things are managed well, nothing happening without a cause. I must be in what is yours, O ruler of all, and if I am there, I am near you' [*S.* 4.23.148]. In this way the true Gnostic is already God [*S.* 4.23.149]; he becomes one, as God is one. God's unity is that of a constant disposition or flow (*theos/thei*) of good things. Man becomes divine by becoming a unity, united with God, free from divisive passions, drawn to God as sailors are drawn to the anchor on which they pull. Self-rule, forever vigilant, assimilates to God as far as possible [*S.* 4.23.152].

Plato saw the godlike state of the man who contemplates the ideas, which are in the mind of God [*S.* 4.25.155]. Yet God is above proof and knowledge. The Son is the unity of all the powers of the Spirit, the Alpha and Omega, who unites all things. To believe in him is to be made one in his divine all-embracing unity [*S.* 4.25.158 – 26.172]. As we have seen, this means freedom from sin, being born to righteousness, serving God in the world, passing from ignorance to knowledge. In this the lack of stages or divisions is the chief point. While at one place God is above proof and knowledge [*S.* 4.25.156], at another he is the first principle of being, of ethics and of logic [*S.* 4.25.162]. The total meaning is that there is only one *arche*, that all things are included under him, and man's chief end is to reach consciously, by faith and knowledge, the highest degree of union with him.

Why has is been possible for some interpreters to miss what Clement is saying? Because the context of the key statements is so obscure that it is ignored, so biblical and ethical that it is not seen to be metaphysically relevant and so dangerous in its wholesale view of God and the world that safety prevails. It is about man becoming God and Clement considers it impossible to talk of such things plainly and also unwise to try; one does not, he says at the beginning of the *Stromateis*, give children swords to play with.[1] So the doxographer isolates his phrases and propositions, avoids the difficulty of the context and misses the point; he cannot accept the warning when his method fails

[1] *S.* 1.1.14.

to deal with apparently contradictory statements, with the ambiguity as to whether God is the *arche* or above the *arche*. The same ambiguity is in Plato's account of the Good.[1] Finally, there is in Wolfson, who shares the error, a manifest and devout desire to show that, once plurality is introduced into God, one cannot be serious about his unity.[2] He has a polemical purpose that is well served by phrases and propositions.

2   Word-event

The distinctive theme of the New Testament is that the Word became flesh, that an event occurred from which man may see the glory of God and find salvation. The New Testament is concerned with a word-event or a speech-occurrence.[3] Words are not signs that point to things, they are not merely representative, but are autonomous. Ebeling has done more than anyone else to investigate this view of language, which clarifies what the New Testament and the fathers meant. Words occur as events in time; they require situations in which they can have meaning, situations to which they can answer. A word occurs in relation to what has preceded, and to what comes after, it. It copes with the past and opens up the future. Words aim at truth. Words that sanctify and heal, that grasp reality, that open up the future, are true words. Jesus, the Word of God, is concerned with man's basic situation, and the mystery of existence. Without this Word man cannot find truth to assess the past or be free for the future. Through this Word man's basic situation is altered and he is able to stand before God. The truth of the Word is shown from the way it verifies or saves men. Man, without God's Word, is in contradiction with himself, but with this Word he finds true existence in the world.[4]

The usefulness of this account lies in the fact that it presents a main theme of the New Testament in a way that is related to

---

[1] *Republic*, 505ff.
[2] Wolfson, *loc. cit.*: 'The other heresies, those which arose within catholic Christianity and were banished from it, had their origin in an attempt to restore the Philonic conception of the unity of God'.
[3] Ebeling, *Nature of faith*, pp. 93ff., and *Word and faith*, pp. 311ff.
[4] Ebeling, *God and Word*, pp. 33–40. E. F. Osborn, 'Ebeling, Word and ...', *ABR*, 17 (1969), 41–53.

both linguistic analysis and existentialism. The peculiar way in which the New Testament speaks about language as event is more intelligible when the careful approach of linguistic analysis is used. Beginning from an awareness that something unusual is being conveyed, it is possible to explain the New Testament viewpoint with freshness and insight.

3   Spirit and letter

In the New Testament 'word' and 'spirit' are joined together in opposition to 'letter'. 'Spirit and letter' is the key to Paul's interpretation of the Old Testament as it has been recently explored by Käsemann.[1] Paul's central antithesis of spirit that gives life and letter that kills, is found in three short accounts: Romans 2: 27–9 and 7: 6; 2 Corinthians 3: 6. Only a careful analysis of these passages enables the key idea to be understood. Letter is the Law of Moses in its written form, seen by the Jew as the source of his own unique salvation and regarded by him as identical with the holy scripture. The scripture was known as 'sacred letters', and Paul was probably the first to refer to it by the singular 'letter'. Jewish interpretation and tradition have, according to Paul, misunderstood the intention of the divine will. The Law confirms this misunderstanding by its demand for works, perverting the relationship between God and the pious Jew, and bringing sin and death. Letter can only mean slavery; freedom comes from the spirit, which is defined christologically and means participation in the event of Jesus Christ.[2] It starts from the revelation of God as one who creates out of nothing and raises the dead; by contrast the letter kills because it ties us to our strength and our own piety, taking us away from the sovereign grace by which alone we can live. The spirit gives life because it is the power that reveals the presence of the risen Lord. The Old Testament may be read under a veil and misunderstood as a demand for works. On the other hand, when the veil is taken away by Christ, the message of justification may be seen. 'Christology interpreted in terms of the doctrine of justification is the criterion for distinguishing

[1] See E. Käsemann, 'The spirit and the letter', in *Perspectives on Paul*, pp. 138–66.
[2] *Ibid.* p. 147.

245

between spirit and letter, both of which may be deduced from scripture.'[1] Having explored the three passages and found these principles, Käsemann turns to Romans 10: 5–13 as an example of Paul's use of the Old Testament. In these verses the antithesis between spirit and letter is shown in different ways.

Paul saw in the antithesis between spirit and letter a key to the understanding of scripture. Yet Paul did not have one fixed exegetical method, any more than he had a dogmatic system. But he did have one theme, which dominates his entire theology, and that one theme is the doctrine of justification. Paul sees man's salvation as the present lordship of Jesus Christ in the justification of the ungodly. For Paul the righteousness of faith can never be just another form of man's piety. It is ultimately christological and shows the way in which Christ works and rules, for the Christ who is now exalted still associates with the godless as he did when incarnate on earth.[2]

4   Powers of the Spirit

Word and Spirit point the way to the distinctive concept of the Logos in the second century. For the Word is the unity of the powers of the Spirit, which are spread through the world in the bodies of believers. The gifts of the Spirit are now at work for Christ in the world; they are the means by which he takes the kingdom to himself. We shall look at 1 Corinthians first and then at Colossians.

The clearest account of the many gifts of the spirit is given by Paul in 1 Corinthians 12. He begins by indicating that every gift is a service or ministry. There are varieties of gifts, but the same Spirit, there are varieties of service, but the same Lord. There are many forms of work, but all of them are the work of the same God. A charisma is not a divine injection that may or may not take effect; it is a service to be performed. 'For there is no divine gift that does not bring with it a task, there is no grace which does not move to action.'[3] Paul goes on to list many

---

[1] *Ibid.* p. 155.
[2] *Ibid.* p. 165.
[3] E. Käsemann, 'Ministry and community in the New Testament', *Essays on New Testament Themes* (London, 1964), p. 65.

varieties of gifts, all with the understanding that what makes a
gift valid is the service it provides. Paul moves in verse 12 to the
idea of body and spirit. Christ is like a single body with its many
limbs and organs, which, many as they are, make up one body.
We were all brought into one body by baptism in one Spirit,
whether we were Jews or slaves or freemen. The one Holy
Spirit has been poured out for all of us to drink. Paul always
links body with spirit, so that spirit is the antithesis of spirituality,[1] and has its effect in visible obedience. Believers are
joined in the one body of Christ, by which he is taking possession of his kingdom. This is not a mystical unity, but a concrete
expression of Christ's sovereignty in the world. The third point
about charismata is their variety [verse 27]. Within the community God has made some apostles, prophets, teachers and
others with many different kinds of gifts. The variety of gifts
comes home too in the earlier notion of their particularity. In
Romans 12 Paul adds to the gifts of inspired speech, faith,
administration and teaching, those of charity, leading, helping
others in distress and fulfilling in various ways a 'household
code' of behaviour. Christian obedience as expressed in ethical
behaviour is seen as charisma, the effect of the grace of God
working through daily life. All is grace. Paul is not systematic
in his list of charismata, because the subject matter is far too
rich to systematise. His account of love gives it some qualities
of charisma, as well as distinctive qualities. If a man has the
gift of healing, he does not need another gift like the gift of
prophecy. On the other hand, whatever gift he has, he still
needs the gift of love. After having spoken of the equality of
gifts, Paul speaks about aiming at higher gifts. There is something, however, that is more important than a system: variety.
The variety of gifts makes unity possible. The body of Christ
indicates the plurality and diversity of gifts. Unity is only
possible through this variety, for like repels like, whereas unlike
needs that which is unlike it. Like makes something like it
superfluous, but that which is unlike another thing depends
upon it. Variety grows into unity, and this is what Paul is
talking about.

To the ideas of service, body and variety, Paul adds the idea
of sovereignty. There are varieties of service, but there is one
Lord. What makes a charisma or gift genuine is the use to which

---

[1] *Ibid.* pp. 68 and 134f.

it is put, its subordination to the sovereign grace of God.[1] 'Grace pushes home its attack to the heart of the world; it liberates it from demons. The whole of life, including death, stands under the promise of *charisma* insofar as it is Christians who are living this life and dying this death.'[2] As Christians stand in obedience under their Lord and are members of his body, they are all endowed with charisma.

What principles of church order govern the relationship between charismata? The inevitable problems that follow a conviction of divine authority may be seen throughout the history of the Church. Paul sets out three principles that govern the relationship between those who exercise charismata.[3]

(1) 'To each his own' [Romans 12: 3; 1 Corinthians 3: 5; 7: 7; 12: 7]. Each has that which he can do. He holds his gift or ministry as a steward and is limited by that which God has given him to do. He is not competent to do everything but grows in understanding of what God has given him to do, and lives within that which is his own. He has a calling, in which he must remain.

(2) 'For one another' [1 Corinthians 12: 25]. The members of the body care for one another. Charisma frees man from self and from striving after his own salvation. This makes him free to care for others. 'When we no longer have to strive for our own salvation, and no longer need to fear external powers, we become free for other people, for whom we otherwise at most find time and attention as allies or opponents.'[4]

---

[1] The more spectacular gifts, which Paul mentions, were not new to the people of Corinth. Ancient Greece knew of the ecstasies of the Thracian Dionysos, the Delphic oracle and the Sibyl. Poets, prophets and priestesses had been inspired to speak above the level of ordinary thought. Paul could have told the Corinthians that all these things were wrong, and sceptical philosophers of the day would have supported him. He took the more courageous step of claiming these gifts for the Father of the Lord Jesus Christ: 'the reign of the old gods was over and the one Lord who had spoken to a small band of exiles from Egypt was now asserting his dominion over the world' (F. D. Maurice, *Collected Essays* [London, 1957], p. 229).

[2] Käsemann, *Essays*, pp. 72f.

[3] *Ibid.* pp. 76ff.

[4] This is best expressed in the magnificent closing pages of Boyce Gibson's *Dostoevsky*, p. 212:

'The question may be asked: how are we to understand *sobornost* –

(3) 'In honour preferring one another' [Romans 12: 10].
The relation of one who has a charisma to another who
has a charisma is the recognition of Christ in his brother.
Humility is central for Paul because grace is central and
the Christian lives in the humility of one who receives.
'What have you which you did not receive?' [1 Corinthians 4: 7]. 'Did the Word of God originate from you?'
[1 Corinthians 14: 36]. All is grace; Paul substitutes the
term *charismata* for *pneumatika*, his opponents' word.

These three principles govern the relationship of the members
of the body of Christ: to each his own; for one another; submission to one another in the fear of Christ. Every Christian is
engaged in concrete opposition to the world, in mission and in
reconciliation so long as he remains a Christian. Yet he must
not take himself too seriously nor believe that he has arrived.
Christians are always men at risk, because they live under the
sign of outpoured grace and that is why they should not leave
one another unsupported.[1]

> the spiritual togetherness of Christians, in which the "I" is both
> submerged and enhanced? It could be taken to mean each man
> doing his own thing in the sight of God along with others each of
> whom is also doing his own thing, all linked with God and there-
> fore moving in harmony, but not deeply aware of each other. That
> interpretation fails to bring out what Dostoevsky was most con-
> cerned for. There is no genuine togetherness without active con-
> cern: "each is responsible for all". It is not enough for the spiritually
> stronger man to be upstanding: he has to be available, and to give
> from his spiritual substance, and in such a way that the weaker
> may receive without being humiliated.'

[1] Käsemann, 'Theologians and laymen', *NT Questions*, p. 294. On the
general theme of the powers of the Spirit, it should be noted that the
move from the unity of the Christian community to the reconciliation
of all things was easy enough for the second century. Two things make
it difficult for us. First, there is the inevitable truth that we no longer
see the disorder of the physical universe as a result of perverse and
evil powers, the overthrow of which would restore peace and harmony. Secondly, there is the separation of the Church as the body
of Christ from the notion of his effective cosmic presence. Neither of
these difficulties is easily solved. In the first place, ecologically, it is
evident that human sin can and does promote disorder in the physical
world. In the second place, the political significance that the Church
assumed in the thought of Cyprian was an element from the beginning, but took over and limited cosmic reconciliation to God's new
commonwealth. This was an obvious reaction to the fury of the

5 Inclusiveness and fulfilment

A recent treatment of the origin of christology shows how central the ideas of inclusiveness and fulfilment are in the New Testament.[1] Both these ideas are clarified by Clement's Logos doctrine and by Irenaeus' account of the summing-up of all things. What is distinctive about Jesus is that he is for his followers alive and present, not merely a great figure of the past, but someone in whom they are included and incorporate. Talking about men as 'in Christ' or incorporated 'in a new humanity' may be difficult [p. 48] yet it was precisely in this way that the early writers understood Jesus. For Paul, the believer's existence in Christ pointed to a unity that derived directly from Christ [p. 72] and 'if the congregation finds itself to be an organic unity, like a well coordinated, living body, this is because of its connection with Christ'. Christ is not identical with the body but he is the reason for it. The body of Christ in the New Testament is the body in which Christ died and the body in which Christians are united. The second depends upon the first; there is no third entity, and the simplicity of this relationship points to a central element in the gospel [p. 80]. We must distinguish between various accounts of the body of Christ, however, and only 1 Corinthians 12: 12 and 6: 15 require us to see Christ himself as the inclusive person, the body to which the Christian is joined. There can be little doubt that the letters of Paul point to the experience of Christ as corporate, so that to be joined to Christ is to become part of an organic whole. This is remarkable, because while the notion of a corporate God was not new, the linking of this concept with the personal view of God in the New Testament is difficult. It points to a new experience of God, which requires dangerous experiment in language [p. 87], for Christ is seen to be more than an individual [p. 95]. Similarly, outside Paul there is evidence of the inclusiveness of Jesus. The Johannine accounts of the vine and branches, of the indwelling of the Spirit, and of the unity of believers in Christ are clear examples.

The inclusive language about Jesus is understood better against the background of Clement and others than when

nations against God's people and shows how wrong it is to link heightened ecclesiology with the fading of apocalyptic hope.

[1] C. F. D. Moule, *The Origin of Christology* (Cambridge, 1977).

viewed solely from the background of earlier writers. It was inevitable that when many people came to know Christ in a distinctive, intimate way, their relationship to one another should come under scrutiny. If Jesus is related to x, y and z in a way that is decisive for each so that the believer no longer lives, but Christ lives in him [Galatians 2: 20], then the question of the relationship of x, y and z to one another is acute. Paul was explicit on this point when the Corinthians failed to see that their relationship to Christ made them a community. He decided to know nothing then but 'Christ, and him crucified', and said indignantly: 'Was Paul crucified for you?' Because the work of their salvation was carried out by Christ alone and not by different religious teachers, they could not divide in any significant way. All things were theirs as they were Christ's and Christ was God's. There was one source of salvation and that implied a new relationship between those who received that salvation, a relationship that excluded the party strife that had occurred at Corinth.

Christians found this relationship with one another hard to define. In *Stromateis* 3, Clement attacks those who want to derive wrong kinds of intimacy from the inclusiveness of Christ. For his Gnostic opponents communion in Christ means community of sexual relations. Clement denies this, and understands the central point better; his phrase 'one saviour individually to each and in common to all' is the heart of the matter.

With this notion of inclusiveness goes the idea of fulfilment. Jesus is the one who fulfils scripture in a way that joins him to those who have gone before and those who come after. As Son of man he is both individual and corporate [p. 132]. Jesus comes to be, through this idea of fulfilment, 'the coping stone of the whole edifice of God's relationship with man' and 'the one who fills the cosmos and fulfils God's design for all creation' [p. 133]. All that Adam and Israel ever meant is fulfilled in Jesus who is the 'ultimate pattern of man's right relationship with God' as well as the reality of that relationship [p. 134].

The ultimacy of Jesus depends upon his relationship to those who believe in him and to the God to whom he joins them. The distinctiveness of Jesus cannot be explained either by the 'divine man' nor the 'Lord' of Hellenistic cult, but only by the new categories that he brought, categories that brought together much of what had been said before. With this fulfilment came too the notion of continuity shared with Jesus into life eternal [p. 153]; and from this life eternal was derived the belief that Jesus was also primordial: he was to all time, and had been from all time.

The pre-existence of Jesus is a consequence of his ultimacy. Here Clement again is able to explain what is obscure within New Testament sources. The ultimacy of Jesus is derived from his unity with the Father. Had he been merely the second cause and not united to the first cause, there need be no pre-existence, but because Jesus is spoken of both as first cause and as second cause, he is seen as one who is from all eternity. Pre-existence is a consequence of the non-derivative nature of Jesus.

Clement's account of the cosmic unity of Christ and of Christ as the first cause, helps to explain what was implicit in the Fourth Gospel and in Paul, by showing on the one hand the relationship of one Saviour, individually to each and in common to all, and on the other hand the ultimacy of the first cause, who is one thing as all things. Similarly, Irenaeus illuminates the notions of inclusiveness and fulfilment by his extensive exposition of the summing-up of all things in Christ.

6 · God as Spirit

A careful comparison of the classical formulation of the doctrine of the trinity with an account of God as Spirit has led one scholar to the conclusion that the second-century account of God as Spirit is more adequate to explain Christian truth than the fifth-century statement of trinitarian doctrine.[1] The three hypostases or persons have placed theologians in many odd positions. For example, a precise distinction between Logos and Spirit has sometimes been made, believers being indwelt by Spirit and the world (non-human creation) being contained by Logos. This is an unfortunate consequence of faulty logic, of referring the interchangeable terms not to the activity of one God but to distinct hypostases [p. 179].

The difficulties of the fourth century with a 'substance' christology have been widely discussed. Now the category of Spirit, as used by Clement, avoids these difficulties, but does

[1] Lampe, *God as Spirit*, p. 228.

not fall into the danger of a reduced christology. Salvation is still a non-transitive, asymmetrical, one–many relation. Christ possesses the Spirit uniquely through his perfect unity with the Father and through being the source and archetype of the presence of the Spirit in believers; they become agents of the Spirit, who reproduces in them the life of Christ. There cannot be a second Christ-event because the fuller the inspiration of a saint the deeper are his dependence on, and sense of inferiority to, Christ.[1]

Further, the danger of the attribution of a universal human nature to Jesus was that it reduced the concrete reality of the incarnation. On the other hand a Spirit christology avoids this reduction. 'It enables us to say that Jesus is authentically human: a man capable of free response to God, inspired and moved by God, and mediating God to others, yet in all respects like ourselves except for the fullness and integrity of his commitment to God's calling.'[2]

7 Beware of philosophy

Two other parts of the New Testament reveal a development from 1 Corinthians 12: Colossians 1 and Ephesians 1 and 2 (which seem to follow from Colossians). In Ephesians, the body of Christ is a cosmic entity spreading through the world. For Paul, the metaphor of the body is used only in a parainetic sense to exhort members to exercise their gifts together for their Lord in the world. The development in Ephesians in no way compromises the lordship of Christ in the world; the Church is his body, but only in him is there the all-conquering peace that breaks down dividing walls. The hymn in Colossians provides a concise statement. Here the cosmic lordship of Christ over all other powers is proclaimed; once again the points of reference are Christ and the cosmos, and his power rules over all.

The most careful recent analyses of the Colossian hymn and

[1] G. W. H. Lampe, 'The Holy Spirit and the person of Christ', in *Christ, faith and history*, ed. by S. W. Sykes and J. P. Clayton (Cambridge, 1972), p. 129.
[2] Lampe, *God as Spirit*, p. 144.

Colossians 1 : 20[1] indicate remarkable similarity with Clement's
account of the cosmic Christ and universal Logos. The hymn
begins with an account of creation, which takes place in Christ,
the Logos, who is the place of all things. It adds a new
eschatological dimension by stressing that creation is 'to him',
that is, it has him as its goal. The christological framework of
creation dominates: only through him, and the love of God he
mediates, can creation be understood.[2] The second strophe
proclaims Christ as the first-born from the dead (parallel to
first strophe: 'first born of all creation') and declares that all
the *Pleroma*, or fullness of divine power, dwelt in him. As a
result of this endowment with all the divine powers or graces,
peace comes to a universe now reconciled.[3] The reconciliation
is total – the elements of earth and heaven, not merely living
things, are all included; there is no break between creation and
reconciliation. All centres on Christ, who is creator and
redeemer and whose resurrection is the new creation; faith
knows that what God's love sees in the world is real because
God's love is stronger than all that stands against it. Man
moves from alienation to reconciliation as he grasps, by faith,
the act of Christ; the reconciliation is not timeless or abstract
but is expressed in daily life, now.

If we look more carefully at Colossians 1 : 20 and the meaning
of cosmic reconciliation, we find the likeness to Clement
becomes still more striking. The rejection of dualism is the same
in the case against Colossian 'philosophy' as in Clement's case
against false Gnostics. The background of the hymn has some
link with the Jewish Day of Atonement; but in the epistle
peace comes from subjection of powers, not from their reconciliation [Colossians 2 : 15]. The writer reinterprets the hymn
on the lines of 1 : 20*b*: 'having made peace by the blood of the
cross, by this bringing peace to things in earth and heaven'.

---

[1] (i) E. Schweizer, *Der Brief an die Kolosser* (Zürich, 1976), pp. 52–74
and 215–23 (= *Brief*).

(ii) E. Schweizer, 'Versöhnung des Alls, Kol. 1, 20', in G. Strecker
(ed.), *Jesus Christus in Geschichte und Theologie, Festschrift H. Conzelmann* (Tübingen, 1975), pp. 486–501 (= 'Versöhnung'). The
following section depends heavily on these two works and on discussions with their author.

[2] Schweizer, *Brief*, p. 63: 'Christus wird so zum Herrn, der dem Leben
überhaupt seinen Sinn schenkt'.

[3] *Ibid.* p. 67: 'Die Folge dieser Einwohnung der Fülle Gottes wird als
Versöhnung des Alls beschrieben'.

The Jewish antecedents clearly link creation and redemption.[1] The peace and stability of the world depend on God and are linked to the cult. On the basis of a near contemporary source[2] it has been claimed that the Colossian heresy can be associated with a form of Jewish Pythagoreanism.[3] Against the strife of the elements man finds liberation through ascetic practices. To the cosmic predicament there are three answers to be found in Colossians: first, the relevant philosophy advocates flight and ascetic purification from the elements of nature; secondly, the writer of the letter points to life above with the risen Christ, a life lived by faith with ethical consequences here and now; thirdly, the hymn declares something more than ethical injunction as it acknowledges a cosmic peace, which is guaranteed once and for all by the resurrection of the first creator. The style of the hymn and the letter reveal a reluctance like that of Clement to engage in direct and precise description. In both cases, highly allusive prose is followed by ethical injunction; in Clement the non-literal mode is even stronger than in the letter.

In the *Extracts from Theodotus* Clement uses the Colossian hymn five times to correct Valentinian errors concerning the person of Christ [7.3; 8.2; 10.5; 19.4; 33.2]. In the same work the Valentinians use the hymn three times. This shows again the inadequacy of merely listing possible sources – the way in which a source is used is the important thing, not the fact of its use. The hymn of Colossians 1 was not enough to guarantee an appreciation of the cosmic sovereignty of Christ. One hundred years later, Valentinians used it and other parts of Colossians to express the same kind of dualism that the letter had intended to destroy.[4] Clement could reply from within the hymn itself; but the letter was too ambiguous and the theme was too important, so he tried new ways of saying the same things. The Fourth Gospel had given him a new concern for Christian unity,[5] which differed from the earthy approach of the Pauline body;

---

[1] Cf. Philo, *Spec. Leg.* 2.188–93. See Schweizer, 'Versöhnung', pp. 490ff.
[2] The tradition is traced by Schweizer, 'Versöhnung', p. 496.
[3] See also Ocellus Lucanus, paras. 19, 22 and 24, with due caution.
[4] From Clement's *Extracts from Theodotus*, it is clear that the Valentinians supported their dualism with Colossians 2: 8; 2: 9; 2: 12; 3: 1–3.
[5] See Käsemann, *Testament of Jesus*, chapter 4, 'Christian unity'; also M. Appold, *The oneness motif in the Fourth Gospel* (Tübingen, 1976).

but he held the two together. The Word and cosmocrator, now exalted on high, drew all men to himself, to unity and to the eternal glory of the Father.

His followers were in the world but not of it. In the suffering of their bodies the cross of Christ went on [Colossians 1: 24]; for in their renewed, universal humanity, Christ was all and in all [Colossians 3: 11]. His kingdom and rule embraced all things; the end was not yet, but the cross, 'the greatest symbol of his power and rule' [*1 A.* 55] declared his sovereignty on every hand. His despised people were to the world as soul to body [*Ad Diog.* 6] and God only delayed the end of the world so that more men might repent; the making of Christians was the only thing that kept the world going [*1 A.* 28; *2 A.* 7.1]. The mystery was the strange unity of life and death that Christ declared; only he who bore the dying of the Lord could show forth the power of risen life [2 Corinthians 4: 10]. The way of the cross led from glory to glory, from Christ's resurrection to that of all men. In this universal process the Son of God was neither one thing as one thing, nor many things as parts, but 'one thing as all things. Therefore indeed to believe in him and through him is to become a unity, being indivisibly made one in him; on the other hand, to disbelieve means to be separated, estranged and divided' [*S.* 4.25.156f.].

Clement was consciously developing a cosmic christology that ran back to the New Testament. Was there anything new in it? His chief contribution is philosophical argument, which is quite foreign to Colossians, where philosophy was the enemy. Platonism explains the meaning of the reconciliation of all things. The mythology of cosmic powers at war could not give adequate content to the concept. What could it mean to reconcile all things? For Clement, as a Platonist, it meant to give them rational and ethical coherence. Somehow the cross of Christ made sense of the world's disorder; it showed how chaotic evil could be overcome and how the world might gain intelligible purpose that was good.

It was all too much. Later generations of Christians turned from the Logos-doctrine to a definition of Christ that safeguarded his humanity and his godhead; the gain and the loss were considerable and it is time to explore again the universal grandeur of the Word, to whom the Father entrusted all things.[1] From the beginning it was precarious. If the forms, which are the objective tests of rationality, are taken up into the Logos, what need is there for argument? The *pigritia perennis* and *lassitudo perpetua* of the Christian man will take their answers straight from the Logos' mouth. Clement's call to rationality and inquiry will not be heard; but until it is heard again, the credibility of the Logos is bound to decline.

[1] Harnack, *History of dogma*, vol. 3, p. 144:

> 'Athanasius' importance to posterity consisted in this, that he defined Christian faith exclusively as faith in redemption through the God–man who was identical in nature with God and thereby he restored to it fixed boundaries and specific contents ... Following on the theology of the Apologists and Origen, it was the efficient means of preventing the complete Hellenising and secularisation of Christianity.'

Such a reduction may have been adequate for Christendom; but those who look back on the end of Christendom are more likely to find an adequate account of their faith in the writers who thought before Christendom began.

Conclusion

Problems

The problems of one ineffable transcendent God group themselves around the idea of a first cause. The persistence of this
idea, with all its difficulties, has been sometimes seen as a
ground for its acceptance. In the second century, a strong
monistic tendency was not peculiar to Christians; but they were
able to make good use of it.[1] In recent discussion, logical
objections to the first cause are tempered by an appreciation of
the question as a religious problem.[2] Everything has a point of
ultimate dependence, as Augustine found at Ostia: 'if one
could hear them, all these things are saying, "We did not make
ourselves, but he who made us is he who abides to eternity"'
[*Conf.* 9.10].

Man and his freedom showed the link between God and man
and the need for God to change human life, while keeping it
human. The term 'deification' was important because it
pointed to the gift of immortality as something that could not
be taken for granted. Freedom was seen to be more important
than free will because it was concerned with a fullness of life
that, unlike self-fulfilment, found its centre in the cross of Jesus.

The world and history go together, for the world belongs to a

---

[1] See above pp. 147ff. In particular, they were able to turn the monistic
tendency against Marcionites, Gnostics and polytheists, who were
less tough-minded on this point. Intelligent opposition from Celsus
may have helped them to see problems rather than merely flatten
any form of plurality in God.

[2] 'Why should anything exist at all? ... Nevertheless, though I
know how any answer on the lines of the cosmological argument
can be pulled to pieces by a correct logic, I still feel I want to go
on asking the question. Indeed, though logic has taught me to look
at such a question with the gravest suspicion, my mind often seems
to reel under the immense significance it seems to have for me'
(J. J. C. Smart, 'The existence of God', in Flew and MacIntyre
(eds.), *New essays*, p. 46).

See also P. Geach, *Three philosophers* (Oxford, 1961), pp. 110f., for a
positive consideration of the central logical issues.

God of hope, who opens the future and gives meaning to history; he is the suffering God, known supremely in the cross of his Son and the death of the martyrs. This is a strange way of defending the world and a strange God of hope; yet this is what the second-century writers held: their God was not a God of earthly prosperity and conquest, but a God of earthly suffering. Their first problem was not earthly failure, but earthly success; they have left us one complete sermon: 'Who is the rich man who is saved?' Yet the world was God's world and God was good. They found their way, as the twentieth century is discovering, in the God of hope and the suffering God. As men of good hope they go on in faith; the world is marked by the sign of the cross, which is woven into the fabric of the universe.

The universal Word represents the final factor in each of the other four problems. Only he could bring man to God, liberate and recreate man, hold the world and history together in the face of darkness and tragedy. The most amazing thing was that he could do this for all men everywhere – there were Christians before Christ. On similar lines in the twentieth century the exclusiveness of the Church is being challenged by the universality of Christ.

But how good were the arguments? The first-cause arguments have been stated more neatly, but their consequences have not been so fully accepted: second-century writers claimed that because there is nothing prior to the first cause, no account can be given of it as an account is given of other things. God is understood by the downward movement of that which comes from him, by the world and its fullness, yet supremely by the cross and its pointlessness. The other chief difference from later statements of the argument lies in the use of first-cause arguments as negative polemic rather than as supporting proofs. They were used to disprove the existence of other gods rather than to prove the existence of a God, to limit a general tendency to transcendence, not to extend it. Their conclusion was not that there must be something beyond the visible universe but that there was one thing and one thing only on which all else depended. In this way the argument entered Christian thought as a reductionist move: the pagans and Marcion should be content with one god and the Gnostics should abandon their fantastic overhead.

In the matters of transcendence and negative theology the most important single truth is that the transcendent ineffable God is not 'abstract' in the ordinary sense. He is all the closer, more intimate, because he is not a measurable block of stone. Justin makes this clear by his arguments from empirical fringes in human experience and by his description of the names of God as 'forms of address'; but the intensity of personal communion is strong in each of the four writers. Clement enters into God, is planted in Christ and lives in continual prayer. This contrasts with a tendency of some twentieth-century theology, which has favoured such terms as 'Ground of Being', a depressingly impersonal title.[1]

On man and his freedom the arguments for free will and the importance of freedom say nearly all that has been said in recent writing. Tertullian's insistence that God's foreknowledge does not deny free will is restated recently with the clarity of formal logic. The most important omission in the second-century arguments for freedom is the political element, which is compensated by apocalyptic. Because tyrants are to be overthrown at the coming of the Lord there is little ground for wanting to overthrow them now; there is rather a desire to convince the civil authorities that Christians are loyal, not disruptive, and not deserving of persecution.

The argument for 'deification' is useful because it indicates how easy it is to misinterpret what has been said whenever the link between meaning and usage is neglected. It would seem inappropriate to attempt to re-establish the term in the twentieth century, because the key words are used so differently. However, the second-century meaning points to an area where recent Christians have been slow to realise the questionable nature of their belief. What effect does God have on human life? Are the phenomena of Christian life observable? Is the Christian expectation of life after death a quaint form of megalomania?

The argument for creation and the discussion of history and hope make good sense to the reader today, and the problem of evil has had a persistence beyond all other problems. The early answers cearly indicate the directions of subsequent answers: free will, good out of evil, growth and development. One

---

[1] Note the critical comments on this term: Dorothy Emmet, 'The ground of being', *JThS.* 15.2 (1964), 280–92.

hesitant early answer, that of retributive justice, serves as a modern reminder that there is yet another problem to be probed and that crude presentations must not obliterate unexamined truths.

The Word does it all: the arguments for the particularity and universality of Jesus are empirical, depending on evidence that is difficult to assess. His particularity remains central despite the slender factual knowledge of the Jesus of history; no one would have written gospels with their quasi-biographical slant if the life and words of Jesus had not been essential to turn the Church from ways of subjective fantasy. And with this particularity goes his universality, for the exalted and the humiliated Lord are identical. The Gospel cannot be anonymous but must be tied to Jesus who, both before and after Easter, confronted his followers as Lord. Their faith and the faith of those who come after repeat the particularity of the event of Jesus, so that the history of Jesus continues to be history on earth.[1]

His universality meant that second-century writers went directly from New Testament to philosophical arguments without being awkwardly conscious of anything new or superfluous. The cosmic, universal Logos was the Jesus of the New Testament. Two recent statements show a similar confidence. Ebeling's account of word-event and de Chardin's account of the cosmic Christ are a beginning, a recognition of what is necessary. Their limited acceptance is not serious unless their enterprise is abandoned; for this kind of statement is a striking need in contemporary Christian thought.

In all the detail and difference there was one theme that ran through all the writers we have considered: the theme of unity. On most issues their position was a defence of unity over against multiplicity: one God, one race of man, one world, one plan of saving history, one Word who held all things in his sway. One God was proclaimed with Deuteronomic passion against pagan, Gnostic and Marcion. One race of men stood against the sectionalism of Jew, Gnostic, Roman and philosopher. One world, God's world, with its fierce mixture of joy and pain, was held against Gnostic and Marcionite. One plan or purpose united the whole of human history in defiance of the divisions of Marcionite, Jew and Gnostic. How did it happen? It happened through the Word, who alone declared the Father, who

[1] Käsemann, *Essays*, p. 47.

healed the broken lives of men in every nation, who held the world together by the power of his cross, who continued in history the saving work of all ages. His universality was the reason for faith. There was no corner of the cosmos and there was no period of history where his lordship did not hold. To be a Christian was to be united in him as he moved forward to the final consummation. Many unwilling opponents could have accepted Christianity without its universal aspirations; but he was no saviour who was not the saviour of all. Universality later hardened into totalitarian exclusiveness, in the face of external pressures; the rediscovery of unity and universality may yet surprise us all.[1]

Method

Obsession with sources is open to criticism on at least two grounds. It is atomistic: it separates words and phrases from their context and links them with different contexts where their meaning is different. It is inconclusive: in the last thirty years the belief that ideas are thoughts in the mind of God has been traced to at least four different origins by more than four different scholars.[2] Yet neither criticism is decisive, for transplants may carry some of their former meaning, which may escape the eyes of the transplanter and influence those who come after him. Provided it is remembered that similar words often have a different meaning and that different words often have a similar meaning, there is value in the exercise. Further, inconclusive results may be preferable to firm conclusions. If x draws proposition A from his reading of Y, the reader may well conclude that x uses A in the same sense as Y, and this conclusion will have slender probability. On the other hand, if x draws proposition A from a variety of sources, the exploration

[1] Küng, *On being a Christian*, p. 478: the Church is 'the community of those who have become involved in the cause of Jesus Christ and who witness to it as hope for all men'; and p. 502: 'it is difficult to see where the differences lie between the Churches, particularly the Catholic Church and the Protestant Churches'.

[2] W. Theiler: Antiochus of Ascalon; C. J. de Vogel: Posidonius; R. E. Witt: Xenocrates; J. Pépin: *De Philosophia*. See J. Pépin, *Théologie cosmique et théologie chrétienne* (Paris, 1964), p. 512.

of these several probabilities will add another historical dimension to the pursuit.

Jew/Greek

One reason for neglect of the second century has been the conviction that the interaction of Christian and Greek thought was a mistake; for the Christian God is not the timeless first principle of Plato. There are several reasons for rejecting such an approach. The use of Plato is wrong: in the second century he was not the idealist whom the early twentieth century pursued; he spoke of a creator God with concern for the world he had made, and his followers rejected Gnostic dualism as firmly as most Christians. The Platonic God was not the Christian God; yet he was closer to the Christian God than the gods of Olympus or the *Pleroma* of the Gnostics could ever be. He was not the God of the Old Testament but he was closer to the Christian God than the anthropomorphic deity of some second-century Jews. The second century like every century had a limited range of conceptual possibilities; but the range is far wider and more subtle than most theologians have seen. Before another general assessment can be made, there needs to be more analysis of specific issues and particular writers.

Problematic elucidation is not the only method of writing the history of philosophy or of Christian thought. It is clearly a useful and illuminating method and its several pursuits can be set out. Retrospective methods, which take the categories of the fourth and fifth centuries and project them back on all literature subsequent to the New Testament, have their uses. But they need to justify and explain what they are doing, to indicate their anachronistic aspects, and to recognise the need for other approaches. The hesitant reaction to Daniélou's first two volumes of the history of doctrine before Nicaea showed how reluctant scholars are to recognise new categories.[1]

[1] A similar reaction greeted the work of J. Pelikan, *The Christian tradition*: vol. 1, 'The emergence of the Catholic tradition (100–600)' (Chicago, 1971).

People

The elucidation of problems within the thought of a particular author and the style of commentary that it requires both provide a deeper insight into the character and mind of the author than could be obtained from a doxographical account. The qualities of each writer stand out more clearly; the differences, which a general history must gloss over, are striking. Justin, with the openness and sincerity commonly attributed to him, has also a tentativeness, an economy with words (except when quoting texts), an enigmatic incompleteness, a stubborn sense of arguing from apparent weakness and hidden universal strength. Irenaeus, the charismatic, who repeats his key ideas endlessly, the visionary, who sees and feels the glory of God, is ruthlessly logical and coarsely sarcastic in his treatment of Gnosticism. Tertullian, who uses words with such freedom and toughness that the Latin language changes in his hands, never finds the security to which he pretends. Clement, with a mind full of past treasure of human wisdom, insists that all men need Jesus, has one foot in heaven, entering God through love, and the other foot in Alexandria, kicking sensualists, pagans and spiritual snobs.

The differences in style and temperament blend with geographical settings. Clement would not have done for Carthage and Tertullian would have been a disaster at Alexandria. Yet nothing is so Christian as that these four incompatibles should fix on the universality of Jesus and his Gospel, on the cosmic lordship of the Logos, as the core of their message: 'All humanity needs Jesus' and 'All men are his.'[1] They also had much in common in the material they handled.[2] We find Justin in each of the other three writers and all use material that has come from common or parallel sources. Tertullian reshapes his material most vigorously and powerfully; Clement can write well but frequently prefers to compile rather than write. Irenaeus insists that he cannot write, clearly compiles, but still has striking phrases and sustained vitality. Justin's style gives less away – his *Apology* is generally restrained and deferential before imperial authority, his *Dialogue* is determined

---

[1] Clement, *Paed.* 1.9.83 and *S.* 7.2.5.
[2] The best single book on this area is P. Prigent, *Justin de l'ancien testament* (Paris, 1964).

by a Jewish audience with a distinctive form of scriptural controversy and the proem to the *Dialogue* is rounded into a Platonic discourse; but the man emerges through practical concern and comment as well as through the use of diverse literary forms.

Does 'the love of truth' describe a common motive in these four different writers? They all claim it as their common concern. Does anything lie behind the impressive phrase? There is Justin's Socratic insistence that love of truth may mean death, Irenaeus' confidence that falsehood only needs to be uncovered in order to be destroyed, Tertullian's conviction that falsehood is fatal and that truth deserves every effort of mind and pen, and Clement's love of inquiry because all truth is part of Christ.

Love of truth

Since at the present moment of history, the crisis facing Christianity and the Churches is linked with a wider crisis facing rationality, humanity and imagination, the theme of the love of truth claims special attention. The world has more to fear from human stupidity than from the more obvious forms of wickedness.[1] So we must look at these last strands of complex argument, lest we regard the most urgent need as a platitude of past tranquillity. The love of truth is central for Justin and that is one reason why he has sometimes been assessed as a simple soul. Justin shows the complexity of the idea; subsequently its various strands are developed by the other three writers. Love of truth begins as something ethical. It means honesty and loyalty to what is true under all circumstances [*1 A*. 2.1]. To live by telling a lie would be wrong, for truth is more important than life [*1 A*. 8.1; 2.2]. This integrity is common ground between Christians and philosophers, for Plato insisted that no man should be honoured above the truth [*2 A*. 3.6] and saw the life of the philosopher as ruled by a desire for truth and a hatred of faslehood [*Republic* 485]. The theme of love of truth dominates the *Apology of Socrates*, and with this widely respected defence Justin wishes to stand.

All this honesty and faithfulness are spelt out in logical terms.

[1] E. Käsemann, 'Love which rejoices in truth', *Colloquium* (1981), 4f.

Anyone who professes to love truth must keep to the rules of argument and not deny what he has admitted in another context. 'You are not however acting rightly nor in the way of a lover of truth when you try to destroy those things about which there has always been argeement between us, namely, that certain commands were established by Moses because of the hardheartedness of your people' [*D*. 67.4]. Without acceptance of common rules of argument, no discussion can take place.

For Justin truth is eschatological and this means at least three things. It means that a man is always under judgement whether he stands before an earthly court or not. What he says and does has final significance and there is no way in which falsehood can permanently decide an issue. Everyone who does not speak the truth he knows will be judged by God. 'As God gave witness by Ezekiel when he said: I have made you a watchman to the house of Judah. If the sinner sin and you do not warn him, he indeed will die in his sin, but I will require his blood at your hands; but if you warn him you will be innocent' [*D*. 82.3]. Secondly, truth cannot be suppressed since it represents ultimate reality: 'For the word of truth and wisdom is more fiery than the sun and filled with greater light than the powers of the sun, penetrating to the very depths of the heart and mind. Whence also the Word says his name shall rise above the un, and again Zechariah says, "Sunrise is his name"' [*D*. 121.2]. This reality is connected with death. Because truth is like this, men endure all kinds of suffering rather than deny it. The cross is the supreme sign of the power of Christ [*1 A*. 55.2] and brings men of every nation to God. Only as testimony to truth is martyrdom significant; just as Socrates' example was tied to truth, so the work of the Christian is never more than pointing to the truth. The refrain of truth runs through the account of Justin'smartyrdom, so that attention is turned from those who are on trial to the truth that they confess. Thirdly, the contrast between truth and falsehood is the contrast between spirit and flesh. The philosophers cannot speak truth about God because they have no knowledge of him [*D*. 3.7]. On the other hand, the prophets saw the truth and spoke it, without regard for human opinion, because they were filled with the Holy Spirit. Belief in the prophets is not optional because the fulfilment of their predicitons compels one to accept what they said as true.

Irenaeus also insists on ethical and logical concern for truth. Piety and love of truth go together [*H*. 2.27.1], but logical argument remains important. Heretics weave ropes of sand and build fantasies on the basis of ambiguity; but one riddle does not solve another riddle and truth can only be found through what is clear and consistent [*H*. 2.9.1]. Those who follow heresies are like sheep, and however proud they may be about what they have received, they resist the need for argument and explanation [*H*. 3.15.2]. Above all, Irenaeus sees truth as set in history and community, as something that runs from Abraham on, for Abraham was the father of those who should believe, and his faith and ours are the same [*H*. 4.20.1]. One truth is to be found in the preaching of the Church, the word of the prophets, and the perfection of Christ. There is a splendid description of truth springing out of the earth at the resurrection of Christ [Psalm 84: 12; *H*. 3.5.1]; wherever truth is found at any stage of human history, it is linked with Christ. Only from him and his gospel has the truth been handed down, and only in him may the truth be found. Spirit and truth mean purity of perception and the community of faith: 'Where the church is, there is the Spirit of God, and where the Spirit of God is, there is the church and every kind of grace; but the Spirit is truth' [*H*. 3.38.1]. History and community are important because they are ruled by Christ, who is the truth.

Irenaeus sees, more forcefully than Justin, the power of error. Certainly for Justin, men live in a world of fantasy and deceit because demons have deceived them, especially through idols. But Irenaeus is still more fearful of error. Heretics wallow in falsehood and have fallen away from life itself, like Aesop's dog who saw his reflection in the water and dropped the bread from his mouth while snatching at its reflection. So heretics drop the bread of life in their attempt to grasp a shadow of the truth [*H*. 2.11.1]. Heresy is a twisted mass of human passions and verbal tricks, which play on names, numbers and letters [*H*. 2.14.3]; it is a disaster because there is a great gulf between truth and error, between God and falsehood [*H*. 2.17]. Truth is tied to God's world and he who loves truth understands God's world and its order [*H*. 2.37.2]; but those who reject truth reject the world that God has made, because they begin and continue in error [*H*. 2.38].

We may add another point. In reaction to the power of error,

Irenaeus holds firmly to a rule of faith. In this simple summary of the living gospel, truth may be found, and those who depart from this rule may quickly be shown to be in error. The Church gives to each Christian at baptism the rule of faith and all that is true may be fitted to this rule [*H.* 1.1.20]. To this truth the Church points continually in her universal teaching and in the testimony of her martyrs.

Tertullian carries on this central obedience to an apostolic rule as the one source of illumination [*Praescr.* 12]. There are two main sources of danger to the Christian. One is idolatry which steals from God what is his and gives it to something else [*Idol.* 1]. The idol appears to be what it is not [*Idol.* 3], and men seem to be ready under the influence of error to worship anything but God himself [*Idol.* 4]. With idolatry must be classed that vast heritage of literature that teaches about the gods of whom men make idols [*Idol.* 10]. The second main danger is heresy and is distinguished from truth by its variety and plurality in contrast to the unity and simplicity of truth [*Praescr.* 28]. Truth and antiquity must go together, since truth must exist before error can corrupt it [*Marc.* 4.4]. Heretics produce and hand down forgeries of the truth. By contrast, the testimony of the martyrs points to the truth that they confess. Tertullian is totalitarian in his claim for Christian truth, and while he uses many spoils of learning, he will not admit any plurality in truth at all; for in the end, God himself is truth.

Clement has a more open love of truth in its ethical, logical and eschatological aspects. For him, as for others, honesty is the only way, argument is important, and the difference between truth and falsehood is the difference between life and death. Yet he breaks new ground in facing the tension between simplicity and argument, between the rule of faith and the wider universe of truth. For Irenaeus, those who wander off into Gnostic woods will be torn apart by savage beasts of error. For Tertullian, there is no need of philosophy after the gospel or of curiosity after Christ. Yet both these writers, like Justin, believed that in the end truth was more powerful than falsehood and that it could stand undefeated against human error. For them, however, this could be a long process; in the short term, error could win, and with its conquests bring pain and death. On the other hand Clement knew that, however many warnings were given, lovers of truth would wander off in search

of new treasures and would not be content to give up inquiry.
To find God was an adventure that called for courage [*Prot.*
10.93]. Certainly simplicity of life must be preserved and there
must be no pretence [*Paed* 2.3ff]. But truth is something to be
bought and sold and all that matters is that the price should
not be juggled in order to gain buyers [*Paed.* 3.11.78f.]. He
who would find and love truth must be strong in soul, discern-
ing truth from falsehood in obedience to the scriptures
[*S.* 7.16.93]. Heretics have confused the picture and made it
more important for the lover of truth to judge clearly and
correctly; but there is still only royal highway on which
men safely travel, while other roads lead to cliffs, dangerous
rivers or deep seas [*S.* 7.15.91]. The Christian soldier has been
placed on guard by the Word himself, and he guards the truth
that brings knowledge and life [*S.* 7.16.100].

At the same time, truth itself has its own power. It sends out
its shadowless light on all who believe, and this light is God's
Spirit, which brings men knowledge [*S.* 6.16.138]. The disease
of heresy can be cured, for truth has power to cut away and
burn up the false infection of heretical opinion [*S.* 7.16.103].
In the end there is only one truth and that is God's. Heretics
and philosophers have broken off part of it and claim that what
they have is the whole truth. The Christian sees the fullness of
Christ and the wholeness of truth, which has its own power to
collect the scattered seeds, ro to bring together the limbs that
have been torn from the one body [*S.* 1.13.57]. Clement
believes that, even in the short term, truth can defeat error.

For this reason, he speaks of truth in two ways.[1] First, there is
the simple rule of faith, the central elements of Christian belief;
this is one, unchanging and sure. From this central simplicity
the universal truth moves out to embrace all knowledge, past,
present and future. Love of truth can never be static but is
always moving on. Dialectic, argument and reason show how
to ask and how to answer [*S.* 1.9.45]. There are times for
silence and words should never be used in strife [*S.* 1.10.49].
But philosophy is a help, not a danger; it may not be the main
course of the meal but after the bread of life it comes as a
dessert [*S.* 1.20.100]. Symbols and allegory open the door to
new worlds of meaning and understanding. Scripture is full of
symbols that convey truth in a more powerful and varied way

[1] See my *Philosophy of Clement*, pp. 113, 26.

than plain statement can achieve. Into this world of unending discovery the Christian makes his way. The love of truth means judgement, reason and discernment. It looks to the objects of thought and judges according to them [*S.* 6.1.3]. As the distinction between truth and falsehood is the distinction between life and death, so he who discerns the truth follows it with a confession that is made perfect in martyrdom.

The love of truth points to the chief fusion of Christianity and Platonism. In Plato's *Symposium*, Eros is the energy that carries the soul to the object of its choice, whether the choice be the lower instincts, the desire for prestige, or the vision of truth. While Plato would agree with Freud that man fails to realise where the basic motive of his life originates, Plato and Freud are ultimately opposed. For Plato, the driving force of the soul belongs to its highest and immortal part. It does not work up from below, but rather sinks from above when the spirit gives way to flesh. 'So when the energy is withdrawn from the lower channels, it is gathered up into its original source.' This is not a sublimation as Freud would claim, the lifting of desire from the lower level whence it came. 'A force that was in origin spiritual, after an incidental and temporary declension, becomes purely spiritual again.'[1] This is the most distinctive and influential theme of Platonism, and it is this theme that has had such a profound influence on Christianity.

Love of truth points to the unusual combination of enthusiasm and rationality. Clement's enthusiasm runs in superlatives from the first invitation of the *Protrepticus* to turn from darkness to light through to the Gnostic peaks of *Stromateis* 7. Irenaeus' charismatic fervour shows in an interest in spiritual gifts, a blunt honesty, a coarse humour, fantastic eschatological hopes and a practical sympathy for Montanism. Tertullian is an obvious enthusiast, who always thinks in superlatives, never imagines that moderation might sometimes be a Christian virtue, turns his savage humour against Marcion as the worst thing the Black Sea ever washed up or against Empedocles as a philosophic fish fried in Mount Aetna, and finally becomes a Montanist himself, only to leave because Montanists are not spiritual enough. Justin is less accessible, but his enthusiasm is indicated by many phrases that express

[1] F. M. Cornford, *The unwritten philosophy and other essays* (Cambridge, 1950), p. 79.

deep devotion and is proved by the ultimate test of martyrdom.

Unlike most religious enthusiasts, the four writers were aggressively rational. Clement argued for the necessity of inquiry against those who wanted mere faith and argued for the rationality of faith against those who despised it; argument was essential since one had to argue to prove the contrary, and logic was a proper object of study. Tertullian, we have seen, was anything but a fideist; he constructed his arguments in harmony with identifiable rules of rhetoric, and argued interminably, even contending for the inferiority of marriage in a discourse addressed to his wife. Justin shapes his *Apology* on a demand for either proof of Christian guilt or release from persecution, and moves by appeal to reason alone. His story of philosophic wandering comes to an end when he is shown that the Platonic account of the soul is inconsistent and that the prophets and the friends of Jesus spoke only truth, without fear or favour. The Jews challenge him to prove that Jesus is Christ. He draws proof from scripture and facts, comparing such proof with mathematical reasoning.

Love of truth, or enthusiasm and rationality, produced a form of Christian thought that differs remarkably from much that came later. It has been argued that in every age there are two main streams of thought and that such sectarianism is to be accepted and even welcomed; the tough-minded will always be at variance with the tender-minded. For a considerable part of its history, Christian thought has been tenderly solicitous of the detail of correct belief. The concern for true doctrine as a corpus of inherited truth is incipient in the second century. By the time of Epiphanius of Salamis it ruled over all and to this day most Christians are tender-minded; but the writers whom we have studied, can only be classed as tough-minded. They argued against established polytheism, Gnostic religion and every form of superstition. They made rough jokes about heavenly aeons, superior piety and revered images. They saw that faith was not a pious work that accepted each article of belief in order to be valid; faith was a response to the total reality of Jesus Christ, whom they called the Word of God. So, as the twentieth century has in part discovered, faith has to be critical of all that does not belong to the central scandal of the gospel.[1]

[1] This was the central theme of Bultmann's work. Edward Schweizer

They all talked too much and knew that they did. Justin goes around and around in argument against Trypho and has to defend his tedious repetitions. Irenaeus mercilessly multiplies biblical evidence for recapitulation – his account is *consummans* but never *abbreviatum*. Tertullian's rhetoric never pauses for breath, he confesses he has no patience, and he never stops to think what his opponent might mean. Clement's proofs from pagan writers are as tedious as any could be, and he observes what every Christian congregation has learned, that 'when words reveal the mysteries of unending life, they are themselves never willing to stop' [*Prot.* 12.123]. Yet they believed in one Word for all men – 'verbum abbreviatum et consummans'.

> We think that Paradise and Calvarie,
> Christs Crosse, and Adams tree, stood in one place;
> Looke Lord, and finde both Adams met in me;
> As the first Adams sweat surrounds my face,
> May the last Adams blood my soule embrace[1].

writes: 'it was clear to him that the crucial decision was not whether this part or that of the life of Jesus was historical or not; but the crucial decision can only be made where one can see, in the whole of the life, death and resurrection of Jesus, God's word directed to oneself' ('Rudolf Bultmann, A tribute', *ABR*, 24 (1976), 2).

[1] 'Hymn to God my God, in my Sicknesse', by John Donne.

Appendix

Alternative methods in the history of ideas in the patristic period

Our five different questions and methods spring from a scheme that is based on three main types, with subdivisions in the third. The first method is polemical: 'Does it make sense?' 'Is it true?'; and regards past writers as contributors to unchanging problems: 'by noticing the strong and weak points of each theory we can discover the direction in which further progress may be made'.[1] The systematic theologian commonly approaches the early centuries with similar direct questions:

'We must raise questions about the truth and falsity of the arguments used in that process and the results achieved by it. And this we can only do from one position and with one set of criteria: that is, from the position of our contemporary world and with the criteria that seem to us appropriate to the subject-matter under review.'[2]

There is an attractive freshness about this approach; for more than a thousand years the fathers had been cited in short authoritative passages. Theology had so often been built upon *catenae* that could not be questioned because they were so close in time to the sources of Christianity. For example, questions of Church order and Roman primacy were argued with extracts from Ignatius, Irenaeus, Cyprian and others. Ascetical theology followed a similar pattern. Just as the biblicist cited his proof-texts from the Bible, so the patristic scholar found his proof-texts in the fathers. In neither case was truth or logical basis questioned and error and misinterpretation were inevitable. The polemical approach places the stress on valid argument and rightly insists that neither antiquity nor sanctity are guarantees of truth or good sense. When, for example, Cyprian's theology is analysed, there emerge weaknesses that make it inappropriate to cite him as a basis for the doctrine of the ministry or the eucharist.[3]

[1] Broad, *Ethical theory*, pp. 1f.
[2] M. F. Wiles, *The making of Christian doctrine* (Cambridge, 1967), pp. 16f.
[3] M. F. Wiles, *Working papers in doctrine* (London, 1976), p. 80.

273

On the other hand, some weaknesses of the method begin to appear in a later interesting study of the development of doctrine in the early Church, where assessment of early arguments is dramatically swift. For example, the bringing together of mathematical and prophetic ideas of unity is questioned because 'it is by no means clear' that they are about the same thing.[1] At least four factors have been neglected. Platonic and Pythagorean accounts of the one first principle had prophetic overtones that increased in the second century; again, the prophetic and mathematical accounts were not monolithic but highly complex and subtle.[2] Further, the history of thought includes the interaction of different ideas to produce something new.[3] Finally elucidation will note in Clement's 'mathematical principle of abstraction' elements such as 'the vastness of Christ' and 'casting ourselves into the void'; what these mean is a matter for imaginative exploration, and until this account of divine unity is explored, what Christian writers said about God is not accessible.[4]

On Origen's definition of divine simplicity we learn that 'traditional trinitarianism is excluded from the outset'.[5] This seems inaccurate in the case of Origen, not to mention others like Augustine and Aquinas, so we need to look at the way in which different trinitarian theologians understand divine simplicity. This is done, to some extent, in the account of the Cappadocians [pp. 135ff.], which shows that it is not excluded from the outset. Yet here again the treatment is too swift to win confidence.

Again, in the area of soteriology, lack of time brings in its revenges. Why must the saviour be wholly God? The prophetic and evangelical account insisted that only God can create and make

---

[1] *Ibid.* p. 26.

[2] See Stead, *Divine substance*, pp. 180–9.

[3] See C. H. Dodd, *The interpretation of the Fourth Gospel* (Cambridge, 1953), pp. 263–85 and 294f. If a student stated in an essay that the Johannine Logos failed because it was by no means obvious that the prophetic creative Word and the Hellenistic rational Logos were the same, he would be judged to have missed the point or to be playfully provocative.

[4] Clement, *S.* 5.11.71. Apart from the inaccessibility of the account of the Christian God, one wonders how much European culture will also be inaccessible. Certainly there will be no chance of understanding why Bach used consecutive unison at the end of the Crucifixion Chorus (*Ich bin Gottes Sohn*) in the Passion according to St Matthew or why after purgatory, Dante is told that he can now follow his purified desire (*Purgatorio*, 27; on Dante, see Murdoch, *The Fire and the Sun*, p. 35 and Cornford, *The unwritten philosophy*, p. 80).

[5] Wiles, *Making of doctrine*, p. 28. Cf. p. 124.

alive, so that there is a fundamental distinction between creator and creature. This found a similar logic in the Platonic distinction between life itself and that which participates in life, between what is participated in and what participates.[1] Putting christology first, it insisted that a saviour must stand on the first side of the antithesis.

The polemicist has no time to assimilate this total argument and asks 'whether it would not be possible for God to be the ultimate author of salvation and man the recipient without the agent or mediator of that salvation being himself necessarily of a fully divine or fully human nature – let alone both'.[2] A simple causal pattern has been substituted for the original argument; this means that so long as God is the ultimate cause of salvation the intermediate causes may be anything but God. Paul and John insisted that there was a difference in the saving work of Christ and that of anyone whom God might use, because Christ was God. The Word was God and with God, the true light shining on every man; John was not the true light but was a man sent by God. Now this element of the argument is completely missed in the restatement that makes salvation an asymmetrical, transitive, many–many relation instead of an asymmetrical, intransitive, one–many relation. Some examples will clarify these terms. The relation of a painter to a wall is asymmetrical; he paints the wall, which does not paint him, unless he be five years of age or less. The relation of disputants is symmetrical. It takes two to make an argument; a 'one-sided' argument has two sides, one of which is much weaker than the other. A transitive relation exists when billiard ball A moves billiard ball B, which moves ball C. A moves C by means of B. An intransitive relation exists between surgeon and patient. If A removes B's appendix and B removes C's appendix, A does not remove C's appendix. A one–many relation exists when a pianist plays to an audience of more than one. A many–many relation exists between two football teams playing a match; a 'one-man' team has many members but one is much better than the others.

Logic can express these relations much more precisely and clearly. A symmetrical relation R fulfils the condition: If $x \, \mathrm{R} \, y$, then $y \, \mathrm{R} \, x$. When this condition never applies, the relation is asymmetrical. A transitive relation R fulfils the condition: If $x \, \mathrm{R} \, y$ and $y \, \mathrm{R} \, z$ then $x \, \mathrm{R} \, z$. When this condition never applies, the relation is intransitive. A one–many relation fulfils the condition 1: If $x \, \mathrm{R} \, y$ and if $w \, \mathrm{R} \, y$, then $w = x$. A many–one relation fulfils the condition 2: If $x \, \mathrm{R} \, y$ and if $x \, \mathrm{R} \, z$, then $z = y$. Any relation that fulfils neither condition 1 nor condition 2 is a many–many relation.[3]

[1] Justin, *D.* 6.1; Clement, *S.* 1.7.38.
[2] Wiles, *Making of doctrine*, p. 107.
[3] See H. Newton-Lee, *Symbolic logic* (New York, 1961), pp. 31–46.

Now Platonism, with its orders of being and becoming helped to express this asymmetrical, intransitive, one–many relation that salvation required (cf. *Republic* 506E). Clement writes, for example: 'and in the spiritual world, that which is oldest in origin, is the timeless and unbegun first principle and beginning of all being, the Son. From him we can search out the still more ultimate cause beyond, the father of all things, the oldest and most beneficent of all.' 'All the powers of the spirit become collectively one thing and come together in the same point – the Son.' 'That the true, only, one, almighty, good God might be manifest from eternity to eternity saving by the son' [*S.* 7.1.2; 4.25.156; 7.2.12]. 'O the great God! O the perfect Child! Son in Father and Father in Son!' [*Paed.* 1.5.24]. The relation between Father and Son is not causal as is their relation to all else.

If another scheme replaces the Platonic scheme, it must provide the same support to the distinctive claim of the Gospel, namely, that when prophets and kings had shown that salvation was not a transitive relation, God came to do the work himself. So the question whether the Christian God needs a divine saviour to do his work is based on a very simple confusion, which is only possible because logical structure is ignored. Salvation is taken as a transitive, many–many relation, when the New Testament sees it as an intransitive, one–many relation. This example of polemical history, which tests ancient arguments by its own definitions, shows the weakness of the method even in the most competent hands. It is doubtful whether any theology can stand the test of a method that cannot let writers speak for themselves, and ignores the detail of an argument. In the work under scrutiny, it is abandoned on practical grounds. The final test of truth, or the only test of true development, is not the ability to answer contemporary objections[1] but a cultural test: whether the church feels she has done her best with the resources at her disposal.[2] This submission to a cultural group is hardly consistent with the polemical toughness of the beginning. The chief strength of the polemical approach is its recognition of the need for argument and its chief weakness lies in its failure to appreciate the complexity of arguments and to comprehend what has been said. 'Too often, indeed, such polemical writing consists in telling men of straw that they have no brains.'[3] The great philosophical advance of our time has been a recognition of the variety of languages or 'forms of life', together with an insistence that this variety should be discovered through analysis of what particular people have said.[4]

[1] Wiles, *Making of doctrine*, p. 16.
[2] *Ibid.* p. 181.
[3] Passmore, 'History of philosophy', p. 13.
[4] D. F. Pears, *Wittgenstein* (Fontana, 1971), pp. 169–80.

The application of this Wittgensteinian principle of imagination and naturalism to early Christian thought is long overdue.

The second main approach asks of a statement or theory: 'How does it reflect the culture in which it emerged?' and interprets all ideas as part of the social setting in which they arose. The most important thing about Hume is that he lived in eighteenth-century Scotland and the most important thing about Plato is that he lived in Greece during the fifth century B.C. Logic is simply the creation of the mind 'to conceal its timidity and keep up its courage, a hocus-pocus designed to give formal validity to conclusions we are willing to accept if everybody else in our set will too'.[1] Such renunciation of argument makes it hard to take this method seriously, yet clearly the cultural historian has something to contribute by exhibiting differences in outlook between various civilisations or periods of history. On this view it is unlikely that an Athenian poet like Plato will have anything in common with a Roman Senator like Cicero, or a mediaeval monk like Aquinas. Philosophy is the product of a civilisation and not a timeless reality. 'The philosophical problems of one age, like the cultural conflicts out of which they take their rise, are irrelevant to those of another.'[2] One weakness of this approach lies in the obvious similarities between some problems of the past and present, and the fact that these similarities determine the direction of much useful research. A good example of this method in theology was noted earlier under the doctrine of deification,[3] which had been considered as intelligible and necessary within the framework of the culture of the Greek Orthodox community, but of little importance or interest outside that community.

Elucidatory methods may be doxographical, retrospective or problematic. The doxographical approach asks: 'What has been said and how is it related to what other writers were saying?' It was established in antiquity by Diogenes Laertius in his work *The Lives and Opinions of Eminent Philosophers*. The only connections that he considers are those within the tradition of each sect of philosophers. This approach has had a wide effect on the study of early Christian thought: the important thing is not the way in which people reacted either to their environment or to philosophical problems with which they were confronted, but rather their connections with what their predecessors and their contemporaries had said. We understand what Justin said about God as creator when we see the parallel

---

[1] Carl Becker, *The heavenly city of the eighteenth-century philosophers* (New Haven, 1932), p. 25, cited by Passmore, 'History of philosophy', p. 14.

[2] Passmore, 'History of philosophy', p. 16.

[3] See above, p. 111.

account in a particular school of contemporary Platonists. We look at the way in which Christian doctrine developed by bringing together ideas from a variety of sources, and are able to understand the background of a thinker, through parallel references and similar ideas in the writings of others. Daniélou's great work brings together the results of fifty years of scholarship, and indicates the ways in which early Christian ideas were similar to those used by other thinkers.[1] This approach has been extremely fruitful and its weaknesses are therefore important.

An odd limitation arises from the fact that, with limited resources in our knowledge of the ancient world, the doxographical approach *seems* to have run out of material *in certain areas*. Andresen compared Justin's opinions with those of second-century Middle Platonism and fixed him with high probability on the line of development.[2] No new data having arisen, those who come after are tempted to push their inquiry far beyond the limits that evidence would impose and indulge in guessing or listing possibilities rather than soberly assessing probabilities. It is not surprising that one writer has spent ten pages discussing whether Justin wore a philosopher's cloak or not, a question that does not deserve extensive treatment.[3]

The second factor of limitation comes from the aggressive and monopolistic nature of doxography in certain hands. One scholar concludes a discussion of Christianity and philosophy by insisting that certain chapters of *To Diognetus* are a collection of commonplaces and not a 'pearl of patristic literature'.[4] So convinced is he by his argument at this point and by his earlier argument that Justin was a vindictive writer, who wanted nothing more than the punishment of his persecutors,[5] that he goes on to claim that Christian thought is better understood by non-Christians than by Christians.[6] Those who have something at stake allow their faith to blunt their critical faculty. Now this is doxography with a vengeance: the *only* important thing is the accurate listing of the opinions of a writer and the parallels found elsewhere. The Christian who sees a meaning in this list of opinions cannot handle them as critically as the unbeliever who is not involved. This might be called the 'honest barman' principle, according to which only a total abstainer may be trusted to serve drinks. Where has it gone wrong? Most interpreters of ancient thought would insist that the ability to think a writer's

---

[1] Daniélou, *Gospel message*.
[2] Andresen, 'Justin', pp. 157–95.
[3] Hyldahl, *Philosophie und Christentum*, pp. 102–12.
[4] Joly, *Christianisme*, p. 201.
[5] *Ibid.* pp. 155–70.
[6] *Ibid.* p. 226.

thoughts after him would produce understanding and that detachment could reduce the historian to a stamp-collector.

It would be easy to say that the critic's zeal for unbelief (he defends Renan's attack on the world-soul concept) gives him the kind of bias that he deplores in believers. That would be a superficial and premature assessment; after all, he is not completely wrong. Non-Christians do see things that believers miss, especially in the study of early Christian thought, but only when they see and assess a whole argument. What is missing here is the ability to analyse, to grasp the logical framework of the many citations. The issue of the punishment of sinners is decided by a list of twenty-three short citations from Justin, announcing the score with glee [p. 167]: 'Twenty-three mentions in ninety little pages!' The question of the originality of the world-soul concept in *To Diognetus* is decided by a list of only twenty-two citations from secular authors but ends with the significant comment that specialist scholars will be able to enlarge 'this dossier' from their memory or their reading [p. 215]. Collection or compilation is the means of deciding the author's meaning. The parallel with stamp-collecting is exact, for each instance is neatly perforated and separated from its context.

Analysis of the logical setting of the two sets of statements is not considered, although in the first case we have the problem that has haunted man from the beginning – 'Is the judgement of this world final?' 'Why do the innocent suffer?' – and in the second case we have the motif of the body of Christ, which is as persistent as it is allusive in early Christian thought.

The criticism fails in both instances. In the first case it fails to see that Justin's hostility to persecutors is tied to his faith in ultimate justice and a need for the solution of the problem of evil. Apart from this problem, his opinions are of little consequence; within this problem the opinions make sense.[1] The second criticism does not see that the world-soul concept is handled in a distinctive way and that the many parallels have little point. The notion of the ongoing body of Christ, of a new spiritual order in the world – these and related notions are misunderstood when attention is paid primarily to historical parallels. The important thing is not what is roughly similar to what a hundred other writers in the ancient world said, but how the concept of Christians as a world soul fits into a total framework that is theistic and not pantheistic. The critic has collected a great number of stamps but he has not begun to do philosophy. Even if his 'honest barman' principle were sometimes justified by Christian myopia, it is certainly false from the philosophical standpoint. The doxographer does not need to understand phil-

[1] See above, p. 156.

osophy, but if he wishes to go beyond the listing of opinions and offer criticism he must know what philosophers or theologians are doing.[1] Philosophers are concerned with problems and not with parallel sets of words. By an aggressive attempt to drive others from the field one doxographer has shown the weakness of his own position.

The deficiency of the approach is confirmed at two other points. The first is the twofold assertion [p. 220] that the metaphor of the soul (in *To Diognetus*) is a commonplace, not an original formulation, and that it is rightly judged to be an expression of Christian pride and intolerance. This claim is internally inconsistent; if the metaphor is a common-place it cannot be an indication of anything specifically Christian. The second weakness is the claim to be 'philosophical' in contrast to 'Christian'. What definition of philosophy would admit a method that simply collected opinions, even if it did not ignore the claims of logical consistency? Plato, Clement and Wittgenstein all wrote philosophy reluctantly and canvassed the claims of careful thought and spoken argument. In criticism of some of his written work, Wittgenstein once said in conversation: 'No. If this were philosophy you could learn it by heart'.[2]

A third limitation is evident when wooden adherence to doxography is contrasted with a flexible approach that takes account of the pattern of argument. We shall look first at the more sensitive approach and then consider a subsequent restriction. A recent account of the earliest Christian thought has one point of obvious relevance for philosophy (Clement's account of creation *ex nihilo*) and this depends on an argument and not on a formula. The claim is that Clement put forward an account of creation out of relative non-being;[3] and while this is ambiguous 'It does not imply that matter is an ultimate principle coeternal with God.'[4] Now in Clement a verbal distinction between absolute and relative non-being is not clear; but that is not important because the context of argument is considered. At this point Clement argues that while several philosophers spoke of matter as a first principle, they said it had no quality or form. Plato boldly went further, and called matter 'non-being'. He spoke mystically about this in the *Timaeus* because 'he knew there was only one real first-principle' [*S.* 5.14.89]. Like others, he took the idea from the invisible and formless earth of Genesis 1: 2. Clement returns to Plato shortly afterwards on the difficulty of finding the maker and father of the universe and ex-

[1] Passmore, 'History of philosophy', p. 30.
[2] Murdoch, *The Fire and the Sun*, p. 23.
[3] *S.* 5.14.89; 5.14.92.
[4] H. Chadwick, 'The beginning of Christian philosophy', in Armstrong (ed.), *Later Greek and early medieval philosophy*, p. 46.

plains the meaning of fatherhood in this context, 'as coming into being from him alone and arising out of what is not' [*S.* 5.14.92].

What emerges is that creation *ex nihilo* cannot be tied to formulae that are capable of various meanings. The concern of Clement in this context and elsewhere is that there should be only one ultimate first principle.[1] This is the point of the argument and this is what creation *ex nihilo* means. One has to go beyond the ambiguous formula to the framework of the argument.

In a more recent account,[2] the strictly doxographical approach leads to a contrary conclusion that Clement's definition is not consistent with creation *ex nihilo*. 'On the contrary, such definition brings him into close connection with Neopythagoreanism and Neoplatonism.'[3] The various accounts of *me on* are collated and Clement's account of matter is seen as reflecting these views.[4] The contrast with the earlier account is remarkable. In the first, the term is understood in the context of the argument in which it stands; the problem of creation out of matter, when there is only one first principle, is Clement's concern and is decisive for his meaning. In the second account the stamp is lifted from its context and placed with Neopythagorean and Neoplatonic issues under the heading *me on*. It is no surprise when accounts of the supreme divinity, who is also outside the realm of being for Plotinus and Pseudo-Dionysius, are placed under the same heading.[5] The accounts must be, 'in some way, analogous' because the same words are used. The simple truth is that, for the writers concerned, they mean the opposite – one falls off the minus end of the scale of being and the other off the plus end. It is fair to say that such an approach to philosophy is beyond description. Yet one must insist that it is the method, not the scholar, that should bear the blame.

Now the mere listing of opinions will be much more concise than any exploration of argument and ambiguities. To give the structure and setting of each argument will involve repetition, which the collection of conclusions avoids. Is the doxographer with his welcome brevity always wrong? No, but without an awareness of the total argument it is impossible to tell where he is right and where he is

[1] Note Clement's comments elsewhere. *Paed.* 1.8.62: 'Nothing exists which God has not caused to exist', *Prot.* 4.63: 'as soon as God merely wills a thing, its existence follows immediately'.

[2] Lilla, *Clement of Alexandria*, pp. 191–9. At no point is the notion of first cause or one first principle mentioned. Yet this is the crux of Clement's argument.

[3] *Ibid.* p. 195.

[4] *Ibid.* p. 196.

[5] *Ibid.* Note that Tertullian scornfully makes the same point [*Herm.* 4], and indicates its absurdity.

wrong. The context of an argument is not only necessary where one must choose between contrary doxographical conclusions. Some- times one does not need to choose; there is a wider synthesis that shows the merit of each conclusion. To find such a synthesis one must go beyond formulae to the total argument and problem. One scholar concludes that 'Justin's basic presupposition is a highly optimistic confidence in human reasoning',[1] while another claims that 'Justin shows a very deep pessimism concerning the capacity of natural reason.'[2] Justin's account of *logos* works on three levels.[3] The Christian participates directly in the Logos who is Christ. Human reason is at a third level and participates in a seed of Logos, which is sown on earth among men. The Christian is on the same level as the seed, while the pagan is one step lower. However, participation is a transitive relation, so it may still be said that all men have participated in the Logos who is Christ. This means that Justin is both optimistic and pessimistic about human reason. Doxography may reach opposite conclusions; only when the con- flicting statements are analysed and the problems emerge, do the contradictions make sense. Justin wants to put Christ above all human teaching yet to show that all truth points to him. It would not do to say either that Christ came to tell men what they already knew or that there had been no preparation for his coming. Further, a complex response was necessary because of the different objections to Christianity. Justin's pessimism about pre-Christian truth is directed against Jews, pagans and philosophers who challenged the absolute Christian claims, while his optimism aimed to unsettle Marcionites who denied all truth prior to Christ.[4]

The doxographer prefers pictures to problems, the stamp-col- lector is interested in what may be seen, not in what may be argued. This emerges in a recent work, where the Christian account of the incarnation is described as 'poetic, anthropomorphic or mytho- logical language', and is contrasted with 'a theological conclusion based on logical argument'.[5] A contrast is made between poetry and myth on the one hand, and theology and logic on the other. However in the discussion of ancient philosophy, no awareness is shown of its logic; it is handled in a poetic or mythological way. The relationship of the transcendent One to a world that is many is seen in pictorial terms. 'Inevitably the solutions involve some kind of system of mediators or a "hierarchy of being" linking the ulti-

[1] Chadwick, 'Christian philosophy', p. 166.
[2] Holte, 'Logos Spermatikos', p. 160.
[3] See my *Justin Martyr*, pp. 140–5, for further comment.
[4] See D. Allen, 'Motives, rationales, and religious beliefs', *APQ* (1966), 112ff., for a useful account of the logic of objection and rebuttal.
[5] Hick (ed.), *The myth*, p. 35.

mate transcendent one, who was even beyond being, with the known world.' The two terms that are considered important are 'emanation' and 'mediation', neither of which has any clear logical significance.[1] Like the philosophers outside the Church, the Christian philosophers saw the *logos* as a mediator 'who was both one and many, sharing in some sense the nature of both, and bridging the gulf between them'. Oddly, the writer continues in a way that shows a complete insensitivity to the difference between pictorial language and logical terminology.[2] 'Logically there was no room in this scheme for the Holy Spirit, but he found his place as another sort of mediating link in the chain of being.' With such a mythological approach to philosophy, it is no surprise that while the different schools were deeply conscious of their radical divergence one from the other, 'From our vantage point they all *look much the same* in principle if not in detail' [p. 25.]

A reference to the 'illogicalities of the scheme as a whole' is made with a persistent total abstention from any discussion of logical issues. Philosophy is a matter of world view, and the contrast between God and the world is overcome by 'a succession of descent', which 'avoided drawing a line between the divine and the created in its hierarchy of existence'[p. 25]. The mediator has to have 'some substantial relationship with what was above and what was below his own rung on the ladder, so providing an effective link. But an ontological distinction, a real line between the divine and the created could not be drawn without insisting that the mediator fell on one side or the other, thus destroying his ability to mediate' [p. 26]. What Arius provides is no different in its achievement of a satisfactory solution because a line has to be drawn at some point. 'Where Arius severed the mediator from God, Athanasius severed him from the world.' Incredibly this discussion goes on to speak of 'inherent illogicalities' and propositions that were 'logically incapable' of making sense of the biblical message of God's involvement with this world [p. 28].

Now it is obvious to anyone who has read a single line of ancient philosophy, and especially of Plato, that despite the words 'substantial' and 'ontological' this account has not begun to look at logical issues. It has not asked what the relationship is between the first cause of things and particular objects, nor the relationship

---

[1] *Ibid.* p. 25. Their pictorial significance seems to exclude discussion of logical issues. Cf. H. Dörrie, 'EMANATION. Ein unphilosophisches Wort im spätantiken Denken', in K. Flasch (ed.), *Parusia, Festschrift für J. Hirschberger* (Frankfurt am Main, 1965), pp. 119–41.

[2] Philosophers from Plato to Wittgenstein have used pictorial language and metaphor, but not without a logical framework of definition and argument.

between final causes, efficient causes and formal causes. For Plato, the forms might be all three kinds of cause, and the ultimate form was the one formal, final and efficient cause of all things. It is true that people have spoken of a Great Chain of Being but not without logical commentary.[1] Plato and the early Christian writers who depended on him were concerned with logical distinctions, which are completely ignored in this treatment. The same may be said of their ethics and metaphysics.

To sum up, doxography here ignores logical questions, is unaware of problems that philosophers and theologians were trying to solve and draws pictures rather than analyses arguments. It is wrong to speak as if philosophy could be embroidered on a tapestry or drawn on a piece of paper. Needlework and sketching may be poetic or mythological ways of expressing certain relations; but when taken in isolation from logical definitions and analysis, they are of no value whatever.[2]

Elucidation may take a second form. The question may be asked concerning the relation of a philosophical opinion, not to its contemporary or antecedent parallels, but to a particular point in the history of thought. Retrospective history of ideas fixes on a certain point as the climax of a development, and interprets earlier ideas according to their anticipation of the central point and later forms according to their faithfulness and accuracy in reproducing it. So the important thing about Justin's belief that the Logos of God appeared to the patriarchs of old is not what this might mean in the framework of his theology, but the fact that having entered Christian tradition it caused difficulty during the Arian controversy. Whatever it did for Justin's argument, 'it must be pronounced a *faux pas* for which his successors had to pay a high price in blood and tears'.[3] The normal point of reference in early Christian thought is the Council of Chalcedon with Nicaea as anticipation, and standard

---

[1] The background of the study is plainly A. O. Lovejoy, *The Great Chain of Being: a study of the history of an idea* (Cambridge, Mass., 1936). Despite criticism of Lovejoy's work elsewhere (p. 144) I do not suggest that he ignored logic. However, something like the cartoon approach under discussion may be found in the work of one of his pupils, Marjorie Nicholson.

[2] Thinking in pictures is notoriously dangerous. Cyprian's use of pictures prevented him from seeing the inevitable conflict between his two definitions of unity. See my discussion, 'Cyprian's imagery', *Antichthon*, 7 (1973), 65f., where Viscount Haldane is quoted: 'The trouble with Lloyd George is that he thinks in images not in concepts' (D. Sommer, *Haldane of Cloan* (London, 1960), p. 360).

[3] H. Chadwick, *Early Christian thought and the classical tradition* (Oxford, 1966), p. 16.

works like that of Kelly[1] move toward this as the climax of development, selecting those elements that are relevant to the final product. Tertullian's account of the distinctions within the Godhead were less important in the general shape of his thought than they were as anticipations of later distinctions. The consequence is that his accounts of three 'persons' and of Christ's two natures have been given more attention than other aspects of his thought. Retrospective histories will always have an important place in the study of the early Church, since there are developments that reach a climax in Nicaea and Chalcedon; but they do not help us enough to understand the second century. For the concerns of the second and fourth centuries were different, just as 'Bach was not trying to write like Beethoven and failing; Athens was not a relatively unsuccessful attempt to produce Rome; Plato was himself, not a half-developed Aristotle'.[2] This weakness is important because the second century has more to give to the twentieth than either the fourth or fifth centuries, for the problems then, as now, were those of a Church in a non-Christian world and in a pluralist society. The issue was not the precise formulation of Christian belief, but rather the plain possibility of any such belief. Cultural histories and retrospective histories are deficient in opposite ways. 'In cultural histories, successive philosophers are unrelated to one another by logical ties; in the story as the retrospective historian tells it, the ties are too tight. Everything fits into a continuous pattern.'[3]

Further, when this method is combined with the polemical, there is a tendency to oversimplify the point of reference so that the systematic theologian imagines that he possesses an unambiguous criterion. Yet the pronouncements of Chalcedon are not entirely coherent. How can two natures 'without division, without separation' be consistent with Leo's account of Word and flesh, where 'The one sparkles with miracles, the other succumbs to injuries'? For example, a review of the recent work, *God as Spirit*, describes the

---

[1] J. N. D. Kelly, *Early Christian doctrines*, (London, 1958). For Harnack, dogma originates when 'an article of faith logically formulated and scientifically expressed, was first raised to the *articulus constitutivus ecclesiae*, and as such was universally enforced in the Church'. This happened, with reference to christology, at the end of the third century and the beginning of the fourth, and Harnack takes this as his point of division (*History of dogma*, vol. 1, pp. 1f.). The principle of selection is therefore to consider those doctrines that led to the dogmas specified.

[2] R. G. Collingwood, *The idea of history* (New York, 1956), p. 329.

[3] Passmore, 'History of philosophy', p. 27.

author as unitarian and adoptionist.[1] A unitarian holds that the Son and the Holy Spirit are not divine, yet for the writer no one could be more divine than they are. An adoptionist holds that the Spirit descends on the man Jesus, and for the writer the idea of God descending and ascending causes confusion and should be rejected. In three pages, the reviewer achieves three formal contradictions. He claims [p. 619] that, for the book, man might be 'as perfect as Jesus and in the same sense' and quotes in support: 'Jesus produces in us a response analogous to his own'. On the same page, he declares that the book's 'notion of redemption is purely exemplarist' and quotes in support: 'Jesus became the pattern of sonship and also the inspiration and power which can create in us a response . . . the interaction of divine Spirit with human spirit presents itself to us and takes effect within us in terms of the character, actions and words of Jesus.' Finally the review claims that Jesus' 'survival of bodily death (and presumably ours also) appears to be irrelevant' and on the next page quotes the book: 'we need not fear . . . that if the bones of Jesus lie somewhere in Palestine we can have no confidence that death has been overcome and in consequence no hope and faith for the future of ourselves or for the ultimate salvation of the human race'.

To sum up, while retrospective histories are important, they always distort because of their fixed angle of vision. Creeds and councils do not provide an unambiguous point of reference and may inspire logical error if personal or political factors are present, as they normally are.

It will now be abundantly clear why these alternative methods have been rejected except as subsidiary to that of problematic elucidation. To leave the matter there would be unsatisfactory, for scholars, like scientists, do not change their methods readily. They see things differently and they see different things. What happens if they refuse to change? There is no way in which the concepts of one method can be translated into another method without remainder. This is why scientists were still doing pre-Newtonian physics twenty years after Newton had published his epoch-making laws of motion. Indeed Darwin wrote at the end of *The Origin of Species*: 'Although I am fully convinced of the truth of the views given in this volume . . . I by no means expect to convince experienced naturalists whose minds are stocked with a multitude of facts all viewed, during a long course of years from a point of view directly opposite to mine'. Yet he was confident because young and rising scientists would see the question impartially.

[1] Review of Lampe, *God as Spirit*, by E. L. Mascall, *JThS*, 29.2 (1978) 617–21.

These difficult transitions have been called 'paradigm changes', 'gestalt switches' or 'scientific revolutions' and their study by philosophers of science like Thomas Kuhn[1] and Paul Feyerabend[2] is of great value to all intellectual disciplines. Elsewhere I have dealt at length with their application to the study of the Bible and historical theology.[3] Here I wish to show that change may be difficult and to indicate one way forward. Difficulties are indicated by the quick replies that proponents of an individual theory may give. The polemicist will claim that what can be said can be said clearly and that common sense is not served by formal symbolic logic as well as by socially acceptable debating moves. Further, he may take a biblicist[4] (one-verse, one-vote) approach to scripture and find texts that might provide a basis for treating salvation as a transitive relation, as for example, John 20: 21; 'As my Father has sent me, so I send you'. He will not be able to handle the counter-evidence; but no biblicist ever can, and he will remain happily in the polemical position. The cultural historian will insist that it is naïve to see permanent problems or types of problems in the history of thought. Conceptual parochialism needs history of ideas to show discontinuity between epochs and to enlarge the scope of theology or philosophy. As indicated above,[5] enlargement implies continuity as well as discontinuity, but it may not be enough to trouble a cultural historian. The doxographer will rightly insist on the priority of what has been said and the need for collecting parallels to clarify historical traditions. How can one assess the originality of a writer without a lot of stamp-collecting, which does no harm and can be looked at objectively? The use of pictures instead of concepts is a good way of explaining or teaching and the dominical use of parables is reassuring. The retrospective historian will claim the need for a fixed point if any continuity is to be traced. The Church has fixed on Nicaea and Chalcedon and it is a continuing

---

[1] T. S. Kuhn, *The structure of scientific revolutions* (Chicago, 1962).

[2] Paul K. Feyerabend, *Against method: an anarchistic theory of knowledge*, Minnesota studies in the philosophy of science, 4, (New Jersey, 1970). See also I. Lakatos and A. Musgrave (eds.), *Criticism and the growth of knowledge* (Cambridge, 1970).

[3] E. F. Osborn, 'Change without decay', in *Imagination and the future: Essays on Christian thought and practice presented to J. Davis McCaughey* (Melbourne, 1980), pp. 167–88.

[4] The technical use of the term is defined by G. Gloege, in *RGG*, vol. 1, col. 1263, as 'a general approach to the bible, which understands it as a self-enclosed whole with parts which are of equal value, and ascribes to it a direct obligating validity for the present'.

[5] See above, chapter 1, p. 14.

function of theology to explain these symbols. All of which is enough to justify resistance to change in method.

To conclude on a practical positive note, problematic elucidation follows most easily upon an awareness of the value of other methods despite their individual inadequacy. Certainly different methods, systems or paradigms are incommensurable; it is impossible to translate without remainder from one to another. Nevertheless translation can lead to some understanding of another approach. Translation is not an adequate metaphor here; it is necessary to apply other methods and see what comes from them. If this is first done in peripheral areas, it will be possible to move on to central or contentious issues, like deification for example. This will produce an appreciation of the ways in which different methods work and in time a recognition of the way in which problematic elucidation shows a limited respect for other methods and indeed uses them all. All this is good epistemology; but when a switch is made to the problematic method it will be made on grounds of logical adequacy and not for any aesthetic, mystical or diplomatic reason.[1] So the argument of this section cannot be set aside and the evidence of the preceding pages must be assessed; for without argument and evidence a change of method would be improper.

[1] For a fuller treatment of these particular issues, see my article, 'Change without decay', pp. 173–88.

Bibliography

Texts and translations

Albinus. *Platonis Dialogi*, Ed. D. F. Hermann, 6 vols. Leipzig, 1921–36, vol. 6, pp. 147–89.

Albinus. *Epitomé*. Ed. P. Louis, Paris, 1945.

Die ältesten Apologeten. Ed. E. J. Goodspeed. Göttingen, 1914.

Apuleius. *De philosophia libri.* Ed. P. Thomas. Leipzig, 1908.

Aristotle. Ed. W. D. Ross. *Physics.* Oxford, 1936.
    Metaphysics. 2 vols. Oxford, 1924.
    De Anima. Oxford, 1961.

Aristotle. Works. Translated under editorship of J. A. Smith and W. D. Ross, 12 vols. Oxford, 1908–52.

Atticus. Fragments, in Eusebius, *Praeparatio evangelica*, XI: 1–2; XV: 4–12. Ed. J. Baudry. Paris, 1931.

Clement of Alexandria. Selections from text with translation, G. W. Butterworth. LCL. London, 1919.

Clement of Alexandria. *Stromateis* 3 and 7. Translated with notes by H. Chadwick, LCC. London, 1954.

Clemens Alexandrinus. Text. Ed. O. Stählin. GCS, 12, 15, 17, 39, Leipzig, 1905–36. 12, 3rd ed., 1972; 15, 2nd ed., 1960; 17, 2nd ed., 1970.

Clemens von Alexandreia. Translation, O. Stählin. BKV II, 7, 8, 17, 19, 20. München, 1934–8.

Clement of Alexandria. Translation, W. Wilson, ANCL, 4, 12, 22, 24. 1882, 1884.

Clement of Alexandria. Text and translation, miscellanies, Book 7. F. J. A. Hort and J. B. Mayor. London, 1902.

Clément d'Alexandrie. Text and translation, notes. SC.
    Le Protreptique, 2 (1949).
    Le Pédagogue, 7 (1960); 108 (1965); 158 (1970).
    Les Stromates, 30 (1951); 38 (1954).
    Extraits De Théodote, 23 (1948).

Corpus Hermeticum. Ed. A. D. Nock and A. J. Festugière. 4 vols. Paris, 1972.

Diognetus, To. *À Diognète.* Ed. H. I. Marrou. SC. 1951.

Irenaeus. *Adversus Haereses.* Ed. W. D. Harvey. 2 vols. Cambridge, 1857.

Irenaeus. *Adversus Haereses.* Ed. A. Stieren. 2 vols. Leipzig, 1848–53.

289

Bibliography

Irenaeus. *Against Heresies*. Text and translation, SC. 34 (1952); 100 (1965); 152 (1969); 210, 211 (1975).

Irenaeus. *Against Heresies*. Translation. ANCL. 5, 9. 1883–4.

Irenaeus. *Démonstration de la prédication apostolique*. Translation, L. Froidevaux. SC, 62. 1959.

Irenaeus. *The demonstration of the apostolic preaching*. Translated with introduction and notes, J. Armitage Robinson. London, 1920.

Irenaeus. Des Heiligen Irenäus Schrift zum Erweis der apostolischen Verkündigung in armenischer Version entdeckt herausgegeben und ins Deutsch übersetzt von K. Ter-Mekerttschian und E. Ter-Minassiantz. TU, 31, 1. Berlin, 1907.

Justin. *Apologies*. Ed. A. W. F. Blunt. Cambridge, 1911.

Justin. *The Dialogue with Trypho*. Translation, introduction, and notes, by A. Lukyn Williams. London, 1930.

Justin. *First Apology*. Translation by E. R. Hardy. LCC, 1. London, 1953. Pp. 242–89.

Justin. *Opera*. Ed. J. C. T. Otto. 3rd ed. Jena, 1876–9.

Justin. Translation. ANCL, 2. 1879.

Maximus Tyrius. Ed. H. Hobein. Leipzig, 1910.

Numenius. Fragments. Texte établi et traduit, E. Des Places. Paris, 1973.

Ocellus Lucanus. Ed. R. Harder. Berlin, 1926.

Oracles Chaldaiques. Texte établi et traduit, E. Des Places. Paris, 1971.

Origen. *Contra Celsum*. Translation and commentary by H. Chadwick. Cambridge, 1953.

Origen. *De Principiis*. Translation and commentary by G. W. Butterworth. London, 1936.

Origen. Works. GCS. 12 vols. Berlin, 1899–1955.

Philo. Works. Ed. L. Cohn and P. Wendland. 6 vols. Berlin, 1896–1915.

Philo. Works. Ed. and trans. F. H. Colson, G. H. Whitaker and R. Markus: index by J. W. Earp. LCL. 12 vols. London, 1929–62.

Plato. Ed. J. Burnet. 5 vols. Oxford, 1900–7.

Plotinus. Ed. P. Henry and H. R. Schwyzer. Vols. 1–2, *Vita Plotini* and *Enn.* i–v. Paris and Brussels, 1951–.

Plotinus. *Enneads*. Ed. E. Bréhier, with French translation, introductions and notes. 7 vols. Paris, 1924–38.

Plotinus. *Enneads*. Ed. R. Harder, continued by R. Beutler and W. Theiler, with German translation and notes. Vols. 1–2 and 5. Hamburg, 1956–.

Plotinus. *Enneads*. Ed. P. Henry and H. R. Schwyzer (ed. minor). Vol. 1, *Enn.* i–iii. Oxford, 1964.

Plotinus. *The Enneads*. Translated by S. Mackenna. 2nd ed. London, 1956.

Plotinus. *Enneads*. An English translation, with notes, of the revised Henry–Schwyzer text, by A. H. Armstrong. LCL. Vols. 1–2. London, 1966.

Plutarch. *Moralia*. Ed. and trans. F. C. Babbitt, et al. LCL. 15 vols. London, 1927–78.

Plutarch. *Moralia*. Ed. G. N. Bernardakis. 7 vols. Leipzig, 1888–96.

Plutarch. *Moralia*. Ed. C. Hubert, M. Pohlenz, etc. Leipzig, 1952–.

Posidonius. *Posidonii Rhodii reliquiae*. Ed. I. Bake. Leyden, 1820.

Proclus. *Elements of Theology*. Ed. and trans. E. R. Dodds. 2nd ed. Oxford, 1963.

Pseudo-Aristotle. *De mundo*. Ed. and trans. D. J. Furley. LCL. London, 1955.

Tertullian. *De Anima*. Edited with introduction and commentary by J. H. Waszink. Amsterdam, 1947.

Tertullian. *Opera*. CChr. SL 1 and 2. Brepols, 1954.

Tertullian. Text, translation and commentary, by E. Evans.
Against Praxeas. London, 1948.
On the Incarnation. London, 1956.
On the Resurrection. London, 1960.
Adversus Marcionem. 2 vols. Oxford, 1972.

Tertullian. Translation, W. P. Le Saint. *Treatises on Marriage and Remarriage*, ACW, 13; *Treatises on Penance*, ACW, 28. London, 1958.

Tertullian. *Treatise Against Hermogenes*. Translation, J. H. Waszink. ACW, 24. London, 1956.

SOURCES CHRÉTIENNES, ed. C. Mondésert. Paris.

Clement of Alexandria. 2 (1949); 32 (1948); 70 (1960); 108 (1965); 158 (1970).

Irenaeus. 34 (1952); 62 (1959); 100 (1965); 152 (1969); 153 (1969); 210 (1974); 211 (1974).

Tertullian. 46 (1957); 173 (1971).

THE ANTE-NICENE CHRISTIAN LIBRARY, ed. A. Roberts and J. Donaldson. Edinburgh, 1879–.

Clement of Alexandria. 4 (1884); 12 (1882); 22 (1886); 24 (1883).

Irenaeus. 5 (1868); 9 (1869).

Justin. 2 (1879).

Tertullian. 7 (1878); 11 (1882); 15 (1880); 18 (1884).

Reference works

Acton, H. B. (ed.). *The philosophy of punishment*. London, 1969.

Ahern, M. B. *The problem of evil*. London, 1971.

Aldama, J. A. 'Adam, typus futuri', *SE*, 13 (1962), 266–80.

Bibliography

Alès, A. D'. 'La doctrine de l'Esprit en S. Irénée', *RSR*, 14 (1924), 497–538.
'La doctrine eucharistique de saint Irénée', *RSR*, 13 (1923), 24–35.
'La doctrine de la récapitulation en S. Irénée', *RSR*, 16 (1916), 185–211.
'Le mot "oikonomia" dans la langue théologique de saint Irénée', *REG*, 32 (1919), 1–9.
'Tertullien helléniste', *REG* (1937), 329–62.
La théologie de Tertullien. Paris, 1905.
Allen, R. E., 'Participation and predication in Plato's middle dialogues', *PhRev.*, 69 (1960), 147–64.
Altendorf, E. *Einheit und Heiligkeit der Kirche*. Leipzig, 1932.
Andresen, C. 'Justin und der mittlere Platonismus', *ZNW*, 44 (1952/3), 157–95.
Logos und Nomos. Berlin, 1955.
'Zur Entstehung und Geschichte des trinitarischen Personbegriffes', *ZNW*, 52 (1961), 1–39.
Armstrong, A. H. *An introduction to ancient philosophy*. London, 1947.
(ed.). *The Cambridge history of later Greek and early medieval philosophy*. Cambridge, 1967.
Armstrong, A. H., and Markus, R. A. *Christian faith and Greek philosophy*. London, 1960.
Aubin, P. *Le problème de la 'conversion'*. Paris, 1962.
Audet, T. A. 'Orientations théologiques chez saint Irénée. Le contexte mental d'une *Gnosis Alethes*', *Tr.*, 1 (1943), 25–54.
Baelz, Peter. *The forgotten dream*. Oxford, 1975.
Bagnani, G. 'Peregrinus Proteus and the Christians', *Hist.*, 4 (1955), 107–12.
Balas, D. L. '*Metousia theou*', *man's participation in God's perfections according to Saint Gregory of Nyssa*. Rome, 1966.
Balthasar, H. U. von. *Herrlichkeit. Eine theologische Ästhetik*, vol. 2. Einsiedeln, 1962.
Love alone: the way of revelation. London, 1968.
Science, religion and Christianity. London, 1958.
Bambrough, R. (ed.). *New essays on Plato and Aristotle*. London, 1965.
Baney, M. *Some reflections of life in North Africa*. Washington, 1948.
Barbel, J. *Christos angelos*. Bonn, 1941.
Bardenhewer, O. 'Zur Mariologie des hl. Irenäus', *ZKTh*, 55 (1931), 600–4.
Bardy, G. *La conversion au Christianisme durant les premiers siècles*. Paris, 1948.
Barnard, L. W. 'God, the Logos, the Spirit and the trinity in the theology of Athenagoras', *SJTh*, 24 (1970), 70–92.
Justin Martyr, his life and thought. Cambridge, 1967.

Barnes, T. D. *Tertullian. A historical and literary study.* Oxford, 1971.

Barrett, C. K. *The signs of an apostle.* London, 1969.

Bauer, W. *Orthodoxy and heresy in earliest Christianity.* ET of 2nd edition, edited by G. Strecker. Philadelphia, 1971.

Becker, C. *Tertullians Apologeticum, Werden und Leistung.* München, 1954.

Bender, W. *Die Lehre über den Heiligen Geist bei Tertullian.* München, 1961.

Bengsch, A. *Heilsgeschichte und Heilswissen. Eine Untersuchung zur Struktur und Entfaltung des theologischen Denkens im Werk 'Adversus Haereses' des hl. Irenäus von Lyon.* Leipzig, 1957.

Benoit, A. 'Un adversaire du Christianisme au IIIe siècle: Porphyre', *RB*, 54 (1947), 543–742.
Saint Irénée, introduction à l'étude de sa théologie. Paris, 1960.

Bentivegna, G. 'L'angelogía di S. Ireneo', *OrChr*, 28 (1962), 5–48.

Beuzart, P. *Essai sur la théologie d'Irénée.* Paris, 1908.

Bickel, E. 'Fiunt, non nascuntur christiani', in *Pisciculi, Festschrift für F. J. Dölger.* Münster, 1939. Pp. 54–61.

Bigg, C. *The Christian Platonists of Alexandria.* Oxford, 1886.

Blum, G. G. 'Der Begriff des Apostolischen im theologischen Denken Tertullians', *KUD*, 9 (1963), 102–21.

Bonwetsch, N. 'Der Gedanke der Erziehung des Menschengeschlechts bei Irenäus', *ZSTh*, 1 (1923), 637–49.

Bratke, F. 'Die Stellung des Clemens Alexandrinus zum antiken Mysterienwesen', *ThStKr.*, 60 (1887), 647–708.

Braun, R. 'Aux origines de la chrétienté d'Afrique. Un homme de combat, Tertullien', *Bulletin Budé*, 5.2 (1965), 189–208.
Deus Christianorum. Recherches sur le vocabulaire doctrinal de Tertullien. Paris, 1962.
'Tertullien et la philosophie païenne, Essai de mise au point', *Bulletin Budé*, 2 (1971), 213–51.

Bréhier, E. *Les idées philosophiques et religieuses de Philon d'Alexandrie.* Paris, 1925.

Brooks, Peter (ed.). *Christian spirituality, essays in honour of Gordon Rupp.* London, 1975.

Brown, R. F. 'On the necessary imperfection of creation: Irenaeus' Adversus Haereses iv, 38', *SJTh.*, 28 (1975), 17–26.

Brown, S. C. *Do religious claims make sense?* London, 1969.

Brox, Norbert. 'Charisma veritatis certum', *ZKG*, 75 (1964), 327–31.
'Juden und Heiden bei Irenaeus', *MThZ*, 16 (1965), 89–106.
Offenbarung, Gnosis und gnostischer Mythos bei Irenäus von Lyon. Salzburg und München, 1966.

Buri, F. *Clemens Alexandrinus und der paulinische Freiheitsbegriff.* Zürich und Leipzig, 1939.

Butterfield, H. *Christianity and history.* London, 1954.

Camelot, P. T. *Foi et Gnose. Introduction à l'étude de la connaissance mystique chez Clément d'Alexandrie.* Paris, 1945.

Campenhausen, H. von. *Ecclesiastical authority and spiritual power.* London, 1969.
The fathers of the Greek church. London, 1963.
The fathers of the Latin church. London, 1964.
The formation of the Christian Bible. London, 1972.
Die Idee des Martyriums in der alten Kirche. Göttingen, 1964.

Capps, W. H. 'Motif-research in Irenaeus, Thomas Aquinas, and Luther', *SJTh*, 25 (1971), 133–59.

Carrington, P. *Christian apologetics of the second century.* London, 1921.

Chadwick, H. *Early Christian thought and the classical tradition.* Oxford, 1966.
'Justin Martyr's defence of Christianity', *BJRL*, 47.2 (1965), 275–95.

Chardin, Teilhard de. *Hymn of the universe.* London, 1965.
Letters to two friends 1926–1952. London, 1970.
The phenomenon of man. New York, 1959.
The realm of the divine. New York, 1960.

Colin, J. 'S. Irénée, était-il évêque de Lyon?' *Latomus*, 23 (1964), 81–5.

Copeland, E. L., 'Nomos and Logos in Ante-Nicene Christianity', *SJTh*, 27 (1973), 51–61.

Cornford, F. M. *The unwritten philosophy and other essays.* Cambridge, 1950.

Cowburn, John. *Shadows and the dark. The problems of suffering and evil.* London, 1979.

Cross, R. C. 'Logos and Forms in Plato', *Mind*, 63 (1954), 433–50.

Crouzel, H. *Théologie de l'image de Dieu chez Origène.* Paris, 1956.

Cullmann, O. *Christ and time.* London, 1951.

Daniélou, J. *A History of early doctrine before the Council of Nicaea:* vol. 1, 'Theology of Jewish Christianity'; vol. 2, 'Gospel message and Hellenistic culture'; vol. 3, 'The origins of Latin Christianity'. London, 1963, 1973, 1977.
Origène. Paris, 1948.
'Philosophie ou théologie de l'histoire?' *DViv.*, 19 (1951), 127–36.
'S. Irénée et les origines de la théologie de l'histoire', *RSR*, 34 (1947), 227–31.

Daniélou, J. and Marrou, H. I. *The first six hundred years:* vol. 1, 'The Christian centuries'. London, 1964.

De Vogel, C. J. 'Did Aristotle ever accept Plato's theory of transcendent ideas?' *AGPh.*, 47 (1965), 261–98.

Decharmé, P., *La critique des traditions religieuses chez les Grecs, Des origines au temps de Plutarque.* Paris, 1964.

Dodds, E. R. *The Greeks and the irrational.* Berkeley, 1951.
    Pagan and Christian in an age of anxiety. Cambridge, 1965.
    'The Parmenides of Plato and the origin of the Neoplatonic
    One', *CQ*, 22 (1928), 129–42.
Dörrie, H. 'EMANATION. Ein unphilosophisches Wort im spätantiken
    Denken', in K. Flasch (ed.), *Parusia, Festschrift für J. Hirsch-
    berger.* Frankfurt am Main, 1965. Pp. 119–41.
    'Die Frage nach dem Transzendenten im Mittelplatonismus',
    in *Les Sources de Plotin*, Entretiens sur l'antiquité classique, 5.
    Geneva, 1960. Pp. 191–242.
    'Die platonische Theologie des Kelsos in ihrer Auseinander-
    setzung mit der christlichen Theologie auf Grund von
    Origenes c. Celsum, 7, 42ff.', *NAWG, PH* (1967), 19–55.
    'Kontroversen um die Seelenwanderung im kaiserzeitlichen
    Platonismus', *Hermes*, 85 (1957), 414–35.
    Review of Carl Andresen, *Logos und Nomos*, *Gn.*, 29 (1957),
    185–96.
Dray, W. H. *Philosophy of history.* Englewood Cliffs, 1964.
Drewery, B. J. *Origen and the doctrine of grace.* London, 1960.
Duméry, H. *The problem of God in philosophy of religion.* Northwestern
    University Press, 1964.
Durrant, M. *Theology and intelligibility.* London, 1973.
Ebeling, G. *God and Word.* London, 1967.
    The nature of faith. London, 1961.
    Word and faith. London, 1963.
Ehrhardt, A. *The beginning.* Manchester, 1968.
Escoula, L. 'Le verbe sauveur et illuminateur chez S. Irénée',
    NRTh., 66 (1939), 385–400 and 551–67.
Farrer, A. *Reflective faith.* London, 1972.
Festugière, A. J. *Contemplation et vie contemplative selon Platon.* Paris,
    1936.
    L'idéal religieux des Grecs et l'évangile. Paris, 1932.
Finé, Heinz. *Die Terminologie der Jenseitsvorstellungen bei Tertullian.*
    Bonn, 1958.
Floyd, W. E. G. *Clement of Alexandria's treatment of the problem of evil.*
    Oxford, 1971.
Foerster, W. *Gnosis, A selection of Gnostic Texts.* 2 vols. Oxford, 1972
    and 1974.
Frédouille, J. C. *Tertullien, et la conversion de la culture antique.* Paris,
    1972.
Frend, W. H. C. *Martyrdom and persecution in the early church.* Oxford,
    1965.
Funk, F. X. 'La question de l'agape', *RHE*, 6 (1906), 5–15.
Fütscher, L. 'Die natürliche Gotteserkenntnis bei Tertullian',
    ZKTh., 51 (1927), 1–34 and 217–51.

Bibliography

Gächter, P. 'Unsere Einheit mit Christus nach dem hl. Irenäus', *ZKTh.*, 58 (1934), 502–32.

Gaiser, K. *Platons ungeschriebene Lehre.* Stuttgart, 1963. 2nd ed. 1968.

Galtier, P. 'Ab his qui sunt undique', *RHE*, 44 (1949), 411–22.
'La vierge qui nous régénére', *RSR*, 5 (1914), 136–45.

Geffcken, J. *Zwei griechische Apologeten.* Leipzig and Berlin, 1907.

Gibbs, Benjamin. *Freedom and liberation.* London, 1976.

Gibson, A. Boyce. *The religion of Dostoevsky.* London, 1973.
Theism and empiricism. London, 1970.

Glover, T. R. *The conflict of religions in the early Roman empire.* London, 1909.

Goodenough, E. R. *The theology of Justin Martyr.* Jena, 1923.

Grant, R. M. 'Gnostic origins and the Basilidians of Irenaeus', *VigChr.*, 13 (1959), 121–8.
Gnosticism and early Christianity. New York, 1959.
'Irenaeus and Hellenistic culture', *HTR*, 42 (1949), 41–51.
(ed.). *Gnosticism: an anthology.* London, 1961.

Greene, W. C. *Fate, good and evil in Greek thought.* Harvard, 1944.

Grillmeier, A. 'Der Gottessohn im Tötenreich', *ZKTh.*, 71 (1949), 1–53 and 184–203.

Gronau, K. *Das Theodizeeproblem in der altchristlichen Auffassung.* Tübingen, 1922.

Gross, J. *La divinisation du chrétien d'après les pères grecs.* Paris, 1938.

Guthrie, W. K. C. 'The development of Aristotle's theology', *CQ*, 27 (1933), 162–71, and 28 (1934), 90–8.

Hager, F. P. *Der Geist und das Eine.* Bern and Stuttgart, 1970.
'Die Materie und das Böse im antiken Platonismus', *MH*, 19 (1962), 73–103.
Die Vernunft und das Problem des Bösen in Rahmen der platonischen Ethik und Metaphysik. Bern, 1963.

Hamilton, J. D. B. 'Justin's *Apology* 66. A review of scholarship and a suggested synthesis', *EThL*, 48 (1972), 554–60.

Hamman, A. 'L'enseignement sur la création dans l'antiquité chrétienne', *RevSR*, 42 (1968), 1–23.

Hanson, R. P. C. *Allegory and event. A study of the sources and significance of Origen's interpretation of scripture.* London, 1959.

Harl, M. *Origène et la fonction révélatrice du verbe incarné.* Paris, 1959.

Harnack, A. von. *Marcion, das Evangelium vom fremden Gott.* Leipzig, 1924.

Hatch, E. *The influence of Greek ideas and usages upon the Christian church.* London, 1914.

Hebblethwaite, Brian. *Evil, suffering and religion.* London, 1976.

Hengel, M. *The Son of God.* ET. London, 1976.

Hesselberg, K. *Tertullians Lehre aus seinen Schriften entwickelt.* Dorpat, 1848.

Hick, John. *Death and eternal life*. London, 1976.
  Evil and the God of love. 2nd ed. London, 1977.
  (ed.). *Truth and dialogue*. London, 1974.
Hirsch, E. D., jr. *Validity in interpretation*. Yale, 1967.
Holl, K. 'Tertullian als Schriftsteller', *Gesammelte Aufsätze zur Kirchengeschichte*, vol. 3. Tübingen, 1928.
Holstein, H. 'La tradition des apôtres chez S. Irénée', *RSR*, 36 (1949), 230–70.
Holte, R. 'Logos spermatikos, Christianity and ancient philosophy according to St. Justin's Apologies', *STL*, 12 (1958), 109–68.
Holz, H. 'Ueber den Begriff des Willens und der Freiheit bei Origenes', *NZSTh*, 12 (1970), 63–84.
Hornus, J. M. 'Étude sur la pensée politique de Tertullien', *RHPhR*, 38 (1958), 1–38.
Houssiau, A. *La christologie de saint Irénée*. Louvain, 1955.
Hunger, W. 'Der Gedanke der Weltplaneinheit und Adameinheit in der Theologie des heiligen Irenäus', *Schol.*, 17 (1942), 161–77.
Hyldahl, N. *Philosophie und Christentum*. Kopenhagen, 1966.
Ivanka, E. von. *Plato Christianus*. Einsiedeln, 1964.
Joly, R. *Christianisme et philosophie*. Brussels, 1973.
Jonas, H. *Gnosis und spätantiker Geist*. Vol. 1, 'Die mythologische Gnosis'. 3rd ed. Göttingen, 1964. Vol. 2, 'Von der Mythologie zur mystischen Philosophie'. Göttingen, 1954.
  The Gnostic religion. Boston, 1963.
Jones, R. M. 'The ideas as the thoughts of God', *ClPh.*, 21 (1926), 317–26.
Jouassard, G. 'Le "signe de Jonas" dans le livre IIIe de l'*adversus haereses* de saint Irénée', in *L'homme devant Dieu, Mélanges offerts au Père Henri de Lubac*. Paris, 1963. Vol. 1, pp. 235–46.
Jüngel, E. *Gott als Geheimnis der Welt*. Tübingen, 1977.
  Gottes Sein ist im Werden. 2nd ed. Tübingen, 1966.
Kahn, J. G. ' "Connais-toi toi-même" à la manière de Philon', *RHPhR*, 53 (1973), 294–306.
Kamenka, E. 'Marxism and the history of philosophy', *HThS*, 5 (1965), 83–104.
Karpp, H. *Probleme altchristlicher Anthropologie*. Gütersloh, 1950.
Käsemann, E. *Essays on New Testament themes*. London, 1964.
  New Testament questions of today. London, 1969.
  Perspectives on Paul. London, 1971.
  The testament of Jesus. London, 1968.
Kenny, J. P. *The supernatural*. New York, 1972.
  'Teilhard de Chardin on original sin', *Colloquium*, 7.1 (1974), 3–16.
King, R. H. *The meaning of God*. London, 1974.
Klebba, E. *Die Anthropologie des hl. Irenäus*. Münster, 1894.

Bibliography

Koch, Hal. *Pronoia und Paideusis*. Berlin, 1932.
'Zur Lehre vom Urstand und von der Erlösung bei Irenäus', *ThStKr*, 7 (1925), 183–214.
Kolping, A. *Sacramentum Tertullianeum*, vol. 1. Regensburg–Münster, 1948.
Krämer, H. J. *Arete bei Platon und Aristoteles. Zum Wesen und zur Geschichte der Platonischen Ontologie*. Heidelberg, 1959.
Platonismus und hellenistische Philosophie. Berlin, 1971.
Der Ursprung der Geistmetaphysik. Untersuchungen zur Geschichte des Platonismus zwischen Platon und Plotin. Amsterdam, 1964.
Küng, H. *On being a Christian*. New York, 1976.
Kunze, J. *Die Gotteslehre des Irenäus*. Leipzig, 1891.
Labhardt, A. 'Tertullien et la philosophie ou la recherche d'une "position pure" ', *MH*, 7 (1950), 159–81.
Lagrange, M. J. *Saint Justin, philosophe, martyr*. 2nd ed. Paris, 1914.
Lampe, G. W. H. *God as Spirit*. Oxford, 1977.
The seal of the spirit. London, 1951.
Langerbeck, H. 'The philosophy of Ammonius Saccas', *JHS*, 77 (1957), 67–74.
Lawson, J. *The biblical theology of St. Irenaeus*. London, 1948.
Lazzati, G. 'Il "de natura deorum" fonte del "de testimonio animae" di Tertulliano', *AeR*, 41 (1939), 153–66.
Introduzione allo studio di Clemente Alessandrino. Milano, 1939.
Lebreton, J. 'Le désaccord de la foi populaire et la theologie savante', *RHE*, 19 (1923), 481–506 and 20 (1924), 5–37.
Leonhardi, G. *Die apologetischen Grundgedanken Tertullians, Ein Beitrag zur Apologie des Christenthums in der kirchlichen Gegenwart*. Leipzig, 1882.
Lewis, C. S. *The problem of pain*. London, 1940.
Lewy, H. *Sobria ebrietas*. BZNW, 9 (Berlin, 1929).
Lieske, A. *Die Theologie der Logosmystik bei Origenes*. Münster, 1938.
Ligier, L. 'Le "charisma veritatis certum" des évêques', in *L'homme devant Dieu. Mélanges offerts au Père Henri de Lubac*. Paris, 1963. Vol. 1, pp. 247–68.
Lilla, S. R. C. *Clement of Alexandria, a study in Christian Platonism and Gnosticism*. Oxford, 1971.
Loofs, F. *Theophilus von Antiochien Adversus Marcionem und die anderen theologischen Quellen bei Irenaeus*. TU, 46.2. Leipzig, 1930.
Lortz, J. *Tertullian als Apologet*. 2 vols. Münster, 1927 and 1928.
Lot-Borodine, M. *La déification de l'homme*. Paris, 1970.
Lubac, H. de. *Histoire et esprit*. Paris, 1950.
Lucas, J. R. *The freedom of the will*. Oxford, 1970.
Mackinnon, D. M. *The problem of metaphysics*. Cambridge, 1974.
Macquarrie, J. *God-talk*. London, 1967.

Manuel, Frank E. *Shapes of philosophical history*. Stanford, 1965.

Markus, R. A. 'Pleroma and fulfilment. The significance of history in St. Irenaeus' opposition to Gnosticism', *VigChr.*, 8 (1954), 193–224.

Marrou, H. I. *Humanisme et christianisme chez Clément d'Alexandrie d'après le Pédagogue*. Entretiens sur l'antiquité classique, 3. Geneva, 1955.

Marten, R. '*Ousia*' *im Denken Platons*. Meisenheim am Glan, 1962.

Mascall, E. L. *The openness of being*. London, 1971.

Maurice, F. D. *Lectures on the ecclesiastical history of the first and second centuries*. Cambridge, 1854.

Mayer, A. *Das Gottesbild im Menschen nach Clemens von Alexandrien*. Rome, 1942.

Mees, M. 'Der geistige Tempel. Einige Überlegungen zu Klemens von Alexandrien', *VetChr.*, 1 (1964), 82–9.

Méhat, A. *Études sur les stromates de Clément d'Alexandrie*. Paris, 1966.

Meijering, E. P. *Orthodoxy and Platonism in Athanasius. Synthesis or antithesis?* Leiden, 1968.

  Tertullian contra Marcion, Gotteslehre in der Polemik. Leiden, 1977.

Merki, H. *Homoiosis theoi. Von der platonischen Angleichung an Gott zur Gottähnlichkeit bei Gregor von Nyssa*. Par. 7. Freiburg in der Schweiz, 1952.

Merlan, P. 'Aristotle's unmoved movers', *Tr.*, 4 (1946), 1–30.

  From Platonism to Neoplatonism. The Hague, 1953.

Mitchell, B. *The justification of religious belief*. London, 1973.

Moingt, J. *Théologie trinitaire de Tertullien*. 4 vols. Paris, 1966–70.

Molland, E. 'Clement of Alexandria on the origin of Greek philosophy', *SO*, 15, 16 (1936), 57–85.

  The conception of the gospel in Alexandrian theology. Oslo, 1938.

Moltmann, J. *The crucified God*. London, 1974.

  Theology of hope. London, 1967.

Monachino, V. 'Intento pratico e propagandistico dell'Apologetica greca del II secolo', *Gr.*, 32 (1951), 187–222.

Monceaux, P. *Histoire littéraire de l'Afrique chrétienne depuis les origines jusqu'à l'invasion arabe*. Vol. 1, 'Tertullien et les origines'. Paris, 1901.

Mondésert, C. *Clément d'Alexandrie, Introduction à l'étude de sa pensée religieuse à partir de l'écriture*. Paris, 1944.

Morgan, J. *The importance of Tertullian in the development of Christian dogma*. London, 1928.

Morris, L. L. *The cross in the New Testament*. Grand Rapids, 1965.

Mortley, R. *Connaissance religieuse et herméneutique chez Clément d'Alexandrie*. Leiden, 1973.

Moule, C. F. D. *The origin of Christology*. Cambridge, 1977.

Bibliography

Murdoch, I. *The Fire and the Sun (Why Plato banished the artists)*. Oxford, 1977.
The sovereignty of Good. London, 1970.

Nautin, P. 'La fin des stromates et les hypotyposes de Clément d'Alexandrie, *VigChr.*, 30 (1976), 268–302.

Nielsen, K. *Scepticism*. London, 1973.

Nisters, B. *Tertullian, seine Persönlichkeit und sein Schicksal*. Münster, 1950.

Nock, A. D. *Essays on Hellenism and the ancient world*, ed. Zeph Stewart. Oxford, 1972.
'Posidonius', *JRS*, 49 (1959), 1–15.

Noeldechen, E. *Tertullian*. Gotha, 1890.

Norris, R. A. *God and world in early Christian theology*. New York, 1965.

O'Hagan, A. P. *Material recreation in the apostolic fathers*. TU, 100. Berlin, 1967.

Ochagavía, Juan. *Visibile patris filius, A study of Irenaeus' teaching on revelation and tradition*. Rome, 1964.

Orbe, Antonio. *Antropología de San Ireneo*. Madrid, 1969.
'El hombre ideal en la teología de S. Ireneo', *Gr.*, 43 (1962), 449–91.
'Ipse tuum calcabit caput (S. Ireneo y Gen. 3.15)', *Gr.*, 52 (1971), 95–150.

Osborn, E. F. 'Elucidation of problems as a method of interpretation, I and II', *Colloquium*, 8.2 (1976), 24–32; *Colloquium*, 9.1 (1976), 10–18.
'Empiricism and transcendence', *Prudentia*, 8.2 (1976), 115–22.
Ethical patterns in early Christian thought. Cambridge, 1976.
'From Justin to Origen, the pattern of apologetic', *Prudentia*, 4.1 (1972), 1–22.
'The God of the Christians', *Colloquium*, 5.2 (1973), 27–37.
'Greek answers to Christian questions', *Colloquium*, 6.2 (1974) 3–15.
Justin Martyr. Tübingen, 1973.
The philosophy of Clement of Alexandria. Cambridge, 1957.
'Teaching and writing in the first chapter of the Stromateis of Clement of Alexandria', *JThS*, 10.2 (1959), 335–43.

Outler, A. C. 'The Platonism of Clement of Alexandria', *JR*, 20 (1940), 217–40.

Pagels, E. H. 'A Valentinian interpretation of baptism and eucharist', *HTR*, 65.2 (1972), 153–69.

Pannenberg, W. (ed.). *Revelation as history*. London, 1969.

Panov, S. 'Apophatische Gotteserkenntnis', *NZSTh.*, 13 (1971), 280–312.

Passmore, John. 'The idea of a history of philosophy', *HThS*, 5 (1965), 1–32.

Man's responsibility to nature. London, 1975.
The perfectibility of man. London, 1970.
Pears, D. F. (ed.). *Freedom and the Will*. London, 1963.
Pelikan, J. *The Christian tradition*. Vol. 1, 'The emergence of the Catholic tradition (100–600)'. Chicago, 1971.
Historical theology: continuity and change in Christian doctrine. New York, 1971.
Pellegrino, M. *Studi su l'antica apologetica*. SeL, 14. Roma, 1947.
Pépin, J. *Idées grecques sur l'homme et sur Dieu*. Paris, 1971.
Théologie cosmique et théologie chrétienne. Paris, 1964.
Phillips, D. Z. *Death and immortality*. London, 1970.
Plagnieux, J. 'La doctrine mariale de saint Irénée', *RevSR*, 44.2 (1970), 179–89.
Plantinga, A. *God, freedom and evil*. London, 1975.
Pohlenz, M. 'Klemens von Alexandreia und sein hellenisches Christentum, *NAWG*, *PH* (1943), 103–80.
Philo von Alexandreia. *NAWG*, *PH* (1942), 409–87.
Die Stoa. Göttingen, 1959.
Prestige, G. L. *God in patristic thought*. London, 1952.
Prigent, P. 'Au temps de l'Apocalypse. I, Domitien. II, Le culte impérial au 1er siècle en Asie Mineure. III, Pourquoi les persécutions?' *RHPhR*, 4 (1974), 451–83; 2 (1975) 215–35; 3 (1975), 341–63.
Justin et l'ancien testament. Paris, 1964.
Prümm, K. 'Göttliche Planung und menschliche Entwicklung nach Irenäus, Adversus Haereses', *Schol.*, 13 (1938), 206–24 and 342–66.
'Mysterion von Paulus bis Origenes', *ZKTh*, 61 (1937), 391–425.
'Zur Terminologie und zum Wesen der christlichen Neuheit bei Irenäus', in *Pisciculi, Festschrift für F. J. Dölger*. Münster, 1939. Pp. 192–219.
Prunet, O. *La morale de Clément d'Alexandrie et le nouveau testament*. Paris, 1966.
Puech, H. C. 'Numenius d'Apamée et les théologies orientales au second siècle', *AIPh.*, 2 (1934), 745–78.
Quacquarelli, A. 'La persecuzione secondo Tertulliano', *Gr.*, 31 (1950), 562–89.
'I presupposti filosofici della retorica patristica', *RThAM*, 34 (1967), 5–17.
Quispel, G. 'Anima naturaliter christiana', *ErJb.*, 18 (1950), 163–9.
Rahner, H. 'Flumina de ventre Christi', *Bib.*, 22 (1941), 269–302 and 367–403.
Rahner, K. 'Die Sündenvergebung nach der Taufe in der regula fidei des Irenäus', *ZKTh*, 70 (1948), 450–5.

'Zur Theologie der Busse bei Tertullian', *Abhandlungen über Theologie und Kirche*. Dusseldorf, 1952.

Ramsey, I. T. *Religious language*. London, 1957.

Rauch, G. *Der Einfluss der stoischen Philosophie auf die Lehrbildung Tertullians*. Halle, 1890.

Raven, C. E. *The creator Spirit*. London, 1928.

Good news of God. London, 1940.

The gospel and the church. London, 1939.

Natural religion and Christian theology. Vol. 1, 'Science and religion'. Vol. 2, 'Experience and interpretation'. Cambridge, 1953.

Science and the Christian man. London, 1952.

Teilhard de Chardin, scientist and seer. London, 1962.

Refoulé, F. 'Tertullien et la philosophie', *RevSR*, 30 (1956), 42–5.

Restrepo-Jaramillo, J. M. 'La doble fórmula simbólica en Tertulliano', *Gr.*, 15 (1934), 3–58.

Reynders, D. B. 'Optimisme et théocentrisme chez Saint Irénée', *RThAM*, 8 (1936), 225–52.

'Parodosis, le progrès de l'idée de tradition jusqu'à S. Irénée', *RThAM*, 5 (1933), 155–91.

'La polémique de Saint Irénée, principes et méthode', *RThAM*, 7 (1935), 5–27.

Rich, A. N. M. 'The Platonic ideas as thoughts of God', *Mn.*, 4.7 (1954), 123–33.

Rist, J. M. *Eros and Psyche: studies in Plato, Plotinus and Origen*. Toronto, 1964.

'A note on Eros and Agape in Pseudo-Dionysius', *VigChr.*, 20 (1966), 235–43.

Plotinus, the road to reality. Cambridge, 1967.

Stoic philosophy. Cambridge, 1969.

Ross, W. D. *Plato's theory of ideas*. Oxford, 1951. 2nd ed. 1953.

Rossi, S. 'Ireneo fu vescovo di Lione', *GIF*, 17 (1964), 239–54.

Sagnard, F. *La gnôse valentinienne et le témoignage de Saint Irénée*. Paris, 1947.

Scharl, E. *Recapitulatio mundi*. Freiburg, 1941.

Schoedel, N. P. 'Philosophy and rhetoric in the Against Heresies', *VigChr.*, 13 (1959), 22–32.

Scholer, D. M. *Nag Hammadi Bibliography*. Leiden, 1971.

Schweizer, E. *Der Brief an die Kolosser*. Zürich, 1976.

'Versöhnung des Alls, Kol. 1, 20', in G. Strecker (ed.), *Jesus Christus in Geschichte und Theologie, Festschrift H. Conzelmann*. Tübingen, 1975. Pp. 487–501.

Skinner, Quentin. 'Meaning and understanding in the history of ideas', *HTh.*, 8 (1969), 3–53.

Smart, Ninian *The concept of worship*. London, 1972.
   Philosophers and religious truth. London, 1969.
Soury, G. *Aperçus de philosophie religieuse chez Maxime de Tyr, platonicien éclectique*. Paris, 1942.
Spanneut, M. *Le stoïcisme des pères de l'église*. Paris, 1957.
Spikowski, L. *La doctrine de l'église dans S. Irénée*. Strasbourg, 1926.
Stead, G. C. *Divine substance*. Oxford, 1977.
   'Divine substance in Tertullian', *JThS*, 14.1 (1963), 46–66.
Stockmeier, Peter. *Glaube und Religion in der frühen Kirche*. Freiburg, 1973.
Story, C. I. K. *The nature of truth in the Gospel of Truth and in the writings of Justin Martyr*. Leiden, 1971.
Struker, A. *Die Gottesebenbildlichkeit des Menschen in der christlichen Literatur der ersten zwei Jahrhunderte*. Münster, 1913.
Stylianopoulos, T. *Justin Martyr and the Mosaic Law*. Montana, 1975.
Tennant, F. R. *The sources of the doctrines of the fall and original sin*. Cambridge, 1903.
Theiler, W. 'Einheit und unbegrenzte Zweiheit von Platon bis Plotin', in J. Mau and E. G. Schmidt (eds.), *Isonomia*. Berlin, 1964.
   'Die Entstehung der Metaphysik des Aristoteles', *MH*, 15 (1958), 85–105.
   Forschungen zum Neuplatonismus. Berlin, 1966.
   'Plotin zwischen Platon und Stoa', in *Les Sources de Plotin*. Entretiens sur l'antiquité classique, 5. Geneva, 1960. Pp. 63–104.
   Die Vorbereitung des Neuplatonismus. Berlin, 1930.
Tibiletti, C. 'Note critiche al testo di Tertulliano de testimonio animae', *GIF*, 12 (1959), 258–62.
Tollinton, R. B. *Clement of Alexandria*. 2 vols. London, 1914.
Tresmontant, C. *Pierre Teilhard de Chardin, his thought*. Baltimore, 1959.
Unnik, W. C. van. *Newly discovered Gnostic writings*. London, 1960.
Vecchiotti, I. *La filosofia di Tertulliano*. Urbino, 1970.
Verriele, A. 'Le plan du salut d'après S. Irénée', *RevSR*, 14 (1934), 493–527.
Vogel, C. J. de. 'On the Neoplatonic character of Platonism and the Platonic character of Neoplatonism', *Mind*, 62 (1953), 43–64.
Völker, W. *Der wahre Gnostiker nach Clemens Alexandrinus*. Berlin and Leipzig, 1952.
Wallis, R. T. *Neoplatonism*. London, 1972.
Ward, K. *The concept of God*. Oxford, 1974.
Waszink, J. H. 'Bemerkungen zu Justins Lehre vom Logos Sper-

matikos', in *Mullus, Festschrift für Theodor Klauser*. Münster, 1964. Pp. 380–90.

'Bemerkungen zum Einfluss des Platonismus im Frühen Christentum', *VigChr.*, 19 (1965), 129–62.

'Der Platonismus und die altchristliche Gedankenwelt', *Entretiens sur l'antiquité classique*, vol. 3. Geneva, 1955. Pp. 137–79.

Weber, K. O. *Origenes der Neuplatoniker*. München, 1962.

Weil, Simone. *Gateway to God*. Fontana, 1974.

Gravity and grace. London, 1972.

Intimations of Christianity among the Ancient Greeks. London, 1957.

Waiting on God. Fontana, 1977.

Wennemer, K. 'Zur Frage einer heilsgeschichtlichen Theologie', *Schol.*, 29 (1954), 73–9.

Whittaker, J. 'Neopythagoreanism and the transcendent absolute', *SO*, 48 (1973), 77–86.

Wickert, U. 'Glauben und Denken bei Tertullian und Origenes', *ZThK*, 62 (1965), 153–77.

Widmann, M. 'Irenäus und seine theologischen Väter', *ZThK*, 54 (1957), 157–73.

Wiles, M. F. *The making of Christian doctrine*. Cambridge, 1967.

Working papers in doctrine. London, 1976.

Wilson, R. McL. *The Gnostic problem*. London, 1958.

Winden, J. C. M. van. *An early Christian philosopher*. Leiden, 1971.

Wingren, G. *Man and incarnation*. Edinburgh, 1959.

Witt, R. E. 'The hellenism of Clement of Alexandria', *CQ*, 25 (1931), 195–204.

Wölfl, Karl. *Das Heilswirken Gottes durch den Sohn nach Tertullian*. AnGr., 112. Rome, 1960.

Wolfson, H. A. *Philo*. 2 vols. Cambridge, Mass., 1947.

The philosophy of the church fathers, vol. 1. Cambridge, Mass., 1956.

Index of biblical citations

Index of citations from ancient authors

Index of citations from modern authors

General index

Adam, 20, 51, 88, 90, 129, 164, 178f, 189, 202, 210
Adam/Christ parallel, 20, 24, 175–81, 189f., 202, 207, 251
Advent, second 10, 185, 192–5, 202, 233–5
Albinus, 29, 35, 37, 241
angels, 59, 97, 137, 139, 175, 211, 223, 225f.
apocalyptic 113, 145, 156f., 198, 250, 260
apostles 8, 19f., 40, 104, 109, 143, 170, 172, 184, 225, 227, 235, 247
Aquinas, 58, 123, 274, 277
argument, 1–4, 11f., 19f., 23f., 33–7, 40, 49, 59ff., 63, 103f., 148, 265–88
Aristotle, Peripatetics, 19, 28, 58f., 70, 123, 241, 285
assimilation to God, *see* likeness to God
attention ('Waiting on God'), 76f.
Augustine 103, 113, 153, 172, 195, 200, 204, 258

Basilides 23, 60, 158f.
bishops 18, 20, 23, 186f., 227f.
body 6, 47, 55, 80, 97–102, 108f., 132f., 213f., 256
body of Christ 213f., 230–4, 237f., 247–50, 253–7

cause, first 4, 7, 28f., 47, 56–64, 98, 125–9, 133, 145, 147f., 219, 238, 252, 258f., 283f.
Celsus, 2, 27–9, 59, 258
charisma, 228, 235–8, 246–9
chiliasm, 21, 193
Christus Victor, 142, 175, 179ff., 185, 196, 209, 219, 221, 234f., 239, 253
Church, 3, 20–3, 90, 107, 109, 177f., 183–9, 233–5, 276, 287
covenant, 170, 173f., 207
creatio ex nihilo, 127f., 147, 245, 280
cross, 3, 42, 61–3, 72–6, 88, 108, 113, 117–19, 122f., 134, 137, 149, 151, 154f., 161–6, 178, 192, 194f., 199, 201, 205, 209, 212f., 215, 227, 230–4, 238, 251, 256, 262, 266

culpa, felix, 89, 130, 199

deification, 88, 111–20, 188, 237, 243, 258, 260
demons, 36, 44, 59, 92, 137, 183, 197, 226f., 238, 247, 267
determinism, 93–7, 120–2
devil, 84, 139–44, 150, 176, 180, 221f., 227, 231
dialectic, 49, 145–7, 219, 229–31
docetism, 61, 162, 212–15, 236
Dostoevsky, 212, 248f.
doxography, 12f., 15, 97, 111, 146, 240–4, 277–84
dualism, 30, 41, 254–6

economy, dispensation, 82, 163–74, 196, 213, 217, 231
elucidation, 12–17, 113f., 264, 274, 277–88
Empire. Roman, 2, 4, 18, 21, 25–7, 41, 136, 186, 264
empiricism, 33f., 64f., 72, 101, 103f., 170, 210
Eve, 88f., 164
Eve/Mary parallel, 174f., 179
evil, problem of 1, 6, 137–44, 154–62, 189, 195–200, 279
exchange formulae, 115, 209–11, 221

faith, 2, 24, 37, 42, 46, 50, 61, 73–6, 98, 104, 149, 151, 180, 186, 197, 224, 230, 243, 261
first principle, 28, 37, 44, 48–50, 70, 98, 103, 195, 223f., 237, 243f., 263
flesh, 8, 61, 83, 97–102, 130–3, 208, 210–15, 219, 237
forms, 44, 145–8, 230, 238, 243, 257, 262, 283f.; *see also* powers
free will and freedom, 1, 5–7, 79, 93–7, 120–3, 129f., 137–42, 151, 160f., 170, 177, 196, 236

Gnosticism and Gnostics, 3, 5, 7, 20, 23, 38–40, 42–4, 54, 59–61, 67, 78, 79, 81, 83, 84, 102–4, 108, 122f., 132,

319

General index

religion, Roman, 2, 5, 8, 9, 21, 26, 28, 32, 41, 50, 56, 59, 186
resurrection, 10, 138, 148f., 182, 233f., 245, 256
retribution, 154–9, 261
righteousness, 169, 177, 191, 210f., 224, 232, 239, 246
rule of faith, 107, 127, 207, 227, 268f.

sacrifice, 47, 151, 166, 179, 194
scriptures, 50, 135, 163, 168–74, 182, 184, 216, 237, 245f., 269
secular, 69, 73, 149, 152f.
sin, 4, 7, 24, 79, 87–93, 95, 110, 112, 123, 133, 139–44, 196–9, 221, 224; original, 90f., 102, 198–200
Socrates, 9, 32f., 35f., 41, 47, 79, 81, 107, 209, 265
sophist, 22, 107, 208
soul, 35, 58f., 80, 85, 90, 97–102, 115, 210
spermatic Logos, 19, 80f., 99, 166f., 201, 203, 206, 220
spirit, 6, 80, 97–102, 150, 186, 191f., 194, 202f., 213, 218, 222f., 225, 231, 233, 235, 245–9, 252f., 286

Stoics, 9f., 19, 79, 85, 87, 96, 105, 135, 138, 140–3, 147, 196, 201, 241
substance, divine, 54f., 67, 217–19, 252
symbolism, symbols, 46, 50, 56, 62, 64, 69f., 193, 224, 239, 269

tradition, 21
truth, 24f., 32, 56, 60, 63, 87, 102–6, 125, 164, 172, 191, 205, 225, 227–31, 233, 273
truth, love of, 19, 23f., 119, 229, 265–71
trinity, 54–6, 186, 217–20

unity, 1, 7, 9, 25, 28, 31–66, 70–2, 82, 92, 119, 125, 140, 145–8, 172, 174, 177, 181, 198, 208, 217f., 220–4, 227, 231–42, 244, 253–5, 261f., 268
universality, 165, 167, 178, 180–2, 194f., 219, 231–40, 256f.

Valentinus, 18, 23, 42, 145, 218, 226, 235, 255

word-event, 216, 244f.
world soul, 134, 238, 241